ZEN WAR STORIES

Following the critically acclaimed *Zen at War* (1997), Brian Daizen Victoria here explores the intimate relationship between Japanese institutional Buddhism and militarism during the Second World War.

Victoria reveals for the first time, through examination of the wartime writings of the Japanese military itself, that the Zen school's view of life and death was deliberately incorporated into the military's programme of 'spiritual education' in order to develop a fanatical military spirit in both soldiers and civilians. Furthermore, it is shown that D. T. Suzuki, the most famous exponent of Zen in the West, was a wartime proponent of this Zen-inspired viewpoint which enabled Japanese soldiers to leave for the battlefield already resigned to death. Victoria takes us on to the naval battlefield in the company of warrior-monk and Rinzai Zen Master Nakajima Genjō. We view the war in China through the eyes of a Buddhist military chaplain. The book also examines the relationship to Buddhism of Japan's seven class-A war criminals, hung by the Tokyo War Crimes Tribunal in 1948.

A highly controversial study, this book will be of interest not only to those studying the history of the period, but also to anyone concerned with the perennial question of the 'proper' relationship between religion and state.

Brian Daizen Victoria is a Senior Lecturer at the Centre for Asian Studies, the University of Adelaide.

THE ROUTLEDGECURZON CRITICAL STUDIES IN BUDDHISM SERIES
General Editors: Charles S. Prebish and Damien Keown

The *RoutledgeCurzon Critical Studies in Buddhism Series* is a comprehensive study of the Buddhist tradition. The series explores this complex and extensive tradition from a variety of perspectives, using a range of different methodologies.

The Series is diverse in its focus, including historical studies, textual translations and commentaries, sociological investigations, bibliographic studies, and considerations of religious practice as an expression of Buddhism's integral religiosity. It also presents materials on modern intellectual historical studies, including the role of Buddhist thought and scholarship in a contemporary, critical context and in the light of current social issues. The series is expansive and imaginative in scope, spanning more than two and a half millennia of Buddhist history. It is receptive to all research works that inform and advance our knowledge and understanding of the Buddhist tradition.

THE REFLEXIVE NATURE OF AWARENESS
Paul Williams

BUDDHISM AND HUMAN RIGHTS
Edited by Damien Keown, Charles S. Prebish, Wayne Husted

ALTRUISM AND REALITY
Paul Williams

WOMEN IN THE FOOTSTEPS OF THE BUDDHA
Kathryn R. Blackstone

THE RESONANCE OF EMPTINESS
Gay Watson

IMAGING WISDOM
Jacob N. Kinnard

AMERICAN BUDDHISM
Edited by Duncan Ryuken Williams and Christopher Queen

PAIN AND ITS ENDING
Carol S. Anderson

THE SOUND OF LIBERATING TRUTH
Edited by Sallie B. King and Paul O. Ingram

BUDDHIST THEOLOGY
Edited by Roger R. Jackson and John J. Makransky

EMPTINESS APPRAISED
David F. Burton

THE GLORIOUS DEEDS OF PŪRNA
Joel Tatelman

CONTEMPORARY BUDDHIST ETHICS
Edited by Damien Keown

INNOVATIVE BUDDHIST WOMEN
Edited by Karma Lekshe Tsomo

TEACHING BUDDHISM IN THE WEST
Edited by V.S. Hori, R.P. Hayes and J.M. Shields

EMPTY VISION
David L. McMahan

SELF, REALITY AND REASON IN TIBETAN PHILOSOPHY
Thupten Jinpa

BUDDHIST PHENOMENOLOGY
Dan Lusthaus

ZEN WAR STORIES

Brian Daizen Victoria

RoutledgeCurzon
Taylor & Francis Group
LONDON AND NEW YORK

by RoutledgeCurzon
2 Park Square, Milton Park, Abingdon, Oxon, OX14 4RN

Simultaneously published in the USA and Canada
by RoutledgeCurzon
270 Madison Ave, New York NY 10016

Reprinted 2004

Transferred to Digital Printing 2005

RoutledgeCurzon is an imprint of the Taylor & Francis Group

© 2003 Brian Daizen Victoria

Typeset in Goudy by LaserScript Ltd, Mitcham, Surrey

British Library Cataloguing in Publication Data
A catalogue record for this book is available from the British Library

Library of Congress Cataloging in Publication Data
A catalog record for this book has been requested

ISBN 0–7007–1580–0 (hbk)
ISBN 0–7007–1581–9 (pbk)

Printed and bound by Antony Rowe Ltd, Eastbourne

DEDICATED TO ALL THOSE
WHOSE LIVES WERE STOLEN FROM THEM
IN THE NAME OF "HOLY WAR"

"Unless the truth is told of the past, its lies and betrayals will infect the future."

(Martin Ball, Australian journalist)

"Why didn't we have the religion of the Japanese, who regard sacrifice for the Fatherland as the highest good?"

(Adolph Hitler, quoted in *Inside The Third Reich* by Albert Speer)

"We too [like the Japanese] are battling to destroy individualism. We are struggling for a new Germany based on the new idea of totalitarianism. In Japan, this way of thinking *comes naturally to the people* [italics mine]!"

(Rudolph Hess, Deputy Führer, quoted in *Tokyo Record* by Otto Tolischus

Every religion seeks to proclaim a truth which transcends the world, but is enmeshed in the very world it desires to transcend. Every religion seeks to remake the world in its own image, but it is always to some extent remade in the image of the world. This is the tragedy of religion.

(Dr Robert N. Bellah, *Tokugawa Religion*)

CONTENTS

CONTENTS

ILLUSTRATIONS

PREFACE

In late 1997 I published a book, *Zen at War*, that sent shock waves throughout Zen communities in the West, for it demonstrated that wartime Japanese Zen masters, almost to a man, had been fervent supporters of Japanese militarism. Moreover, these masters claimed the Buddha Dharma was itself synonymous with that militarism. What was especially disconcerting to some readers was the fact that many of those Japanese Zen masters who first introduced Zen to the West, especially in the postwar era, turned out to have been some of the strongest proponents of Japanese militarism, cloaking their support in the guise of such phrases as "the unity of Zen and the sword."

I remember being deeply moved by one reader whose pained reaction was posted on the Internet. He said simply, "What the hell went wrong?" He went on to add that if my book had any failing, it was that while I had done a good job in revealing the wartime deeds and acts of Japan's leading Zen figures, I had failed to interpret or explain what it all meant within the context of Buddhism as a whole; that is to say, is Zen, if not Buddhism, a totalitarian or 'fascist' faith?

This book is meant to address, at least to some degree, the question of "what went wrong." However, rather than using the survey approach that characterized my earlier book, each chapter in the present volume focuses on discrete events or personalities. Any disjunction between chapters resulting from this approach will hopefully be compensated for by the opportunity to take a more in-depth look at the material. In any event, I have tried to include sufficient background information in each chapter so that the reader will find it unnecessary to have read *Zen at War* in order to make sense of what is presented here: each book stands by itself, although, taken together, they give a much broader and deeper picture than either of them does alone.

Approach

I caution readers that this book, especially its first part, is not intended as a description of the nature of Zen (or Buddhism as a whole) in any theoretical or abstract sense. Rather, it describes what a number of prominent Japanese Zen leaders *believed* or *interpreted* Zen to be, primarily in the 1930s and 1940s. On the other hand, material in the second part has a broader focus, showing that Buddhist support for Japanese militarism was by no means limited to the Zen school alone.

Let me also point out that my conflated use of the words "Buddhism," "Mahāyāna Buddhism," and "Zen" is done if not quite purposely then at least consciously – I seek to introduce readers to the way in which these terms were used by the principals themselves at the time. If contemporary scholars of Buddhism must of necessity distinguish between these terms, we must also recognize that for most believers of Buddhism (or any religion for that matter) their "sectarian viewpoints" represent, at least to them, the essence if not the totality of their faith. This attitude was embodied in the 1930s by Sōtō Zen Master Iida Tōin (1863–1937) who wrote: "Zen is the general repository for Buddhism."[1] Thus, in seeking to understand the (Zen) Buddhist faith of those introduced in this book, we must, at least initially, seek to understand Buddhism as they themselves understood it.

No doubt some readers will be disappointed to learn that despite the title of this book, *Zen War Stories*, there are only two chapters (chapters 1 and 9) that relate actual "battlefield tales." As far as Zen is concerned, it is only Zen Master Nakajima Genjō who describes his experience on the naval battlefield. Nevertheless, I dare to call the entire book by this name because every chapter in Part I does describe one or another aspect of Zen's support for Japanese militarism. The material in Part II, as previously noted, reinforces the fact that the Zen school was by no means the only Buddhist organization in Japan to have lent its support.

As this book reveals, the major focus of the Zen school's wartime support was on the "home front" in what was designated at the time as *shisō-sen*, lit. "thought warfare." Hence the bulk of this book seeks to illuminate this critical dimension of modern-day "total war." The reader will, therefore, not find any tales here of Zen-inspired soldiers wielding their samurai swords (or bayonets) in order to "mindlessly," "selflessly," and "compassionately" strike down their opponents *à la* D. T. Suzuki and his ilk. Instead, this book is primarily about the ideology, especially the *spiritual* ideology, that sustained and "inspired" Japan's soldiers on the battlefield and its civilians at home.

Stance

To my mind, a critical analysis of just how the Buddha Dharma was used to legitimate Japanese militarism is far, far more important than revelations about the militarist connections of any one particular Zen master. Nevertheless, since the appearance of *Zen at War*, a number of western Zen teachers have invested considerable time and effort in defending their particular Zen lineage from the charge of war collaboration. Yet, with the laudable exception of David Brazier in his recent book *The New Buddhism*, few of these teachers have analyzed, let alone criticized, the doctrinal interpretations of the Buddha Dharma once used by Japanese Zen masters to justify the mass killing of their fellow human beings.

While I make no claim to have provided such detailed analyses myself, each chapter in this book does include my own interpretation of the material presented. No doubt some readers will take offense at what they perceive as my "moralistic" if not "judgmental" stance. In contemporary academe it often seems that "detached (if not indifferent) objectivity" is the only acceptable stance for the academic author to adopt.

As a reaction to what in times past has often been the bigoted, if not hypocritical, stance taken by western scholars toward Asia in general, and Asian religion in particular, I am very sympathetic to those who demand the highest standards of objectivity from Asianists. I well remember having been first introduced to the study of Buddhism through the works of Christian missionary scholars who claimed:

> According to Buddha, complete annihilation is man's *summun bonum*; whence it follows, that atheism, materialism, or the most absolute scepticism, is in reality the sole doctrine of Buddhism. The followers of Buddhist doctrine at the present day are delivered up to ignorance and immorality, and their rulers are tyrannical and cruel. The doctrine of Śākyamuni, after its expulsion from India, is followed in connection with all the iniquities and absurdities of the idolatrous worship with which it is allied.[2]

As recently as 1963, the distinguished German scholar of Zen, Heinrich Dumoulin, concluded his *A History of Zen Buddhism* as follows: "As a mystical phenomenon, the *satori* experience is imperfect. No human effort to attain enlightenment, no matter how honest and self-sacrificing, can ever lead to the perfect truth, but only the eternal Logos 'who coming into the world enlightens every man' (John 1:9)."[3] In light of prejudiced statements like these, who would not cry out for unbiased scholarship?

Nevertheless, Buddhism has been, from its inception more than 2,500 years ago, a profoundly moral religion, with no more important precept than abstention from taking life. Stanza 130 of the *Dhammapada*, for example, records Śākyamuni Buddha as saying:

> All tremble at punishment,
> Life is dear to all
> Comparing others with oneself,
> One should neither kill nor cause to kill.[4]

Furthermore, in the Mahāyāna tradition, the *Brahmajala Sūtra* teaches that followers who take the vows of a bodhisattva should not participate in war. This sūtra, as Peter Harvey notes,

> forbids detention of anyone, or the storing of any kind of weapons, or taking part in any armed rebellion. [Followers] should not be spectators of battles,

nor should they kill, make another kill, procure the means of killing, praise killing, approve of those who help in killing, or help through magical chants.[5]

Yet, despite injunctions of this kind, modern-day exponents of Buddhism to the West like D. T. Suzuki have not hesitated to claim that Zen, as the essence of Buddhism, "transcends morality."[6] However, not all Zen practitioners agree, for as American Sōtō Zen Master John Daido Loori notes:

Enlightenment and morality are one. Enlightenment without morality is not true enlightenment. Morality without enlightenment is not complete morality. . . . Somehow, teachers in the East and West have tended to shy away from writing about the precepts, perhaps fearing being categorized as moralists.[7]

Whatever other faults this book may have, shying away from a discussion of the precept forbidding the taking of life is not one of them. And as far as being judgmental is concerned, it was Śākyamuni Buddha who, responding to a query from a professional soldier, informed him that were the latter to die on the battlefield he could expect to be "reborn in a hell or as an animal" for his transgressions.[8] Inasmuch as I make no claim to omniscience for myself, I do not know in what state, or even if, the protagonists in this book will be reborn. But, like the Buddha himself, I do not hesitate to judge them on the basis of their deeds, whether of body or speech.

Precautions

This said, I do recognize the ever-present danger of misinterpreting the historical record. That is to say, I am dedicated to the proposition that the material presented in this book be neither twisted nor distorted to serve the writer's own prejudices. Toward this end, to the greatest extent possible my protagonists present their story in their own words, not mine. Of necessity, this requires the frequent use of long quotations, a practice some readers may find tiresome if not repetitive. While I regret this, I do so in the hope that whatever other faults this book may have, taking quotations out of context is not one of them. This book may therefore even be regarded as a "sourcebook" of wartime pronouncements by Zen and other institutional Buddhist leaders, both lay and clerical.

Closely related to the above has been my attempt to include any material that might serve to counteract, or even justify, what might otherwise be regarded as the pro-war stance of those introduced. Who better to defend themselves against the charge of war collaboration than those implicated? This said, it must be pointed out that nearly all of the justifications included in this book were originally written with a Japanese audience in mind. What may serve to convince Japanese readers may not be equally convincing to non-Japanese.

Finally, I have endeavoured to make it clear to readers where my own commentary both begins and ends. Hopefully, whether or not readers agree with me, there will at least be no confusion as to what is historical fact versus my interpretation of the same. While not expecting unanimity of opinion, I do hope the reader will be prompted to further explore the critically important issues raised here. Like its predecessor *Zen at War*, this book is but a further step on the road to understanding the reasons behind the slavish subservience of Zen leaders to Japanese militarism. Thus, this book is not designed to end debate on Zen-endorsed "holy war" but to provoke it.

ACKNOWLEDGEMENTS

In writing this book I have once again enjoyed the support and understanding of a number of academic colleagues, as well as fellow Buddhists who, like myself, continue to struggle with the meaning of the events I describe, not least in terms of its meaning for their own spiritual life. I would particularly like to express my appreciation to Stuart Lachs and David Loy who, thanks to the magic of the Internet, were able to read and critique early drafts of particular chapters in this book. They have been true "Dharma friends." I am also indebted to historians Herbert Bix and Yoshida Yutaka at Hitotsubashi University in Tokyo for sharing with me their penetrating insights into the wartime period as well as helping me locate relevant documents. John Makeham, a colleague at the University of Adelaide, contributed to my understanding of the influence of indigenous Chinese thought on the development of East Asian Buddhism. Nevertheless, any faults and omissions contained in this book are entirely my own.

As in *Zen at War*, I have continued the practice of writing Japanese names in the traditional manner, i.e. family name first and personal name last. Further, after first mention, Buddhist priests are referred to by their religious rather than family names – for example, Nakajima Genjō in chapter 1 is referred to as Genjō after first mention. The only exceptions to this are references to Zen Masters Harada Daiun Sōgaku and his disciple Yasutani Haku'un who are best known in the West by their surnames. As for rendering Chinese into English, I have employed the *pin-yin* system of romanization though, on occasion, I have augmented this with the older Wade-Giles system in the interest of clarity.

Notes referring to material found on the same or immediately adjoining pages of a single source have sometimes been telescoped together. In such cases, the last numerical citation in a paragraph refers to all preceding quotations lacking a citation. Complete source citations are provided in the appendices under "Bibliography." Macrons have been used to indicate long vowels, with the exception of such words as Tokyo and Bushido, which are already familiar to English readers. Sanskrit terms are rendered complete with diacritical marks.

I have been most fortunate to have had an understanding and patient, not to mention knowledgeable, editor in Rachel Saunders at RoutledgeCurzon. In addition, the patient advice and support provided by the series editor,

Charles Prebish, has proved invaluable. Finally, I wish to thank you, my reader, for investing both your time and money in this book. I very much look forward to hearing your reactions and critiques, for over the years readers have been among my very best teachers.

Part I

1

THE ZEN MASTER WEPT

In late January 1999 I travelled to the village of Hara in Japan's Shizuoka Prefecture to visit Zen Master Nakajima Genjō (1915–2000), the 84-year-old abbot of Shōinji temple and head of the Hakuin branch of the Rinzai Zen sect. Shōinji is famous as the home temple of Zen Master Hakuin Ekaku (1685–1768), the great medieval reformer of Rinzai Zen. Although I didn't know it at the time, Genjō had little more than another year to live.

Genjō, I learned, had first arrived at Shōinji when he was only twelve and formally entered the priesthood at the age of fifteen. Eventually he became a Dharma successor of Yamamoto Gempō (1866–1961), who was abbot of both Shōinji and nearby Ryūtakuji temples, and one of the most highly respected and influential Rinzai masters of the modern era. In the immediate postwar period, Gempō was selected to head the entire Myōshinji branch of the Rinzai Zen sect.

In the course of our conversation, Genjō informed me that he had served in the Imperial Japanese Navy for some ten years, voluntarily enlisting at the age of twenty-one. Significantly, the year prior to his enlistment Genjō had his initial enlightenment experience (*kenshō*).

Having previously written about the role of Zen and Zen masters in wartime Japan, I was quite moved to meet at last a living Zen master who had served in the military. That Genjō was in the Rinzai Zen tradition made the encounter even more meaningful, for as readers of *Zen at War* will recall, none of the many branches of that sect have ever formally expressed the least regret for their fervent support of Japanese militarism. Given this, I could not help but wonder what Genjō would have to say about his own role, as both enlightened priest and seasoned warrior, in a conflict that claimed the lives of so many millions.

To my surprise, Genjō readily agreed to share his wartime experiences with me, but, shortly after he began to speak, tears welled up in his eyes and his voice cracked. Overcome by emotion, he was unable to continue. By this time his tears had triggered my own, and we both sat round the temple's open hearth crying for some time. When at length Genjō regained his composure, he informed me that he had just completed writing his autobiography, including a description of his years in the military.

Genjō promised to send me a copy of his book as soon as it was published. True to his word, at the beginning of April 1999 I received a slim volume in the mail entitled *Yasoji o koete* (*Beyond Eighty Years*). The book contained a number of photos including one of him as a handsome young sailor in the navy and another of the battleship *Ise* on which he initially served. Although somewhat abridged, this is his story.[1] It should be borne in mind, however, that his reminiscences were written for a Japanese audience.

In the Imperial Navy

Enlistment

I enlisted in the Imperial Japanese Navy in 1936. On the morning I was to leave, Master [Yamamoto] Gempō accompanied me as far as the entrance to the temple grounds. He pointed to a nearby small shed housing a water wheel and said

Look at that water wheel, as long as there is water, the wheel keeps turning. The wheel of the Dharma is the same. As long as the self-sacrificing mind of a bodhisattva is present, the Dharma is realized. You must exert yourself to the utmost to ensure that the water of the bodhisattva mind never runs out.

Master Gempō required that I leave the temple dressed in the garb of an itinerant monk, complete with conical wicker hat, robes, and straw sandals. This was a most unreasonable requirement, for I should have been wearing the simple uniform of a member of the youth corps.

I placed a number of Buddhist sūtras including the *Platform Sūtra of the Sixth Zen Patriarch* in my luggage. In this respect I and the master were of one mind. While I had no time to read anything during basic training, once assigned to the battleship *Ise* I did have days off. The landlady where I roomed in Hiroshima was very kind, and my greatest pleasure was reading the recorded sayings of the Zen patriarchs.

In the summer of 1937 I was granted a short leave and returned to visit Master Gempō at Shōinji. It was clear that the master was not the least bit worried that I might die in battle. "Even if a bullet comes your way," he said, "it will swerve around you." I replied, "But bullets don't swerve!" "Don't tell me that," he remonstrated, "you came back this time, didn't you?" "Yes, that's true ..." I said, and we both had a good laugh.

While I was at Shōinji that summer I successfully answered the Master's final queries concerning the *kōan* known as "Zhaozhou's *Mu*" [in which Zhaozhou answers "*Mu*" (nothing/naught) when asked if a dog has the Buddha nature]. I had grappled with this *kōan* for some five years, even in the midst of my life in the navy. I recall that when Master Gempō first gave me this *kōan*, he said: "Be the genuine article, the real thing! Zen priests mustn't rely on the experience of others. Do today what has to be done today. Tomorrow is too late!"

4

Plate 1 Rinzai Zen Master Nakajima Genjō as a young priest. Courtesy Nakajima Genjō.

Plate 2 Rinzai Zen Master Nakajima Genjō wearing the uniform of a Japanese Imperial Navy sailor attached to the battleship *Ise*. Courtesy Nakajima Genjō.

Plate 3 View of Nakajima Genjō's ship, the Japanese Imperial Navy battleship *Ise*. Courtesy Nakajima Genjō.

Plate 4 Shōinji Temple located in the village of Hara in Shizuoka Prefecture. Both Zen Master Nakajima Genjō and Inoue Nisshō trained here. In prewar Japan this temple was headed by Rinzai Zen Master Yamamoto Gempō. Courtesy Nakajima Genjō.

6

Master Gempō next assigned me the most difficult *kōan* of all, i.e. the sound of one hand. [Note: this *kōan* is often wrongly translated as "the sound of one hand *clapping*"] "The sound of one hand is none other than Zen Master Hakuin himself. Don't treat it lightly. Give it your best!" the master admonished.

Inasmuch as I would soon be returning to my ship, Master Gempō granted me a most unusual request. He agreed to allow me to present my understanding of this and subsequent *kōans* to him by letter rather than in the traditional personal encounter between Zen master and disciple. This did not represent, however, any lessening of the master's severity but was a reflection of his deep affection for the Buddha Dharma. In any event, I was able to return to my ship with total peace of mind, and nothing brought me greater joy in the navy than receiving a letter from my master.

War in China

In 1937 my ship was made part of the Third Fleet and headed for Shanghai in order to participate in military operations on the Yangzi river. Despite the China Incident [of July 1937] the war was still fairly quiet. On our way up the river I visited a number of famous temples as military operations allowed. We eventually reached the city of Zhenjiang where the temple of Jinshansi is located. This is the temple where Kūkai, [ninth-century founder of the esoteric Shingon sect in Japan], had studied on his way to Changan. It was a very famous temple, and I encountered something there that took me by complete surprise.

On entering the temple grounds I came across some five hundred novice monks practicing meditation in the meditation hall. As I was still young and immature, I blurted out to the abbot,

> What do you think you're doing! In Japan everyone is consumed by the war with China, and this is all *you* can do? [The abbot replied,] And just who are you to talk! I hear that you are a priest. War is for soldiers. A priest's work is to read the sūtras and meditate!

The abbot didn't say any more than this, but I felt as if I had been hit on the head with a sledgehammer. As a result I immediately became a pacifist.

Not long after this came the capture of Nanjing (Nanking). Actually we were able to capture it without much of a fight at all. I have heard people claim that a great massacre took place at Nanjing, but I am firmly convinced there was no such thing. It was wartime, however, so there may have been a little trouble with the women. In any event, after things start to settle down, it is pretty difficult to kill anyone.

After Nanjing we fought battle after battle and usually experienced little difficulty in taking our objectives. In July 1940 we returned to Kure in Japan. From then on there were unmistakable signs that the Japanese Navy was about to plunge into a major war in East Asia. One could see this from the movements of the ships though if we had let a word slip out about this, it would have been fatal. All of us realized this so we said nothing. In any event, we all expected that a big war was coming.

In the early fall of 1941 the Combined Fleet assembled in full force for a naval review in Tokyo Bay. And then, on 8 December, the Greater East Asia War began. I participated in the attack on Singapore as part of the Third Dispatched Fleet. From there we went on to invade New Guinea, Rabaul, Bougainville, and Guadalcanal.

A losing war

The Combined Fleet had launched a surprise attack on Hawaii. No doubt they imagined they were the winners, but that only shows the extent to which the stupidity of the navy's upper echelon had already begun to reveal itself. US retaliation came at the Battle of Midway [in June 1942] where we lost four of our prized aircraft carriers.

On the southern front a torpedo squadron of the Japanese Navy had, two days prior to the declaration of war, succeeded in sinking the British battleship *Prince of Wales* and the battle cruiser *Repulse* on the northern side of Singapore. Once again the navy thought they had won, but this, too, was in reality a defeat.

These two battles had the long term effect of ruining the navy. That is to say, the navy forgot to use this time to take stock of itself. This resulted in a failure to appreciate the importance of improving its weaponry and staying abreast of the times. I recall having read somewhere that Admiral Yamamoto Isoroku [1884–1943], commander of the Combined Fleet, once told the emperor: "The Japanese Navy will take the Pacific by storm." What an utterly stupid thing to say! With commanders like him no wonder we didn't stand a chance.

In 1941 our advance went well, but the situation changed from around the end of 1942. This was clear even to us lower-ranking petty officers. I mean by this that we had started to lose.

One of our problems was that the field of battle was too spread out. The other was the sinking of the American and British ships referred to above. I said that we had really lost when we thought we had won because the US, learning from both of these experiences, thoroughly upgraded its air corps and made air power the centre of its advance. This allowed the US to gain air superiority while Japan remained glued to the Zero as the nucleus of its air wing. The improvements made to American aircraft were nothing short of spectacular.

For much of 1942 the Allied Forces were relatively inactive while they prepared their air strategy. Completely unaware of this, the Japanese Navy went about its business acting as if there were nothing to worry about. Nevertheless, we were already losing ships in naval battles with one or two hundred men on each of them. Furthermore, when a battleship sank we are talking about the tragic loss of a few thousand men in an instant.

As for the naval battles themselves, there are numerous military histories around, so I won't recount them here. Instead, I would like to relate some events that remain indelibly etched in my mind.

Tragedy in the South Seas

The first thing I want to describe is the situation that existed on the islands in the south. Beginning in 1943 we gradually lost control of the air as the US made aerial warfare the core of its strategy. This also marked the beginning of a clear differentiation in the productive capacity of the two nations.

It was also in the spring of that year that my ship was hit by a torpedo off the coast of Hainan island. As I drifted in the South China Sea, I groaned caught in the realm of desire, hovering between life and death. *Kōans* and reciting the name of Amitābha Buddha were meaningless. There was nothing else to do but totally devote myself to Zen practice within the context of the ocean itself. It would be a shame to die here I thought, for I wanted to return to being a Zen priest. Therefore I single-mindedly devoted myself to making every possible effort to survive, abandoning all thought of life and death. It was just at that moment that I freed myself from life and death.

This freedom from life and death was in reality the realization of great enlightenment (*daigo*). I placed my hands together in my mind and bowed down to venerate the Buddha, the Zen Patriarchs, their Dharma descendants, and especially Master Gempō. I wanted to meet my master so badly, but there was no way to contact him. In any event, all of the unpleasantness I had endured in the navy for the past seven years disappeared in an instant.

Returning to the war itself, without control of the air, and in the face of overwhelming enemy numbers, our soldiers lay scattered about everywhere. From then on they faced a wretched fate. To be struck by bullets and die is something that for soldiers is unavoidable, but for comrades to die from sickness and starvation is truly sad and tragic. That is exactly what happened to our soldiers on the southern front, especially those on Guadalcanal, Rabaul, Bougainville, and New Guinea. In the beginning none of us ever imagined that disease and starvation would bring death to our soldiers.

As I was a priest, I recited such sūtras as Zen Master Hakuin's *Hymn in Praise of Meditation* (*Zazen Wasan*) on behalf of the spirits of my dying comrades. Even now as I recall their pitiful mental state at the moment of death I am overcome with sorrow, tears rolling uncontrollably down my cheeks.

Given the pitiful state of our marooned and isolated comrades, we in the navy frantically tried to carry them back to the safety of our ships. I recall one who, clutching a handful of military currency, begged us to give him a cigarette. Our ship's doctor had ordered us not to provide cigarettes to such men, but we didn't care. In this case, the soldier hadn't even finished half of his cigarette when he expired. Just before he died, and believing that he was safe at last, he smiled and said, "Now I can go home."

Another soldier secretly told me just how miserable and wretched it was to fight a war without air supremacy. On top of that, the firepower commanded by each soldier hadn't changed since the 1920s. It was both heavy and ineffective, just the opposite of what the Americans had. Thus the inferiority in weapons only further contributed to our defeat.

It was Guadacanal that spelled the end for so many of my comrades. One of the very few survivors cried and cried as he told me: "One morning I woke up to discover that my comrade had cut the flesh off his thigh before he died. It was as if he were telling me to eat it."

There were so many more tragic things that happened, but I can't bear to write about them. Forgive me, my tears just won't let me.

Characteristics of the Japanese military

In the past, Japan was a country that had always won its wars. In the Meiji era [1868–1912] military men had character and a sense of history. Gradually, however, the military was taken over by men who did well in school and whose lives were centred on their families. It became a collection of men lacking in intestinal fortitude and vision. Furthermore, they suffered from a lack of Japanese spirit and ultimately allowed personal ambition to take control of their lives.

In speaking of the Japanese spirit I am referring to the august mind of the great Sun Goddess Amaterasu. Forgetting this, men in the military were praised as having spirit when they demonstrated they were physically stronger than others. This turned the Japanese Spirit into a joke!

Nevertheless, officers graduated from the naval academy thinking like this and lorded it over their pitiful subordinates. The officers failed to read those books so important to being human, with the result that by the end of the war the Japanese Navy had turned into a group of fools.

As for enlisted men, volunteers were recruited at such a young age they still hadn't grown pubic hair on their balls. Gutless men trained these recruits who eventually became senior enlisted men themselves and the cycle repeated. And what was the result? A bunch of thoughtless, senior enlisted personnel! I was dumbfounded, for it meant the end of the Japanese Navy.

If only the officers at least had thoroughly read Sunzi's *Art of War* and books on western and Chinese history. If they had firmly kept in mind what they learned from such books it would have influenced their military spirit whether they wanted it to or not. How different things would have been had this kind of study been driven home at the naval academy.

If, prior to our invasion, a senior officer had taken six or so junior officers with him to thoroughly survey such places as New Guinea, Rabaul, Guadalcanal etc., I don't think they ever would have sent troops there. The same can be said for our naval attachés stationed abroad. Things would have been different had they thoroughly investigated the latent industrial and military potential of the countries they were assigned to.

The national polity of Japan is characterized by the fact that ours is a land of the gods. The gods are bright and like water, both aspects immeasurable by nature. Furthermore, they undergo constant change, something we refer to in the Buddha Dharma as a "mysterious realm." Eternal and unbroken, these gods have existed down to the present-day. Stupid military men, however, thought: "A country that can fight well is a land of the gods. The gods will surely protect such a country." I only wish that the top echelons of the military had absorbed even a little of the spirit of the real national polity.

The Japanese military of recent times was an organization that swaggered around in the name of the emperor. To see what it was like earlier, look at [army hero of the Russo-Japanese war of 1904–5] Field Marshal Ōyama Iwao [1842–1916] from the Satsuma clan, the very model of a military man. Likewise, [naval hero of the Russo-Japanese war] Admiral Tōgō Heihachirō [1847–1934] was a true man of war.

I will stop my discussion at this point by tearfully acknowledging just how hellish the world was that these more recent stupid officers produced. Thus it is only with my tears that I am able to write these sentences, sentences I send to my beloved war comrades who now reside in the spirit world.

Final comments

This was a stupid war. Engulfed in a stupid war, there was nothing I could do. I wish to apologize, from the bottom of my heart, to those of my fellow soldiers who fell in battle. As I look back on it now, I realize that I was in the navy for a total of ten years. For me, those ten years felt like an eternity. And it distresses me to think of all the comrades I lost.

Author's remarks

Upon reading Genjō's words, I could not help but feel deeply disappointed. This disappointment stemmed from the realization that while I and Genjō had shed tears together, we were crying about profoundly different things. Genjō's tears were devoted to one thing and one thing only – his fallen comrades. As the reader has observed, Genjō referred over and over again to the overwhelming sadness and regret he felt at seeing his comrades die not so much from enemy action as from disease and starvation.

One gets a strong impression that as far as Genjō is concerned what was "wrong" about the "Greater East Asia War" was not the war itself, but that, unlike its earlier wars, Japan had been defeated. Whereas previously, Japanese military leaders had been "men of character," the officers of his era were a bunch of gutless bookworms seeking only to advance their own careers. The problem was not that Japan had invaded China and occupied numerous Asian countries, let alone attacked the USA, but that his superiors had recklessly stationed troops in areas, especially in the South Seas, that were indefensible once Japan lost air superiority.

While at a purely human level I can empathize with Genjō's sense of loss, my own tears were not occasioned by the deaths of those Japanese soldiers, sailors, and airmen who left their homeland to wreak havoc throughout Asia and the Pacific. Rather, I had cried for all those, Japanese and non-Japanese alike, who so needlessly lost their lives due to Japan's aggressive policies.

Nanjing massacre

To my mind, the most frightening and unacceptable aspect of Genjō's comments is his complete and utter indifference to the pain and suffering of the *victims* of Japanese aggression. It is as if they never existed. The one and only time Genjō refers to the victims, i.e. at the fall of Nanjing, it is to tell us that no massacre occurred. Had Genjō limited himself to what he, as a shipboard sailor at Nanjing, had personally witnessed, one could at least accept his words as an honest expression of his own experience. Instead, he claims, without presenting a shred of evidence, that the whole thing never occurred.

Yoshida Yutaka, one of Japan's leading scholars on events at Nanjing, described the Japanese Navy's role as follows:

> Immediately after Nanjing's fall, large numbers of defeated Chinese soldiers and civilian residents of the city attempted to escape by using small boats or even the doors of houses to cross the Yangzi river. However, ships of the Imperial Navy attacked them, either strafing them with machine-gun fire or taking pot shots at them with small arms. Rather than a battle this was more like a game of butchery.[2]

In addition, Japanese military correspondent Omata Yukio provides a graphic eyewitness account of what he saw happen to Chinese prisoners at Nanjing lined up along the Yangzi riverbanks:

> Those in the first row were beheaded, those in the second row were forced to dump the severed bodies into the river before they themselves were beheaded. The killing went on non-stop, from morning until night, but they were only able to kill 2,000 persons in this way. The next day, tired of killing in this fashion, they set up machine guns. Two of them raked a cross-fire at the lined-up prisoners. Rat-a-tat-tat. Triggers were pulled. The prisoners fled into the water, but no one was able to make it to the other shore.[3]

Needless to say, Genjō was not the only Japanese military man to deny that anything like a massacre ever took place at Nanjing. One of the commanders leading the attack on the city, Lt. General Yanagawa Heisuke (1879–1945), later dismissed all such allegations as based on nothing more than "groundless rumours." His soldiers, he claimed, were under such strict military discipline that they even took care to wear slippers when quartered in Chinese homes.[4]

These denials notwithstanding, the numerous eye-witness accounts, including those by western residents of the city, not to mention such recent books as Iris Chang's 1997 *The Rape of Nanking*, graphically document the widespread brutal and rapacious conduct of the Japanese military at Nanjing if not throughout the rest of China and Asia. It therefore borders on the obscene to have a self-proclaimed "fully enlightened" Zen master like Genjō deny a massacre took place at Nanjing while admitting "there may have been a little trouble with the women."

Compare Genjō's admission with an interview for the 1995 documentary film *In the Name of the Emperor* given by Azuma Shirō, the first Japanese veteran to publicly admit what he and his fellows soldiers had done in Nanjing:

> At first we used some kinky words like *Bikankan*. *Bi* means "hip," *kankan* means "look." *Bikankan* means, "Let's see a woman open up her legs." Chinese women didn't wear underpants. Instead, they wore trousers tied with a string. There was no belt. As we pulled the string, the buttocks were exposed. We "*Bikankan*." We looked. After a while we would say something like, "It's my day to take a bath," and we took turns raping them. It would be all right if we only raped them. I shouldn't say all right. But we always stabbed and killed them. Because dead bodies don't talk.[5]

In attempting to explain the rationale behind the conduct of Japanese soldiers at Nanjing, Iris Chang, among others, points to their religious faith as one of the key factors in making such conduct possible. She writes: "Imbuing violence with holy meaning, the Japanese Imperial Army made violence a cultural imperative every bit as powerful as that which propelled Europeans during the Crusades and the Spanish Inquisition."[6] (Chapter 9 contains yet another eye-witness account of Japanese military brutality in China.)

From a doctrinal point of view, Japan's Shinto faith cannot escape culpability for having turned Japan's military enterprise into a "holy war." That is to say, it is Shinto that has long asserted that Japan is a divine land ruled over by an emperor deemed to be a divine descendant of the Sun Goddess Amaterasu. Thus, any act sanctioned by this divine ruler must necessarily be a divine undertaking. Yet, as this book and my earlier *Zen At War* amply demonstrate, this world view was adopted *in toto* into the belief system of Japan's Buddhist leaders, most especially those affiliated with the Zen school. Genjō's contemporary reference to Japan as a "land of the gods" is but further evidence that, at least as far as he was concerned, it still is.

Pacifism

Genjō's encounter with the Chinese abbot of Jinshansi is, at least in terms of his Buddhist faith, one of the most memorable parts of his memoirs, for it clearly reveals a head-on clash of values. On the one side stands Buddhism's *universal* commitment to non-killing. On the other side is the Japanese military's willingness to engage in mass killing as an instrument of national policy. Genjō was a Buddhist priest, yet he was also a member of the Japanese military. What was he to do?

"I felt as if I had been hit on the head with a sledgehammer," Genjō states before adding "as a result I immediately became a pacifist." As promising as his dramatic change of heart first appears, nowhere does Genjō demonstrate that it had the slightest effect on his subsequent conduct, i.e. on his willingness to fight and kill in the name of the emperor. This suggests that *in practice* Genjō's newly found pacifism amounted to little more than "feel good, accomplish nothing" mental masturbation.

In fact, during a second visit to Shōinji in January 2000, I personally queried Genjō on this very point: I asked him why he hadn't attempted, in one way or another, to distance himself from Japan's war effort following his change of heart. His reply was short and to the point: "I would have been court-martialled and shot had I done so."

No doubt, Genjō was speaking the truth, and I for one am not going to claim that I would have acted any differently (though I *hope* I would have). This said, Genjō does not hesitate to present himself to his readers as the very embodiment of the Buddha's enlightenment. The question must therefore be asked, is the killing of countless human beings in order to save one's own life an authentic expression of the Buddha Dharma, of the Buddha's enlightenment?

An equally important question is what Genjō had been taught about the (Zen) Buddhist attitude toward warfare *before* he entered the military. After all, he had trained under one of Japan's most distinguished Zen masters for nine years before voluntarily entering the navy, apparently with his master's approval. Although Genjō himself does not mention it, my own research reveals that his master's attitude toward war and violence is all too clear. As early as 1934 Yamamoto Gempō proclaimed: "The Buddha, being absolute, has stated that when there are those who destroy social harmony and injure the polity of the state, then killing them is not a crime."[7] Gempō's wartime actions will be introduced in further detail in chapters 6 and 11.

If there is some truth in the old adage, "Like father, like son," then one can also say, "Like master, like disciple." Thus if Genjō may be faulted for having totally ignored the moral teachings of Buddhism, especially those forbidding the taking of life, then he clearly inherited this outlook from his own master. But were these two Zen priests exceptions or isolated cases in prewar and wartime Japan?

Like *Zen At War* before it, this book will show that they were not. In reality, Genjō and Gempō were no more than two representatives of the fervently pro-war attitudes held not only by Zen priests but nearly all Japanese Buddhist priests and scholars regardless of sectarian affiliation.

Neither must it be forgotten that Genjō's preceding comments were not written in the midst of the hysteria of a nation at war, but as recently as 1999, more than fifty years later. Like Genjō, today's Japanese political leaders still find it extremely difficult, if not impossible, to acknowledge or sincerely apologize for, let alone compensate the victims of, Japan's past aggression. This fact was revealed once again in April 1999 when a new government-sponsored war museum opened in Tokyo. Known as the *Shōwa-kan*, this museum features exhibits devoted exclusively to the wartime suffering of the Japanese people themselves. As in Genjō's case, the immense suffering of the *victims* of Japanese aggression is totally ignored.

If there is anything that distinguishes Genjō from his contemporaries, either then or now, it was his self-described conversion to pacifism in China. Genjō was at least conscious of a conflict between his priestly vows and his military duties. This was a distinction that very, very few of his fellow priests ever made. On the contrary, during the war leading Zen masters and scholars claimed, among other things, that killing Chinese was an expression of Buddhist compassion designed to rid the latter of their "defilements."[8]

Moral blindness

For those, like myself, who are themselves Zen adherents, it is tempting to assign the moral blindness exhibited by the likes of Genjō and his master to the xenophobia and ultranationalism that so thoroughly characterized Japan up until 1945. On the other hand, there are those who describe it as reflecting the deep-seated, insular makeup of the Japanese people themselves.

While there is no doubt some degree of truth in both these claims, it is also true that Zen has a very long history of "moral blindness," reaching back even prior to Zen's introduction to Japan. Japanese Zen inherited the antinomian assertions prevalent in Chinese Chan (Zen) circles as early as the eighth century that those who are enlightened transcend all duality including life and death as well as good and evil. Enlightened beings are therefore no longer subject to the moral constraints enjoined by the Buddhist precepts on the unenlightened.

Significantly, Chan's break with traditional Buddhist morality did not go unchallenged. Liangsu (753–93), a famous Chinese writer and lifelong student of Tiantai (J. Tendai) Buddhism criticized this development as follows:

> Nowadays, few men have true faith. Those who travel the path of Chan go so far as to teach the people that there is neither Buddha nor Dharma, and that neither good nor evil has any significance. When they preach these doctrines to the average man, or men below average, they are believed by all those who live their lives of worldly desires. Such ideas are accepted as great truths which sound so pleasing to the ear. And the people are attracted to them just as *moths in the night are drawn to their burning death by the candle light*[9] [Italics mine].

In reading Liang's words, one is tempted to believe that he was a prophet able to foresee the deaths over a thousand years later of millions of young Japanese men who were drawn to their own burning deaths by the Zen-inspired "light" of

Bushido. And, of course, the many more millions of innocent men, women and children who burned with (or because of) them must never be forgotten.

It is only when we become aware of Zen's deep-seated antinomianism as expressed in the preceding quote that Genjō's attitude as expressed in his recollections becomes comprehensible. It is in fact the key to understanding why both Genjō and his master were equally convinced that it was possible to continue on the road toward enlightenment even while contributing to the mass carnage that is modern warfare.

In Genjō's case it is even possible to argue that his experience of "great enlightenment" was actually hastened by his military service, specifically the fortuitous American torpedo that sank his second ship, the military fuel tanker *Ryōhei*, and set him adrift while killing some thirteen of his shipmates.[10] Where else was he likely to have found both *kōans* and reciting the name of Amitābha Buddha "meaningless" and been forced, as a consequence, to "totally devote [him]self to Zen practice within the context of the ocean itself ... making every possible effort to survive, abandoning all thought of life and death."

As Zen continues to develop and mature in the West, Zen masters like Genjō remind us of a key question remaining to be answered – *what kind of* Zen will take root? The scandals, often of a sexual nature, that have rocked a number of American Zen (and other Buddhist) centers in recent years may seem a world apart from Zen-supported Japanese militarism. The difference, however, may not be as great as it first appears, for I suggest the common factor is Zen's long-standing and self-serving lack of interest in, or commitment to, Buddhism's ethical precepts. If this seems too broad or sweeping a conclusion to reach on the basis of just one Zen master's war recollections, I invite the reader to read further.

2

MONKS AND SOLDIERS MOVE ON
THEIR STOMACHS

The relationship between Zen and the Imperial military was as broad as it was deep. This chapter reveals just how thoroughly the Imperial military was influenced by Zen monastic life – even down to such practical matters as soldiers' mess kits. Readers of *Zen At War* will recall that it was Sōtō Zen Master Sawaki Kōdō (1880–1965) who pointed out in June 1944 that Zen monasteries and the military "truly resemble each other closely."[1]

At the time I recorded Kōdō's words, I thought he might have been guilty of some "wishful thinking" in identifying Zen monastic life with the military. However, on discovering the following episode in the 1985 book *Time of the Wintry Wind (Kogarashi no Toki)*. I realized that the "close resemblance" was, historically speaking, neither fabrication nor mere coincidence. Whereas in other instances it can be argued that it was the personal choice of military men to practice Zen, what follows is one example of a situation in which all Japanese soldiers were destined, albeit indirectly, to become "Zen practitioners."

The following episode forms part of chapter 3 of *Kogarashi no Toki* and is presented here in slightly condensed form. I wish to express my gratitude to the book's author, Ōe Shinobu, for having given his permission for this material to be translated and included here. Before recounting the episode, however, let us take a brief look at the situation facing the Japanese military at the time.

Toward "total war"

In 1907, Japan was once again at peace, having emerged victorious from the Russo-Japanese War of 1904–5. Unlike its earlier war with China in 1894–5, however, victory had not come easily nor decisively. In fact, having lost 100,000 men and spent some two billion yen on the war, Japan's ostensible victory was so fragile that during peace negotiations it had no choice but to forego all war reparations from Russia. This was so deeply resented at home that anti-peace riots broke out in Tokyo resulting in the imposition of martial law.

Though dismayed at the cost of the war, there was nevertheless an upsurge in national pride among the general populace. After all, for the first time in modern history, Japan, an Asian nation, had forced a western imperialist country to give up some of its economic interests in Asia, especially those in Korea and Manchuria. The Japanese military basked in the glory of this accomplishment even as its leaders reflected soberly on just how close to defeat they had come. The more visionary among them realized that future victories would depend on Japan's ability to quickly and effectively mobilize the resources of the entire country, military and civilian alike, in the war effort. It was the dawn of the age of "total war."

One of those visionary military leaders was an up-and-coming Lieutenant Colonel by the name of Tanaka Gi'ichi (1864–1929). Tanaka had first distinguished himself as a military strategist during the Russo-Japanese War. One reason for his success was his thorough knowledge of Russian military organization, strategy, and tactics. Tanaka had acquired this knowledge, including fluency in Russian, during an earlier four-year sojourn in Czarist Russia (1898–1902) where he had been the first Japanese officer to study Russian military affairs. Tanaka would later rise to the rank of full general, serve as Minister of the Army in two cabinets, and as prime minister from 1927–9.[2]

In May 1907, however, Tanaka was the commander of the Third Infantry Regiment located in Tokyo. With the support of the highest echelons of the military, Tanaka was determined to initiate a program of military renewal, beginning with his own unit. Thus he took the unprecedented step of ordering two platoons of his men to provide logistical support for the first annual meeting of the "Patriotic Women's Society" (*Aikoku-fujin-kai*) to be held outdoors. Recognizing that his use of the military to aid a voluntary civilian organization would be controversial, Tanaka justified his action as follows:

> The age when wars are fought by the military alone has come to an end. During the Russo-Japanese War we mobilized one million men of whom only 200,000 were active duty soldiers. The rest were reservists ... family men with wives and children to support....
>
> The reason that a major power like Russia lost to us was because Russian civilians were involved in revolutionary disturbances at home. We have reached a stage where the military that has built a close relationship with the civilian populace during peacetime will emerge victorious in war. No doubt, however, we will hear complaints about our actions from those useless muddleheads who still believe wars are won by military power alone.[3]

As Tanaka predicted, complaints were forthcoming, some from the country's major newspapers. With the backing of his superiors, however, he weathered the storm and steadfastly stuck to his agenda for military reform, the next target of which was the military's internal regulations. The regulations then in effect had been taken verbatim from those in use by the Prussian army in 1894.

Internal Regulations

A committee was established for the revision of the internal regulations on 25 July 1907. Tanaka explained the committee's purpose as follows:

> The emperor's army is like a boat that floats on the sea of the people. It is our duty as officers to ensure that it doesn't lose its way. ... Without the people's support the ship will sink, but there cannot be the slightest doubt that it is we officers who are responsible for determining the ship's destination.[4]

Given the overwhelming power of the Japanese military in setting the political agenda during the Asia-Pacific War, Tanaka's words seem almost prophetic, though he no doubt would not have regarded them as such. They remind us once again of just how deeply imbedded militarism's roots were in modern Japan, predating the attack on Pearl Harbour by more than thirty years.

Returning to Tanaka, he determined that the revision of the internal regulations should be based on four fundamental principles:

1 Everything in the military was to be standardized.
2 "Spiritual education" (*seishin kyōiku*) was to be heavily stressed.
3 Military discipline was to be promoted.
4 Ethical training based on a sense of family was to be made of primary importance.[5]

Of particular interest is the increased emphasis Tanaka placed on "spiritual education." This is no doubt a reflection of the fact that one of the chief lessons Japanese military leaders drew from the carnage of the Russo-Japanese War was the critical role played by morale or spirit on the battlefield.[6] Tanaka not only sought to incorporate spiritual education into the military's revised internal regulations, promulgated in 1908, but upon becoming a section chief in the Military Affairs Department of the Army Ministry in 1909, he successfully urged the adoption of a new set of general service regulations that also exalted the military spirit, using the medieval warrior code of Bushido as a model.

In the eyes of military leaders like Tanaka, victory hinged not so much on modern weaponry as it did on the individual soldier's willingness to sacrifice himself in the attack. Something as readily and freely available as "spirit" was especially attractive to a military leadership who found themselves engaged in a never-ending struggle for funding in a peacetime economy. At the same time, it gave new life to Japan's traditional samurai culture, as embodied in the Bushido code, which stressed the twin virtues of absolute loyalty to one's superiors and duty unto death. This renewed emphasis on Japan's traditional warrior spirit dovetailed nicely with the heightened nationalism of the general populace.

Japan's military leaders sought not only to indoctrinate the Bushido code into their troops but hoped to discover indigenous models for as many things related to the military as possible. Having previously slavishly modeled themselves on the Prussian military, the Japanese military found itself with anomalies like western-style eating utensils that were clearly inappropriate for a culture where cooked rice remained the main staple of a soldier's diet. Lightweight, durable bowls for rice, not plates for meat and potatoes, were what was needed. But where were such items to be found? As we join the story, Imperial Infantry Major Kishi Yajirō (1874–1938), Lt. Col. Tanaka's assistant, was about to find out.

A Visit to Kenchōji

Major Kishi was at a loss as to how to go about improving the provision of soldiers' rations. At that point Regimental Commander Tanaka suggested that he visit a Zen temple to see how they fed their novice monks (*unsui*). Using his connections, Kishi arranged to inspect the dining area at the Rinzai Zen monastery of Kenchōji in Kamakura in the late fall of 1907.

That evening, on his way back to Tokyo by train, Kishi recalled what he had seen during his visit to Kenchōji. He was told that the foundation of Buddhist practice was to cut oneself off from the secular world, eat pure and simple food, and devote oneself totally to Buddhist practice. In Buddhism the purpose of eating was the maintenance of one's health in order to realize enlightenment. In doing this, one should bear in mind that eating was itself an expression of enlightenment. It was for this reason that in the Buddhist precepts there were various regulations related to the taking of meals. Of all sects, he was told, it was the Zen sect that had most faithfully observed these regulations.

In the Tang era (618–c.907) the Zen monk Baizhang (720–814) established a set of monastic regulations known as the *Baizhang Qinggui*. Most of these regulations were eventually lost, but those left were gathered together by the Zen priest Changlu Zongze during the Northern Song Dynasty (960–1126) and republished as the ten-volume *Chanyuan Qinggui*. In Japanese Zen it was these regulations that were adopted as the basis of monastic life. In the Zen sect, eating was regarded as being synonymous with the Buddha Dharma and for that reason was considered to be extremely important.

As Kishi previously had but little knowledge of Zen, he was surprised to hear all this and asked, "I've heard that one principle of the Zen sect is to eat plain food."

The priest assigned to look after Kishi was the monastery's kitchen supervisor (*tenzō*). The kitchen supervisor replied:

Needless to say, we abstain from meat and fish. In the morning we eat rice gruel together with sesame seed mixed with salt and pickled radishes. Lunch consists of barley boiled together with partially milled white rice, *miso* soup, and pickles. In addition, there is something we call *yakuseki* (lit.

20

medicine stone) consisting of leftovers that, in principle, require no further cooking. In the secular world this would be called the evening meal.[7] When the monks have been engaged in physical labour we may add one or two dishes of cooked vegetables to their lunch and evening meals.

Having said this, the kitchen supervisor went on to stress the following:

> Although plain food is unpretentious, it doesn't mean that it is simply coarse food prepared in any old way. It seems that people in the secular world often mistakenly regard plain food as being nothing more than coarse food. From our point of view, however, even seemingly luxurious food is merely coarse food if carelessly and thoughtlessly prepared. It seems the secular world has a lot more such food than we do.

With this the kitchen supervisor broke into a smile and continued:

> Please forgive me for having gone on so about the *Chanyuan Qinggui*, but I would like you to understand that from the time of Baizhang, Zen monasteries have had a system in which there are six monastic offices designed to assist the head priest. Taken together, they are responsible for all of the monastery's affairs.
>
> One of the six positions is that of kitchen supervisor. I serve as the kitchen supervisor for Kenchōji. According to the *Chanyuan Qinggui*, the kitchen supervisor is responsible for feeding all of the monks residing in the monastery in order to enhance their practice of the Way as much as possible. At times this may call for certain innovations, the aim of which is to promote the joy they experience on realizing the unity of all things.
>
> Pardon the personal reference, but the office of the kitchen supervisor is, by virtue of his responsibility for meal preparation, a very important one. From ancient times this position has been filled by a dedicated senior monk who is held in high regard by all the monks in the monastery. The *Chanyuan Qinggui* states that the kitchen supervisor should decide questions relating to the acquisition of foodstuffs and the content of the menu in consultation with the monastery's head administrator. This indicates just how important the provision of meals is.

Kishi felt that he had been taught an important lesson. In the military's current regulations governing internal matters there was absolutely nothing related to culinary affairs. In the military, the physical condition of soldiers is synonymous with their readiness for war. Therefore the provision of meals was even more important than in the Zen school. In light of this, how was it possible, he asked himself, that the military's internal regulations lacked so much as a single provision on culinary affairs?

In the current internal regulations there was, it is true, provision made at the battalion level for a mess commissioner. However, the duties of the mess commissioner were defined as follows: "To supervise the battalion's cooks, control all rations-related financial transactions, and take care of rations-related administrative matters."

That is to say, the title was that of a mess commissioner but the duties were those of a Zen monastery's head administrator. There was no provision made for a position equivalent to that of kitchen supervisor.

Kishi asked: "What should the mental attitude of a kitchen supervisor be as it relates to providing food?" The kitchen supervisor responded:

> The *Chanyuan Qinggui* states that if the "six flavours" are not pure, and the "three virtues" are not present, then the rationale for the kitchen supervisor's service to his fellow monastics disappears. The six flavours refer to the six characteristics of monastic food, i.e. its degree of 1) chewiness, 2) acidity, 3) sweetness, 4) bitterness, 5) saltiness, and 6) seasoning. Further, the three virtues of monastic food refer to its: 1) taste, 2) cleanliness, and 3) compliance with the Buddhist precepts. That is to say, it should be pleasant to the palate, prepared in a sanitary manner, and use only those foodstuffs that are in accord with the Buddhist precepts.

Sitting in the train, Kishi took out his notebook and wrote the following down in pencil:

1 Matters concerning the mess commissioner.
2 Matters concerning the establishment of culinary regulations.

The scene that had left the deepest impression on Kishi was of the monks going to the midday meal carrying their own bowls. This was known as *takuhatsu* (lit. "requesting bowls") while the use of bowls in the meal itself was called *gyōhatsu* (bowls for religious practice). Up until then, Kishi had associated the word *takuhatsu* with monks in training who recited sūtras in front of the homes of laity while accepting alms of either rice or money in their iron bowls. While this understanding was correct as far as it went, he learned for the first time that the term *takuhatsu* was also used in connection with the taking of meals. The iron bowl, as an eating utensil, was regarded as a symbol of the enlightenment-seeking mind.

Kishi remembered having asked: "I seem to recall that the phrase, 'assuming the mantle of one's master' is derived from the Zen school."

"Yes," the kitchen supervisor replied, "this practice began with Bodhidharma (fifth-century CE?), the first Zen patriarch in China, who gave his robes and bowls to his disciple Huike (487?–593?) as proof that he had transmitted the Dharma to him."

Hearing this, Kishi thought to himself that inasmuch as Zen monastic life was designed so that a large group of trainees might live a hygienic and orderly lifestyle on an ongoing basis, there was plenty of scope to put it into practice within a military context.

On the train returning to Tokyo, Kishi continued thinking about just how to incorporate the monks' eating bowls into barrack's life.

"Use aluminum!" he thought as he slapped his knee.

Aluminum was already being used to make pots for cooking rice in the field. Its ease of handling had been demonstrated during the Russo-Japanese war.

This said, it was also true that all of the raw materials used for making aluminum had to be imported. Furthermore, in wartime aluminum was so rapidly consumed that there was never enough even for just cooking pots and canteens. Nevertheless, as far as daily use in a barrack's environment was concerned, it was far more hygienic and durable than the pasteboard eating utensils then in use even if it was not as long lasting as bowls made out of iron.

At that time the eating utensils used by common soldiers were called "*menko*" (pasteboard). As far as army regulations were concerned, they were regarded as kitchen fixtures and formally designated by two Chinese characters that could be pronounced as either "*mentsū*" or "*mentu.*" This designation referred to something that was round and able to hold a full serving of rice. This utensil was actually made out of thin pieces of such woods as Japanese cedar and cypress that had been bent into a circular shape with a bottom attached. In some districts it was known as "*wappa.*"

At the time of this story, *mentsū* were more commonly known for being used by beggars. It was because ceramic rice bowls and wooden lacquer bowls were so easily broken that *mentsū* had been adopted as eating utensils by the military at the beginning of the Meiji period. However, just why the pronunciation of the word "*mentsū*" had been changed to *menko* is unknown.

The only thing that can be said with certainty is that the designation of eating utensils as *menko* was something that occurred following the adoption of *mentsū* by the military. In any event, this custom continued even after the eating utensils changed to aluminum and in fact survived until the dissolution of the Imperial military in 1945.

Revision

Returning to Major Kishi, he gave an oral report on the outcome of his visit to Kenchōji to Regimental Commander Tanaka. He then prepared a written report by way of reference for the revision of the military's internal regulations. His report contained the following recommendations for improving the provision of rations and cooking in a barrack's environment:

1 A basic principle should be to make it clear that all activities, whether sitting, lying down, sleeping or eating are opportunities for the soldier to cultivate his spirit.
2 It should be clearly stated that the provision of rations is one of the duties of the battalion commander.

3 The primary responsibility of the battalion mess commissioner should be changed from supervising the disbursement of funds to taking responsibility for the quality, storage, and acquisition of rations.

4 Regulations should be established for a noncommissioned officer to be in charge of culinary affairs.

5 A chapter dealing with culinary affairs should be created. This chapter should contain the following main points:

(a) It must be made clear that food should be nutritious, easily prepared, and plain.

(b) It must be realized that the purpose of culinary affairs in the military is to achieve the goals listed above as well as to quickly prepare tasty food on the battlefield.

(c) The brigade's accountant and mess commissioner should investigate such things as the market price of food, exerting themselves to the utmost to provide good quality food.

(d) The major reason for leftover rice or side dishes is the presence of unhealthy soldiers or poor tasting food. The brigade commander and mess commissioner must watch this carefully, conducting frequent inspections and continuously endeavouring to improve the quality of the food.

(e) The mess commissioner should place primary importance on nutrition, selecting good tasting items while bearing in mind the amount budgeted for rations. The commissioner is also responsible for preparing the following week's menu and submitting it to the brigade commander.

(f) The mess commissioner should frequently visit the kitchen area to taste the food prior to its being served, checking on such things as the quality of the cooking, the quantity of the food, and the cleanliness of the eating utensils.

6 It is permissible to discard the present pasteboard utensils and replace them with bowls made of aluminum. From the point of view of both durability and hygiene, such bowls are far superior to pasteboard. Furthermore, in order to realize the basic principle concerning eating in a barrack's environment, eating utensils must not be seen to lack dignity. From this aim as well, it is clear that pasteboard is regarded as inappropriate by the general populace.

Regimental Commander Tanaka immediately began experimenting with the use of eating utensils made of aluminum. As expected, they were both convenient and hygienic, superior in every respect. Based on this, the entire military gradually switched over to aluminum utensils.

However, as far as ordinary soldiers were concerned, even though such things as their washbasins were now made out of aluminum, they were still considered "pasteboard." Soldiers were sensitive to the fact that when one touched utensils made of aluminum one got the feeling of cold, military efficiency combined with religious asceticism. Out of this came a song by an unknown author that

24

gradually spread throughout the military. Its lyrics accurately captured the change that had taken place:

> Oh how we dislike the military
>> With its metal teacups and metal chopsticks!
> We are not Buddhas
>> What a pity they feed us as if we were!

Author's remarks

Those wishing to defend Zen from the charge of collaboration with the modern Japanese military from an early date might well say of the preceding episode that the responsibility for the influence of Zen monastic life on the military cannot fairly be apportioned to Zen leaders themselves. After all, it was Japanese military leaders who came seeking "inspiration" from Zen, not the other way around.

This said, I cannot but recall the evident pride of one of my own Zen masters, Asada Daisen, abbot of Jōkuin temple in Saitama Prefecture, when he first told me some twenty-five years ago of the way in which Zen monasteries had served as a model not just for the Japanese military's mess kits but its organizational structure as well. Writer, and former Rinzai Zen priest, Mizukami Tsutomu (b. 1919) described this organizational influence as follows:

> Zen monasteries attach greater importance to the length of one's Zen training than they do to one's calendar age. Even older monks must follow the lead of younger ones if the latter have been in training for longer. This is a fundamental rule, one that applied to the life of novice monks (*unsui*) as well. In light of this it is understandable that when, in the past, the military was drafting regulations to govern its internal affairs, it looked to Zen monastic regulations for guidance.[8]

Historically speaking, the close relationship between Zen and the military is hardly surprising, for its origins can be traced as far back as the Kamakura period (1185–1333) when Zen was first introduced into Japan as an independent school. Zen rapidly found favour with the warrior class, many of whom schooled themselves in this tradition up to and including the emergence of Japan's modern imperial soldiers, especially its officer corps. D. T. Suzuki explained the attraction of Zen to warrior/soldiers as follows:

> Zen discipline is simple, direct, self-reliant, self-denying; its ascetic tendency goes well with the fighting spirit. The fighter is to be always single-minded with one object in view: to fight, looking neither backward or sidewise. To go straight forward in order to crush the enemy is all that is necessary for him. . . . A good fighter is generally an ascetic or stoic, which means he has an iron will. This, when needed, Zen can supply.[9]

Should the Zen-trained warrior be worried that he might be breaking the fundamental Buddhist precept against the taking of life, the great Rinzai Zen Master Takuan (1573–1645) dismissed such concern in the following letter written to his warrior patron, Yagyū Tajima no kami Munenori (1571–1646):

> The uplifted sword has no will of it own, it is all of emptiness. It is like a flash of lightning. The man who is about to be struck down is also of emptiness, and so is the one who wields the sword. None of them are possessed of a mind which has any substantiality. As each of them is of emptiness and has no 'mind' (*kokoro*), the striking man is not a man, the sword in his hands is not a sword, and the 'I' who is about to be struck down is like the splitting of the spring breeze in a flash of lightning.[10]

As these quotes and the above episode attest, Japanese Zen and martial figures enjoyed a close and intimate relationship long before the outbreak of the Asia-Pacific War in December 1941.

3

THE ZEN OF ASSASSINATION

Just as in the case of the rise to power of the Nazi party in Germany, the growth of Japanese militarism took place in concert with the repression of domestic dissent, including dissent within the military itself. While this book, like *Zen At War* before it, is primarily concerned with the close relationship that existed between Japanese Zen leaders and the Japanese military during the Asia-Pacific War (and before), it is noteworthy that Zen leaders also played an active role in curbing domestic dissent to Japan's expansion on to the Asian continent. Of particular interest, if only because of the major impact it had on Japanese society, is the role played by a small number of Zen masters and their lay disciples in the domestic assassinations that were such a prominent feature of public life during the early to mid-1930s.[1]

The following is an introduction to this question. It examines the role played by one prominent Sōtō Zen master, Fukusada Mugai, in the assassination of a major military leader. While Mugai neither pulled the trigger of an assassin's pistol nor wielded an assassin's sword, he was nevertheless convinced, like his lay disciple Lt. Colonel Aizawa Saburō, that Zen Buddhism justified killing his fellow Japanese in the name of the Buddhist-inspired phrase "destroying the false and establishing the True" (*haja kenshō*).[2]

The assassination of Major General Nagata Tetsuzan

Brief historical introduction

The Manchurian Incident of September 1931 set off a chain of events that led in the first instance to the establishment of the Japanese puppet state of *Manzhouguo* (*Manchukuo*) in February 1932 and eventually to the outbreak of full-scale war with China in July 1937. Japanese aggression abroad, however, did not imply unanimity of opinion at home, for widely diverse groups of civilian politicians, ultranationalists, leftists, and military officers of various ranks, continued their attempts to bend domestic and foreign policy to their particular viewpoints and ideologies. In short, in the early to mid-1930s, Japan was still some distance away from the monolithic emperor-centred, military-dominated society it would become by the end of the decade.

In seeking to understand how the military, together with sympathetic bureaucrats and corporate allies, ultimately emerged triumphant in Japanese society, it is crucial to understand the role played by the domestic assassinations of both civilian and military figures. Although assassination is the ultimate form of political intimidation, in Japan of the 1930s (and before), right-wing inspired violence rarely resulted in anything more than a short prison sentence for the "patriotic" perpetrator(s) involved, at least that is, up through the major military uprising staged by a group of young military officers and their troops on 26 February 1936. This uprising succeeded in killing three leading cabinet ministers, wounding a fourth, and injuring a number of others, some critically, before it was finally suppressed.[3] It is also noteworthy that no matter how disparate the views of the assassins were, the one thing they and their supporters always agreed on was their deep concern for the "welfare of the nation."

One of the military assassins active during this period was Lt. Colonel Aizawa Saburō (1889–1936) of the 41st Infantry Regiment in Fukuyama, a member of a group of relatively young army officers who, at least in their own eyes, were characterized by their complete and total devotion to a uniquely divine emperor. Appropriately, they designated themselves as the "Young Officers' Movement" (*Seinen Shōkō Undō*) and willingly identified themselves with the larger "Imperial Way Faction" (*Kōdō-ha*) that included some of Japan's top-ranking military officers.

Imperial Way Faction members further attached the pejorative label "Control Faction" (*Tōsei-ha*) to those officers of any rank who, by refusing to join with them, stood in the way of the realization of their goals. It should be noted, however, that the military's leadership was also split on the basis of such things as age, education and family background, and even former clan affiliation. In addition, there was a sometimes fierce rivalry, especially for funding but also including strategy, between the Army and the Navy.

Inasmuch as this is not a discussion of military factionalism, let it suffice here to note that members of the Imperial Way Faction sought to bring about a "Shōwa Restoration," i.e. the direct rule of the emperor, something they believed would result in land reform, the overthrow of the corrupt, "privileged classes" and a more equitable distribution of the nation's wealth through the nationalization of big business. In theory at least, their goals shared much in common with Nazi "national socialism," and like the Nazis they were fully prepared to employ violence, especially political assassination, to bring about a government to their liking. As for foreign policy, they were strongly anti-communist and therefore regarded the Soviet Union, rather than the USA, Great Britain and other western powers, as the chief threat to the Japanese Empire, especially to growing Japanese interests in Manchuria.

By comparison, members of the Control Faction were generally more accepting of the status quo, at least at home. They accepted a basically capitalist society but wanted the government to intervene more actively in the private sector to ensure their military-related, economic goals were achieved. Believing that it was possible to advance the military's interests through close cooperation with Japan's leading financial combines (*zaibatsu*) and government bureaucrats, they were generally opposed to political assassination, at least domestically. In the foreign policy arena, however, they advocated ever greater advancement onto the Asian continent, including further encroachments on a fractionalized and militarily weak China. They also came to favour proposals for the forcible acquisition of such strategic raw materials as oil and rubber from the colonized countries of Southeast Asia, even at the risk of war with the western masters of these countries.

Both military factions, it must be stressed, were equally committed to the maintenance and, if possible, the expansion of Japan's own colonial possessions. In this sense the struggle within the military was not one of "good guys" versus "bad guys," or even "moderates" versus "radicals." In the end, however, what may be termed the more realistic, if not opportunistic, stance of the Control Faction meant that its leaders eventually gained the upper hand in the military (and then the government), gradually purging members of the Imperial Way Faction from positions of leadership beginning as early as January 1934.

Predictably, this purge of leaders produced a strong backlash, especially among those younger and more radical officers associated with the Young Officers' Movement within the Imperial Way Faction. Having been one of the few high-ranking officers to oppose the ongoing purge, General Mazaki Jinzaburō (1876–1956), then Inspector General of Military Training, was a hero (or "saviour") to the Young Officers, among them Lt. Colonel Aizawa Saburō. Thus, when in July 1935 Aizawa learned that General Mazaki had himself been purged, the former took it upon himself to seek revenge. As a mid-ranking officer, Aizawa later claimed that he had acted in order to save younger officers from ruining their careers by taking matters into their own hands (as some of them nevertheless did on 26 February 1936).

The man Aizawa chose for assassination was Major General Nagata Tetsuzan (1884–1935), Director of the Military Affairs Bureau at the War Office. Nagata was known not only for his brilliant mind, but equally for his attention to detail and the calm and thoughtful manner in which he reached decisions. None of these, however, were qualities that appealed to the deeply-felt yearnings of Aizawa and his comrades for a swift and thoroughgoing restructuring of Japanese society, the particulars of which even they were unsure of. That is to say, to have had a detailed plan for social reform would have impinged on the prerogatives of the emperor, something that was unthinkable for loyal subjects (although not necessarily for the highest-ranking officers of the Imperial Way Faction). Inasmuch as Nagata actively opposed their call for a "Shōwa Restoration," he had to be eliminated.

On 19 July 1935 Aizawa, then forty-six, called on Nagata for the first time, verbally demanding that the general step down because of his role in ousting Mazaki. Nagata not only refused to do so but in retaliation arranged for Aizawa to be transferred to Taiwan. This in turn prompted Aizawa to consider more drastic action, for he realized that once in Taiwan he would be in no position to influence the course of events.

At approximately 9.20 a.m. on 12 August 1935, Aizawa entered the War Ministry from the rear and went to the first floor office of an old friend, Lt. General Yamaoka Shigeatsu (1882–1954), head of army maintenance. Ostensively he had come to inform the general of his imminent departure for Taiwan. After sharing some tea, Aizawa asked Yamaoka if Nagata were in his office on the second floor. Upon being informed that he was, Aizawa excused himself and, at 9:45 a.m., burst in on Nagata, sword in hand.

Nagata did not immediately realize what was about to happen, for he was deep in conversation with Colonel Niimi Hideo, chief of the Tokyo Military Police. Ironically, the topic of their conversation was what to do about the growing discontent in the army.[4] Quickly coming to his senses, Nagata jumped up and headed for the door, successfully dodging Aizawa's first blow. He was, however, unable to escape the next, a thrusting blow from the back that momentarily pinned the general to the door. Not yet dead, Aizawa then delivered a final blow to his victim's head as the latter lay outstretched on the floor.

Although unarmed, Col. Niimi had initially attempted to aid Nagata but suffered a disabling cut to his left arm. For his part, Aizawa, a former swordsmanship instructor at the military academy, later confessed to having been embarrassed by the manner in which he had despatched the general. "I had failed to kill Nagata with one blow and as a fencing master I felt deeply ashamed," he said.[5] Ashamed or not, Aizawa calmly left the general's office and returned to General Yamaoka's office where he informed his startled friend what had taken place. Noticing that Aizawa was bleeding, Yamaoka arranged for the colonel to be taken to the Ministry's medical dispensary. There, while being treated for a minor cut to his left wrist, Aizawa was arrested by the military police.

Aizawa Saburō and Zen

Aizawa first encountered Zen at the Rinzai temple of Zuiganji located near Matsushima in Miyagi Prefecture. At the time, Aizawa was a 26-year-old second lieutenant attached to the 29th Infantry Regiment headquartered in the northern Honshū city of Sendai. On a Monday morning in the spring of 1915, Aizawa's company commander, Prince Higashikuni Naruhiko (1887–1990), paternal uncle to Emperor Hirohito, addressed the assembled company officers as follows: "Yesterday I visited Zuiganji in Matsushima and spoke with the abbot, Matsubara Banryū [1848–1935]. He informed me that Buddhism was a religion that taught exerting oneself to the utmost in service to the country."[6] As simple as this statement was, it nevertheless proved to be the catalyst for Aizawa's Zen practice, for as he later related: "I was troubled by the fact that I knew so little of what it meant to serve the country."[7]

Aizawa therefore decided personally to visit Banryū to seek further clarification of this matter. On doing so, Banryū related to him the well-known example of Kusunoki Masashige (1294–1336), a loyalist military leader during the period of the Northern and Southern Courts (1332–90). Defeated in battle and facing death, Masashige is said to have made a vow to be reborn seven times over in order to annihilate the enemies of the emperor. Banryū went on to inform Aizawa that if he truly wished to acquire a spirit like that of Kusunoki he "must study the Buddha Dharma and especially practice Zen meditation."[8] Inspired by these words, Aizawa determined to do exactly that, though he first encountered the practical problem that Zuiganji was located some distance from Sendai making it impossible for him to meditate there on a daily basis.

The result was that Aizawa sought out an equally well-known Sōtō Zen master resident in the city of Sendai itself, Fukusada Mugai (1871–1943), abbot of the large temple complex of Rinnōji. Mugai, however, following a time-honoured Zen tradition, initially refused to accept Aizawa as his lay disciple. "If you're just coming here for character-building, I don't think you'll be able to endure [the training]," Mugai told him.[9] Refusing to be dissuaded, Aizawa eventually gained Mugai's acceptance. In fact, shortly after Aizawa began his training, Mugai granted him, in a highly unusual gesture, permission to board in the priests' quarters just as if he were a neophyte monk (unsui).

Some months later Aizawa encountered yet another barrier to his Zen practice when his regimental superiors decided it was improper for him to actually live at the temple. Hearing of this, Mugai set about finding alternative living quarters for his military disciple. It was in this way that Aizawa came to board with Hōjō Tokiyoshi (1859–1929), then president of Tōhoku Imperial University and yet another of Mugai's lay disciples. With this arrangement in place, Aizawa continued to train under Mugai through the spring of 1917.

As to what he gained from his Zen training, Aizawa later testified at his pre-trial hearing: "The result of [my training] was that I was able to deeply cultivate the conviction that I must leave my ego behind and serve the nation."[10] When, during the court-martial itself, the judge specifically asked which one of Mugai's teachings had influenced him the most, Aizawa immediately replied: "Reverence for the emperor [is] absolute."[11] As for Mugai's attitude toward his military disciple, one of Aizawa's close officer friends described it as "just like the feelings of a parent for his child."[12]

Not surprisingly, Aizawa felt the same about Mugai. This is revealed, among other things, by the fact that even after his imprisonment, Aizawa arranged for medicine to be sent to Mugai upon hearing of his master's illness. In fact, it was this illness that prevented Aizawa from realizing his final wish – that Mugai be present to witness his execution. Having failed in this, Aizawa's last message to Mugai read: "I pray that you will fully recover from your illness just as quickly as possible."[13]

Given the closeness of the master-disciple relationship between Aizawa and Mugai, it is not surprising to learn that Mugai was the second person to visit

Aizawa in prison after the latter's arrest, i.e. on 4 September 1935. Mugai subsequently visited him once again on the 10th. The entries in the prison's visitor log describe Mugai as Aizawa's "teacher to whom is owed a debt of gratitude" (*onshi*). The purpose of the visits was recorded as a "sympathy call" (*imon*).

Court martial

Aizawa's public court martial began on 28 January 1936 at the headquarters of the 1st Division in Tokyo, and received wide press coverage. Testifying on the general background to his act, Aizawa stated:

> I realized that the senior statesmen, those close to the throne, and powerful financiers and bureaucrats were attempting to corrupt the army for the attainment of their own interests; the Imperial Army was thus being changed into a private concern and the supreme command was being violated. If nothing was done I was afraid the army would collapse from within. The senior statesmen and those close to the throne are indulging in self-interest and seem to be working as the tools of foreign countries who watch for their chance to attack Japan.[14]

It should be noted that the "[right of] supreme command" referred to in this passage meant that the military was, constitutionally-speaking, not subject to the control of the civilian government. Rather, in theory at least, it was directly under the emperor's command (and that of his designated representatives). In practice, this meant that anyone (other than the emperor) who sought to interfere with, or restrict the military in any way could be charged with "violating" not simply the military's prerogatives but the right of command of the emperor himself – a charge akin to treason.

In light of this, why did Aizawa choose to assassinate another military man, indeed his lawfully-appointed superior officer? Was he not thereby violating the very right of supreme command he claimed to be defending? To this charge Aizawa replied:

> I marked out Nagata because he, together with senior statesmen, financial magnates and members of the old army clique like Generals Minami and Ugaki, were responsible for the corruption of the army. The responsibility for the army rested on Nagata, the Director of the Military Affairs Bureau. He was the headquarters of all the evil. If he would not resign there was only one thing to do. I determined to make myself a demon and finish his life with one stroke of my sword.[15]

With this in mind, let us turn to the "spiritual" dimension, or motivation, which lay behind Aizawa's act. Here Aizawa testified as follows:

The emperor is the incarnation of the god who reigns over the universe. The aim of life is to develop according to His Majesty's wishes, which, however, have not yet been fully understood by all the world. *The world is deadlocked because of communism, capitalism, anarchism, and the like.* As Japanese we should make it our object to bring happiness to the world in accordance with His Majesty's wishes. As long as the fiery zeal of the Japanese for the Imperial cause is felt in Manchuria and other places, all will be well, but let it die and it will be gone forever. Democracy is all wrong. Our whole concern is to clarify Imperial rule as established by Emperor Meiji [Italics mine].[16]

Although the above words appear to leave little room for a "Zen connection" to the incident, the phrase "The world is deadlocked . . ." will shortly be seen to be pregnant with the "flavour" of Zen. More to the point, however, is the following short, yet key comment Aizawa made in describing his state of mind at the moment of the assassination itself: "I was in an absolute sphere, so there was neither affirmation nor negation, neither good nor evil."[17]

Is this a manifestation of the Zen spirit? The well-known western exponent of Japanese culture and Zen, Reginald Blyth (1898–1964) would certainly have recognized it as such. In postwar years he wrote: "From the orthodox Zen point of view, . . . any action whatever must be considered right if it is performed from the absolute."[18]

Mugai's defense

Mugai appeared as a witness for the defense at the ninth hearing held on 22 February 1936. Following his court testimony, Mugai returned to the witness waiting room where he told a reporter for the *Yomiuri Shimbun*:

> Although I don't intend to discuss the incident itself, I would like to say that I have known Aizawa's parents for the past thirty years. For this reason there is no one better acquainted with Aizawa's childhood and character than I am. While it is true that Aizawa's Zen practice is still immature in some respects, I think that the decisive action he took in accomplishing his great undertaking transcended both life and death. Even should he receive the death penalty, Aizawa will be satisfied, for as long as his ideas live on, life and death are of no concern to him.[19]

If the preceding comments leave some doubt as to what Mugai really thought of his disciple and his "great undertaking," Mugai later clarified his position in a pamphlet entitled *A Glimpse of Lt. Colonel Aizawa (Aizawa Chūsa no Hen'ei)*. In a section labelled "Comments by Fukusada Mugairōshi," Mugai wrote:

> Aizawa trained at Rinnōji for a period of three years starting when he was still a lieutenant. In applying himself to his practice with untiring zeal, he

acted just as if he were a Zen priest, something quite impossible for the ordinary person to do. His character was honest and pure, and from his youth he had, through his Zen training, continually strengthened his resolve to "destroy the false and establish the True" as he sought the Buddha Way. I believe the recent incident was truly a reflection of the purity of mind he had acquired over a period of more than twenty years since having been a young officer. That is to say, he was burning with his ideal of destroying the false.[20]

If the preceding comments still strike the reader as relatively vague, especially as regards Mugai's assessment of Aizawa's motive in killing General Nagata, Mugai was prepared to be more specific, including his own estimation of the problems then facing Japan. He wrote:

Aizawa frequently lamented the existing state of corruption in our country. Military morale, he noted, had deteriorated to the point that he was concerned about the nation's safety. Whenever Aizawa came to Sendai he visited me without fail, and, in addition, frequently wrote me letters overflowing with his intense concern for the welfare of the nation. Especially in the last two or three years he spoke of his inconsolable sorrow. And in this regard I felt the same as he did.[21]

And finally, Mugai was ready to tell his readers just how truly wonderful his disciple was. That is to say, he was ready to praise Aizawa's "superb spirit" coupled with his "resolute and steadfast faith":

It is clear that Aizawa thought day and night of how to break the deadlock facing the nation in the present emergency. I believe Aizawa felt compelled to express his spirit as he did. He intended to sacrifice himself from the outset in hope of single-handedly purifying the military through eradicating the source [of the problem]. I recognize, however, that many of those who today think only of their own personal advancement find his action difficult to understand. For my part, I fully understand why he acted as he did.

Aizawa's act was definitely not one of madness. Without discussing whether it was right or wrong, I know that, prior to acting, he had repeatedly given the matter serious thought. His was not a rash undertaking nor one, as many now say, of seeking fame for himself. Neither, I am convinced, was it one of simple blind faith. There is no doubt that, given Aizawa's purity of character and self-sacrificing devotion, he felt compelled to do what he did in the face of present-day corruption.

I believe in Aizawa. The consistency of Aizawa's character lies in his readiness to serve sovereign and country on the basis of a resolute and unshakable faith that enabled him to transcend life and death. I am certain this is not a question of placing too much confidence in him, for I know that many of his former classmates [at the military academy] also recognize the nobility of his spirit.[22]

Execution

In light of Mugai's admiration for his disciple, it was only natural that the close relationship between these two lasted even beyond the grave. That is to say, following Aizawa's execution by military firing squad on 3 July 1936, it was Mugai who bestowed on his disciple a posthumous Buddhist name (*kaimyō*) consisting of nine Chinese characters, numerically speaking the highest honor a deceased Japanese Buddhist layman can receive. The meaning of the characters also reveal the esteem Mugai had for his disciple: "layman of loyalty and thoroughgoing duty [residing in] the temple of adamantine courage."

Mugai bestowed this auspicious posthumous name on Aizawa in spite of the fact that a general order had been issued which forbade both elaborate memorial services and the erection of shrines or monuments in his memory. Thus, by honoring a man the army had branded a "traitor to the nation" (*kokuzoku*), Mugai himself became the subject of an investigation by the military police. Although hospitalized at the time, upon being informed of the investigation Mugai said, "Are there any traitors in the realm of the dead? ... If they [the military police] have any complaints, tell them to have the Minister of the Army come here and lodge them in person!"[23]

Aizawa had yet a second connection to Zen following his death. A portion of his cremated ashes were retained in Tokyo and interred in a common grave for all twenty-two former officers and civilian sympathizers who were executed for their part in the 26 February 1936 military uprising referred to above. The grave site is located at the Sōtō Zen temple of Kensōji in Azabu, Tokyo, founded in 1635 by the Nabeshima family, the former feudal lord of Hizen (present-day Saga Prefecture).

It was only in the postwar years that relatives of the deceased were allowed to openly hold memorial services at Kensōji. In 1952 these relatives erected a tombstone over the common grave which included the names of the deceased as well as the following inscription: "Grave of the Twenty-two Samurai." In 1965 this same group erected a statue of the bodhisattva of compassion, Avalokiteśvara (*Kannon*), with right hand raised, at the spot in Yoyogi, Tokyo where the executions took place. This statue was dedicated to the memory of both the executed rebels and their victims. Even today, memorial services are held at Kensōji on 26 February and 12 July (the day on which most of the victims were executed).

The organizational name chosen by the relatives for their undertakings is *Busshin-kai* (Buddha Mind Association). One is left to ponder the connection between "Buddha mind" and political assassination.

Conclusion

In evaluating the above, it should be noted that Mugai was far from the first modern Zen master to heap lavish praise on a military disciple. The noted Meiji period Rinzai Zen master, Nantembō (1839–1925), for example, praised his own famous disciple, Army General Nogi Maresuke (1849–1912), as follows:

> I have no doubt that Nogi's great accomplishments during the Sino-Japanese and Russo-Japanese Wars were the result of the hard [Zen] training he underwent. The ancient Zen patriarchs taught that extreme hardship brings forth the brilliance [of enlightenment]. In the case of General [Nogi] this was certainly the case.... All Zen practitioners should be like him.... A truly serious and fine military man.

And Nantembō went on to add: "There is no bodhisattva practice superior to the compassionate taking of life."[24]

This said, Mugai was certainly unique in praising a military man who had been labelled a traitor to his country. It is abundantly clear, however, that Mugai did not regard Aizawa as such. On the contrary, he was convinced, as was Aizawa himself, that such acts were necessary in order to "break the deadlock facing the nation in the present emergency." Although the historical validity of this statement is questionable, what is of interest here is the almost uncanny resemblance between Mugai's thought and that of D. T. Suzuki. Only two years later, i.e. in 1938, Suzuki would claim:

> Zen has no special doctrine or philosophy, no set of concepts or intellectual formulas, except that it tries to release one from the bondage of birth and death, by means of certain intuitive modes of understanding peculiar to itself. It is, therefore, extremely flexible in adapting itself to almost any philosophy and moral doctrine as long as its intuitive teaching is not interfered with. It may be found wedded to anarchism or fascism, communism or democracy, atheism or idealism, or any political or economic dogmatism. It is, however, generally animated with a certain revolutionary spirit, and *when things come to a deadlock* – as they do when we are overloaded with conventionalism, formalism, and other cognate isms – Zen asserts itself and *proves to be a destructive force* [Italics mine].[25]

In supporting the actions of an assassin, it can be said that Mugai demonstrated just how "extremely flexible" Japanese Zen of the 1930s was "in adapting itself to almost any philosophy and moral doctrine...." In this context the question must be asked if there was anything in Suzuki's interpretation of Zen that would have argued against Mugai's endorsement of his disciple's action.

I suggest there is nothing. That is to say, the type of Zen advocated by Suzuki, Mugai, and other Zen leaders of that period was, under the right conditions, just as amenable to supporting assassination at home as it was to supporting Japan's aggression abroad. In arguing this I would point to yet another of Suzuki's statements:

> Zen did not necessarily argue with them [warriors] about the immortality of the soul or righteousness or the divine way *or ethical conduct,* but it simply urged *going ahead with whatever conclusion rational or irrational a man has arrived at.* Philosophy may safely be left with intellectual minds; Zen wants to act, and the most effective act, once the mind is made up, is to go on without looking backward. In this respect, Zen is indeed the religion of the samurai warrior [Italics mine].[26]

Whether Aizawa's act was rational or not is yet another contestable point, but for both Suzuki and Mugai the question of 'rationality' was, in any event, of little or no consequence. Furthermore, like Suzuki, Mugai did not wish to consider "whether [his disciple's act] was right or wrong." For both Suzuki and Mugai there was only one direction for the Zen practitioner to proceed – straight ahead "without looking backward."

In pointing out the similarity in thought between Mugai and Suzuki, I am not suggesting these two men were either acquaintances or directly influenced each other's thinking. This said, it is interesting to note the existence of an indirect link between the two men in the person of Hōjō Tokiyoshi. As noted above, Mugai had arranged for Aizawa to reside in Hōjō's home during the period he trained at Rinnōji. Not only was Hōjō then president of Tōhoku Imperial University, he was also the same man who, as D. T. Suzuki's former high school mathematics teacher, had first introduced Suzuki to Zen.

One indication of Hōjō's own Zen orientation is that he originally trained as a layman under the noted Rinzai Zen master, Imakita Kōsen (1816–92), abbot of Kamakura's Engakuji monastic complex. In the 1870s Kōsen had been a leading figure in promoting reverence for the emperor and unquestioning loyalty to the state by virtue of his role as a "national evangelist" for the Meiji government's ill-fated Ministry of Doctrine. No doubt it was Hōjō's influence that led Suzuki to train at Engakuji beginning in 1891, first under Kōsen until the abbot's death the following year, and then under Kōsen's successor, Shaku Sōen (1859–1919).

Be that as it may, Suzuki's connection to Hōjō did not end in high school, for the latter eventually resigned his university presidency to become head of the prestigious Gakushūin (Peers' School) in Tokyo in June 1917. It was at Gakushūin that Suzuki once again found himself under Hōjō's tutelage, for Suzuki had been an English teacher at this same school ever since his return to Japan from the United States in 1909.

While I have no evidence indicating this indirect link was anything more than coincidence, I suggest it reveals something about the intellectual climate within Zen circles of that era. That is to say, it was perfectly acceptable to represent Zen as being a "destructive force" as long as that destruction was in the service of some alleged "greater good," most especially in the service of the state and its policies. Although it was unusual for this destructiveness to be directed against representatives of the state, even this was not unprecedented, for Zen-related figures had already been deeply involved in the so-called "Blood Oath Corps Incident," i.e. the assassination of two government and financial leaders in early 1932.[27] This incident will be discussed in more detail in chapter 11.

Borrowing Suzuki's words once again, it can be argued that this was the inevitable price Japanese Zen in the 1930s had to pay for its willingness to be found "wedded to anarchism or fascism, communism or democracy, atheism or idealism, or any political or economic dogmatism."

4

ŌMORI SŌGEN

The Dr. Jekyll and Mr. Hyde of Zen

Another Zen figure closely connected to the events described in the previous chapter is Ōmori Sōgen (1904–94). Sōgen has been lauded as the "greatest Zen master of modern times," whose very life is "worthy to be considered a masterpiece of Zen art."[1] As extravagant as these claims may sound, Sōgen was unquestionably an accomplished master of the traditional arts of swordsmanship (*kendō*) and calligraphy (*shodō*), not to mention a prolific author of books and articles on Zen. He also served as president of Rinzai Zen sect-affiliated Hanazono University and was the founder of the Chōzenji, International Zen Dōjō (Training Centre), in Hawaii. Needless to say, Sōgen also claimed Buddhist enlightenment as his own, having had his initial enlightenment experience at the of age twenty-nine while yet a lay disciple of another highly regarded Rinzai Zen master, Seki Seisetsu (1877–1945).

Readers of *Zen At War* will recall that I touched on the wartime activities of both Seki Seisetsu and his equally famous disciple Yamada Mumon at some length.[2] As for Sōgen, I noted that he was closely connected to the Tōyama family, the head of which, Tōyama Mitsuru (1855–1944), was the dean of Japan's prewar and wartime ultranationalists for whom intimidation, blackmail, and assassination, both at home and abroad, were routine occurrences.[3] What I didn't know at the time was the important role Sōgen played in the events that both preceded and followed Aizawa Saburō's assassination of General Nagata Tetsuzan as described in the previous chapter.

Yet, simply because Sōgen was an acquaintance of Japan's most notorious ultrarightist, or associated with persons involved in political assassination, should that detract from his reputation as a Zen master? Is it fair to judge Sōgen, or any person, solely on the basis of the company they keep?

Obviously the answer to these questions is no. But, as the reader will soon see, there is much more that is suspect about Sōgen than simply his wartime friends. As this chapter will show, Sōgen was himself a significant ultranationalist leader not only in prewar and wartime Japan but in the postwar period as well. Before exploring this "dark side" of Sōgen, however, let us first become better acquainted with the "official" version of his life as related by his numerous admirers. After all, what makes the "good" Dr. Jekyll such a fascinating character is that he lived in the same body as the "evil" Mr. Hyde.

Plate 5 Rinzai Zen Master Ōmori Sōgen.

Ōmori as the "Good" Dr. Jekyll

Perhaps more than any other modern Zen master, Ōmori Sōgen may be said to personify what D. T. Suzuki, among others, held to be a Zen ideal – the "unity of Zen and the sword" (*Zenken ichinyo*). In fact, when in 1958 Sōgen published a book promoting this unity, Suzuki praised it, saying, "I was enthralled by Mr Ōmori's *Zen to Ken* (*Zen and the Sword*). . . . With this, for the first time, we can speak of *Ken* and Zen as one."[4]

That Sōgen was an accomplished swordsman there can be no doubt, for he began his practice of *kendō* (the Way of the sword) at the age of fourteen or fifteen and subsequently trained under some of Japan's best-known masters, including Maeno Jisui (1870–1940), Oda Katsutarō, and Yamada Jirōkichi, fifteenth generation head of the Jikishin Kage school of swordsmanship. Further, Sōen studied calligraphy under Yokoyama Setsudo (1884–1966) of the Jubokudō school. In time, the two of them founded their own school of calligraphy known as the *Hitsuzendō* (Way of Brush and Zen).

Sōgen's connection to Zen was no less illustrious than his mastery of the above arts. He commenced his Zen training at the age of nineteen under Maeno Jisui who, like so many teachers of swordsmanship, was also an experienced lay Zen practitioner in the Rinzai tradition. As to why he took up Zen, Sōgen explained:

Honestly speaking, the reason I entered the Way of Zen from the Way of the sword had nothing to do with any lofty ideals on my part. Instead,

40

being short, I realized that I had no hope of standing up to opponents taller than me if I couldn't compensate for their physical advantage by acquiring superior spiritual power. In short, I entered the Way of Zen due to the fear I experienced when sword fighting. I hoped to overcome that fear.[5]

Subsequently, in the late spring of 1925, Sōgen met Seki Seisetsu, head of the Tenryūji branch of the Rinzai Zen sect. Sōgen continued his training under this distinguished master for the next twenty years, i.e. until the latter's death in October 1945. It was in 1933, following eight years of intensive struggle with the *kōan "Mu,"* that Sōgen had his initial enlightenment experience. Sōgen related his "breakthrough" as follows:

> I finished *zazen* and went to the toilet. I heard the sound of the urine hitting the back of the urinal. It splashed and sounded very loud to me. At that time I thought, "Aha!" and I understood. I had a deep realization.[6]

Sōgen added that thanks to his breakthrough, he realized that he was at the centre of absolute nothingness (*zettai-mu*) as well as at the centre of the infinite circle. "To be at the centre of the infinite circle in this human form," he claimed, "is to be BUDDHA himself."[7]

During the war years Sōgen remained a civilian and supported himself and his family as an instructor of swordsmanship. The year 1945, however, dealt a double blow to Sōgen, for not only did Japan lose the war but his own master, Seki Seisetsu, passed away. These events, especially Japan's surrender, became the catalyst for Sōgen's decision to formally enter the Rinzai Zen priesthood. "The first half of my life ended when Japan lost the war," he explained, "[so] according to the samurai code, I became a Buddhist priest."[8]

Seisetsu was succeeded by his chief disciple, Seki Bokuo (1903–91). In 1946, Sōgen, at the age of forty-two, entered the priesthood as Bokuo's disciple. In little more than two years he completed the *kōan* training he had started as a layman and received *inka-shōmei*, a certificate attesting to his full enlightenment. Bokuo then directed Sōgen to become the abbot of Kōho-in, a small temple located in Tokyo's Higashi-Nakano district.

Kōho-in might be called the perfect temple for someone like Sōgen, for though it had been founded as recently as 1943, it was built on land where Yamaoka Tesshū (1836–88) once lived. Yamaoka was not only one of the Meiji period's best known practitioners of swordsmanship, calligraphy, and Zen, but he contributed to the relatively bloodless transition from the Tokugawa Shogunate to the new Meiji government. Thus, what Kōho-in lacked in terms of institutional history was made up for by the character and accomplishments of the man who had lived in its precincts. In Sōgen's eyes, Yamaoka was the very "model of a Japanese."[9]

Life at postwar Kōho-in, however, was far from easy, for as a new temple it lacked traditional parishioners to support it. Thus, Sōgen was forced to turn elsewhere for his primary source of income, and eventually became a civil magistrate in Tokyo, serving in this position for some twenty years. He did, however, find time to write and, as mentioned above, it was through his books that he became acquainted with D. T. Suzuki. Suzuki thought so highly of Sōgen that when he was asked by a high government official to recommend a Zen teacher for then Crown Prince Akihito (now Emperor Akihito), Suzuki reportedly said, "Mr Ōmori would be the best."[10]

In 1970 Sōgen became a professor at Hanazono University in Kyoto where he taught a course entitled "The Practice of Zen." The core of the course was the practice of *zazen* coupled with lectures on such Zen classics as the *Hekigan-roku* (*Blue Cliff Record*) and the *Roankyō* (*Donkey-Saddle Bridge*). He went on to serve as the university's president from 1978 to 1982. During these years he led a Wednesday evening *Zazen* Club that was started on behalf of the members of the university's *Kendō* Club but grew in popularity to take in members of other martial arts clubs, the all-male pep squad, and the general public.

It was also during these years that Ōmori commenced a series of visits to the West, most especially Hawaii, initially at the invitation of the Japanese-American Rinzai Zen master, Tanoue Tenshin (b. 1938). In 1972 this led to the establishment of Chōzenji, International Zen Dōjō, in Hawaii as "a place of Zen training where persons of any race, creed, or religion who are determined to live in accordance with Buddha Nature (the Inner Self or the Way) may fulfil this need through intensive endeavour."[11] In Japan, Sōgen founded Seitaiji, a Zen training centre for both clerics and lay people, in 1975 in Yamanashi Prefecture.

Until he suffered a debilitating stroke in December 1988, Sōgen carried on a busy schedule of lecturing, Zen instruction, and martial arts demonstrations that seldom saw him at his primary residence in Kōho-in for more than a few days at a time. Prior to his stroke, in August 1979, he visited Europe as part of a spiritual exchange entitled "The Fount of East-West Culture." This visit was made possible by the well-known authority on Japan, Trevor Leggett of the BBC and Father Kadowaki, a Catholic priest who had practiced Zen under Sōgen's guidance. Had he not fallen ill during the tour, Sōgen would have had an audience with the Pope.

In October 1979, Sōgen elevated Chōzenji, now located on two-and-a-half acres of land in Hawaii's Kalihi Valley, to the position of a *Daihonzan* (great main temple), thereby creating a new line of Zen with Tanoue Tenshin as its head. Ever faithful to his belief in the unity of Zen and the sword, Sōgen included the following paragraph in the canon for Chōzenji:

Zen without the accompanying physical experience is nothing but empty discussion. Martial ways without truly realizing the "Mind" is nothing but *beastly behaviour*. We agree to undertake all of this as the essence of our training [Italics mine].[12]

After six years of laying bedridden at Kōho-in, Sōgen died on the afternoon of 18 August 1994.

Ōmori as the 'evil' Mr. Hyde

While all too brief, the preceding description demonstrates that Sōgen enjoyed a distinguished career as a master of Zen, swordsmanship, and calligraphy, among his other religious and literary accomplishments. Yet there was also another, and less known, side to Sōgen's life – that of political activist. Here, too, Sōgen distinguished himself from his peers, for he is the only Zen master to have his own fifteen-line entry in the 1991 Japanese publication, *Dictionary of the Right Wing* (*Uha Jiten*). Instead of a master concerned with the "life-giving sword" (*katsujin-ken*) of Zen, we encounter someone who from the 1920s took an active part in the ultra-right's agenda to eliminate parliamentary democracy through political assassination at home and promote Japan's imperialist aims abroad. In short, a man willing to kill all who stood in the way of his political agenda, yet claiming the enlightenment of the Buddha as his own.

Sōgen's statement

But, what exactly did Sōgen believe in so strongly that he was willing to kill on its behalf? Fortunately, Sōgen himself left behind a statement that, though far from providing the whole story, serves to introduce his political thought. It also affords him the opportunity to put the best possible face on his political past (at least for a Japanese audience). Sōgen's views are contained in his foreword to a 1974 enlarged edition of *A Major History of the Right Wing [Dai-Uha Shi]* originally published in 1966 by right-wing leader Arahara Bokusui (b. 1905). It is included here in its entirety.

> From the time I knocked on Tōyama Mitsuru's door as a youth of twenty until war's end at age forty-two, I was, at least to some extent, actively involved in national affairs and endeavoured to train our youth. Yet, during this period I never once referred to myself as a rightist. The reason for this is not because I was too proud to be placed in the rightist category. Instead, it was because I am of the opinion that if the left wing designates Communism and its adherents, then its opposite, the right wing, must naturally refer to capitalism and those who would defend it.
>
> [Rightist leader] Maeda Torao often said, "We are not rightists. If compelled to call ourselves something, we are the "imperial wing." In truth, our position was, to the best of our ability, to clarify the national polity and achieve a restoration of the Imperial Way. It was definitely not our intent to either defend capitalism or become running dogs for the military authorities.

On the one hand, it is true that in its initial stages Japanese capitalism contributed to the national interest by creating a "rich country." Yet, in its later stages it became a part of the financial machinery of Britain and the US and ended up creating a feudal plutocracy, throwing the national polity into confusion. Its true character was revealed by both the Washington [Naval Arms Reduction] Treaty [of 1922] and the London [Naval] Treaty [of 1930].

As for a "strong military," this was a demand of the Meiji state. It was precisely the step by step realization of this goal that made it possible, thanks to both the Sino-Japanese and Russo-Japanese Wars, to smash the surging waves of European expansionism, thereby enhancing the radiant glory of our nation before the whole world. However, when this goal next produced a "military clique" linked to the feudal plutocracy, it became a force that disturbed the emperor's right of supreme command [of the military].

If one lacks a proper understanding of this history, it is impossible to appreciate the self-sacrificing conduct of those who, seeking a Restoration [of political and economic power to the emperor], engaged in a series [of political assassinations] starting with the Blood Oath Corps [in early 1932] and extending through [the Young Officers' Uprising of] 26 February 1936.

So-called progressive commentators criticize these incidents as having been aimed at either the defense of capitalism or the expansion of the military's influence. However, their arguments contain many discrepancies and half-baked inconsistencies. If one followed their reasoning, it would be utterly impossible to understand why the list of persons to be overthrown included senior officials in the government and the Imperial Household Department, as well as military leaders and financial magnates.

In desperation, these commentators seek to fool everyone with talk about military factionalism and personal ambition. But no sane person would believe that a large number of pure-minded youth together with their even more numerous military units would throw away their irreplaceable lives on behalf of one or two ambitious persons or as part of a factional struggle.

For example, at the time of the 26 February Incident, Isobe [Asaichi] wrote in his heart-rending prison diary: "Please overthrow the military clique!" by way of an appeal to the Japanese people. Similarly, just before Shibukawa [Zensuke] was executed he is said to have shouted: "People of Japan, don't be deceived by the military clique!" Would anyone dare claim these words represent nothing more than the resentment felt by the pawns of the military clique at having been betrayed by their masters? Be serious!

Nothing was dearer to myself and my comrades than the elimination of the privileged classes who stood in opposition to the national polity. That is to say, we sought to eliminate the military, financial and political cliques who, having created a feudal plutocracy, placed themselves between the emperor and the people. In this way we believed that the benevolence of the August Mind of His Majesty would pour down on all the people just as the rays of the sun in spring flood the earth with warmth. The feudal plutocracy, on the other hand, was like a black cloud blocking the sunlight.

In times past, this is what the Restoration [of political and economic power to the emperor] was all about. For example, at the time of the Taika Reforms [of 645 CE], powerful families owning both the land and the people on it were the black clouds. At the time of the Meiji Restoration [in 1868], the Tokugawa Shogunate, ruling by force of arms, was responsible for having destroyed the parent-child relationship that previously existed between the sovereign and the people. Hence, our predecessors did away with these black cloud-like entities and in so doing were able to clarify the national polity, contributing to the accomplishment of a forthcoming Restoration that will once again allow the sun to shine resplendently.

I am speaking here of a Shōwa Restoration, the central thesis of which is the overthrow of the feudal plutocracy through the return of property to the emperor. This in turn would make it possible to dispose of capitalism within the context of the national polity and enable the economy to occupy its proper position in society. For this reason it is clear that the Restoration forces can never be described as simply being right wing as opposed to left wing. If one must label these forces, then, as Mr Maeda said, there is no alternative but to call them the "imperial wing."

After the rise of Communism, the theory of national socialism became popular among those who opposed it. National socialism, premised on an affirmation of the state, is an ideology requiring the state to put socialism into operation. However, while at first glance this ideology appears to be quite reasonable, from the point of view of the pure-minded members of the Imperial Way, it was rejected as something akin to "refrying an eel that has already been cooked." That is to say, it was seen as being totally unnecessary.

From the point of view of Japan's ancient history and tradition, the emperor is the nucleus at the centre of the state. And the Great August Mind of His Majesty is something that pours down on the people just as a parent offers unlimited affection to his child. Out of this comes the expression: "Heavenly gods, if there be sin, blame me, for these are the people whom We have given birth to."

In a country such as ours, it follows that politics ought to be thoroughly based on the people. For someone like myself, the [left-wing] idea that the state was an organ for class exploitation was no more than a nonsensical delusion of little importance. The Japanese state, graced by His Majesty, has from its beginnings naturally incorporated (and ought to incorporate) the good points and advantages of socialism. Hence there was no need for us to take up these matters again. It was for this reason that we viewed national socialism as "refrying an eel that has already been cooked."

Later on, the totalitarianism of the Nazis and Fascists became popular, but this was incompatible with Japan's traditional thought that held Japan to be a single, indivisible body. The progressives swept aside those of us who loved Japan and esteemed the state as right-wing fascists and totalitarians. How ignorant they were!

Totalitarianism is a system that, unwilling to admit the uniqueness of the individual within the whole, sees the individual as being in opposition to the whole, discriminating between the two. While totalitarianism takes an organic view of society, it does not accept the independence of the cells that make up the social organism. Instead, the cells are expected to submit unilaterally to the whole. In this respect, totalitarianism is completely different from the standpoint of this country that has as its ultimate aim uniting together as one with our divine emperor while respecting the independent existence of each individual.

Nevertheless, as the war intensified, there was a tendency, no doubt related to the need to prosecute the war, for Japan's military and political leaders to gradually embrace totalitarianism. There is abundant material, however, showing how this tendency produced serious rifts between civilian restorationists outside the government and officials inside.

In rough outline, then, these are the reasons I deny being a rightwinger. Yet, it is true that we were anti-Communist, and therefore opposed to the left wing. In that sense it is not unreasonable to label us as the right wing. However, as detailed above, it is equally clear that it was not our intent to defend capitalism. Nor did we ever intend to establish a dictatorship in contravention to the principles of democracy. On the contrary, we were convinced that the political principles of Japan rejected despotism.

For that reason, we claimed to follow the Imperial Way that consists of the great doctrine of the mean as the highest righteousness. Seen in this light we are decidedly not right-wingers. However, this doctrine does not necessarily mean that we occupy a position equidistant from both wings. That is to say, the doctrine of the mean is not some kind of neutrality ever ready to compromise. Rather, because it is the way of Truth, it is only natural that when, as at present, society is excessively tilted to the left, it takes the form of a tilt to the right.

In today's Japan, at a time when the people of our nation have lost their spirit and society as a whole is tilted to the left, were we to remain exactly in the middle, the ship [of state] would capsize. In this situation it is necessary for us to make a seat for ourselves on what appears to be the right in order to preserve the ship's stability. Understood in this sense we are the right wing.

At this point in time I am a priest, that is to say, someone who has forsaken the secular world. Thus, I am hardly the appropriate person to write a foreword for a book as graphic as this one. But, in consideration of the bonds that existed between myself and the author in the past, I dared to write down an outline of my thoughts by way of an introduction to this book (March 1966).[13]

For those readers unfamiliar with the history and terminology of the prewar period, the meaning of a number of the above passages may be obscure at best. Nevertheless, the deep reverence Sōgen had for the emperor is clearly revealed in such statements as "we believed the benevolence of the August Mind of His Majesty would pour down on all the people...." While it can be argued that something approaching emperor-worship is not necessarily a bad thing in itself, the uncritical attitude Sōgen displayed toward the imperial institution suggests that at the very least we are dealing with matters of faith rather than objective analysis.

Historical record

Kinki-kai

When compared with the historical record, Sōgen's words will be seen as comprising a curious blend of truth, half-truth, and downright fabrication. To demonstrate this, however, we first need to review Sōgen's connection to the Japanese right, beginning with the first right-wing organization he joined, i.e. the Kinki-kai (Imperial Flag Society), in May 1927 at the age of twenty-three.

The Kinki-kai had just been formed for the purpose of pushing for the creation of a totally emperor-centric society. Among other things, this entailed the abolishment of political parties and the transfer of the nation's wealth, especially industrial wealth, from the private sector to the emperor for disposal as befits a "benevolent father." As Sōgen himself indicated above, this latter demand lay at the heart of his political agenda from then on. The justification for restoring the nation's wealth to the emperor was described in the first tenet of the Kinki-kai as follows: "We believe that Japan is one sacred, indivisible body consisting of the emperor, our benevolent father and a living god, and we the masses, his loyal retainers and children."[14] At its peak, the Kinki-kai had some seven hundred members and published its own organ, *Japanese Thought* (*Nihon Shisō*).

Not content with mere membership of a right-wing organization, Sōgen helped found the Kinnō Ishin Dōmei (League for Loyalty to the Emperor and the Restoration) on 11 February 1932. Inasmuch as Sōgen served as the League's secretary-general, its three founding principles may rightly be seen as reflecting his thinking, at least at the time:

I   Taking the establishment of our nation as a matter of first importance, we march forward in a movement dedicated to making a prosperous country through the historic Restoration (of economic and political power to the emperor).

47

II We cry out for the nation's democratic financial machinery to be restored to the emperor as the second phase of the Meiji Restoration.

III Restoring the spirit of the Taika Reforms [of 645 CE], we eagerly await the placing of all private production under the emperor's firm control as well as the completion of the Japanization of all aspects of the nation including its politics, economy, culture, etc.[15]

Significantly, Sōgen did more than merely participate in, or found, emperor-centric organizations. Utilizing his prowess as a master swordsman, he was also willing to both support, and personally engage in, violence to achieve his political goals. This is most clearly demonstrated by his involvement in a July 1933 anti-government plot known as the Sacred Soldiers Incident (*Shinpeitai Jiken*).

Shinpeitai Jiken

The aim of this attempted *coup d'état* was to bring about the Shōwa Restoration through the creation of a Cabinet composed of members of the Imperial family. Toward this end, a group of mostly civilians drawn from various right-wing organizations intended to assassinate the entire existing Cabinet, the presidents of the two major political parties, the Superintendent-General of the Metropolitan Police, together with other leading politicians and financial magnates. Though none of the radical young officers in the Army were directly involved, Navy Commander Yamaguchi Saburō was scheduled to bomb the Cabinet from his plane.

The scale of this plot was unprecedented as demonstrated by the fact that the police, who uncovered the plot only hours beforehand, arrested a total of ninety-five persons armed with ninety-eight swords, and backed by some four hundred armbands to identify all participants. Interestingly, one of the plot leaders arrested was Maeda Torao (1892–1953). The reader will recall that Sōgen previously expressed his approval of Maeda's claim that their movement was not right wing at all, but merely the "imperial wing."

The conspirators also prepared a large number of leaflets, some of which were to be scattered from Commander Yamaguchi's plane, to justify their actions. The leaflets contained three main principles, the third of which read: "The sacred soldiers will annihilate the financial magnates, political parties, and traitors surrounding the sovereign together with their watchdogs, who continue to block the development of the basic principles of our imperial state." This statement was followed by the following five slogans:

I   Establish politics by the emperor!
II Establish an economy in accordance with the Imperial Way!
III Long live the restoration of the Imperial Way!
IV Exterminate the Communist movement!
V   Annihilate financial magnates and political parties![16]

Returning to the perpetrators, by rights there should have been one more arrestee, together with his sword. This was Sōgen who recounted how he avoided arrest as follows:

> The police were looking for me as one of the top leaders in the affair. I was on the list of people to arrest. I had to hide, so I left for Nagoya with only the *kimono* I was wearing and my short sword. In Nagoya I was caught in a police cordon and was searched, but my sword was carefully hidden under my arm. The detective did not find it. . . . From then, I went from place to place and hid.[17]

The fact that Sōgen had time, before being stopped by the police, to get as far away as Nagoya, more than three hundred kilometres to the southwest of Tokyo, reveals an important fact about his involvement in this incident. That is to say, Sōgen had decided, albeit at the last minute, against participating in the plot and was therefore not present when the main body of conspirators was arrested. Sōgen explained what led him to drop out as follows:

> One of the leaders of this incident, Mr Suzuki [Zen'ichi], asked me to join them. But after listening to what he said, there were several points I could not agree with. One of their targets was General Araki, a man that I respected.[18]

General Araki Sadao (1877–1966) was then Minister of War, a position he had held in two successive Cabinets, beginning in December 1931. Sōgen's objection to killing Araki is explained by the fact that, together with General Mazaki Jinzaburō, Araki was regarded as the leader of the Imperial Way faction in the military. He was highly respected by the Young Officers for the premium he placed on military spirit as expressed in the Bushido code. He was also the author of the Japanese military's redesignation as the "Imperial (or Emperor's) military" (*Kōgun*).

Nevertheless, Araki's performance since assuming the position of Minister of War was from the point of view of Japan's ultranationalists far from satisfactory. That is to say, the civilian-dominated governments of which Araki was a part consistently blocked his moves to significantly increase military expenditures let alone put into effect the political and economic reforms required of the Shōwa Restoration. The dissatisfaction with Araki's lack of effectiveness reached the point that at least the leadership of the Sacred Soldiers was ready to see him die alongside the other despised civilian Cabinet members. Sōgen, on the other hand, perhaps because of his close ties to members of the Young Officers' Movement, viewed Araki's assassination as unwarranted.

Japanese historian Hori Yukio reports that an additional factor influencing Sōgen was his belief that "the time was not yet ripe."[19] This may account for Sōgen's own statement that he found himself in disagreement with "several points" of the plot. Here too, Sōgen's opinion may have been influenced by supporters of the Young Officers' Movement, specifically his close friend, Nishida Mitsugi (1901–37), a former military officer. In the fall of 1933 Nishida is known to have counseled patience to yet another group of plotters composed of young officers, non-commissioned officers, soldiers and civilians. In Nishida's opinion the timing for such an uprising was "premature."[20]

Whatever its causes, Sōgen's decision to drop out of the plot at the last minute was clearly fortuitous, for otherwise he would have been arrested alongside his fellow conspirators. Yet, it must not be forgotten that Sōgen, literally with sword in hand, had been prepared to take part in the mass assassination of at least the civilian members of the Cabinet, plus many other political and financial leaders, with no apparent objection to the murderous nature of his task. It should be noted that Japan's civilian politicians, primarily because of their power over the budget, were still able to exercise a degree of control over the military. It was exactly for that reason, together with their ongoing support of the capitalist status quo, that they had to be eliminated.

In short, while Sōgen may have disagreed with his fellow conspirators over tactics, he had no quarrel with them over ultimate goals or the use of violence to achieve those goals. As a master swordsman, Sōgen was fully prepared to wield his sword in his self-appointed role as judge, jury and executioner of those whom he saw as preventing the implementation of his political ideals. Neither should it be forgotten that this incident occurred in the same year that Sōgen had his first enlightenment experience. That is to say, it occurred in the year he realized: "To be at the centre of an infinite circle in this human form is to be BUDDHA himself."

Jikishin Dōjō

Despite having narrowly avoided arrest, Sōgen quickly resumed his right-wing activities. On 1 January 1934 Sōgen opened the Jikishin Dōjō (lit. "Direct Mind" Training Centre) in the Koishikawa district of Tokyo. The Dōjō was created with the support of a number of right-wing activists aligned with the Imperial Way Faction, especially the Young Officers' Movement, and included such men as Nishida Mitsugi, Kobayashi Junichirō (1880–1963), and yet another former officer, Shibukawa Zensuke (1905–36). And in the role of Dōjō "advisor" was Tōyama Ryūsuke, the sickly eldest son of the grand old man of Japan's ultranationalists, Tōyama Mitsuru.

Appropriately, Sōgen headed the new Dōjō, appropriately that is, because the Dōjō incorporated all of his skills and interests. Namely, under one roof it became possible to practice Zen, *kendō, jūdō,* and calligraphy, all in preparation for the realization of the Shōwa Restoration. Given the nature of its program, it is not surprising that right-wing historian Arahara Bokusui described the Dōjō as "giving the impression of having been the inner citadel of the Imperial Way Faction among all the patriotic organizations of the day."[21] This impression was given concrete expression in the Dōjō's founding statement:

Based on our respect for the Founder of the Empire [i.e. mythical Emperor Jimmu], we reverently seek to promote the prosperity of our glorious Imperial Throne by respectfully revealing the fundamentals of statesmanship and investigating through our own persons the essentials of governance. The spread of the emperor's work is the national policy of Japan while the mission of the people is to assist in this endeavour. It is for this reason that we have taken it upon ourselves, first of all, to aid each other in cultivating divine justice. Therefore, we have established the Jikishin Dōjō in order to resolutely promote the true practice of the Way of the warrior.

We pray that by hiding nothing, we will encounter excellence; by exerting ourselves to the utmost, we will foster our talents; and by pointing directly at the source of the mind received from our ancestors, we will encounter our divine, immortal native spirit. Furthermore, we have made the reverent accomplishment of the [Shōwa] Restoration a pledge of steel in which mundane, personal interests have no place.[22]

An ordinary day at the Dōjō began with wake-up at 6 a.m., followed by cleaning and then approximately forty-five minutes of *zazen*, i.e. the time required for one stick of incense to be consumed. This in turn was followed by a morning worship service consisting of the recitation of Shinto prayers (not Buddhist sūtras) before the Centre's main altar on which was enshrined a large tablet of the Sun Goddess, mythical progenitress of the Imperial family. To the left of the main altar were three rows of photographs of Japan's greatest military heroes and right-wing civilian leaders. To the right was an alcove in which, together with a flower arrangement and traditional Japanese swords, was hung a large scroll reading: "Enemy Countr(ies) Surrender!" (*Tekikoku Kōfuku*).

From 4 to 6 p.m. every afternoon there was martial arts practice. *Jūdō* was taught on Monday, Wednesday, and Friday, while *kendō* was on Tuesday, Thursday, and Saturday. Thursday afternoon was reserved for study circles while calligraphy was practiced on Sunday afternoon. In addition, from the fifteenth of every month there was a five-day period of intensive Zen meditation, i.e. *sesshin*, commencing at 4 a.m. and lasting until 10 p.m. each day. The purpose of the *sesshin* was described as "the realization of our great pledge [to achieve the Shōwa Restoration] by acquiring an indestructible and adamantine body of indomitable resolve through introspection and Zen practice."[23] Further, in justifying this rigorous training schedule, Sōgen wrote:

In Bushido, as a traditional Way transmitted from ancient times, a person throws his mind and body into Bushido. Forgetting himself and becoming one with the Way, he completely transforms the small self into the Way of the warrior. He then lives the Great Life."[24]

More will be said about the transformation of the "small self", etc. in chapter 7.

For Dōjō students, the "Great Life" clearly entailed a great deal of right-wing political activism, activism that would eventually bring imprisonment or death to many of its participants. Initially, however, the Dōjō's activism took the form of publishing right-wing organs, the first of which was a monthly magazine entitled *Essence* (*Kakushin*). The initial issue was published on 18 September 1934 with the lead article entitled "Destroy the False and Establish the True – Risk Your Life in Spreading the Dharma – the Great Essence of the Shōwa Restoration." The article contained the following call to action:

> The [Shōwa] Restoration is a holy war to destroy the false and establish the True and applies equally to [Japan's] domestic and foreign affairs. The [army manual] *Essentials of Combat* (*Sentō Kōyō*) states: "The essence of victory lies in integrating various combat elements, both material and immaterial, so as to concentrate and give full play to power superior to that of your enemy at a strategic point."
>
> In this instance, "various combat elements, both material and immaterial" refer to the unity in speech and action of all military and civilians involved in the Restoration Movement and other patriotic activities. The "enemy" refers to the enemy amongst us, that is to say, today's ruling powers who, with the backing of various financial cliques and elder statesmen, command the services of bureaucrats, big and small, as well as the police. The basis of power superior to this enemy is the force of all those dedicated to destroying the false and establishing the True. This force is to be found in the great unity of the people's forces composed of the civilians and military of this imperial land....
>
> As a practical matter, we recognize that the Restoration can only be put into effect through the realization of a new Cabinet of national unity centred on a unified army and navy. We must therefore support and promote the Imperial Army and Navy as the main force backing the Restoration while reverently seeking the promulgation of an Imperial Order that will promptly disperse the black clouds engulfing us. This is the proper duty of all citizens who cooperate with, and support, imperial policy.
>
> Duty is heavier than mountains while death is lighter than feathers. Given this, how is it possible that the epoch-making, great undertaking [of the Shōwa Restoration] can be accomplished without the valiant, dedicated spread of the Dharma at the risk of your life?[25]

The Buddhist influence on this article is as unmistakable as its political extremism. In addition to its call to "spread the Dharma," readers will recall the frequent references in the previous chapter to "destroy(ing) the false and establish(ing) the True." This phrase first appeared in a famous Chinese Buddhist treatise entitled *Sanlun Xuanyi* [*Profound Meaning of the Three Treatises*] written by the Sui Dynasty priest, Jicang (643–712). It forms one of the fundamental tenets of the Sanlun (Three Treatises) school based on the Mādhyamika philosophy of

Nāgārjuna. However, the "destruction" called for in this school originally had nothing to do with taking the lives of other sentient beings. Instead, it referred to "destroying" the *mind of attachment*, such "destruction" being in and of itself the establishment of the True.

Needless to say, doctrinal "subtleties" of this nature were of no interest to Sōgen and his associates, for they sought to use Buddhism as a means of bolstering their claim that the Restoration Movement was part of a "holy war." Not only that, by calling on readers to risk their lives on behalf of the Shōwa Restoration, the article's unspoken assumption was that killing the "enemy amongst us" was a necessary part of that process. This last point was not lost on police censors who impounded the magazine's first issue only two days after its publication.

Aizawa Saburō

Despite ongoing police interference, the Dōjō added a second magazine, *Imperial Spirit (Kōki)* to its list of publications and then, on 23 November 1935, established a monthly newspaper, *Great Essence (Taiganmoku)*. As Arahara noted: "Under the guidance of Nishida Mitsugi and other Young Officers, and using their sharp editorial style, this newspaper made propaganda for the Pure Japanism Movement."[26] Needless to say, this newspaper was also strongly supportive of Lt. Colonel Aizawa, introduced in the previous chapter, who was then awaiting court martial for the assassination of General Nagata in August 1935. Although Aizawa was not directly associated with the Dōjō, his "direct action" against a man seen as the leader of the Control Faction was eagerly embraced as a further step on the road to the Shōwa Restoration. Israeli historian Ben-Ami Shillony describes the Dōjō's role at this time as follows:

> The ex-military activists of the Young Officers' Movement, Nishida Mitsugi, Shibukawa Zensuke, Muranaka Kōji, and Isobe Asaichi, became the "brain trust" of Aizawa's defense, trying hard to make the most of it for their cause. They founded a special organization, the Jikishin Dōjō (Sincere Spirit Seminary) for propagating "the ideals of Aizawa" and wrote articles in Nishida's *Taiganmoko*, which hailed the defendant as a forerunner of the Shōwa Restoration.[27]

On the one hand it must be pointed out that Shillony's description contains two errors, the first being his claim that the Jikishin Dōjō was founded specifically to support Aizawa. As we have seen, the Dōjō had already been in existence for more than a year and a half prior to Nagata's assassination. Second, while in theory it is possible to translate the Dōjō's name as "Sincere Spirit Seminary," this translation misses the traditional Zen meaning of the title, fully expressed in Sino-Japanese as "pointing *direct*(ly) at the human *mind*, seeing one's nature, and realizing Buddhahood" (*jikishi ninshin, kenshō jōbutsu*). No doubt, Shillony, like so many historians of modern Japan, was simply unaware of the Buddhist, especially Zen, background to terms like these.

Nevertheless, Shillony is quite correct in identifying the Dōjō as being at the heart of the movement seeking to create popular support for Aizawa and his "ideals." This is hardly surprising since not only did all of these men share the same political agenda, but they were personal friends as well. In fact, Aizawa had stayed at Nishida Mitsugi's house the night before he assassinated General Nagata. The morning of the attack Nishida told Muranaka and Isobe:

> Aizawa stayed with me last night after arriving in Tokyo from Fukuyama. This morning he said he was going to the Ministry of War to see Nagata. Knowing what kind of person Aizawa is, I think he may do something.[28]

The Dōjō published a number of leaflets on Aizawa's behalf, some anonymously, in which the Zen emphasis on "transcendence" played an important role. One of these leaflets described Aizawa's actions as stemming from his desire to "clarify the national polity, cleanse the military, and bring about the Restoration revolution." The leaflet also identified ongoing support for capitalism and the rule of law as two of the elements then present in Japan that were "opposed to the national polity" and thus had to be eliminated. Significantly, the "rule of law" was held to be synonymous with "individualism and liberalism" (*kojinshugi-jiyūshugi*), both of which were regarded in right-wing circles as "unJapanese" imports from the West.[29]

The strong attack on the rule of law is hardly surprising in that a successful Shōwa Restoration would have meant the suspension of any semblance of the rule of law, at least as contained in the Meiji Constitution of 1889. That is to say, all political parties were to be dissolved and, accordingly, policy debate would become not only unnecessary but a sign of disloyalty. Instead, the emperor, aided by his (mostly military) advisors, would rule directly as the "benevolent father" he was held to be. Thus, while it can be argued that there was a populist element of government "for the people" in the proposed Shōwa Restoration, there was not the slightest hint of a government either "of the people" let alone "by the people."

More to the point, in Aizawa's case the rule of law had to be suspended if he were to escape the death penalty, for in killing a superior officer he was clearly guilty of having committed a capital offense. Thus the same leaflet contained the following demand: "The fate of those parties who, having transcended the law, have sacrificed themselves for the Restoration that also transcends the law, must itself transcend the law."[30]

26 February Incident

As noted in the previous chapter, one of the Dōjō's demands, i.e. that Aizawa's court martial be open to the public, was successful; and the first hearing was held on 28 January 1936. Yet by this time Aizawa's trial was no longer the main focus of the Dōjō's activities. Rather, the time for large-scale action had come at last; and on the evening of the trial's opening, Dōjō activists Isobe Asaichi and Muranaka Kōji met with their active military counterparts to plan what would become the largest military revolt in modern Japanese history – the Young Officers' Uprising of 26 February 1936. Although Nishida Mitsugi initially felt that the time was still not ripe, he was evenually won over and all of the Dōjō's activists devoted themselves to the uprising's success.

Just how important the role played by these activists was, is revealed by the fact that the uprising was planned by only five men, three ex-military civilians and two officers. All three civilians, i.e. Nishida, Isobe, and Muranaka, were also key figures in the Jikishin Dōjō.[31] Further, Isobe and Muranaka comprised two of the three members of the committee that drew up the political demands to be submitted to the Minister of War once the uprising was underway. At a more practical level, Shibukawa Zensuke and his wife spent the night of 23 February at a Japanese inn located in Yugawara, Kanagawa Prefecture, to observe the movements of Lord Keeper of the Privy Seal, Count Makino Nobuaki (1863–1949), one of the "evil advisors" surrounding the throne slated for assassination.

What Sōgen's exact role was in all this is unknown. It may well have been limited in that the uprising's leaders made a conscious decision to exclude civilians, at least those who were not former military officers, from the initial phase of operations. Shillony suggests this decision was made because "civilian terrorists were held in lower public esteem than military officers and their involvement could impair the heroic image that the rebels wished to create."[32] As for Sōgen himself, he later admitted that "during the [26] February Incident, the persons involved in the incident had come to me for advice." Yet, he also claimed, "but I said, 'Now is not the time. You must wait a little longer,' and opposed the action."[33] Once again, we find Sōgen opposed to the *timing* for political assassination, not its use.

Sōgen's associates, however, had no such reservations. For example, Isobe and Muranaka once again donned their military uniforms to help lead the revolt. In addition, on the uprising's first day, Nishida, Shibukawa and other civilians gathered at the home of another and much better known Buddhist supporter of the Young Officers, Kita Ikki (1883–1937). Kita was better known because, inspired by the teachings of Nichiren (1222?–82), he was one of the chief ideologues to whom the Young Officers turned for guidance, especially as to the nature of an emperor-centric, yet populist-oriented Shōwa Restoration. (More will be said about the role played by Nichiren and his adherents within Japanese militarism in chapter 9.)

During the four days of the Uprising, the civilian supporters used Kita's house as a liaison centre between the twenty-one rebel officers and the more than 1,400 men they commanded. These supporters provided the rebels with encouragement and advice as well as information from the outside world. They also published three issues of a *Shōwa Restoration Bulletin* (*Shōwa Ishin Jōhō*) in which they appealed to the people of Japan to rise up in armed revolt on the one hand and to sympathetic officers stationed outside of Tokyo to commit their units in support of the "glorious uprising in the capital."[34] Before any of these things could occur, however, the revolt was bloodlessly suppressed, apart from two officer suicides, on 29 February.

The revolt had collapsed for one key reason. Despite support for its goals from Imperial Way Faction generals like Araki Sadao, and most especially Mazaki Jinzaburō, Emperor Hirohito was dead set against it from the outset. Awakened in the early morning of 26 February and informed of what had taken place, Hirohito told his chief aide-de-camp: "They have killed my advisors and are now trying to pull a silk rope around my neck.... I shall never forgive them, no matter what their motives are."[35]

True to his word, shortly after the uprising's collapse, Hirohito insisted on a Special Court-Martial to try those involved. In the end, a total of thirteen officers, together with Dōjō activists Isobe, Muranaka, Shibukawa, and Nishida, and including Kita Ikki, faced a military firing squad. As the American historian Herbert Bix notes, it was Hirohito's resolute decisiveness that "abruptly ended the period in which alienated 'Young Officers' had tried to use him as a principle of reform to undermine a power structure they could not successfully manipulate."[36]

As for Sōgen, this time he was unable to avoid arrest and, together with four additional Centre members, was held at the Otsuka Police Station on suspicion of having fanned the revolt. Sōgen described one of his interrogation sessions as follows:

> The prosecuting attorney said that I had agitated the emperor's army. I asked, "Do you really think that an ordinary citizen like myself could agitate the soldiers of the emperor? If you think that, you are really showing contempt for the army." When I said that, the prosecuting attorney began to tremble.
>
> I continued, "During the 26 February Incident, you called them (those who participated in the incident) revolutionary soldiers, in other words, you were calling them the enemy. If that is so, according to military law, in the event that the general staff office is occupied by enemy forces, even if just temporarily, the person in charge must be punished. Was the commander in chief, Naninnomiya (an aristocrat) punished? If he has not yet been punished, he should be punished before me."
>
> When I said that, the prosecutor's face turned blue.[37]

Unbowed, Sōgen was finally released after two months in detention, the police unable to amass sufficient evidence to convict him of any offense. By this time, however, the trials of both the military and civilian rebels had begun. Given that all the military court hearings related to these cases were now closed to the public, there was a strong likelihood that the accused would be sentenced to death. Furthermore, because martial law was still in effect, including strict censorship provisions, direct appeals to the public on behalf of men whom the emperor himself had branded as "mutineers" (*bōto*) were out of the question. This, however, did not stop Sōgen from trying.

Specifically Sōgen and two of his students from the Dōjō, Kuroda Sueo and Kaneko Nobuo, got their hands on a number of memoranda written by Isobe Asaichi that had been smuggled out of prison by his wife when she visited him. One read in part:

> Appeal to the patriots of Japan. Help us destroy the members of the military clique in power [i.e. the Control Faction] which is the enemy of the true Restoration. . . . Annihilate them in order that the Restoration may be realized. I shall fight to the end![38]

Sōgen and his students proceeded to mimeograph these memoranda and mail copies throughout Japan. Not content with this, they hit on a unique method of distributing them to the larger public. According to a postwar Allied intelligence report entitled *The Brocade Banner*, Sōgen and Kuroda "distributed the appeals like Gideon Bibles in the toilet compartments of the Tokaido Line trains."[39] Given his earlier spiritual "breakthrough" in a urinal, it is almost comical to picture Sōgen making his way from one toilet to the next armed with nothing more than leaflets.

Unsurprisingly, the police were not amused by Sōgen and his student's activities. Eventually both of them were arrested together with fifty-eight other rightists who had engaged in similar acts. They were convicted and sentenced to prison where Sōgen remained for one year before being placed on probation for three years. Later, in 1940, he received a full pardon. As the following reveals, Sōgen found his time in prision quite beneficial, both mentally and spiritually:

> A solitary cell in a prison is a great convenience. Everything can be done in one room: the toilet is there; you can eat there; you can even study there. While I was there, I didn't think that I should read all the time, so during the day I read books, and at night I did *zazen*.[40]

Sōgen was later gratified to find that his Zen master, Seki Seisetsu, approved of his conduct.[41] That is to say, on the day of his release from prison Seisetsu visited Sōgen at the Dōjō and said, "You had a long *sesshin*. You had much hardship, but you did well."[42] Seisetsu then took his disciple out to dinner. Sōgen summed up his prison experience as follows: "Since there is no other place where one can study so leisurely, everyone should do the right thing and get into prison."[43] In light of Sōgen's actions up to that point, one can but express surprise that he had not succeeded in "do[ing] the right thing" earlier.

Wartime activities

In postwar years Sōgen's disciples claimed that their master "had tried his best to prevent Japan's involvement in World War II."[44] If this were true, it must be said that he had a strange way of showing his opposition. That is to say, not long after his release from prison, he resumed his right-wing activities, only this time as a loyal supporter of Japan's military actions in China and Asia. In August 1940 he helped found the Youth League for the Construction of the (Imperial Rule) Assistance Structure (Yokusan Taisei Kensetsu Seinen Renmei). When the participants in this group couldn't agree on a common agenda, Sōgen left to form yet another organization, the Japanism Youth Council (Nipponshugi Seinen Kaigi), founded in September 1940. Finally, in July 1944 Sōgen took up an administrative position in the (Imperial Rule) Assistance Manhood Group (Yokusan Sōnen Dan).

This last organization was a service group of the Imperial Rule Assistance Association (IRAA), a government-sponsored mass organization modelled on the Nazi Party that had been established in October 1940. Like its Nazi counterpart, its purpose was to replace all political parties and factions and create one united, war-affirming body, based on the slogan of "100 million [citizens of] one mind" (*ichi-oku isshin*). However, as noted in the *Brocade Banner*, the IRAA and its supporting organizations were beset from the outset with internal policy and organizational differences, not to mention petty personal jealousies, all of which combined to reduce their effectiveness in rousing and sustaining the people, especially as it became clear that Japan was losing the war. Nevertheless, they did at least succeed in "regimenting and herding the populace behind the war effort" even if the old struggles for power remained as active as ever.[45] Whatever reservations he may have had, there can be no doubt that Sōgen was an integral part of this overall effort.

This said, in fairness to Sōgen it should be pointed out that in mid-1940 he made direct contact with the aristocratic Prince Konoe Fumimarō (1891–1945), then in the midst of forming his second Cabinet. Sōgen repeatedly pleaded with him to choose either General Ugaki Kazushige (1869–1956) or General Mazaki Jinzaburō as his new Minister of War. Konoe, however, refused Sōgen's advice and eventually stopped inviting him to his advisors' meetings. For Sōgen, his failure to sway Konoe became a source of lifelong regret. As he later wrote: "I should not have given up. I should have persevered and *even used intimidation if necessary* [Italics mine].[46]

Sōgen further claimed that his plea to Konoe had been motivated by his earnest desire "to prevent the war."[47] Inasmuch as Japan had already been engaged in full-scale warfare with China since July 1937, it is reasonable to assume that what Sōgen had in mind was preventing war with the USA and its western allies. This is in accord with the Imperial Way Faction's unyielding belief that Japan's primary enemy was Russia and its Communist ideology. Thus, Sōgen may genuinely have wanted to prevent a misguided attack on the USA.

However, even had Sōgen been successful, this would have done nothing to save the colonized peoples of Taiwan, Korea, and Manchuria; for Generals Ugaki and Mazaki's careers reveal that they were as dedicated to the maintenance and, if possible, the expansion of the Japanese Empire as any of Japan's other military leaders. Ugaki, for example, had willingly accepted appointment as governor general of Korea in 1931.[48] Further, neither Sōgen's writings nor those of the many right-wing organizations of which he was a part contain the slightest hint of opposition to Japanese imperialism. For geographical, historical and ideological reasons, Russia, not the USA, was seen as the chief threat to the maintenance and expansion of the Japanese Empire. Thus, Sōgen's effort "to prevent the war" was in reality an effort to prevent war *with the wrong enemy!*

Nevertheless, even Sōgen's disciples admit that their master had a change of heart following Japan's attack on Pearl Harbour. Hosokawa Dōgen, one of Sōgen's Dharma successors and current abbot of Hawaii's Chōzenji, notes that Sōgen was determined to see the war through to the end. "Winning or losing was not the point. He [Sōgen] felt that something that had been started should be carried through to the end," Dōgen wrote.[49] In light of the many millions of lives lost in seeing the war "through to the end," this must surely be one of the most inane justifications for the mass slaughter of human beings ever written.

Sōgen's total commitment to Japan's war effort is further demonstrated by his attempt to preempt the emperor's pre-recorded radio broadcast scheduled for noon on 15 August 1945. "Since I wanted to resist till the end," Sōgen stated, "I was going to obstruct the emperor's broadcast [in which he would announce Japan's surrender]. For that reason I often went to the Imperial Headquarters to incite the soldiers."[50] Needless to say, Sōgen would have had to be very well connected indeed to even know that such an unprecedented broadcast was planned.[51]

Had Sōgen and his ilk succeeded in preventing Japan's surrender, an Allied invasion of Japan would have become inevitable. As chapter 7 describes in detail, this would have resulted in almost unimaginable carnage, most especially for those millions of Japanese civilian men and women of all ages required to fight the Allied invaders armed with little more than sharpened bamboo spears. But that was of no concern to Sōgen, for whether one was trying to prevent a war or fight it, he claimed that "if one trains in Zen, one must do everything thoroughly and completely. . ."[52]

Postwar activism

When Japan finally surrendered, Sōgen's initial impulse was to commit suicide. Surprisingly for someone schooled in Bushido, Sōgen had no intention of using a sword to slowly and painfully disembowel himself in the traditional manner. Instead, "I had decided to kill myself instantly with a pistol," he explained.[53] However, early on the morning of the appointed day, his old calligraphy teacher,

Yokoyama Setsudo dropped by the Dōjō, now relocated in Tokyo's Setagaya district. Yokoyama also intended to kill himself because in his opinion: "These days all Japanese have become hopeless cowards." Yet Yokoyama subsequently had a change of heart and, after waking Sōgen, said, "The reason we lost the war is because there was some weak point.... It won't be too late to die after we completely investigate the reason." Sōgen replied, "I agreed right away, but if he hadn't come, I would have committed *seppuku* (suicide)."[54]

As previously noted, Sōgen stated that after Japan's defeat he had decided to enter the Rinzai Zen priesthood "according to the samurai code." What he neglected to mention, however, was that as a practical matter, apart from suicide, he had very few other options. In the first place this was because his prominent role in Japan's ultranationalist movement brought him to the attention of the Allied Occupation authorities. While the Allies did not indict him as a war criminal, they did include his name on a list of persons purged from public life including employment even as a school teacher. In addition, as the practice of the martial arts was also proscribed, Sōgen's career as an instructor of the martial arts came to an abrupt end. Practically speaking, the Zen priesthood was one of the few remaining positions open to him.

Priestly status, however, by no means spelled the end of Sōgen's right-wing activism. Thus, on 1 April 1952, four weeks prior to the formal end of the Allied Occupation, Sōgen held a meeting with ten other former right-wing leaders to discuss rebuilding the Right in a soon-to-be independent Japan. Subsequently, this group met regularly for about a year under the name of the East Wind Society (Tōfū-kai). Sōgen and his associates felt that in its weakened state, the Right could only influence events if it spoke with a united voice.

With the goal of creating a united Right, Sōgen became one of the founders, and first committee chairman, of the Kantō District Council of the Restoration Movement (Ishin Undō Kantō Kyōgi-kai), founded in July 1953. Similar to the prewar years, the goals of this new umbrella organization included the creation of a "racial state" (*minzoku kokka*), the ousting of the Communist Party and its allies, and the purging of corrupt political parties, financial magnates, and government bureaucrats.

Despite Sōgen's best efforts, the old rivalries soon appeared, and by May 1954 it became necessary to create yet another umbrella organization fostering right-wing unity, the General Federation of Citizens for the Salvation of the Nation (Kyūkoku Kokumin Sōrengō). Once again, Sōgen served as the committee chairman of this group. Nevertheless, by December 1956, so many of the constituent right-wing organizations in the federation had dropped out that a further name change became necessary. The end result was called simply, the General Federation of Citizens (Kokumin Sōrengō).

Never one to give up, in January 1958 Sōgen became a permanent director of the New Japan Council (Shin-Nippon Kyōgi-kai). As its name suggests, this was the most mainstream of the many right-wing organizations of which Sōgen had been a part. In fact, it has been described as a "vehicle for the unification of the right wing with Japan's financial circles and the Liberal Democratic Party (LDP)."[55] The LDP, of course, is the conservative (and corrupt) political party that has ruled Japan on an almost uninterrupted basis for the past half-century.

On the one hand, Sōgen was now aligned with financial magnates like Takasugi Shin-ichi (1892–1978), chairman of the board of directors of Mitsubishi Electric Co. and Council finance chairperson. On the other hand, Sōgen's longstanding anti-Communism was reflected by the following tenet of the Council's charter: "This Council will endeavour to expel Communism, defeatism and all plots by foreign countries that threaten the peace and freedom of our citizens."[56] In this context, the Council was particularly critical of the left-leaning Japan Teachers' Union (Nikkyōso) and demanded that education be "normalized" (*seijō-ka*) in accord with what it called the "proper ethics for teachers."[57]

In addition, the Council demanded that Japan's postwar "peace" constitution be revised in order that Japan might once again maintain a full-fledged military. This was coupled with a demand for the maintenance of the Japan–US Mutual Security Treaty that came up for renewal in the face of strong left-wing opposition in 1960 and again in 1970. In the face of this opposition the Council also called for the establishment of a law to "preserve public peace and order," thereby enhancing the power of police to control anti-Treaty demonstrations. As Hori Yukio commented: "In the final analysis, the Council became the mouthpiece for the ideology of [Japan's] political and financial circles who sought to steer Japan to the right by creating a sense of crisis."[58]

This is not to say that Sōgen cut himself off from his old roots altogether, for in October 1961 he became a director of the postwar version of the infamous (and deadly) Black Dragon Society, now renamed as the Black Dragon Club (Kokuryū-kurabu). The original Black Dragon Society (Kokuryū-kai) had been created in 1901 to block Russian penetration into the Far East on the one hand and promote Japanese advancement onto the Asian continent, especially Manchuria, on the other. The postwar Black Dragon Club sought to "succeed to the spirit of the [prewar] Black Dragon Society and promote the Restoration." It also aimed at "comforting and exalting the spirits of the society's former members."[59] Although the Club never attracted more than one hundred and fifty members, Sōgen no doubt felt more at home there than he did in the New Japan Council where he sat alongside the corrupt politicians and financial magnates he had so long opposed.

Finally, it is noteworthy that the last entry regarding Sōgen in the *Dictionary of the Right Wing* states that he eventually became President of Rinzai Zen-affiliated Hanazono University. While at first glance this appears to be unconnected to Sōgen's right-wing activism, in reality it was not; for it had been Sōgen's right-wing reputation that brought him to the university in the first place.

That is to say, in 1970, left-wing student activism was on the rise throughout Japan, centred on opposition to the extension of the Japan–US Mutual Security Treaty and a demand for an increased student voice in campus affairs. Hosokawa

Dōgen describes the circumstances under which Sōgen was asked to teach at Hanazono University as follows:

> During this time [1970] there was unrest at universities all over Japan. Hanazono University was no exception. Along with Ritsumeikan University, it was a well known base for the students in the Japanese Red Army. Within the university there was strife.... As a result, [Sōgen] Roshi became a professor at that university.[60]

Although he had dropped out of university as a youth, who better than Sōgen to suppress left-wing student activism. Sōgen could not, of course, accomplish this task on his own so he reached out to a group of students he knew, from past experience would readily support him – students of the martial arts. Even today martial arts' students at Japan's universities regard themselves as the embodiment of the wartime "Spirit of Japan" (*Yamato-damashii*) and are decidedly right-wing in their political orientation. Sōgen therefore began a weekly *Zazen* Club, initially for members of the *Kendō* club but then expanded to include the *Karate* and *Kenpō* clubs as well as the all-male pep club. Since these students were more than willing to use their martial arts skills to intimidate left-wing students, it did not take long for university "strife" to end.

Finally, with the strong backing of these right-wing students, Sōgen the university dropout became Sōgen the university president in 1978. It would appear Sōgen learned something from his earlier failure to intimidate Prince Konoe after all.

Conclusion

In evaluating Sōgen's life, especially his manifestation as Mr. Hyde, I am reminded of the following claim made by Bernard Phillips of Philadelphia University in his book *Zen and Western People*: "Aside from Zen, there is no other universal religion." Phillips justified this rather surprising claim as follows:

> It is true that many other religions have emphasized a universal religion; but all of the other religions have been influenced by the time, place, and character of the region. Other religions have been instrumental in a specific nation, during a specific time, and in a specific area. They did not play a part in the lives of all mankind or in all endeavours. They all made the mistake of trying to create an absolute form or absolute creed. The reason is that the forms and creeds of these religions lost their absoluteness and are restricted historically or were the product of a certain geography, certain society, and economic environment.[61]

Needless to say, here Phillips embraces without reservation the view promoted by such Zen representatives as D. T. Suzuki that Zen transcends not only things like concepts, ethics and time, but history itself. As Suzuki wrote: "Zen does not affirm or negate temporal actuality. Actuality has historicity, with which the ultimacy of Zen has no dealings."[62]

One cannot help but wonder if Phillips, let alone Suzuki, would argue that when Imperial Way Faction supporters, under Sōgen's "enlightened" guidance, daily practiced *zazen*, worshipped the Sun Goddess, practiced swordsmanship etc., in preparation for staging a violent Shōwa Restoration, that Zen was *not* "the product of a ... certain society"?

What is even more interesting about Phillips' quotation is that Sōgen himself employed it in a series of talks given at Hanazono University on the *Roankyō*, a collection of teachings by the famous warrior-turned-Zen priest, Suzuki Shōsan (1579–1655).[63] Sōgen invoked Phillips to show that even westerners recognized that Zen alone contains "the basic principle that will save the world."[64]

Based on Sōgen's clear acceptance of assassination as the preferred method for achieving his political aims, let alone his wartime support of Japanese militarism, one might well ask if it was not Sōgen himself who made Zen "instrumental in a specific nation"? If this is what is really required to "save the world," I think I am not alone in suggesting the world would be better off, much better off, left "unsaved."

Hosokawa Dōgen writes: "The life of Ōmori Roshi is the manifestation of traditional and true Zen. After eight years of arduous training, he experienced this absolute negation and for the rest of his life tried his best to use his experience of absolute negation in every possible circumstance."[65] If Sōgen, as Mr. Hyde, represents "traditional and true Zen" then it must be said that Zen faces a very bleak future, not least of all morally. Bleak, that is, unless one happens to agree that Zen ought to be "united as one" with what was in reality a deadly form of emperor-worshipping fascism. Of course, if D. T. Suzuki is correct, there is no reason to be alarmed about this since Zen can be readily "wedded to anarchism or fascism, communism or democracy, atheism or idealism, or any political or economic dogmatism."

If the word "fascism" seems too strong a term to employ in regard to Sōgen and his ilk, I would point to the writings of Maruyama Masao, one of postwar Japan's most distinguished political scientists. After describing the features of prewar and wartime Japanese society that clearly made it fascist in nature, Maruyama identifies the three stages of fascism's development:

1 the preparatory stage, between 1919–31, when various fascist societies of civilians existed on the margins of Japanese politics;
2 the mature stage, from 1931–36, when fascism was endorsed by young officers and manifested in acts of terrorism;
3 a stage of consummation, from 1936–45, when fascism was adopted by Japan's ruling elite.[66]

Maruyama also identifies three distinct types of political personality involved in this process who "serv[ed] to formulate not only the fascist period but the entire political world of Imperial Japan." Designating the three as the "Shrine," the "Official," and the "Outlaw," he described their respective roles as follows:

> The Shrine represents authority; the Official, power; and the Outlaw, violence. From the point of view of their position in the national hierarchy and of their legal power, the Shrine ranks highest and the Outlaw lowest. The system, however, is so constituted that movement starts from the Outlaw and gradually works upwards. The Shrine is often a mere robot who affects other people by "doing nothing" (Ch. *wu wei*).
>
> The force that "holds aloft" the Shrine and that wields the real power is the Official (civilian or military). His rule over the powerless people is based on the legitimacy that descends from the Shrine. He in his turn is being prodded from behind by the Outlaw.[67]

Needless to say, the "Outlaw" encompasses Japan's civilian ultranationalists whose emperor-centric, fascist-promoting societies gathered steam in the 1920s and then, bolstered by their youthful military supporters, burst on the scene as terrorists in the 1930s. While not the only legitimating body in Japanese society, Emperor Hirohito was nevertheless the ultimate "Shrine" who legitimated the entire system ruled over by the "Official," both military and civilian. As Herbert Bix notes, Hirohito was "*the reason* the system worked."[68]

Sōgen, due to his right-wing affiliations in the 1920s and his involvement in terrorist violence in the 1930s, clearly falls in the Outlaw type. In evaluating the influence he and his ilk had on turning Japan into a fascist state, it is important to remember "that movement start[ed] from the Outlaw and gradually work[ed] upwards." This said, it is also true that in the biggest Outlaw act of them all, i.e. the 26 February Young Officers' Uprising, the Outlaws, Sōgen included, *appear* to have failed miserably.

Appearances, however, can be deceiving, for as David Titus notes in *Palace and Politics in Prewar Japan*: "The Outlaw(s) of the unsuccessful Shōwa Restoration were instruments of pressure used to consolidate a bureaucratic monolith in government and then discarded."[69] More concretely, Herbert Bix adds:

> Interestingly, in their concept of total war the thinking of the [uprising's] leaders and their senior commanders in the Army Ministry and the Army General Staff was strikingly similar: Both wanted state control of industrial production in order to fully mobilize the nation's resources.... The emperor and most of his advisers concurred with the demands of the Army and Navy for accelerated military buildup and state-directed industrial development.[70]

Nevertheless, it can be argued that Sōgen and his fellow Outlaws never meant it to turn out this way. Yet, planned or not, Titus argues:

The winners [of the uprising] were the Army's Control Faction Officials and their colleagues in the Navy and the civil bureaucracy: they capitalized on the successful use of Outlaw violence by the Imperial Way Faction against moderate Officials, and on the mistakes of the Imperial Way Faction's Officials in the way they did so, to consolidate bureaucratic "fascism from above."[71]

If the military and civilian bureaucrats, including the emperor, represented "fascism from above," it is equally important to recognize, as Maruyama Masao asserts, that the violence unleashed by the Outlaws represented "fascism from below" and further, that in "suppressing fascism from below, ... fascism from above made rapid progress."[72]

As we have seen, despite his initial reservations, Sōgen went on to align himself as completely with "fascism from above" as he had with "fascism from below." No doubt he was sustained in this by his belief that "if one trains in Zen, one must do everything thoroughly and completely." And, of course, there was his equally firm belief that "with regard to their ultimate goals and aims, the sword and Zen are one."[73]

Dr. Jekyll or Mr. Hyde? Or both?

5

ZEN MASTER DŌGEN GOES TO WAR

The militarist and anti-Semitic writings of Yasutani Haku'un

In reviewing the history of Zen's introduction to the West – and in particular to the United States – it can be argued that the vast and varied terrain of the Zen landscape was funnelled through just a handful of Japanese teachers. Of these, Yasutani Haku'un (1885–1973) is undoubtedly one of the most significant.

In 1965 Yasutani's American disciple, Philip Kapleau, compiled *The Three Pillars of Zen*. The first section is devoted to Yasutani's instructions for beginning students and continues to this day to be an important source of Zen teachings. Although Yasutani travelled to the West seven times in the 1960s, it was largely this widely-read and influential book that made him so important to the growing Zen movement. This led to Yasutani becoming a major player in the transmission of Zen from Japan to the West.

However, like Ōmori Sōgen in the previous chapter, there is another side to Yasutani, one that was almost totally unknown in the West until the appearance of *Zen at War* in 1997. There Yasutani was introduced as "no less a fanatical militarist and anti-communist than his master."[1] This passage was, however, a quotation from another book, *Nihon Fashizumu-ka no Shūkyō* (*Religion under Japanese Fascism*), written by the late Rinzai Zen-affiliated scholar-priest Ichikawa Hakugen (1902–86).[2] But was this a fair or objective assessment of this distinguished master whose lectures on Zen have been highly praised by such luminaries as Huston Smith, professor of philosophy at MIT, and Ruth Fuller Sasaki, director of the First Zen Institute of America? Could Yasutani, had he once been a "fanatical militarist," gone on to exercise such a profound influence on the development of Zen in the West, particularly in the USA?

To be sure, it would be difficult to find fault with Hakugen's similar characterization of Harada Daiun Sōgaku (1870–1961), Yasutani's own Sōtō Zen master. Among many similar quotes included in *Zen At War*, this is demonstrated by Harada's call for ten years of "fascist politics" in Japan while maintaining that "the Japanese people are a chosen people whose mission is to control the world," and "it is necessary for all one hundred million subjects [of the emperor] to be prepared to die with honour."[3] Perhaps Harada's most memorable wartime quote is:

Plate 6 Sōtō Zen Master Yasutani Haku'un. Photograph by Francis Haar
© Tom Haar, Francis Haar Estate.

[If ordered to] march: tramp, tramp, or shoot: bang, bang. This is the manifestation of the highest Wisdom [of enlightenment]. The unity of Zen and war of which I speak extends to the farthest reaches of the holy war [now under way]. Verse: I bow my head to the floor in reverence of those whose nobility is without equal.[4]

Yet, this still does not address the question of whether or not Yasutani should be so readily lumped together with his master. Was not Hakugen attempting to discredit Yasutani by employing the time-worn tactic of "guilt by association"? What proof did Hakugen offer in support of his identification of Yasutani as a "fanatical militarist"?

In actual fact, Hakugen included in his book only a few right-wing comments made by Yasutani in postwar years. Among other things Yasutani was quoted as claiming that due to their left-wing stance, Japan's trade unions and four opposition parties "had taken it upon themselves to become traitors to the nation" and, similarly, that "the universities we presently have must be smashed one and all."[5] Granted that these and similar postwar quotes suggest that Yasutani embraced, at the very least, a very conservative political agenda, does this by itself justify the label of fanatical militarist?

67

It was, first of all, my desire to answer this question that served as the catalyst for further research in Japan at the beginning of 1999. I suspected I would find the answer in any of Yasutani's writings that dated from the war years. If ever there was a time when Japanese Zen masters, like the leaders of other Buddhist sects, expressed a militarist ideology, it was around the time of Japan's surrender on 15 August 1945. Yet, had Yasutani written anything of substance during this period, and even if he had, would it still be accessible?

What I discovered is that Ichikawa Hakugen was indeed mistaken in his characterization of Yasutani as "no less a fanatical militarist" than his master. On the contrary, Hakugen should have written: "Yasutani was an *even more* fanatical militarist, not to mention ethnic chauvinist, sexist, and anti-Semite, than his master!"

Not only that, Yasutani transformed the life and thought of Zen Master Dōgen (1200–53), the thirteenth-century founder of the Sōtō Zen sect in Japan, into a propaganda tool for Japanese militarism. He portrayed Dōgen as a paragon of both loyalty to the emperor and dedication to the nation's "defense," reinterpreting certain events in Dōgen's life so as to make the latter appear to have been among Japan's earliest advocates of restoring political power to the emperor, thereby laying the groundwork for the loyalist actions of the Meiji era reformers some six hundred years later. Similarly, Dōgen's interest in spreading the true Dharma in order to "protect the nation" was recast by Yasutani into backing for Japan's wartime goal of exercising hegemony over all of Asia through establishing the "Greater East Asia Co-prosperity Sphere" under the slogan of the "eight directions under one roof" (*hakkō ichi-u*).

Yasutani's wartime writings

In February 1943 the firm of Fuji Shobō in Tokyo published a book written by Yasutani entitled: *Dōgen Zenji to Shūshōgi* (Zen Master Dōgen and the *Treatise on Practice and Enlightenment*). The *Shūshōgi*, promulgated by the Sōtō Zen sect in 1890, was created to provide the sect's lay adherents with a relatively easily understood digest of Zen Master Dōgen's teachings concerning Buddhist practice and enlightenment.

The publication date, February 1943, is significant because it occurred only two months before Yasutani, at the age of fifty-eight, received formal Dharma transmission from his master, Harada Sōgaku. Equally important, this book was published at a time when it was becoming clear that the war was no longer going well for Japan, meaning that ever greater sacrifices would be required of the Japanese people.

What follows are excerpts from this book. In format the book was very traditional, consisting as it did of Yasutani's sentence by sentence, section by section commentary on the *Shūshōgi*'s text. This said, Yasutani made it clear from the outset that he was not interested in merely presenting yet another traditional interpretation of Dōgen's life and thought. Instead he wanted to "clarify the true

Dharma of Zen Master Dōgen," something he maintained had heretofore been misunderstood both within and without Zen Buddhist circles in Japan. In this, we catch an early hint of the rationale Yasutani would use in the postwar era, i.e. 1954, to justify his own break with the traditional Sōtō Zen sect and the creation of an independent Zen sectarian organization known as the Sanbōkyōdan (Three Treasures Association).

Be that as it may, inasmuch as Yasutani's book was composed of some 416 pages in all, what follows is clearly only a very small portion of the total. In having focused on Yasutani's war-related statements, it can be argued that the following material does not fairly represent the overall book. Nevertheless, the quotations below were contained, as the appended page numbers indicate, in what was at the time the most comprehensive statement of the Sōtō Zen sect's position on the Asia-Pacific War. I make this claim inasmuch as Ōmori Zenkai (1871–1947), then former administrative head of the Sōtō Zen sect, contributed a calligraphic endorsement that served as the book's *frontispiece*. More will be said about Ōmori in chapter 7 of this book.

On the book's purpose

In describing the purpose of his book, Yasutani wrote:

> Asia is one. Annihilating the treachery of the United States and Britain and establishing the Greater East Asia Co-prosperity Sphere is the only way to save the one billion people of Asia so that they can, with peace of mind, proceed on their respective paths. Furthermore, it is only natural that this will contribute to the construction of a new world order, exorcising evil spirits from the world and leading to the realization of eternal peace and happiness for all humanity. I believe this is truly the critically important mission to be accomplished by our great Japanese Empire.
>
> In order to fulfil this mission it is absolutely necessary to have a powerful military force as well as plentiful material resources. Furthermore, it is necessary to employ the power of culture, for it is most especially the power of spiritual culture that determines the final outcome. In fact, it must be said that in accomplishing this very important national mission the most important and fundamental factor is the power of spiritual culture....
>
> It is impossible to discuss Japanese culture while ignoring Buddhism. Those who would exclude Buddhism while seeking to exalt the Spirit of Japan are recklessly ignoring the history of our imperial land and engaging in a mistaken movement that distorts the reality of our nation. In so doing, it must be said, such persons hinder the proper development of our nation's destiny. For this reason we must promulgate and exalt the true Buddha Dharma, making certain that the people's thought is resolute and immovable. Beyond this, we must train and send forth a great number of capable men who will be able to develop and exalt the culture of our

imperial land, thereby reverently assisting in the holy enterprise of bringing the eight corners of the world under one roof (pp. 1–2).

On the Spirit of Japan

The Spirit of Japan is, of course, unique to our country. It does not exist in either China or India. Neither is it to be found in Italy or Germany, let alone in the US, England and other countries.... We all deeply believe, without the slightest doubt, that this spirit will be increasingly cultivated, trained, and enlarged until its brilliance fills the entire world. The most remarkable feature of the Spirit of Japan is the power derived from the great unity [of our people]....

In the event one wishes to exalt the Spirit of Japan, it is imperative to utilize Japanese Buddhism. The reason for this is that as far as a nutrient for cultivation of the Spirit of Japan is concerned, I believe there is absolutely nothing superior to Japanese Buddhism.... That is to say, all the particulars [of the Spirit of Japan] are taught by Japanese Buddhism, including the great way of "no-self" (*muga*) that consists of the fundamental duty of "extinguishing the self in order to serve the public [good]" (*messhi hōkō*); the determination to transcend life and death in order to reverently sacrifice oneself for one's sovereign; the belief in unlimited life as represented in the oath to die seven times over to repay [the debt of gratitude owed] one's country; reverently assisting in the holy enterprise of bringing the eight corners of the world under one roof; and the valiant and devoted power required for the construction of the Pure Land on this earth....

Within Japanese Buddhism it is the Buddha Dharma of Zen Master Dōgen, having been directly inherited from Śākyamuni, that has emphasized the cultivation of the people's spirit, for its central focus is on religious practice, especially the great duty of reverence for the emperor (pp. 7–11).

On Dōgen's life

The Buddha Dharma of Zen Master Dōgen is thoroughly and completely, from beginning to end, characterized by the great duty of reverence for the emperor. While it can be said that this is a feature of Japanese Buddhism as a whole, the great duty of reverence for the emperor is especially thoroughgoing in the Buddha Dharma of Zen Master Dōgen, pulsing through its every nook and cranny. It must be said that this spirit was a natural expression of Zen Master Dōgen's [noble] lineage. Having said this, because Dōgen thoroughly disliked such illusory things as fame and fortune, he didn't make a big fuss about this issue....

The reason that Dōgen intensely sought after the Buddha Dharma was definitely not for his own personal salvation. That is to say, braving the billowing waves, he travelled to faraway great Song China in search of the true Dharma of the Buddha because, being deeply angered by the tyranny exercised by the military government in Kamakura and deploring the hardship endured by the Imperial House, he was consumed by his reverence for the emperor and concern for what he might do to ensure the welfare of this imperial land. If one thoroughly examines what Zen Master Dōgen accomplished during his lifetime, it is clear that he was determined to cultivate the foundation of the people's spirit, causing them to awake to the true Spirit of Japan (pp. 21–2).

On Dōgen's thought

The Buddha Dharma of Zen Master Dōgen is thoroughly and completely characterized by the great spirit of reverence for the emperor and protection of the nation. For Zen Master Dōgen, the fundamental method for realizing and practicing this spirit is to have all the people practice *zazen* properly. The proper practice of *zazen* consists in the practice of *zazen* with the proper mental attitude. By nature, the body and mind are one, not two. For this reason, if the mind is proper, then one's physical posture will be proper. If one's mind and posture are proper, then one's thoughts and feelings will, as a matter of course, become proper. If one's thoughts and feelings become proper, then one's original mind naturally manifests itself. If one's original mind manifests itself, then as Japanese it is inevitable that the Spirit of Japan, consisting as it does of reverence for the emperor and protection of the nation, will be enhanced. It is for this reason that Zen Master Dōgen recommended the proper practice of *zazen* to all our citizens. . . .

In other words, Zen Master Dōgen taught that when our citizens maintain their bodies and minds properly, then the Way of the warrior is put into practice, the Way of the farmer is put into practice, the Way of the factory worker is put into practice, the Way of the merchant is put into practice, and, most especially, the Way of the loyal subject is thoroughly put into practice. The reason for this is that when the body and mind are properly maintained, illusory thoughts of seeking fame and fortune will not arise, nor will distracting ideas of selfishness and personal feelings occur. When illusory and distracting ideas disappear, then one's original mind and nature reveal themselves. That is to say, one's divine nature will manifest itself; the virtue of the Buddha will manifest itself. It is for this reason that Zen Master Dōgen so earnestly recommended the proper practice of *zazen* (pp. 29–30).

The precept forbidding killing

At this point the following question arises: What should the attitude of disciples of the Buddha, as Mahāyāna bodhisattvas, be toward the first precept that forbids the taking of life? For example, what should be done in the case in which, in order to remove various evil influences and benefit society, it becomes necessary to deprive birds, insects, fish, etc. of their lives, or, on a larger scale, to sentence extremely evil and brutal persons to death, or for the nation to engage in total war?

Those who understand the spirit of the Mahāyāna precepts should be able to answer this question immediately. That is to say, of course one should kill, killing as many as possible. One should, fighting hard, kill everyone in the enemy army. The reason for this is that in order to carry [Buddhist] compassion and filial obedience through to perfection it is necessary to assist good and punish evil. However, in killing [the enemy] one should swallow one's tears, bearing in mind the truth of killing yet not killing.

Failing to kill an evil man who ought to be killed, or destroying an enemy army that ought to be destroyed, would be to betray compassion and filial obedience, to break the precept forbidding the taking of life. This is a special characteristic of the Mahāyāna precepts (pp. 245–6).

The precept forbidding stealing

In making China cede the island of Taiwan, and, further, in annexing the Korean peninsula, our Great Japanese Imperial Empire engaged in the practice of a great bodhisattva, a practice that reveals itself through compassion and filial obedience. That is to say, it is this practice that provides the basis for seeking the great stabilization of East Asia, ensuring, first of all, the greatest happiness for the inhabitants of Taiwan and Korea; and secondly, bringing peace of mind and happiness to the various peoples of East Asia; not to mention producing peace and happiness for all humanity.

I hear that there are those among our brethren on the Korean peninsula who, ignorant of the noble purpose of our actions, rob people of their belongings (of course there are such people in mainland Japan as well) and even go so far as to say, "Japan is a great robber who has stolen Korea. Why make such a big fuss when we steal a few things!" I really would like to have the opportunity to thoroughly explain to people who think like this the truth and spirit of what I have written above, quickly dispelling their misunderstanding.

In a similar manner we must thoroughly and completely explain the great ideal of the founding of our nation, that is to say, the great spirit of the eight directions of the world under one roof. In so doing we will not only be able to clarify the understanding and conviction of our own people but, furthermore, make the various peoples of the world understand and acquiesce to our ideals. In truth, it is our Japanese Mahāyāna Buddhism that is fully equipped with the superb homilies necessary to accomplish this task (pp. 254–5).

On the Jews

While much of what Yasutani wrote above was echoed by innumerable wartime Zen leaders, there was one area in which he had less company: Yasutani was one of only a few Zen masters to integrate virulent anti-Semitism into his pro-war stance. The following are a few representative quotes, the first of which manages to mix Confucian social values together with its sexism and anti-Semitism:

1   Everyone should act according to their position in society. Those who are in a superior position should take pity on those below, while those who are below should revere those who are above. Men should fulfill the Way of men while women observe the Way of women, making absolutely sure that there is not the slightest confusion between their respective roles. It is therefore necessary to thoroughly defeat the propaganda and strategy of the Jews. That is to say, we must clearly point out the fallacy of their evil ideas advocating liberty and equality, ideas that have dominated the world up to the present time (p. 9).

2   Beginning in the Meiji period, perhaps because Japan was so busy importing western material civilization, our precious Japanese Buddhism was discarded without a second thought. For this reason, Japanese Buddhism fell into a situation in which it was half dead and half alive, leaving Japanese education without a soul. The result was the almost total loss of the Spirit of Japan, for the general citizenry became fascinated with the ideas of liberty and equality as advocated by the scheming Jews, not to mention such things as individualism, money as almighty, and pleasure-seeking. This in turn caused men of intelligence in recent years to strongly call for the promotion of the Spirit of Japan (pp. 10–11).

3   We must be aware of the existence of the demonic teachings of the Jews who assert things like [the existence of] equality in the phenomenal world, thereby disturbing public order in our nation's society and destroying [governmental] control. Not only this, these demonic conspirators hold the deep-rooted delusion and blind belief that, as far as the essential nature of human beings is concerned, there is, by nature, differentiation between superior and inferior. They are caught up in the delusion that they alone have been chosen by God and are [therefore] an exceptionally superior people. The result of all this is a treacherous design to usurp [control of] and dominate the entire world, thus provoking the great upheavals of today. It must be said that this is an extreme example of the evil resulting from superstitious belief and deep-rooted delusion (p. 19).

From the book's conclusion

At this point in time, nothing is more urgent than the clarification of the true Dharma of Zen Master Dōgen, thereby extolling the great duty of reverence for the emperor, and, at the same time, rectifying numerous unsound ideas, cultivating proper belief among the Japanese people as leaders of the Orient, one hundred million [people] of one mind, equipped with a resolute and immovable attitude.

In this connection I have provided a brief and simple outline of Zen Master Dōgen's Buddha Dharma. Nothing could bring me greater joy than if, through the dissemination of this book, the true Dharma becomes known once again, resulting in the total and complete exaltation of the Spirit of Japan and benefiting both the state and humanity.

Moreover, I am convinced this will become the spiritual foundation for the establishment of the Greater East Asia Co-Prosperity Sphere, the standard for cultural activities, and the pillar for the construction of a new world order (p. 416).

Dōgen as a paragon of imperial loyalty

Undoubtedly the most striking, if not deeply disturbing, aspect of Yasutani's wartime writings as introduced above is his anti-Semitism. Before examining this critically important topic, however, let us first examine Yasutani's attempt to turn Zen Master Dōgen into a paragon of imperial loyalty. Was Dōgen the man Yasutani made him out to be?

Inasmuch as Yasutani devoted an entire book to setting forth his interpretation of Dōgen, it would require at least the same if not more space to fully examine his claims, an impossible task in a single chapter. Therefore let us focus on just one of Yasutani's key claims to see if it can withstand the scrutiny of modern scholarship. I refer to Yasutani's claim that Dōgen was "consumed by his reverence for the emperor."

Yasutani supported this claim by alluding, first of all, to Dōgen's noble birth though conveniently omitting the fact that the oldest sources containing Dōgen's biographical details fail to name his father let alone his mother. Even today reputable scholars like Nakaseko Shōdō and James Kodera put forth strong cases for two different candidates, i.e. Minamoto Michitomo and Minamoto Michichika respectively. Furthermore, as Heinrich Dumoulin has pointed out, the background of Dōgen's mother is "completely uncertain."[6] In light of Yasutani's adulation for both Dōgen and the emperor, however, it is difficult to imagine that this master would have had much use for such scholarly "quibbling."

Be that as it may, of far more importance to an understanding of Dōgen's political orientation is his alleged visit to Kamakura, the country's military and political capital, in the winter of 1247–48. According to Yasutani the purpose of Dōgen's visit was as follows:

Dōgen's only objective in going to Kamakura was to urge the restoration of imperial rule. Inasmuch as this request was refused, Dōgen no longer had any reason to remain in Kamakura. Not only that, but we can respectfully infer that it was [Dōgen's] intense desire not to accept so much as a grain of rice from the Kamakura government, the greatest robber of the day (p. 28).

And what proof did Yasutani offer in support of this assertion? In other words, how did Yasutani seek to convince his readers that Dōgen had advocated the restoration of political power to the emperor?

Surprisingly, Yasutani offers evidence that on the surface would appear to contradict the very idea that Dōgen went to Kamakura in the first place. Yasutani quotes the following exchange contained in a collection of Dōgen's sayings known as the *Shōbōgenzō ZuimonkI (Record of Things Heard)*:

Someone suggested that in order for the Buddha Dharma to prosper, [Dōgen] should travel to Kamakura. [Dōgen] replied:

I will not go. In the event there is someone who seeks the Buddha Dharma, that person should be willing to cross over mountains, rivers and seas to study it. It would therefore be inappropriate for me to agree to travel on behalf of someone lacking in this aspiration (p. 25).

Yasutani's point in quoting this passage is to show that Dōgen must have had a very serious purpose in eventually going to Kamakura in spite of his initial misgivings. The serious purpose was, in Yasutani's eyes, Dōgen's commitment to restore the emperor to power.

Yasutani also offers a second exchange that appears at first glance to be much more pertinent to the question in hand. The exchange in question is said to have occurred on 25 September 1381 and involved Rinzai Zen Master Gidō Shūshin (1325–88), abbot of Kyoto's Tenryūji monastery, and Shōgun Ashikaga Yoshimitsu (1358–1408). Addressing Gidō, Yoshimitsu said: "In the event of a [political] upheaval, I would like to forsake the world. That is to say, I would like to do just what the abbot of Eiheiji [i.e. Dōgen] recommended that [Kamakura Regent] Hōjō Tokiyori do" (p. 26).

Inasmuch as Yasutani built his case for Dōgen's one-man 'imperial-restoration movement' on nothing more than the two preceding quotes, it is clear that he had a very weak case indeed. In fact, Yasutani himself appears to have recognized this fact inasmuch as he admitted that Dōgen failed to leave a record of his visit for posterity. This, however, Yasutani attributed to Dōgen's personal character: "Dōgen never divulged the details of his visit [to Kamakura] to the outside world because he didn't wish to publicize himself and because he was very meticulous and thorough" (p. 26).

Making sense out of "nonsense"

By this time, readers may be wondering how a man whose lectures and writings on Zen have been so highly praised in the West could have put forth an interpretation of a key episode of Dōgen's life based on such fragmentary, even contradictory, evidence. Even were it true that Dōgen visited Kamakura to urge Hōjō Tokiyori to become a monk, it requires a giant if not gigantic leap in logic to interpret this as motivated by Dōgen's desire to see political power restored to the emperor. Here, however, it may be well to remember that Yasutani also taught: "Buddhism has clearly demonstrated that discriminative thinking lies at the root of delusion . . ."[7]

Yasutani's interpretation notwithstanding, with the spread of non-sectarian-based scholarship in postwar years, the question of whether or not Dōgen ever went to Kamakura in the first place has become the focus of attention and debate. Foremost of those who deny such a visit took place is Yanagida Seizan (b. 1922), Japan's preeminent scholar on the history and early development of Chan/Zen in China.

On 18 November 1980 Yanagida commenced a series of twenty articles in the Buddhist newspaper *Chūgai Nippō* under the overall title of "Tabū e no Chōsen" (Challenging Taboos). As the title of the series suggests, it has long been taboo in Japan to challenge certain key articles of "faith" associated with Japan's major religious figures, regardless of their sectarian affiliation. For the Sōtō sect, Dōgen's visit to Kamakura is one of those defining events in his life that fits within that category.

Due to limitations of space I can give but the barest of introductions to Yanagida's research. Not surprisingly, his research focuses on a careful examination of the historical materials that refer to this event. Yanagida notes, for example, that the only historical material alleging that Dōgen visited Kamakura is connected with Eiheiji, the monastery Dōgen founded in 1246: there is no outside, independent verification of his visit dating from the time it is alleged to have occurred. This is especially suspicious inasmuch as the official history of this period, commissioned by the Kamakura military government and entitled *Azuma-kagami*, makes no mention whatsoever of Dōgen's visit in spite of the fact that it details Tokiyori's relationship with various other Zen masters.

Yanagida further points out that not even all of the Eiheiji biographical materials agree on this issue. One biography of Dōgen formulated by Gien (d. 1314) and entitled *Eihei Genzenji Goroku* makes no mention of Dōgen's having either left Eiheiji for Kamakura or his return. On the other hand, while it is true that the *Eihei Kōroku* does contain an entry mentioning this trip, Yanagida suspects this entry may be a later addition to the original text exactly because the travel dates are so clearly recorded, unlike other entries in which references to the exact dates of events are missing. Yanagida also suggests that it is doubtful that Dōgen would have absented himself from Eiheiji for an entire winter, i.e. during one of a Zen monastery's two key training periods.

These and a number of other factors led Yanagida to conclude: "Dōgen's visit to Kamakura never happened."[8] Furthermore, he suggested the following rationale lay behind the creation of Dōgen's mythical trip to Kamakura:

As time went by, the number of biographical materials gradually increased. When the person in question was the great founder of a sect, this increase was even more pronounced. The authors [of these biographical materials] had to be responsive to the different interests of their readers. These readers, regarding themselves as children of the age of the degenerate Dharma, burned with an extremely intense faith that was not necessarily related to their biological age. The background to their broad interests is to be found here. I think this is the meaning of the phrase "killing a person with kindness."

Living biographies take on a life of their own, and readers seek after a new and comprehensive image [of their subject]. They are not interested in Dōgen as a linguist or as a skin and bones philosopher. It was absolutely necessary for Dōgen to have travelled to Kamakura, just as it was absolutely necessary for him to have expounded [the Buddha Dharma] to a famous general like Tokiyori.[9]

While there is, no doubt, room for further scholarly debate on whether Dōgen actually visited Kamakura, in light of Yanagida's research and absent additional proof that he went, I am persuaded that the whole episode was the invention of subsequent sectarian advocates. These advocates saw Dōgen's alleged visit to Kamakura as proof that even while their sectarian founder was still alive, his greatness had been recognized by no less than the most powerful secular figure of his day.

With this background in mind, it is not difficult to understand the rationale behind Yasutani's insistence that Dōgen's "only objective in going to Kamakura was to urge the restoration of imperial rule." In fact, I suggest this is the key to unlocking the rationale behind Yasutani's overall effort to transform Dōgen's life and thought, Zen, Japanese Buddhism, Mahāyāna Buddhism and the Buddha Dharma itself, into a comprehensive system dedicated to the fervent and unconditional support of Emperor Hirohito and Japanese military aggression. In 1943, with Japan engaged in a losing war throughout Asia, it was "absolutely necessary" for Yasutani to have done so.

This said, it must be admitted that at least one of Yasutani's comments was, historically speaking, completely accurate. I refer to Yasutani's obvious pride in noting that for hundreds of years Japanese Zen priests had, following their recitation of the sūtras, chanted the following verse: "We reverently pray that the sacred life of His Excellency, the Reigning Emperor, may extend for ten thousand years; ten thousand years; ten, ten thousand years" (p. 23).

Yasutani's anti-Semitism

To think of anti-Semitism in the West is to be reminded of the Holocaust as perpetrated by the Nazis. Does this mean that in addition to his militarist stance, Yasutani was a "closet-Nazi"?

While not discounting a Nazi influence on Yasutani, it should be noted that in Japan, as in Europe, the history of anti-Semitism predates the emergence of the Nazis. This said, the unique feature of Japanese anti-Semitism is that it developed in a country where, at least in the prewar era, there were almost no Jewish residents, and no Japanese citizens of Jewish descent. Thus, Japan presents us with the rare spectacle of an anti-Semitism without Jews!

However, the fact that Japan lacked Jews does not mean that Japan, as one of the Axis powers, was simply aping, in some abstract or meaningless way, the racist ideology of its Nazi ally. As David Goodman pointed out in his book, *Jews in the Japanese Mind*:

> Anti-Semitism [in Japan] was not used to persecute Jews, nor was it by any means central to Japan's wartime ideology, but it did influence the way the Japanese viewed the war and was employed by the government on the home front to *silence dissent and enforce ideological conformity* [Italics mine].[10]

The parallels between the Japanese government's use of anti-Semitism and Yasutani's own views are all too clear. The reader will recall that in his book Yasutani explained his desire to "rectify numerous unsound ideas, cultivating proper belief among the Japanese people as leaders of the Orient, one hundred million [people] of one mind, equipped with a resolute and immovable attitude."

Yet, just how did the promotion of hatred of the Jews, or more accurately, hatred of "the demonic *teachings* of the Jews" serve to silence dissent and enforce ideological conformity?

Anti-Semitic propaganda

Readers familiar with the development of anti-Semitic thought in the West, including Nazi Germany, will immediately recognize the important role played by *The Protocols of the Elders of Zion*, a work claiming to be the original minutes of twenty-four secret sessions of Zionist "Elders" meeting in Basel, Switzerland in 1897. The purpose and goal of these sessions was nothing less than the takeover of the entire world in order to install a Jewish despot. The Elders are presented as believing that only a despot can rule society effectively and only force can ensure social order.

The Zionist leaders determined to further their plot for world conquest through support for liberalism, including a liberal education, as well as democratic institutions. They reckoned that pluralism and democracy would inevitably be accompanied by ever-growing social and political dissent, leading eventually to the disintegration of society. At that point, Jewish financiers would use the power of the capital they controlled to force the collapse of the already weakened Gentile states, setting the stage for the unification of the world under their own rule. Article 10 of Protocol 5 expresses these sentiments as follows:

> In order to put public opinion into our hands we must bring it into a state of bewilderment by giving expression from all sides to so many contradictory opinions and for such a length of time as will suffice to make the *gym* [Gentiles] lose their heads in the labyrinth and come to see that the best thing is to have no opinion of any kind in matters political, which is not given to the public to understand, because they are understood only by him who guides the public. This is the first secret.[11]

It was in this way that, as Yasutani would later phrase it, the allegedly socially disruptive ideas of "freedom and equality" became an expression of "the demonic teachings of the Jews."

Historically speaking, the *Protocols* were a total fabrication by agents of Russian Czar Nicholas II (reigned 1894–1917). The *Protocols* were introduced to Russia as early as 1903 to prove the existence of a nefarious Jewish plot to overthrow the Tsar and take control of the country. The *Protocols* did not, however, become influential until after the Russian Revolution of 1917 when they proved to be a useful propaganda tool in building a counter-revolutionary movement opposed to the Bolsheviks, whose leaders, it was claimed, were all Jews.

It was in this context that the *Protocols* first came to the attention of the Japanese Army, sent to Siberia in August 1918 to fight alongside soldiers from such countries as the USA, England, and France, in support of the counter-revolutionary White Russian and Ukrainian troops. Needless to say, the Japanese Army, like the Japanese government, also feared the spread of Bolshevism, i.e. Marxism, into Japan and seized on the *Protocols* as an effective method of countering domestic voices demanding such things as social equality, land reform, and freedom from economic exploitation.

One of the earliest Buddhist voices to echo the Japanese military's anti-Semitic propaganda was Tanaka Chigaku (1861–1939), a one-time Nichiren sect priest who later founded the National Pillar Society (*Kokujū-kai*) in 1914, a lay Buddhist organization dedicated to promoting what Tanaka called "Nichiren-ism" (*Nichiren-shugi*). Included in Tanaka's ultranationalist program was the adoption of an economic system similar to Nazi national socialism though centered, like all Nichiren-related movements, in exclusive faith in the *Lotus Sūtra* as promulgated by Nichiren (1222–82).

Tanaka had a number of prominent disciples, perhaps the best known of which was Lt. General Ishiwara Kanji (1889–1949), the officer primarily responsible for planning and executing the Manchurian Incident of 1931. This incident led first to the Japanese military takeover of the whole of Manchuria and eventually to full-scale warfare with China in 1937. In the same year that Japan went to war with China, Tanaka had the following to say about Jews:

> At present sixty to seventy per cent of the world's money is said to be in Jewish hands. There are many poor and penniless countries that end up having to accept capital from abroad in order to get by, and consequently they have to submit to Jews in order to borrow the money they need.
>
> Typically Jews invest in transportation facilities, electric plants, railroads, and subways.... The reason for this is based on the plan contained in the *Protocols* to constantly foment revolution in various countries, eventually leading to their collapse. It is then that the Jews will be able to take over.[12]

As with Yasutani, Tanaka argued that Jews were fomenting social unrest in order to rule the world. He went on, again like Yasutani, to point out that Jews advocated liberalism, especially within academic circles, as part of their plan to destroy the people's moral sense. Even the 1936 Olympic Games were, according to Tanaka, part of the Jewish conspiracy; for spectators at Olympic events went wild with enthusiasm, the first step on the road to a life of debauchery. This in turn undermined the people's moral sense even more, making them easy targets for revolution – "a truly dreadful prospect."[13]

Helped by men like Tanaka, anti-Semitism spread rapidly throughout Japanese society despite the near total absence of Jews. The US ambassador to Japan, Joseph Grew (1880–1965) gloomily noted that an anti-Semitic propaganda exhibition held in Tokyo toward the end of 1938 had been something of a success.[14] By the 1940s, anti-Semitic ideas became so widespread that the famous writer Tokutomi Iichirō was able to utilize them in his 1944 book *A Citizen's Reader for Certain Victory* (*Hisshō Kokumin Tokuhon*) to justify his assertion that Japan and Japan alone was capable of serving as "the model, the pattern, the standard for the world." Not only that, Japan was destined "to lead the whole world along the path of virtue."[15]

But why Japan? Did not the USA, with its greater national wealth and power, not to mention its democratic institutions, have a superior claim to world leadership? Not according to Tokutomi, for in his view American democracy was only a charade in which real political power rested in the hands of the rich. And behind the rich stood the "evil and ugly plutocracy of the Jews."[16]

The Buddhist connection

In Japan, institutional Buddhist leaders had played a prominent role in the ideological struggle against anarchism, socialism, and communism since the late Meiji period (1868–1912). In 1911, for example, Toyota Dokutan (1840–1917), the administrative head of the Myōshinji branch of the Rinzai Zen sect, condemned Japanese socialists and anarchists for having "fallen into the trap of believing in the heretical idea of 'evil equality'" (*aku byōdō*). [17]

Even earlier, in 1879, the noted Shin sect priest and scholar Shimaji Mokurai (1838–1911) wrote an essay entitled "Differentiation [Is] Equality" (*Sabetsu Byōdō*). Shimaji asserted that distinctions in social standing and wealth were as permanent as differences in age, sex, and language. Thus, socialism and the like were fatally flawed because they emphasized only social and economic equality. That is to say, socialists failed to understand the basic Mahāyāna Buddhist teaching that "differentiation is identical with equality" (*sabetsu soku byōdō*).[18]

Needless to say, socialism and its like were seen as imports from a West that threatened Japan's existence not only externally, through force of arms, but internally, through ideological subversion. One of the most outspoken proponents of this point of view was Lt. General (and Viscount) Torio Tokuan (1847–1905). General Torio was the founder of the Yuima-kai, a lay society established in 1881 to promote Zen practice among Japan's military leaders. Headquartered at the Rinzai Zen monastery of Shōkokuji in Kyoto, this society actively pursued its nationalist and militarist mission on an ever-expanding scale up until Japan's defeat in 1945.

Torio's ideological orientation is well illustrated by the following excerpt from a newspaper editorial he wrote for Japan's *Daily Mail* in 1890:

The adoption of the [occidental] principles of *liberty and equality* in Japan would vitiate the good and peaceful customs of our country, render the general disposition of the people harsh and unfeeling, and prove finally a source of calamity to the masses....

Though at first sight occidental civilization presents an attractive appearance, adapted as it is to the gratification of selfish desires, yet, since its basis is the hypothesis that men's wishes constitute natural laws, it must ultimately end in disappointment and demoralization....

Occidental nations have become what they are after passing through conflicts and vicissitudes of the most serious kind.... Perpetual disturbance is their doom. Peaceful equality can never be attained until built up among the ruins of annihilated western States and the ashes of extinct western peoples [Italics mine].[19]

Underlying comments like the above is an interpretation of the Buddhist doctrine of *karma* which held that differences in social and economic status were not the result of either social injustice or exploitation but were, instead, solely the reward (or punishment) for an individual's past actions in either this or previous lives. Rinzai Zen Master Shaku Sōen (1859–1919), D. T. Suzuki's master and the abbot of Engakuji, expressed this viewpoint as follows:

We are born in a world of variety; some are poor and unfortunate, others are wealthy and happy. This state of variety will be repeated again and again in our future lives. But to whom shall we complain of our misery? To none but ourselves![20]

A marriage made in hell

Given this background, what happened next was all too predictable. That is to say, Yasutani's anti-Semitism, like that of other Japanese Buddhist leaders, represented the "marriage" or "personalization" of the two preceding strands of reactionary thought in prewar Japanese society. This marriage made it possible for Yasutani and others to identify foreign and potentially socially destabilizing liberal and left-wing ideas with a foreign and alien people – the Jews – a people allegedly espousing liberty and equality as part of their nefarious plot to take over the world, Japan included.

Seen in this light, Yasutani's anti-Semitic remarks are no mere aberration or afterthought, let alone a mere aping of the anti-Semitism of Japan's Nazi ally. Rather, his remarks go directly to the heart of the "home-grown" reactionary social role that Japanese institutional Buddhism played in Japanese society following the Meiji period (and before).

Sexism

In this connection, reference must also be made to Yasutani's dictum that "men should fulfil the Way of men while women observe the Way of women, making absolutely sure that there is not the slightest confusion between their respective roles." Here, too, Yasutani was but reiterating the longstanding sexist attitudes of Japan's male Buddhist leaders, regardless of sectarian affiliation. As Okano Haruko has noted:

> In Japan, as in many other societies, religions – in this case Shinto, Buddhism, and Confucianism – have contributed significantly to the development and maintenance of separate gender roles and of gender inequality. These religions have encouraged people to accept a notion of ethics which proclaims that people are born with differing abilities and into different statuses within society, thereby serving to maintain the prevailing social order. . . . Buddhism [was] the most influential of the three in shaping the image and role of women and supporting sexism in Japanese society.[21]

Significantly, as Okano herself points out, it was only Zen Master Dōgen, among all the founders of Japan's traditional Buddhist sects, who clearly opposed religious discrimination against women. In the "Essence of Worship" (Raihai-tokuzui) chapter of the *Shōbōgenzō*, Dōgen wrote:

> Though of humble appearance, a person who has awakened to the Bodhi [Wisdom-seeking]-mind is already the teacher of all mankind. Even a little

girl of seven can become the teacher of the four classes of Buddhists and the compassionate mother of all beings; for [in Buddhism] men and women are completely equal. This is one of the highest principles of the Way.[22]

Needless to say, Yasutani had no more use for what would today be seen as a feminist viewpoint than he had, in the "Merit of Entering the Priesthood" (Shukke Kudoku) chapter of the *Shōbōgenzō*, to Dōgen's references to Japan as no more than a "little country" located in a "remote place," i.e. in comparison with countries like India and China. More importantly, nowhere in Yasutani's writings is there the slightest reference to Dōgen's statement in the same chapter that "although in this small and remote country there is a king in name, he lacks virtue and is completely overcome with greed."[23]

That Japan, as a "land of the gods" ruled eternally by a "living god," i.e. the emperor, could ever have been merely a "little country" under the control of a greedy and virtueless ruler was as unacceptable to Yasutani as was the idea of sexual equality. The reason for this is not hard to fathom, for Yasutani and his peers, like their masters before them, had wholeheartedly embraced the role of "ideological shock troops" for Japanese aggression abroad and thought suppression at home. As such they were dedicated to an unwavering and unremitting struggle against all forms of thought, left-wing or merely "liberal," that did not completely and totally subsume the individual to the needs and purposes of a hierarchically-constituted, patriarchal, totalitarian state.

Liberalism

It is important to remember that in prewar Japan it was liberalism, not socialism or communism, which formed the last effective barrier to the rule of the military and its bureaucratic allies. This reality is best reflected in the successful 1935 attempt to drive the renowned constitutional scholar, Professor Minobe Tatsukichi (1873–1948) of Tokyo University, from public life. In the eyes of his right-wing critics, Professor Minobe committed the unforgivable sin of interpreting the Japanese constitution to mean that the emperor was not identical with the state, but was, instead, a subordinate "organ" (*kikan*) of it.

Had Minobe's interpretation prevailed, it would have served as a brake on the emperor's power in that the government of the day would have been responsible to *both* the emperor and the Diet (i.e. parliament), and thereby to the electorate. This would have enhanced the power and prestige of not only the civilian government but the Japanese people as a whole.

Needless to say, Minobe's interpretation did not survive the right-wing onslaught. True to form, the Japanese military, especially the Imperial Military Reserve Association (*Teikoku Zaigo Gunjin-kai*), played the leading role in denouncing Minobe. Typical of the Reserve Association's denunciations was the following:

A non-Japanese, blasphemous, Europe-worshipping ideology which ignores our three-thousand-year-old tradition and ideals is rife. This *liberalism* which threatens to turn us into western barbarians (*yōi*) is basic to Minobe's beliefs. His books must be burned to show how we [reservists] feel about his servile *individualism* [Italics mine].[24]

Minobe, it should be noted, was not only a leading constitutional scholar but also a member of Japan's House of Peers, the upper chamber of the Diet. Thus, when in September 1935 Minobe reluctantly resigned from all of his official positions, including both his professorship and seat in the Diet, the last major ideological impediment to the military's control of Japan was eliminated. Nevertheless, while liberalism had been blocked in the short term, the danger of its reemergence, like that of communism and socialism, was always there. Recognizing this, the Ministry of Education published a tract in July 1941 entitled *Shimmin no Michi* (*The Way of the Subject*) which called for overthrowing "the old order based on the dominance of individualism, liberalism, and dialectical materialism."[25]

Needless to say, the danger of internal discontent became especially acute from 1943 onwards as the possibility, if not the likelihood, of Japan's defeat became ever clearer. Thanks to men like Yasutani, however, any internal dissent that did exist never became an organized force. It can be argued, however, that the very success these men enjoyed spelled Japan's defeat, for as the historian Edward Drea has argued, underlying all Japanese strategy was what turned out to be a colossally wrong assumption: "Americans [were] products of liberalism and individualism and incapable of fighting a protracted war."[26] Ironically, it was exactly these two features, attributed to Jews in particular and westerners in general, that turned out to be one of the main sources of the fighting spirit of allied soldiers. They understood what it meant to fight (and die if necessary) for "liberty."

The question remaining to be examined is whether or not Japan's surrender on 15 August 1945 brought an end to Yasutani's anti-Semitic and ultranationalist crusade.

Yasutani's postwar ideology

In postwar Japan it was no longer acceptable to be an explicit anti-Semite let alone a "militarist." This said, the US-dominated Occupation authorities did share one fundamental value with Japan's wartime leaders, i.e. their fear and hatred of Communism. Furthermore, these former enemies had long recognized that applying labels like "Communist," "Communist stooge", etc. to any political movement challenging the status quo was an effective way to demonize and destroy it. Similarly, they knew that religious leaders could be counted on to endorse and promote any crusade directed against "godless" Communists and their materialist ideology.

In light of the abject poverty prevailing in postwar Japan, it is hardly surprising that the left-wing promise of economic and social betterment for the working class attracted large numbers of supporters. The Japanese Left grew so powerful that in April 1947 it succeeded in electing a Socialist-led government headed by Katayama Tetsu (1887–1978), albeit under the supervision of the Occupation authorities.

This unprecedented development, though short-lived, set off alarm bells in both Washington and among Japan's right-wing forces, many of whom as seen in the previous chapter had been closely allied with the military during the war years. This led, by fair means and foul, to a resurgence of conservatism, one result of which was that by 1957, only six years after the end of the Allied Occupation, Japan found itself led by a prime minister, Kishi Nobusuke (1896–1987), who had been arrested in December 1948 under suspicion of being a Class A war criminal.

Japan's eventual disavowal of left-wing parties in the postwar era is due, at least in part, to the ongoing efforts of Japan's institutional Buddhist leaders, including many leading Zen masters. For example, as we have seen, in 1954 Ōmori Sōgen became head of a major federation of newly-reconstituted ultranationalist organizations. In 1974 Asahina Sōgen (1891–1979), head of the Engakuji branch of the Rinzai Zen sect, was one of the founders of the "Association to Protect Japan" (Nihon o Mamoru Kai). This organization sought to "exalt patriotism" and rid Japan of so-called "biased education," especially any suggestion in school textbooks that Japan had engaged in aggressive warfare, let alone committed atrocities in Nanjing and elsewhere.

Similarly, in 1976 Zen Master Yamada Mumon (1900–88), head of the Myōshinji branch of the Rinzai Zen sect, helped establish the "Society to Repay the Heroic Spirits [of Dead Soldiers]" (Eirei ni Kotaeru Kai). Yamada asserted that since Japan's fallen soldiers had clearly been involved in a "holy war," the government should reinstate financial support for enshrining their "heroic spirits" (eirei) in Yasukuni Jinja, a major Shinto shrine located in the heart of Tokyo.

Given this background, it is hardly surprising to learn that Yasutani, like his Zen contemporaries, continued his own struggle against left-wing and liberal thought in the postwar era. For example, in March 1971 Yasutani wrote:

> Those organizations which are labelled right-wing at present are the true Japanese nationalists. Their goal is the preservation of the true character of Japan. There are, on the other hand, some malcontents who ignore the imperial household, despise tradition, forget the national polity, forget the true character of Japan, and get caught up in the schemes and enticements of Red China and the Soviets.[27]

If the preceding is representative of Yasutani's ongoing struggle against the Japanese Left, then the following, written in September 1972, reveals his ongoing opposition to liberalism of any kind, not least of all in education:

The universities we presently have must be smashed one and all. If that can't be done under the present constitution, then it should be declared null and void just as soon as possible, for it is an un-Japanese constitution ruining the nation, a sham constitution born as the bastard child of the Allied Occupation Forces.[28]

One notable characteristic of both of these quotes is that they were written in Japanese for a purely domestic audience. In addition, the second of these quotes, in its disdain for a western-style liberal education, bears the unmistakable imprint of the views of Yasutani's own master, Harada Daiun Sōgaku. In March 1934 Harada wrote:

At present, the thoughts and [religious] faith of the ordinary people are totally confused. We patriots, nay, all of the Japanese people, must immediately rouse ourselves in order to fundamentally reform all levels of Japanese education, from primary and intermediate schools up through the various types of universities.... These schools all know how to make shallow, cosmopolitan-minded persons but they have completely forgotten how to make Japanese. The cardinal point of education in Japan ought to be to make Japanese.[29]

US visits

Chauvinistic comments like the above were noticeably absent from Yasutani's "Dharma talks" given during his numerous visits to the USA in the 1960s. Yet perhaps such comments were not as entirely absent as it first appears, for in 1969 Yasutani shared the following thoughts with his American disciples:

Western-style social sciences have been based on a deluded misconception of the self, and they attempt to develop this "I" consciousness. This is dichotomy. As a result, they have reinforced the idea of dichotomy between human beings which has led to conflicts and fighting. They have even created a crisis which may destroy all of mankind.[30]

In seeking to understand why Yasutani chose to attack western-style social sciences, it is crucial to understand that in Japan the social sciences have long been regarded with deep suspicion if not outright hostility by the right wing. As David Goodman notes:

Beginning in the 1920s, Marxism was virtually synonymous with social science in Japan, that is, with the systematic analysis of society against a broad historical background, and to turn one's back on it was therefore to abandon the effort to deal rationally with the world. Thus Japanese intellectuals rejected Marxism and embraced irrational nationalism.[31]

I suggest that Japanese intellectuals were not the only ones to have "abandoned the effort to deal rationally with the world." That is to say, Yasutani's own eagerness to "embrace irrational nationalism" is all too plain to see, both during the war and even after it. As D. T. Suzuki pointed out:

> [Zen] simply urges going ahead with whatever conclusion rational or *irrational* a man has arrived at. Philosophy may safely be left with intellectual minds; Zen wants to act, and the most effective act, once the mind is made up, is to go on without looking backward. In this respect, Zen is indeed the religion of the samurai warrior [Italics mine].[32]

For his part, Yasutani is quoted in Kapleau's *Three Pillars of Zen* as having taught: "Thought is the sickness of the human mind."[33]

The postwar legacy of anti-Semitism

In one sense it can be argued that Yasutani's anti-Semitism, like that of his contemporaries, had very little to do with flesh and blood Jews at all. Thus in wartime Japan the near total absence of Jews was no hindrance to a government-endorsed campaign of anti-Semitism of which Yasutani was merely one representative. It must be remembered that Japanese militarism, like its Nazi counterpart, was fundamentally a reactionary movement that sought to create a totalitarian society as a counter to liberalism, democracy, socialism and communism, both at home and abroad. Thus, in Japan, criticism of the Jews was merely a convenient method of "personalizing" the struggle against western thought in general and left-wing ideologies in particular. As John Dower explains:

> The single most corrupting feature of western thought was identified as being preoccupation with the self, or the individual, as opposed to the larger collectivity. From this egocentrism and individualism stemmed most of the ills of the modern age: utilitarianism, materialism, capitalism, liberalism, socialism, and communism among them. Innumerable public and private statements ... explained the rationale for purging Japan of these degenerate and corrupting influences.[34]

For this reason, in the postwar period it was a relatively simple matter for Yasutani to substitute the words "western-style social sciences" for the words "scheming Jews" and carry on his ultranationalist and right-wing crusade as if nothing had changed. In one sense he was simply reverting back to the conservative if not reactionary social agenda of institutional Buddhist leaders from the mid to late Meiji period onwards. It can only be described as highly ironic that Yasutani's western disciples, some of whom are themselves from Jewish backgrounds, failed to notice the substitution.

The Nazi connection

I note that my discovery of Yasutani's wartime writings in early 1999 was no accident – I owe my discovery to comments made by Rinzai Zen Master Shimano Eido (b. 1932) on the occasion of Yasutani's death in 1973. In the Summer/Fall issue of that year's *ZCLA Journal*, Eido wrote:

> During World War II ... the German government sent Professor Durckheim to Japan to study Japanese culture, especially Zen Buddhism. After arriving in Japan, Professor Durckheim searched for an appropriate book to study and finally, with the assistance of Professor [Fumio] Hashimoto, he found a book called *Dogen Zenji and Shushogi*, published in 1943.... So impressed was Durckheim that he visited Yasutani Roshi's temple with Professor Hashimoto. Yasutani Roshi entertained them by preparing a Japanese bath which they all took together.[35]

As innocent as this story appears, Eido omitted some significant facts about both Professor (and Count) Karlfried Graf Durckheim (1896–1988) as well as Professor Fumio Hashimoto (b. 1909). First of all, Durckheim was no ordinary professor visiting Japan on some cultural exchange program. Instead, from 1935 through to the end of 1937, Durckheim had been a member of the then Nazi Ambassador to England (and later Foreign Minister) Joachim von Ribbentrop's (1893–1946) so-called "Brain Trust." Unfortunately for Durckheim, it was discovered that he had a Jewish grandmother, cutting short his career at the highest levels of the Nazi foreign service. Although he did not lose his job, he was demoted and given a choice between attending to the needs of German youth organizations abroad or serving as a cultural envoy to Japan.

Durckheim chose the latter assignment and departed for Japan in June 1938 for an initial nine-month stay. He returned to Japan a second time at the beginning of 1940 and remained there through the end of the war. It was during this latter period that Durckheim first met Yasutani. That these two men became acquaintances was primarily due to the presence of Hashimoto Fumio, who was then not a professor but a former higher school teacher of German serving as a translator for the German embassy in Tokyo.

Hashimoto described his relationship to Durckheim as follows:

> When Durckheim first arrived in Japan, he was surrounded by Shintoists, Buddhist scholars, military men and right-wing thinkers, each of whom sought to impress him with their importance. The Count found it difficult to determine which of them was the real thing, and I stepped in to serve as his adviser. In addition, a great number of written materials were sent to him, and my job was to review them to determine their suitability....
>
> In the end what most interested the Count was traditional Japanese archery and Zen. He set up an archery range in his garden and zealously

practiced every day. In addition, he went to Shinkōji temple on the outskirts of Ogawa township in Saitama Prefecture where he stayed to practice Zen for a number of days. His instructor in *zazen* was the temple abbot, Master Yasutani. I accompanied the Count and gladly practiced with him.[36]

Durckheim's interest in the relationship of the military arts to Zen was not limited to his own practice of archery. He attended a number of lectures on this topic and held extended discussions with such leading military figures as Imperial Navy Vice-Admiral Teramoto Takeharu and Imperial Army General Araki Sadao. As previously mentioned, Araki was well known for both his fierce anti-Communism and the importance he placed on promoting the Spirit of Japan among both military men and civilians, particularly school-age youth. In postwar years, Araki would be tried as a Class A war criminal and sentenced to life imprisonment.

Hashimoto relates that it was he who first took an interest in Yasutani because of his master's strong emphasis on both the practice of *zazen* and the realization of enlightenment. This emphasis on practice was a new revelation for him, for until then his only knowledge of Buddhism had come from scholars who "had never properly done *zazen* or realized enlightenment."[37] In particular, Hashimoto was impressed by Yasutani's 1943 book on Zen Master Dōgen and the *Shūshōgi* which revealed "the greatness of this master [i.e. Yasutani] and the profundity of Buddhism."[38] So impressed was Hashimoto by this book that not only did he provide Durckheim with a detailed description of its contents but went on to translate the entire book into German.

Thus, Yasutani's book was clearly the catalyst for Durckheim to train at Shinkōji. While there is nothing particularly sinister in this, it is clear that Durckheim could not help but have been aware of Yasutani's militarist and anti-Semitic rhetoric as previously introduced. Given that, his Jewish grandmother notwithstanding, Durckheim was a cultural envoy for the Nazis, it is hardly surprising that he would have been "so impressed" by Yasutani's writings.

While Yasutani was demonizing the Jews in Japan in 1943, the Nazis had long since started to herd Jews into concentration camps in preparation for their extermination. This is not to claim, of course, that Yasutani, any more than Durckheim or Hashimoto, was directly responsible for either the Nazi-perpetrated Holocaust or Imperial Japan's own "home-grown" massacres, e.g. the December 1937 "Rape of Nanjing" among many others. Nevertheless, in Yasutani's case there is a disturbing parallel, for history reveals that the journey from "demonized other" to massacre, if not to gas chamber, is very short indeed.

It is also noteworthy that Yasutani went even further than the Japanese government of his day by asserting that his emperor-worshipping, pro-war, imperialistic, sexist and anti-Semitic sentiments were nothing less than the "true Buddha Dharma." In so doing, it is no exaggeration to say that Yasutani had, consciously or not, so completely subordinated himself to the state that he was indeed "self-less." He not only rendered unto Caesar what was Caesar's, but proffered the entirety of the Buddhist faith as well. Not content with that, he urged the entire Japanese nation to do likewise.

Conclusion

Even this cursory glance at Yasutani's wartime writings reveals that he was more than willing to twist and distort Zen Master Dōgen's life and thought; the Mahāyāna precepts; Jewish identity, etc. in order to present a picture of the "true Buddha Dharma" that was indistinguishable from the aims and goals of Japanese militarism. Further, as readers of *Zen At War* will recognize, Yasutani was only one of many Zen masters and other institutional Buddhist leaders in wartime Japan to have done so.

If there is anything that distinguishes Yasutani from his fellow priests, it is simply the thoroughness of his subordination of all aspects of the Buddha Dharma in general, and the Zen tradition in particular, to the ideology of the totalitarian (or fascist) state. The strength and frequency of his anti-Semitic remarks, while not unique among his contemporaries, are yet another distinguishing feature of this overall pattern.

For those looking for some kind of "saving grace" in Yasutani's ultranationalist ideology it may be found in the fact that, as noted above, even following Japan's defeat in 1945, Yasutani continued his right-wing ideological crusade unabated. This suggests at least a certain degree of integrity or consistency in his approach. The caveat here, of course, is that while his right-wing statements continued unabated in the Japanese language, they were conspicuously absent from remarks directed toward westerners.

The "bifurcation" of Yasutani's exposition of the Buddha Dharma to Japanese and western audiences cannot but raise the question of Yasutani's underlying integrity. There may, however, be more continuity in Yasutani's statements to the two groups than appears at first glance as, for example, when words like "western-style social sciences" are recognized as what we would today call a "politically correct" substitution for "scheming Jews." Furthermore, when in the mid-1960s an American student asked Yasutani what to do in the event he were drafted to serve in Vietnam, Yasutani simply answered: "If your country calls you, you must go."[39]

Yasutani was not, of course, the only Zen master to reflect a "split personality" in statements directed toward either Japanese or western audiences in the postwar era. Rinzai Zen masters Yamada Mumon and Ōmori Sōgen, previously introduced, come immediately to mind as Zen masters who acted similarly.[40]

Postwar Japanese political leaders have also manifested the same kind of split personality, though usually not in one and the same person: almost every time one leading Japanese politician makes some kind of apology for Japan's past military aggression, another politician will almost simultaneously offer a justification or rationalization for Japan's wartime acts. In some sense it may be said that Zen masters like Yasutani only reflect the overall split in the entire Japanese nation, or at least its leadership.

It should be noted however, that the Zen tradition has long played the role of "ideological policeman" for the state. In 1608, for example, it was Rinzai Zen Master Ishin Sūden (1569–1633), abbot of the major monastic complex of Nanzenji, who formulated a decree banning Christianity on behalf of the Tokugawa government. As in the case of the later anti-Christian movement spearheaded by Buddhist leaders during the middle part of the Meiji period (1868–1912), Christianity's call to faith in a truly transcendent and universal deity was regarded as a threat to the absolute loyalty an imperial subject owed his sovereign.

It is possible to argue that even today, more than fifty years after the end of the Asia-Pacific War, little has changed in this regard. For example, when Josh Baran, a former Sōtō Zen sect priest, visited Japan in March 1998, he met with Toga Masataka, director of the Institute of Zen Studies at Rinzai sect-affiliated Hanazono University in Kyoto. "In Japanese Zen," Toga explained, "loyalty is most important. Loyalty to one's teacher and the tradition is more important than the Buddha and Dharma."

In commenting on Toga's words, Baran pointed out:

> The Buddha never taught that loyalty was more important than truth or compassion. Blind loyalty outside the *zendo* can and did have disastrous results. Until key assumptions can be questioned, the roots of warrior Zen remain alive and well.[41]

My own research leads to a similar conclusion. Thus, it can be said that in today's Japanese Zen tradition, as demonstrated so vividly by Ōmori Sōgen, the unity of Zen and the sword, i.e. the belief in "holy war," lives on. One cannot help but believe that Zen masters Yasutani Haku'un and Harada Daiun Sōgaku, among many others, would be pleased.

6

CARRYING ZEN TO CHINA

Many readers will recognize this title as a variation of the familiar maxim: "carrying coals to Newcastle." Just as one would question the reason for transporting coal to a major coal-producing area like Newcastle, it is necessary to question why leaders of the Japanese Zen school thought it necessary in the 1930s to reintroduce Zen to China, the land of its birth.

To be sure, Japanese Buddhist leaders of all sects had established Buddhist "missions" in China, some as early as 1876.[1] The Japanese government lent its support to these efforts; for, as a pan-Asian religion, Buddhism was seen as a useful tool in promoting the unity of East Asian peoples under Japanese hegemony. In addition, from the Meiji period onwards, leading Japanese Buddhists maintained that Buddhism in China and the rest of Asia was backward, passive, and indifferent to social needs while Japanese Mahāyāna Buddhism was activist, socially engaged, and scientific – the world's only "true Buddhism."[2]

Consequently, Buddhist leaders, conjuring up a Japanese version of "the white man's burden," felt themselves duty-bound to bring Japan's "true Buddhism" to the benighted peoples of Asia and even the West, whether the latter wanted it or not.

With this background in mind, let us examine a missionary effort led by Rinzai Zen Master Yamamoto Gempō, first introduced in chapter 1. As early as 1932, Gempō had justified the political assassination of "even good people" in the name of Buddhism. Given this, it is hardly surprising that this master would lend his prestige to the promotion of Japanese colonial policy abroad. More telling, in postwar years leaders of the Myōshinji branch of the Rinzai Zen sect rewarded Gempō for his wartime efforts by selecting him to head their influential branch from 1947–9.

Cultural exchange

Japan's formal recognition of its puppet state of *Manzhouguo* (*Manchukuo*) in September 1932, followed by its ever-increasing military and economic intervention in north China, heightened anti-Japanese feelings on the part of

Plate 7 Nakajima's master Rinzai Zen Master Yamamoto Gempō.
Courtesy Nakajima Genjō.

the Chinese government and people. To counter this militant Chinese nationalism, the Japan–China Buddhist Research Association dispatched, in June 1935, an eleven member delegation, including Gempō, to promote "international friendship" between Japan and China. Seeking to promote a feeling of pan-Asian solidarity, Gempō and his fellow priests visited some of China's most famous temples and met many prominent Buddhists.

In July 1935, prior to returning to Japan, Gempō decided to visit Xinjing (present-day Changchun), the newly created capital of *Manzhouguo*. Upon arrival, the Manchurian government's vice minister of foreign affairs held a dinner banquet on his behalf. Significantly, the vice minister, Ōhashi Chūichi, was not Manchurian, but Japanese. Ōhashi's nationality was no accident for Japanese vice ministers, aided by a staff of Japanese secretaries, stood immediately behind and in control of all native Manchurian Cabinet ministers.

Among the dinner guests was the adjutant general of the occupying Japanese *Guandong* (*Kwantung*) army; the local branch head of the Mitsubishi financial combine; the vice-president of the central bank of Manchuria; a judge of the Manchurian Supreme Court; other senior military officers and business leaders; and government officials and legislators, numbering more than twenty in all. As it turned out, these leaders had more on their minds than simple hospitality, for

93

their goal was to ensure "the proper exaltation of the spirit of both the Japanese military and other Japanese residents of Manchuria."[3] They believed this could be accomplished if Gempō would agree to create a branch temple of the Rinzai Zen sect-affiliated Myōshinji in Xinjing.

New branch temple

Gempō immediately accepted their request, though he first had to return to Japan to secure permission from the head of Myōshinji. This in hand, construction began quickly and Gempō's personal residence was completed on 7 July 1936, while the dedication ceremony of the new *zendo* (meditation hall) was held on 29 November of the same year. This ceremony was attended by no less a figure than Zhang Zhonghui, prime minister of *Manzhouguo*, together with his cabinet ministers, the mayor of Xinjing and, of course, a bevy of Japanese government vice ministers, Japanese embassy personnel, and other local leaders.

Although no Japanese military officers were present at the opening ceremony, the *Guandong* army had played a key role in the temple's actual construction, especially of Gempō's living quarters and the meditation hall. In addition, Hanaya Tadashi (1894–1957), *Guandong* army staff officer and yet another youthful instigator of the Manchurian Incident of 1931, donated the first 500 yen toward the temple's construction. The total construction costs came to more than 50,000 yen, a large sum in those days; but, with the military taking the lead, the remaining funds were readily raised from various Japanese companies doing business in Manchuria, notably the quasi-governmental South Manchuria Railroad Company.

Controversy

The naming of the new temple turned out to be a contentious issue, for the temple's major patrons, the officers of the *Guandong* army, did not want the new temple to have the word "temple" in its title. Instead, they favoured calling it a "spiritual training centre" (*shūyō dōjo*). However, as far as Gempō and his superiors at Myōshinji in Kyoto were concerned, the new temple was definitely meant to be a branch of the head temple and should be designated as such.

The officers' demands reflected a controversy that had been going on since the early days of the Meiji period. It was then that, for the first time in Japanese history, institutional Buddhism as a whole was subjected to a major repression, including destruction of thousands of temples and the forced laicization of like numbers of priests. Although this anti-Buddhist movement was short-lived, post-Meiji Japanese Buddhism remained suspect as a "foreign" and therefore "non-Japanese" religion. The result was that many military men, especially in the officer corps, were wary of being seen to place their faith in anything that even hinted at less than total devotion to a Shinto-inspired divine emperor who, descended from the Sun Goddess, ruled over a divine land.

This said, Zen was different. As will be detailed in chapter 7, Zen had long been an integral part of Japan's warrior culture and therefore Zen training, particularly the practice of meditation, was regarded as a method of spiritual empowerment. In turn, this spiritual empowerment was believed to enhance the practitioner's martial prowess on the battlefield. Yet, while Zen training *per se* was acceptable to the military, as much as possible of its Buddhist "facade" was to be discarded.[4]

Resolution

A solution acceptable to both parties was eventually worked out: the new temple would have two signboards – one identifying it as a spiritual training centre, another identifying it as a Zen temple (i.e. Myōshinji Shinkyō Betsuin). Gempō managed to unite these two positions when he later created a temple stamp engraved with both names and centred on the figure of Bodhidharma, the legendary sixth-century founder of Zen (Chan) in China.

In postwar years, some of Gempō's disciples attempted to portray this incident as an early indication of Gempō's opposition to war, or at least to the Japanese military. Further, they claimed that soon after the new temple was completed, Gempō invited leading military figures in for a discussion on how to enhance the spirit of Japanese military and civilians resident in Manchuria. This time, however, Gempō's anti-war remarks so enraged his military guests that one of them threatened to kill him with his sword. Gempō responded: "Well, you're a military man, aren't you? A military man wins when he cuts down his opponent as quickly as he can. So why don't you go ahead and strike me!"

There is only one trouble with this story – it never happened – or in the more circumspect words of Gempō's disciple and biographer, Takagi Sōgo: "This theatrical story is far removed from the truth."[5] Instead, Takagi indicates that the following incident, at which he was present, was typical of Gempō's relationship to the military:

> Not long after the temple was complete, I took a few rough and ready warrior types from the military, who had just arrived in Xinjing from Mukden [present-day Shenyang], to visit Zen Master [Gempō]. These young officers spouted their theories and sought to challenge Gempō with their arguments. Gempō, however, responded to them calmly, showing not the least sign of agitation. There was, of course, no question of his having said anything like "Strike me!" After that we all drank *sake*.[6]

Takagi also writes that Major General Tanaka Ryūkichi (1893–1972) and then Lt. Colonel Tsuji Masanobu (1901–61?) were among Gempō's many military visitors and drinking companions.[7] General Tanaka is best known for having secretly instigated the Shanghai Incident of 1932 by arranging for five Japanese Nichiren priests and novices resident in that city to be beaten so badly by supposed "anti-Japanese" Chinese thugs that one of the priests later died. This served as the excuse for landing thousands of Japanese marines, ostensibly to defend Japanese interests in Shanghai and punish Chinese residents for their hostile attitude toward Japan. During the postwar Tokyo war crimes trials, Tanaka testified as a cooperative witness for the Allies in what turned out to be a ploy to ensure that Emperor Hirohito's wartime role would never be examined. Lt. Colonel Tsuji's wartime exploits will be detailed in chapter 11.

General Yamashita

Gempō's most famous military acquaintance was Army General Yamashita Tomoyuki (1888–1946). While Yamashita would later earn the title of "Tiger of Malaya" for his successful campaign in February 1942 to capture Singapore, 1936–7 saw him serving as a brigade commander in Seoul, Korea. As important as his position was, his transfer from Tokyo nevertheless represented punishment for having sympathized with the abortive Young Officers' Uprising of 26 February 1936.

Gempō met General Yamashita on his way back to Manchuria from Japan. Yamashita, honoured by his visit, asked Gempō for a calligraphic specimen on which he wanted inscribed his favourite phrase: "Do your best and leave the rest to fate." Gempō readily acceded to the General's request but suggested a slight alteration to the latter part of the text in order to eliminate its passive character. The text now read: "Do your best and act *in accordance with* fate." Yamashita found the altered text even more to his liking and thereafter kept Gempō's calligraphy wrapped around his stomach as a sort of good luck charm.[8] While he survived the war unscathed, Yamashita was nevertheless executed as a war criminal in February 1946 for having had ultimate command responsibility for the sacking of Manila and other atrocities committed during the final days of Japan's occupation of the Philippines.

Gempō's call on Yamashita had been no accident; for the former was appointed, on 21 August 1937, by Myōshinji officials as the superintendent-general (*sōkan*) of a delegation of five Rinzai priests who were to pay "sympathy calls" (*imon*) on members of the imperial military stationed on the continent. For this purpose, Gempō took off his Buddhist robes and put on the plain, military-style uniform, including billed hat, that was rapidly becoming standard wear for all civilians in wartime Japan. During his travels, Gempō was accompanied by one of his chief disciples, Nakagawa Sōen (1907–84), yet another priest whose postwar admirers have sought to portray as a war opponent.

Nakagawa Sōen

Sōen was not merely Gempō's attendant, for he, too, made the rounds of various Japanese enterprises in Manchuria urging employees, then designated as "industrial warriors" (*sangyō senshi*), to increase production on behalf of Japan's war effort. Sōen described both his own and his master's efforts as having been motivated by "the spirit of eight corners of the world under one roof" (*hakkō ichiu*), the ubiquitous wartime slogan used to justify Japan's attempt to bring Asia, if not the world, under its control.[9]

Sōen visited the Manchurian Mining Company, a major producer of such strategically important raw materials as gold, copper, zinc and molybdenum. This company, with headquarters in Xinjing and mining operations throughout Manchuria, was owned and operated by the Nissan financial combine (*zaibatsu*) from 1937 onwards. More importantly, it is well known, if not infamous, for its utilization of a slave labour force made up of Chinese peasants, prisoners of war, and criminals, all subjected to inhuman living and working conditions.

One of the company officials responsible for directing this labour force was Yamada Kōun (1907–89). Yamada served as the company's personnel manager in 1941 and later became the deputy director of the General Affairs Department in 1945. Yamada was also Sōen's former schoolmate and a lay Zen practitioner, initially training under Gempō's successor at Myōshinji Betsuin during the war years.

Following repatriation to Japan at war's end, Yamada trained under Rinzai Zen Master Asahina Sōgen (1891–1979), Sōtō Zen Master Harada Sōgaku (1870–1961), and finally, Yasutani Haku'un, whose chief Dharma heir he became in 1961. In 1967 Yamada succeeded to the leadership of the Sambō-kyōdan (Three Treasures Association), an independent, lay-oriented Zen sect that Yasutani had created in Kamakura in 1954. Significantly, one common thread uniting all of Yamada's Zen teachers was their fervently-held ultranationalism, both during the war and even after it.[10]

Gempō's activities

Gempō's efforts, like those of his disciple Sōen, were not limited exclusively to the military. He, too, was expected to enhance the patriotic spirit of the many Japanese civilian residents of Manchuria. One form this took was the construction of a memorial hall on the grounds of Myōshinji Betsuin temple for all those Japanese who had died in the process of creating Japan's puppet state. The impetus for this memorial came from a delegation of civilians who first came to see Gempō shortly after the new temple's construction. They said: "The reason we are able to live in this foreign country without any fear or want is due to the more than 10,000 heroic spirits [*eirei*] who earnestly sacrificed themselves in order to preserve and pacify our country. For this reason we would like to build a memorial hall to pray for their repose."[11] Although the initial steps were taken for the construction of this memorial, work eventually came to a halt due to the worsening war situation.

Gempō, who suffered from poor eyesight, had been ill throughout much of his life. In 1939, aged seventy-four, he contracted an ear disease which led to his resignation as abbot of Myōshinji Betsuin in January 1940 and subsequent return to Japan. It did not, however, lead to any lessening of his close relationship with the Japanese military. For example, Gempō eventually turned over most of his home temple of Ryūtakuji near the city of Mishima in Shizuoka Prefecture for military use. The Buddha Hall, for example, became an army hospital for the seriously wounded while the bell tower was used as a food warehouse for an army regiment stationed in Mishima. Further, for the benefit of his lay parishioners, Gempō had a special Rinzai Zen sūtra booklet printed in 1942 which ended with the following words: "I pray for victory in the Great East Asian War.... Gempō."[12]

Turning toward peace

If there is anything that distinguished Gempō's war support from that of his contemporaries, it was his relatively early recognition that Japan was losing the war. When Tokyo came under air attack for the first time in 1943, Gempō reportedly told one of his disciples: "Well, Japan is really done for now!" Yet, when asked what might be done to stop the war, Gempō cautioned patience, pointing out:

> Events have their own momentum and direction. If you try to oppose that momentum or change direction before the time is ripe, you will accomplish nothing. When people are running to the east you must run to the east with them. When they are running west, you must do likewise.[13]

Gempō clearly followed his own advice, for he never publicly spoke out against the war. Yet by April 1945, with Tokyo and other cities being progressively reduced to ashes by Allied fire bombing, Gempō reached the conclusion that the time to act, if only indirectly, had come. Accordingly, when 77-year-old Admiral Suzuki Kantarō (1867–1948) sought his advice on whether or not to end the war, Gempō replied:

> In terms of *sumo*, Japan is like a champion wrestler (*ōzeki*). When a champion loses, he loses like a champion – in a dignified way. Given the present state of affairs, Japan must figure out how to win by losing. Today you are the only person capable of accomplishing this great task. Although I know that a person of your pure and unblemished character is not suited for politics, I nevertheless hope that you will, even at the risk of your life, render this final public service.[14]

Admiral Suzuki may well have taken Gempō's advice to heart, for only a week later he accepted a request from Emperor Hirohito to become the next prime minister. Just how deeply touched the Admiral was by Gempō's words is revealed by the fact that early on the morning of 12 August 1945 he sent a special messenger to inform Gempō of Japan's imminent surrender three days later.

Aware of the difficult situation Suzuki found himself in, Gempō immediately gave the messenger a note of encouragement to be delivered to Suzuki. The note contained phraseology that was, in part, identical with the emperor's famous radio broadcast of 15 August 1945 announcing Japan's surrender. Specifically, it contained the following words: "Your true public service is set to begin from this point onwards. Please be careful of your health and work for the reconstruction of our country while enduring what is hard to endure and practicing what is hard to practice."[15]

Based on this, Gempō's disciples later maintained that the following passage of the emperor's radio address was influenced by Gempō's note:

> The hardships and sufferings to which Our nation is to be subjected hereafter will be certainly great. We are keenly aware of the inmost feelings of all ye, Our subjects. However, it is according to the dictate of time and fate that We have resolved to pave the way for a grand peace for all the generations to come while *tolerating what is hard to tolerate and enduring what is hard to endure* [Italics mine].[16]

In addition to the possible influence of Gempō's words on this key wartime document, what is revealing about the preceding incident is just how well-connected this Rinzai Zen master was to one of the most powerful figures in Japan. It was connections like this that led Gempō's disciples to claim that their master's influence on national events continued even into the postwar period. Specifically, they asserted that Gempō made a key contribution toward resolving the single most contentious question facing Japan's postwar government – the appropriate role for the emperor within the new constitution. It was Gempō, they claimed, who made possible the preservation of the chrysanthemum throne at a time when the Allied Occupation authorities were thought to favour Emperor Hirohito's removal.

Emperor's new clothes

In early 1946, Narahashi Wataru (1902–73) was chief cabinet secretary in the government of Prime Minister Shidehara Kijūrō (1872–1951). Narahashi was already acquainted with Gempō, having first been introduced by a mutual friend.[17] Narahashi described his postwar relationship with Gempō as follows: "I visited Gempō-rōshi on two or three occasions to hear what he had to say. I was exceedingly charmed by his humanity and deeply impressed with his intuitive way of thinking, something that transcended mere knowledge."[18]

According to Narahashi's version of events, 1946 found him facing an impossible situation. As mediator (*matomeyaku*) of the Constitutional Revision Committee (Kempō Kaisei I'in-kai), headed by Minister of State Matsumoto Jōji (1877–1954), it was his responsibility to come up with a draft proposal for the new Japanese constitution – a proposal that would be acceptable to both his fellow committee members and the Allied Occupation authorities. While the provisions for the establishment of a democratic form of government went relatively smoothly, none of the committee's initial proposals for the continuation of the emperor's position were acceptable to the Allies. According to Narahashi, the Allies, under pressure from the Soviet Union among others, wished to see the emperor's position eliminated in the new constitution.[19] Narahashi described the reasoning behind what he claimed to be the Allied position as follows:

> Because the Japanese people believed the emperor to be a god, they calmly died on his behalf, crying out, "May the emperor live for ten thousand years!" Claiming that it had to make the August Virtue of His Majesty shine throughout the world, Japan adopted [the slogan of] "the eight corners of the world under one roof" and committed aggression. The emperor is the cause of all of this. Without removing him, true democracy, in which sovereign power resides in the people, cannot exist; and Japan will be unable to find acceptance in the world as a peaceful nation.[20]

For Narahashi and his politically conservative fellow committee members, such Allied thinking concerning the emperor was totally unacceptable. In their eyes the imperial system had to be saved at all costs. But how? At this point Narahashi thought of seeking Gempō's advice and asked the Occupation authorities for a delay of four or five days in order to come up with a mutually acceptable solution. Narahashi found Gempō recuperating at a hot springs resort in Nagaoka and provided the following description of their meeting at a local inn:

> I found [Gempō]-rōshi seated beside a charcoal brazier, a bottle of *sake* by his side. The moment I entered his room he said, "You've come about the emperor, haven't you. I think that if the emperor takes an interest in politics or the government of the day, there will be no end to internal struggles. This is because there are those [politicians] who engage in factional disputes claiming to have the emperor's backing because they received an Imperial Edict."
>
> "Therefore the emperor must transcend all political considerations and shine in the heavens like the sun. In the future we must have a politics that brings to fruition truth, goodness, and beauty based on the Imperial will. If politics are conducted prudently and reverently, then even with an emperor, we can still have a fine, democratic country. The emperor will be like a symbol shining in the sky."[21]

Narahashi claimed to have been deeply impressed by this proposal for a symbolic emperor system and pleased, subsequently, to find that it was acceptable to both his fellow committee members and the Occupation authorities. Narahashi noted that General Douglas MacArthur (1880–1964), Supreme Commander of the Allied Forces in Japan, particularly welcomed this proposal since the latter was personally sympathetic to the emperor and hoped to find a formula that would preserve the emperor's position (*sans* political power) within a democratically constituted Japan. The result, as incorporated in Chapter I, Article 1, of the 1947 Japanese constitution, was that the emperor became "the symbol of the State and of the unity of the people."[22] According to Narahashi, the imperial throne was saved due to a combination of General MacArthur's "wisdom" and Gempō's "great intuitive contribution."[23]

Conclusion

In Chapter XVII, verse 228 of the *Dhammapada*, Śākyamuni Buddha is recorded as having said: "There never was, there never will be, nor is there now, a person who is always to be blamed, or a person who is always to be praised."

In evaluating Yamamoto Gempō, or other Zen and Buddhist figures introduced in this book, it is important to remember that none of them had horns, much less tails, i.e. they were not the devil incarnate. Instead, like most human beings East and West, they were readily captured by the values and prejudices of the societies and ages of which they were a part. In this respect they may best be described as having been all too "ordinary," claims to enlightenment notwithstanding. It was their very ordinariness, however, that contributed to the deaths of millions of human beings. Thus, if Gempō is to be credited with having urged Japan to surrender as early as April 1945, then, as seen in chapter 1, he must also be held responsible for having justified, as early as 1934, the killing of those "who destroy social harmony and injure the polity of the state."

Even Gempō's plea for Japan's surrender is more problematic than it first appears. That is to say, was Admiral Suzuki Kantarō, as Japan's new prime minister from April 1945, really motivated to seek peace as a result of Gempō's entreaty? In December 1945 Suzuki responded to Allied questioning about the attitude toward peace of the six-member Supreme War Council of which he was a member as follows:

> The Supreme War Council, up to the time [that] the atomic bomb was dropped, did not believe that Japan could be beaten by air attack alone.... [They] proceeded with the one plan of fighting a decisive battle at the landing point and were making every possible preparation to meet such a landing. They proceed[ed] with that plan until the atomic bomb was dropped, after which they believed the United States ... need not land when it had such a weapon; so at that point they decided that it would be best to sue for peace.[24]

Furthermore, as military historian Richard Frank notes, upon becoming prime minister, "Suzuki promptly signed a pledge presented by a delegation of generals from Imperial Headquarters committing himself to prosecute the war to the bitter end, ... and to exert every possible effort to totally mobilize the nation."[25]

The above notwithstanding, it is possible that at a personal level the Admiral hoped to bring an early end to the war as Gempō had urged. Nevertheless, it appears that the atomic bombs dropped on Hiroshima and Nagasaki played a far more important role in bringing peace than the appeal of a Zen master.

Surrender

The alleged influence of Gempō's words on the content of the emperor's surrender rescript is yet another example of what might best be described as the "wishful thinking" of Gempō's disciples. Chaen Yoshio, author of a book devoted exclusively to the surrender rescript, records that the emperor himself was the source of the words in question. At approximately 2 a.m. on the morning of 10 August 1945 the emperor addressed an emergency Imperial Conference as follows:

> If we continue on as we have, both the Japanese people and Japan will perish. When I think of the people, the military, the war dead and their families, I feel heartbroken. Thus, *enduring what is hard to endure*, I wish to open the way toward peace for all time [Italics mine].[26]

The man charged with drawing up the surrender rescript, Sakomizu Hisatsune (1902–77), chief cabinet secretary in the Suzuki government, states that immediately after the end of the above conference, he set to work on the rescript's first draft with the express purpose of "including His Majesty's words just as they were" into the text of the document.[27] Thus, assuming that Chaen's attribution is accurate, whatever credit is due for calling on the Japanese people to "endure what is hard to endure," i.e. both surrender and the subsequent Allied Occupation, rightfully belongs to the emperor, not Gempō.

Symbolic emperor

Far more importantly, Gempō's contribution to the creation of the postwar symbolic emperor system cannot be taken at face value despite the credentials of the man who made this claim, i.e. Narahashi Wataru, chief cabinet secretary in the postwar Shidehara government. For one thing, staff members of the US State Department's Office of Far Eastern Affairs were producing memoranda referring to the emperor as "a symbol of Japanese national unity" as early as December 1942.[28] Further, Joseph Grew (1880–1965), former US ambassador to Japan and wartime head of the State Department's Office of Far Eastern Affairs, had long urged the retention of the emperor as "purely a symbol."[29]

Japanese historian Nakamura Masanori notes that due to his ten year's residence in Japan, Grew exerted a powerful influence on the views of General MacArthur.[30] One sign of this influence was revealed in a secret telegram that MacArthur sent to US Army Chief of Staff Dwight Eisenhower on 25 January 1946. The thrust of the telegram was to argue against indicting Hirohito as a war criminal and contained the following passage: "[Hirohito] is a symbol which unites all Japanese. Destroy him and the nation will disintegrate."[31]

While none of the preceding references offers conclusive proof that Article 1, Chapter 1 of the 1947 Japanese constitution providing for a symbolic emperor system was an American invention, it does strongly suggest that the American influence was far stronger than Narahashi admitted. Yet, if this were so, why would Narahashi claim otherwise?

The following statement made by Narahashi suggests the answer: "The initial drafts [of the constitution] were created by Japanese so it was a Japanese constitution."[32] Countering this claim, the historian Hugh Borton states that "an analysis of the official Japanese text indicates that the original text was in English rather than in Japanese."[33] Nakamura adds that at 10 a.m. on the morning of 13 February 1946 high-ranking members of General MacArthur's staff arrived at the residence of Foreign Minister Yoshida Shigeru (1878–1967) to present both him and Minister of State Matsumoto Jōji with a draft of the constitution that had been written by the Government Section of Allied Headquarters. Matsumoto claimed to have been "really quite surprised" by the use of the word "symbol" in Article 1, Chapter 1 of this American draft, the text of which read as follows: "The Emperor shall be *the symbol of the State and of the Unity of the People*, deriving his position from the sovereign will of the People, and from no other source [Italics mine].[34]

The discrepancy between Narahashi's claim and Burton and Nakamura's research is obvious, but it is well documented that the committee on which Narahashi served did come up with an initial draft for a new constitution as Narahashi claimed. The provisions of this draft, however, merely altered some of the phraseology of the former Meiji constitution, leaving the emperor's powers unchanged; and it was quickly rejected by MacArthur. Instead, MacArthur, as noted above, ordered his Government Section to produce a draft incorporating his own views, giving the section only one week to do so.[35] Narahashi acknowledges the existence of this American draft, but asserts nevertheless that the source of the relevant wording in Article 1 stemmed from Gempō as transmitted to the Occupation authorities by himself.[36]

In attempting to resolve these conflicting versions of events, it must be admitted that, with the principals now dead, a final resolution is all but impossible. Even after exhaustive study, historian Nakamura Masanori admitted that he had been unable to determine precisely the origins of the symbolic emperor system. "Having got this far, I found that I had reached a dead end," he writes.[37] Thus, there is no way to prove definitively that Gempō's proposal either did, or did not, contribute to the wording of Article 1.

There is, however, further evidence that needs to be taken into account. First, according to historian Herbert Bix, Narahashi was the type of man who not only exaggerated his own role in events but was quite capable of inventing meetings that never happened.[38] More importantly, it was clearly in his and his fellow committee members' self-interest to claim that the Japanese side had come up with, or at least made a substantial contribution to, the new constitution if for no other reason than to save face, a key consideration in Japanese culture.

Narahashi's description of events had the added advantage of allowing the Japanese side to take credit for having saved the emperor system, albeit one stripped of political power due to Allied pressure. Thus, making Gempō the inspiration for the creation of the symbolic emperor system may have been the proverbial fig leaf required to disguise the new constitution's foreign origins. After all, who was more authentically "Japanese" than a Zen master?

Gempō's wartime role

In assessing Gempō's overall wartime role it should not be forgotten that he unhesitatingly turned over much of his temple complex to the Imperial Army while earnestly praying for Japan's victory. Yet the most telling of Gempō's wartime actions was the establishment of a temple in the capital of the puppet state of *Manzhouguo*. Gempō's action was, of course, not the least unusual; for, as has been noted earlier, institutional Buddhist leaders had been establishing temples on the Asian continent from the late 1800s. Like Gempō, these leaders were ever ready to work hand in hand with both the Japanese government and military in seeking to establish Japanese hegemony in Asia if not throughout the world.

The creation of Myōshinji Betsuin was, nevertheless, somewhat unique; for it was clearly a temple dedicated almost exclusively to meeting the spiritual needs of the Japanese residents of *Manzhouguo*. While this appears to be a legitimate goal for any religious body, it was the leadership of the Japanese Army, the *de facto* rulers of this puppet state, who took the lead in establishing what they regarded as a "spiritual training centre." Accordingly, the Army's goal, accepted by Gempō, was "the proper exaltation of the spirit of both the Japanese military and other Japanese residents of Manchuria." Not only that, this temple was slated to become a centre valorizing the thousands of Japanese "heroic spirits" who were alleged to have died in the process of establishing *Manzhouguo*. Seen in this light, the militarist character of Myōshinji Betsuin is unmistakable.

Gempō is also recorded as having travelled throughout Manchuria on a number of occasions.[39] Although neither he nor his biographers mention it, one of the sights Gempō could not have missed were the ubiquitous street booths located on the downtown streets of major Manchurian cities. Men, women, boys and girls lined up at these booths to thrust their arms through a hole in the canvas to receive a shot of their choice of morphine, cocaine, or heroin.

These booths, as well as the legally licensed opium-smoking dens, had come under the control of Japanese dope-peddlers from the late 1920s with the result that by 1938, one out of every forty Manchurians was hooked on drugs. Drug addiction served to weaken Manchurian resistance to Japanese control while enriching the dope-peddlers, their patrons among the Japanese secret police, and the Japanese-controlled Opium Monopoly Bureau. By contrast, in Japan proper, where the use of narcotics was strictly proscribed, only one out of every 17,000 Japanese was addicted.[40] If ever there were a time for religious leaders to speak out against drugs, it was in 1930s Manchuria. Yet Gempō and his fellow Buddhist missionaries remained silent even though they collectively laid claim to being Asia's most "socially engaged" Buddhists.

It can be justly argued that the role played by Buddhism in general, and Zen in particular, as the spiritual vanguard of Japanese militarism was not all that different from what various Christian missions had previously done on behalf of western imperialist expansion into Africa, Asia and the Americas. While some may gain solace in pointing out that other religions were as guilty as their own, it can never excuse the conduct of Zen adherents who claimed to have realized the same enlightenment Śākyamuni Buddha first experienced some 2,500 years earlier.

The key issue is not simply the way in which leading Zen figures like Gempō actively collaborated with Japanese imperialism and military aggression, for the issue runs far deeper than that. As chapter 7 will reveal, the real problem is that certain key aspects of Zen doctrine lay at the very heart of the Japanese military spirit.

7

ZEN "SELFLESSNESS" IN JAPANESE MILITARISM

SECTION ONE: THE GENERAL AND THE ZEN MASTER

On 8 January 1941, then Army Minister Tōjō Hideki (1884–1948) promulgated the *Field Service Code* (*Senjinkun*). More than any other wartime document, this 32-page Code encapsulated Japan's "do or die" military spirit. Section Eight of chapter 2, for example, contained the injunction: "Never accept alive the shame of capture; die, so as not to leave the disgrace of such an offense." This alone resulted in the pointless deaths of tens, even hundreds of thousands of Japanese soldiers, not to mention civilians, who chose suicide over surrender.

The Code was distributed to every soldier, and it's effectiveness is suggested by these sobering statistics on Axis soldiers taken prisoner of war during World War II on all fronts. While the International Red Cross recorded 9,451,000 German and 4,906,000 Italian POWs, the corresponding figure for Japan was only 208,000, i.e. slightly more than 2 per cent of the German figure.[1] In addition, many of those Japanese soldiers who ended up as prisoners were emotionally scarred for life, believing they had brought shame on themselves and their families by being captured alive.

Further evidence is contained in a December 1945 US military document entitled: "Report on a Survey of Japanese Prisoners' Attitudes towards the War." Of the 1,953 prisoners interviewed, more than two-thirds considered they had committed a shameful act and did not wish their families to be notified of their whereabouts. Seventy-five per cent expressed the wish to either commit suicide or be executed.[2]

On the evening preceding the Code's promulgation, General Tōjō gave a newspaper interview which he concluded as follows: "The entire Code has a great deal in common with the spirit of the *Hagakure* though our officers and men must clearly recognize the present situation prevailing in East Asia."[3] The "present situation" Tōjō referred to was the fourth year of a costly, stalemated war with China. As the war dragged on, there had been a noticeable deterioration in the conduct of Japanese troops as epitomized in the events surrounding the fall of the Nationalist Chinese capital of Nanjing in December

1937. The atrocities committed there, i.e. the "Rape of Nanjing," were but one in a long series of similar acts.

By 1938, Japanese military leaders recognized the need to do something to curtail the rapacious conduct of their soldiers. One of their first steps was a major expansion in the number of infamous "comfort women" (*ianpu*) stations designed to cater, in a controlled manner, to the sexual appetites of soldiers in the field. These comfort stations, serviced primarily by impoverished Korean women, had the added "benefit" of maintaining battle readiness by reducing the incidence of venereal disease among the rank and file.

In addition, Japan's military leaders hoped that the creation of a new *Field Service Code* would effect a revival of the ideals associated with the traditional Bushido warrior code as expressed in such writings as the *Hagakure*. In his classic 1938 work, *Zen and Japanese Culture*, D. T. Suzuki described the *Hagakure* as follows:

> There is a document that was very much talked about in connection with the Japanese military operations in China in the 1930s. It is known as the *Hagakure*, which literally means "Hidden under the Leaves," for it is one of the virtues of the samurai not to display himself, not to blow his horn, but to keep himself away from the public eye and be doing good for his fellow beings. To the compilation of this book, which consists of various notes, anecdotes, moral sayings, etc., a Zen monk had his part to contribute.
>
> The work started in the middle part of the seventeenth century under Nabeshima Naoshige, the feudal lord of Saga in the island of Kyūshū. The book emphasizes very much the samurai's readiness to give his life away at any moment, for it states that no great work has ever been accomplished without going mad – that is, when expressed in modern terms, without breaking through the ordinary level of consciousness and letting loose the hidden powers lying further below. These powers may be devilish sometimes, but there is no doubt that they are superhuman and work wonders. When the unconscious is tapped, it rises above individual limitations. Death now loses its sting altogether, and this is where the samurai training joins hands with Zen.[4]

The Zen monk Suzuki referred to was Yamamoto Jōchō (1659–1719), a former samurai of the Nabeshima fief in Kyushu who entered the priesthood on the occasion of his lord's death in 1700. Suzuki is more than a little misleading in noting that a Zen monk did no more than "contribute" to the compilation of the *Hagakure*, for in reality Jōchō dictated all eleven chapters of this work to a young samurai admirer over a seven-year period beginning in 1710. Though neither systematic nor closely reasoned, the *Hagakure* nevertheless forcefully and repeatedly expressed the selfless "loyalty unto death" demanded of the warrior.

As in the *Hagakure*, there was also a Zen influence on the "modern version" of that work. The following is a discussion of that influence, the first part of which

107

looks at the Zen influence on the person primarily responsible for the Code, Imperial Army General Imamura Hitoshi (1886–1968). The second part examines the Code's underlying ideology as interpreted both by the imperial military itself and leading Zen masters. When the two parts are considered as a whole, it will be clear that the Zen influence on the *Field Service Code* was not merely deep-rooted but even foundational.

General Imamura Hitoshi and Zen

General Imamura Hitoshi was widely recognized as one of the most intelligent strategists in the Imperial Army. Following the Japanese attack on Pearl Harbour in December 1941, he commanded the 16th Army as it successfully drove colonial power Holland out of the oil-rich "Dutch East Indies," i.e. today's Indonesia. War's end found him in command of some 76,000 troops on the islands of Rabaul, New Ireland, and Bougainville in the southwest Pacific.

Imamura has been credited with saving the lives of many thousands of his troops by encouraging them to grow their own food even prior to being cut off from supplies from Japan in the latter stages of the war. Unlike many top Japanese military leaders, Imamura did not commit suicide at the war's end but worked closely with Australian military authorities to ensure an incident-free surrender and the early repatriation of his troops. This accomplished, Imamura did attempt, in July 1946, to take responsibility for Japan's defeat by first taking poison and then cutting his throat with a razor blade. Unsuccessful, he was subsequently tried as a war criminal and found guilty of having failed to prevent the maltreatment of Asian forced labourers under his command. Sentenced to ten years imprisonment, he was incarcerated for nine years before gaining release in 1954.

Imamura's troops revered him as epitomizing the essence of the Bushido spirit. Even General Douglas MacArthur agreed with their assessment, for during the allied occupation of Japan he was so moved by Imamura's ongoing concern for his former soldiers that he commented: "This is the first time since coming to Japan that I feel I have encountered the true Bushido spirit."[5] On the other hand, at his earlier trial as a war criminal, the presiding judge said: "I believe the reason that the leaders of the Japanese military could never act realistically was because of Bushido. Defendant Imamura... believing as you do in conceptions and values from the middle ages places you beyond redemption."[6]

At the time of the *Field Service Code*'s promulgation in January 1941, Imamura was in charge of the Tokyo headquarters of the Department of Military Education, a position he held for more than eight months. As Tōjō noted in the newspaper article mentioned above, it was this department that had written the Code. By virtue of his position, Imamura was the key figure in the Code's final formulation, a fact Imamura himself attested to when he later wrote: "I, too, took up the pen and spent about three months giving firm shape to the Code."[7]

Early Zen interest

Imamura's interest in Zen can be traced back at least to 1907, shortly after his graduation from officer candidate school. As a newly commissioned second lieutenant, Imamura was assigned to an infantry unit in the northern Honshū city of Sendai. He was befriended there by First Lieutenant Itagaki Seishirō (1885–1948). Imamura greatly admired Itagaki not only because of the latter's skill at both swordsmanship, i.e. *kendō*, and gymnastics, but because, as a platoon leader, he exhibited brilliant combat leadership.

One Sunday afternoon, Imamura noticed a book on Zen laying on Itagaki's desk. Picking it up, Imamura said, "I am prone to becoming agitated and quarrelling with people. Do you think I can overcome this shortcoming through Zen?" Itagaki replied, "I've noticed you do have a tendency to flare up. But since you are aware of this weakness, I think you can overcome it."[8]

Saying this, Itagaki lent Imamura his book on Zen, and after that the latter continued to read about Zen on his own. At the time, however, Imamura didn't feel Zen was helping him much in overcoming his temper, but he seemed to believe that Itagaki had benefited from his Zen practice. Imamura later wrote: "Although I don't know how much longer Itagaki continued his Zen practice . . . I do know that as he gained rank he received the respect and trust of an ever-increasing number of people. Unlike me, he didn't worry about trifles, nor did he show his feelings in front of others."[9]

Itagaki subsequently rose to the rank of full general and served the government in various capacities including Minister of the Army in 1938–9, Chief of the Army General Staff in 1939, and a member of the Supreme War Council in 1943. He first distinguished himself while still a colonel by helping to plan the 1931 Manchurian Incident, a successful Japanese military plot to occupy all of Manchuria and establish a puppet government. He was also an early proponent of a military alliance with Nazi Germany. In the postwar period he was tried and convicted as a Class A war criminal by the Tokyo War Crimes Tribunal and hanged in 1948. Itagaki will be discussed further in chapter 11.

It must be stressed that in the Japan of 1907, there was nothing at all unusual about two young officers being attracted to Zen. It was already well known that both Imperial Army Generals Nogi Maresuke (1849–1912) and Kodama Gentarō (1852–1906), heroes of the victorious Russo-Japanese War of 1904–5, were longtime Zen practitioners.[10] Nantembō (1839–1925), Nogi's Rinzai Zen master, had even designated his illustrious military disciple as one of his "Dharma descendants" in recognition of his fully enlightened state. As Sōtō Zen scholar-priest Nukariya Kaiten (1867–1934) wrote a few years later in 1913: "It is Zen that modern Japan, especially after the Russo-Japanese War, has acknowledged as an ideal doctrine for her rising generation."[11]

Ōmori Zenkai

For a deeper understanding of Imamura's interest in Zen, we must turn to the first volume of his war memoirs published in 1960. There, in his only extended discussion of any religion, Imamura devotes thirty-eight pages to Zen. In particular, he singles out Sōtō Zen priest Ōmori Zenkai (1871–1947) as having contributed the most to his understanding of Zen. Zenkai was, however, no ordinary priest; for over his long career he served as a professor, dean, and finally president of Sōtō Zen sect-affiliated Komazawa University from 1934–7; administrative head of the Sōtō sect in 1940–41; and then chief abbot of both of the Sōtō sect's head temples, Sōjiji and Eiheiji.

Imamura's relationship to Zenkai was one of many years standing, dating back to August 1921. Surprisingly, their first meeting was not in Japan but on the deck of a ship steaming through the Indian Ocean. Both men were on their way back to Japan after separate sojourns in Europe. Imamura had served for nearly three years as a military attaché at the Japanese embassy in London while Zenkai had been engaged in research on early Buddhist sūtras preserved in England and on the continent. Surprisingly for that period, Zenkai spoke both fluent English and German, for from 1904 to 1911 he had studied the philosophy of religion at West Virginia State and Washington universities in the US and Leipzig University in Germany.

In explaining the events leading up to their shipboard meeting, Imamura noted that it was so hot in the cabins that many of the passengers preferred sleeping on deck in lounge chairs. This led one of Imamura's fellow officers, Captain Homma Masaharu (1887–1946), to a discovery – there appeared to be a Buddhist priest on board who came up on deck shortly after four in the morning to recite sūtras. Homma said: "I was totally captivated by his recitation of the sūtras and soon entered into a selfless realm. It was not just the quality of his voice, but there was a kind of power that drew me in."[12]

The Captain Homma who so rapidly entered a "selfless realm" would later become Lt. General Homma, the man executed by the Allies in April 1946 for authoring the Bataan Death March and bombing of undefended Manila.

For his part, Imamura decided to get up early the next morning to see if the suspected Buddhist priest was all Homma made him out to be. Imamura wasn't disappointed:

> I became absorbed in his voice. I don't know whether I should say I was in a selfless realm, or in a trance, but in any event I was so absorbed in the sound of his voice that I lost all sense of time and had no idea how long his sūtra recitation lasted.[13]

Imamura did recognize, however, that Zenkai had first recited the short *Heart Sūtra* and then the *Shūshōgi*. Imamura was particularly struck by the latter sūtra's opening words: "To understand life and clarify death is of critical importance to a Buddhist. If the Buddha exists within life and death there is no life and death. . . ." The reader will recall that the *Shūshōgi*, a uniquely Sōtō Zen scripture, was discussed in chapter 5. That Imamura immediately recognized this sūtra is one indication of just how well acquainted he was with the Sōtō Zen sect. From then until their arrival back in Japan some weeks later, Imamura never missed Zenkai's early morning recitations.

Not content with the role of passive listener, Imamura introduced himself to Zenkai and was pleased to discover how approachable he was, totally lacking in the stern demeanour he expected of a Zen master. This in turn led Imamura to query Zenkai about a problem that had bothered him for some time. Imamura was worried about the demands for democracy and workers' rights that had been growing in Japan since the end of World War I.

According to Imamura, this new democratic way of thinking was even finding its way into the military as evidenced by the fact that lower-ranking soldiers had begun to question their superiors about things they found unreasonable in military life and society as a whole. What, Imamura wanted to know, would Zenkai say to soldiers who asked why it was that some Japanese children were born into rich families where they had plenty while "poor children don't have enough to eat and are unable to seek medical treatment when they get sick"?[14]

Zenkai thought about this question for a moment and then recited a verse from an unnamed Buddhist sūtra he felt contained the answer:

> The sun in the heavens has no self,
> Flowers and branches have their order.[15]

In other words, natural phenomena like the sun play no favourites, providing life-giving warmth to all without distinction. Despite this, not all buds on a tree blossom at the same time. That is to say, the buds on the branches on the south side of the tree blossom before those on the north side. Should the branches on the north side of the tree dislike having to wait their turn and all crowd onto the south side, the tree would become unbalanced and crash to earth, destroying the chance for the buds on any of the branches to bloom.

Zenkai claimed the same can be said about human society. If everyone will but wait and work diligently, good fortune will eventually come their way. In fact, Zenkai claimed to have proof of this. He recalled having once trained at a temple that had records on its parishioners going back for some four hundred years. Looking through these records he discovered that in cycles of approximately one hundred years each, families that had been tenant farmers became small landholders; small landholders became large landowners; and large landholders fell into tenancy. Explain to your soldiers, Zenkai said, that "adversity improves one's character, while a life of ease tends to make one negligent."[16]

Imamura was quite taken with Zenkai's explanation and subsequently often used it in instructing his military subordinates. For example, in 1926 Imamura, now a Lt. Colonel, was sent to Korea, a Japanese colony, to serve with the 74th

Regiment. While there he became concerned about what he regarded as the luxurious lifestyle led by some of his officers and senior enlisted personnel. This lifestyle was made possible because, being stationed outside of Japan proper, higher ranking personnel were entitled to salary supplements. Using Zenkai's words, Imamura warned them that by using their money to purchase luxuries for themselves, instead of saving it for such things as their children's education, they were denying their children "the chance to blossom."

Imamura noted with satisfaction that a number of his subordinates took his advice to heart and expressed their gratitude to him for having shared Zenkai's teaching. This led Imamura to conclude: "I was overjoyed that the Buddhist virtue of Zen Master Ōmori had reached from Japan all the way to a rural regiment stationed in Korea."[17]

Zen Master Shaku Sōen

At this point in his narrative Imamura related an anecdote that Zenkai shared with him concerning Rinzai Zen Master Shaku Sōen (1859–1919). Shaku Sōen was not only D. T. Suzuki's Zen master and abbot of the major Rinzai monastery of Engakuji in Kamakura but was widely regarded as the greatest Rinzai Zen master of his day.[18] The anecdote in question had a significant impact on Imamura's thinking in that he claimed to have understood for the first time the meaning of the Zen phrase "the ordinary and the Buddha are one."[19]

The incident Zenkai described happened to him when he was still a young student priest studying in the USA. At the time Sōen was on a short tour of the USA and needed an English-speaking guide. Zenkai was a natural candidate for the job, and one of the sites they visited was the Natural History Museum in Chicago. After touring the museum for about two hours, they entered a large room containing mounted specimens of various animals and reptiles. Zenkai explained:

> Zen Master Shaku Sōen immediately stopped and his whole body started to shake. His face turned pale and perspiration dripped from his forehead. He gave the appearance of being in deep distress. "Are you feeling ill?" I asked as I reached to steady him. "Yes, I am. Let's go back to the hotel."[20]

Only after they had returned to their hotel did Sōen reveal what was wrong. It so happened that Sōen was petrified by snakes, and there had been a giant snake, coiled lifelike, in a tree in the large room they had entered. Sōen confessed:

> No matter how small it is, I still get frightened when I see a snake. I have been this way since childhood, and even though I am now an adult and have practiced Zen for many years, I am unable to get rid of this fear. I am truly ashamed.[21]

Adding to Sōen's shame may well have been his awareness that since the time of Śākyamuni Buddha there have been numerous stories of accomplished monks converting such potentially malevolent spirits as snakes and dragons (Skt. *Nāga*) to the Buddha Dharma, thereby securing their protection in return.

As far as Zenkai was concerned, Sōen's conduct was nothing to be ashamed of. On the contrary, he regarded it as confirmation of Zen Master Dōgen's teaching that "one must continue to practice Zen for one's entire life." More importantly, he was deeply impressed with Sōen's honesty in having openly confessed his fear of snakes to a young monk like himself. "This was possible," Zenkai claimed, "because Sōen had reached an enlightened state.... It reveals the ordinariness of the extraordinary."[22]

For his part, Imamura readily agreed with Zenkai's favourable interpretation of Sōen. In fact, he thought something similar could be said of Zenkai who had initially been ignored by his fellow first-class passengers because he "looked just like a farmer."[23] More importantly, Imamura believed the ordinariness of the extraordinary could also be seen at work in the military, noting: "Among those soldiers who are given to bragging in peacetime, few demonstrate true bravery on the battlefield. On the other hand, among those who are normally reserved and courteous there are many who are brave."[24]

Zen writings

Imamura departed from his conversations with Zenkai at this point to record what had impressed him over the years in his readings on Zen. The discussion that followed made it clear that Imamura had not only read but given considerable thought to the teachings of major Zen figures, starting with the semi-legendary Bodhidharma and the early Chan (Zen) patriarchs in China and extending to Zen Masters Dōgen and Hakuin (1685–1768) in Japan. Imamura claimed, however, to have done no more than "untie the strings of a few Zen writings and meditate just a little on my own without the benefit of a master's guidance."[25]

Not surprising for a military man, many of Imamura's Zen-related comments had to do with how best to face death, including a discussion of Ryōkan (1758–1831), a Sōtō Zen monk famous for his poetry, eccentric lifestyle, and love of children. At the age of seventy four, Ryōkan was approaching death, suffering from severe stomach pains brought on by diarrhea. Finding him lying in pain in his hermitage, one of the villagers thoughtlessly asked: "Ryōkan! Does even a priest like you who has forsaken the world suffer so when he dies?" Ryōkan opened his eyes and quietly repeated the following seventeen syllable *haiku*:

Ura o mise	Show me what is out in back,
Omote o mise	Show me what is out in front,
Chiru momiji	Falling maple leaves.

Imamura interpreted this poem to mean that Ryōkan had simply resigned himself to die according to nature's dictates. And Imamura concluded: "I am deeply impressed with someone like Ryōkan who, having totally identified himself with the oneness of the ordinary and the Buddha, could demonstrate such a wonderful state of mental preparedness."[26]

Hakuin

While Imamura devoted less than a page to Ryōkan, he spent some five pages discussing Hakuin, previously introduced in chapter 1. Clearly, the vigorous nature of Hakuin's Zen practice attracted Imamura to this great seventeenth-century reformer of the Rinzai Zen tradition. Needless to say, it was Hakuin's own encounter with life and death that made the deepest impression.

Imamura noted that Hakuin had his first enlightenment experience at the age of twenty-four. Although Hakuin was confident, even proud, of his enlightenment, he nevertheless went to visit Zen Master Dōkyō Etan (aka Shōjū-rōjin, 1642–1721) to have his enlightenment confirmed. In Etan's eyes, however, Hakuin's understanding was still limited, not least of all by the latter's pride. At length, Hakuin was himself overcome by self-doubt, if not self-loathing, leading to a famous episode that Imamura described as follows:

> One day Hakuin was out collecting alms in the castle village of Iiyama [in present-day Nagano Prefecture]. As he made his rounds, reciting Buddhist sūtras as he went, he stopped before the gate of a house. "Get out of here!" yelled a man who was sweeping the garden inside the gate. Hakuin, however, was lost in thought and, failing to hear the man shouting at him, continued reciting sūtras. The man in the garden grew even angrier and shouted at the top of his voice: "I told you to get out of here, now go!"
>
> Hakuin, still lost in thought, just stood there reciting sūtras. The man, his anger now transformed into rage, came out of his gate and, suddenly lifting up his bamboo broom, gave Hakuin a big whack on the head. The young priest's conical wicker hat split in half, and he fell to the ground unconscious.
>
> A passerby eventually found Hakuin and kindly looked after him until he revived. At that point Hakuin, clearly recognizing that he was still not fully enlightened, said: "Death is fine, and life is still better. Life is fine, and death is still better."[27]

Imamura records that Etan was overjoyed when Hakuin later informed him of the day's events and the realization he had come to. For his part, Hakuin broke into tears, deeply grateful for Etan's harsh but loving guidance that had led to his breakthrough. Imamura concluded his own examination of Hakuin's life by noting: "Hakuin had smashed the extraordinary and, for the first time, identified with the oneness of the ordinary and the Buddha."[28]

While Imamura's overall discussion of Zen ends with the above episode, Imamura's relationship to Zenkai clearly went beyond a simple shipboard acquaintanceship. Imamura's biographer, Tsunoda Fusako, records that Imamura arrived back in Japan in 1921 a changed man. In her view, Zenkai had contributed significantly to this change:

> Following Imamura's return from England, there was an abrupt change in his character – he mellowed. There are various reasons for this, first that he was approaching middle age and second his meeting with Ōmori Zenkai. While it is true that Imamura didn't go on to practice Zen extensively after their meeting, this Zen priest nevertheless exercised a big influence on him for his entire life.[29]

As Zenkai's daughter, Ume, later recorded: "General Imamura came to visit father a number of times. These were always short visits, but the two of them really seemed to enjoy their time together."[30] Whether directly related or not, Imamura also moved his ancestral grave site to the major Sōtō Zen temple of Rinnōji in his hometown of Sendai in 1938. The reader will recall, this is the same temple where military assassin Lt. Col. Aizawa Saburō had first trained under the guidance of Zen Master Fukusada Mugai.

Finally, when Imamura was allowed to return to Japan in 1949 to complete his prison sentence, he immediately inquired about Zenkai's whereabouts only to learn that his old friend had died two years earlier. Thereafter, whenever Imamura was asked for a piece of his calligraphy, he typically inscribed the eight-character phrase Zenkai first taught him:

> The sun in the heavens has no self,
> Flowers and branches have their order.

Having adopted Zenkai's karmic viewpoint, Imamura remained convinced that, despite the wartime deaths of millions upon millions, many of which Imamura had been directly involved in, the world was just as it "ought to be."

Ōmori Zenkai and war

In the 1930s and 1940s, Zenkai went on to become one of the Sōtō sect's strongest supporters of Japanese militarism. For example, just before the outbreak of full-scale war with China in July 1937, Zenkai, then president of Komazawa University, addressed an assembly of student-priests as follows: "In light of the crisis facing this nation, you must rouse yourselves to defend and protect the state, solemnly determined to do your very best!"[31]

On 15 January 1941, only seven days after the promulgation of the *Field Service Code*, Zenkai, as administrative head of the entire Sōtō sect, wrote:

Today the most important mental attitude required of us is the realization that our bodies have been consigned to us by His Majesty [the emperor].... It is this realization that distinguishes our national character from that of western nations with their emphasis on individualism and liberalism.... It is only when we proceed to give ourselves completely to the state in humble service that we are able to practice the Way of a loyal subject....

The core of the Buddha Way is to turn away from self. In other words, subjugation of self is its fundamental principle. It is due to the existence of self that strife occurs. It is due to the existence of self that self-interest and egoism exist. Zen Master Dōgen, the founder of the Sōtō sect, kindly taught us: "To study the Buddha Way is to study the self. To study the self is to forget the self" ....

All of us have a very strong attachment to life. However, it is not until we discard this attachment that we are able to acquire the noble spirit of sacrificing our lives for the state.... The heart of the practice of the Buddha Way is to forget self. It is in killing the idea of the small self that we are reborn as a true citizen of Japan.[32]

Zenkai went on to describe at length just how important Zen selflessness had been to empowering Japanese warriors over the centuries. He further noted that when one was willing to die selflessly for the state, victory was assured. Like General Tōjō Hideki and D. T. Suzuki, Zenkai also found in the *Hagakure* the embodiment of the Bushido spirit, especially Jōchō's famous words: "I have discovered that Bushido means to die." This led Zenkai to conclude: "Without eliminating one's attachment to life, it is impossible to acquire a truly strong spirit."[33] As far as Zenkai was concerned, this was exactly what Zen had to offer.

Conclusion

Zenkai's ostensibly Buddhist justification for social inequality as introduced above was certainly not unique to him but, on the contrary, was quite typical of Buddhist leaders at the time.[34] Zenkai himself came from a family of wealthy landowners in Fukui Prefecture who completely financed his many years of education abroad. Applying Zenkai's logic, this should have made him an example of someone whose "life of ease" made him "negligent."

Furthermore, one is left to speculate whether Zenkai would have told a starving or indebted tenant farmer, forced to sell his daughter into prostitution (as was then quite common), that everything would be fine in a hundred years or so. And if he had, just how much solace would father, mother or daughter have derived from that?

Despite General Imamura's undoubted admiration for Zenkai, there is nothing in Imamura's memoirs to indicate that the latter directly influenced the content of the *Field Service Code*. Nor does Zenkai claim to have done so. At most, the evidence suggests that Imamura's relationship to Zenkai, coupled with his general interest and knowledge of Zen, formed part of what might best be described as the "spiritual background" of the Code.

Yet, based on his repeated use of the term, one critical insight Imamura received from Zenkai in particular, and Zen in general, can be identified, i.e. the oneness of the ordinary and the Buddha. In other words, the fundamental identity of the unenlightened and enlightened states. Failing to realize this fundamental identity, the unenlightened mistakenly regard these as two separate states, believing they must first discard or transcend the former in order to achieve the latter. The Mahāyāna school of Buddhism, however, centred as it is on Mādhyamika philosophy, teaches that "there is not even the subtlest something separating the two."[35]

For Imamura, nowhere was this insight of greater significance than in his view of the proper mental state needed to face death. Ryōkan was admirable for his willingness to simply let nature take its course. Hakuin, however, was even more admirable. The oneness he achieved of the ordinary and the Buddha was best expressed when he said: "Death is fine, and life is still better. Life is fine, and *death is still better.*"

In Hakuin, Imamura found a man who was totally "unattached" to both life and death, a man who had transcended life and death in that, for him, both states were equally desirable. Given that Imamura, as a military officer, faced the ever-present possibility of his own death on the battlefield, let alone responsibility for sending large numbers of his soldiers to their deaths, what could be more attractive than the acquisition of this mental state. This is not to mention the acquisition of the "truly strong spirit" that Zenkai spoke of.

As the second part of this chapter reveals, it is precisely in the Zen view of life and death that the major Zen influence on the *Field Service Code* is to be found. In fact, the evidence will show that the Zen view of life and death, grounded in selflessness, lay at the very heart of the military spirit the Code incorporated.

SECTION TWO: ZEN – THE FOUNDATION OF MILITARY SPIRIT

In January 1941, the same month in which the *Field Service Code* was promulgated, the Department of Military Education issued a set of four thick booklets, under anonymous authorship, designed to provide the officer corps with guidance for the implementation of the Code. This guidance was crucial in that the primary responsibility for so-called "spiritual education" (*seishin kyōiku*) in the Imperial Army lay with company commanders. They were expected to gather the roughly one hundred and fifty men in their units together on a weekly basis for morale-building talks. The booklets would provide them with the necessary background information on how to explain each section of the Code.

The second of the four booklets contained an explanation of the military's view of life and death on the battlefield, corresponding to Section Seven, chapter 2 of the Code. This section of the Code read as follows:

> That which penetrates life and death is the lofty spirit of self-sacrifice for the public good. Transcending life and death, earnestly rush forward to accomplish your duty. Exhausting the power of your body and mind, calmly find joy in living in eternal duty.[36]

Appropriately, the accompanying booklet's commentary was entitled "Death and Life Are One" (*Shisei Ichinyo*), a Zen phrase closely related to Imamura's "the ordinary and the Buddha are one." The commentary begins by pointing out just how critical a proper understanding of life and death is to the maintenance of military discipline:

> The view of life and death held by officers and enlisted personnel is one of the roots of military discipline, the true value of which is first demonstrated under a hail of bullets. It is those who, having transcended life and death, maintain a serene state of mind that are first able to perform their duties well.... That is to say, what is to be esteemed is duty, not life. One should take as one's ideal the realization that even though the body perish, one lives on in the eternal life of the nation through the oneness of life and death.[37]

If the above represents the "ideal" to which all imperial soldiers were expected to adhere, the question remains as to the origin(s) of this ideal. In the nationalistic fervour of wartime Japan, it was not sufficient to merely explain what the individual soldier ought to think or believe. It was also necessary to demonstrate that the stated ideal was truly "Japanese," i.e. deeply rooted in traditional Japanese culture and values. In this connection it is not surprising to learn that the booklet's authors insisted: "It is the Bushido of our country... that is the core of the unique warrior spirit of the Japanese people."[38]

This said, the question still remains, where did the values incorporated in Bushido come from? The booklet's authors were convinced they knew:

> It was the Zen sect that furnished the warrior spirit with its ideological and spiritual foundation. The Zen sect overthrew the earlier belief in rebirth in Amitābha Buddha's western Paradise [as taught by the Pure Land school of Buddhism] and replaced it with the teaching that one's very mind is the Buddha, coupled with a call to rely on one's own efforts [to achieve salvation]. It caused people who were vainly yearning for rebirth in the innumerable lands of Amitābha's western Paradise to immediately focus on the here and now, to reflect on the original nature of the self. That is to say, the Zen sect emphasized the dignity and power of the self and concluded

that belief in gods, Buddhas, paradises, or hells outside of the self was total delusion.

On the one hand it can be said that it was only natural for warriors to be able to fearlessly and calmly enter the realm of life and death based on their prior experience on the actual battlefield. Nevertheless, it is also true that the teachings of the Zen sect exerted a strong influence on the warrior spirit. . . .

It can therefore be said that the time-honoured, traditional spirit of our country [as embodied in Shinto mythology] was tempered by the belief in the oneness of life and death that had been incorporated into the Zen training of the warriors of the Kamakura period [1185–1333]. . . . Thus becoming the deeply and broadly-held view of life and death of the Japanese people. . . .

It is this view of life and death that is one of the primary factors in the maintenance of strict military discipline in the midst of a rain of bullets. Coupled with this, of course, is the sublime greatness of the imperial military's mission, making it possible to sacrifice one's life without regret in the accomplishment of that mission.[39]

Despite the preceding total identification of the Zen view of life and death with the Japanese military spirit, it can still be claimed that this, after all, represents the Japanese military's understanding of Zen, not Zen's understanding of itself, or at least not the understanding of Zen held by leading Zen figures. Wasn't the Japanese military guilty of having willfully distorted Zen teaching concerning life and death to suit itself? For an initial answer to that question let us turn to no less a Zen authority than D. T. Suzuki.

D. T. Suzuki's view

In light of the wide respect D. T. Suzuki continues to enjoy in the West, some readers will be surprised to learn that he was one of the first Zen leaders to address the question of the Zen view of life and death in the period following the promulgation of the *Field Service Code*. Suzuki had, furthermore, actively promoted the idea of a link between Zen, Bushido, and the modern Japanese military from as early as 1906, following Japan's victory in the Russo-Japanese War of 1904–5. It was then that Suzuki wrote:

The *Lebensanschauung* of Bushido is no more nor less than that of Zen. The calmness and even joyfulness of heart at the moment of death which is conspicuously observable in the Japanese, the intrepidity which is generally shown by Japanese soldiers in the face of an overwhelming enemy; and the fairness of play to an opponent, so strongly taught by Bushido – all these come from the spirit of Zen training, and not from any such blind, fatalistic conception as is sometimes thought to be a trait peculiar to Orientals.[40]

Despite Suzuki's attempt to prevent Zen from being mistakenly regarded as a form of Oriental fatalism, he was quite willing to identify Zen with the warrior's calmness and "joyfulness of heart" at the moment of death. As readers familiar with Suzuki's *Zen and Japanese Culture* will recognize, he later went into great detail about the Zen influence on the development of Bushido. Yet his previous writings hardly prepare one for the contents of a wartime article Suzuki published in 1942 entitled: "The Japanese People's View of Life and Death."

Suzuki began his article by admitting that the Japanese people had possessed a unique national character prior to the introduction of Buddhism, something Shintoists called either the "spirit of Japan" (*Yamato-gokoro*) or a "pure and clear spirit" (*seimei-shin*). While the positive side of this national character was its "aesthetic simplicity," in Suzuki's eyes it lacked such components as "ethical justice," "spiritual tenaciousness," and "universal religious compassion." More importantly, it had not developed to the point of recognizing the oneness of life and death as derived from the Buddhist teaching of non-attachment.[41]

In Suzuki's view, the arrival of Buddhism, especially Zen, in Japan produced a profound change. That Zen exerted the greatest influence was because it had integrated the unique sensitivities and thought-patterns of both the Indian and Chinese peoples in such a way that they could be readily assimilated and cultivated by the Japanese. The result was that the Japanese people's pre-Buddhist recognition of "life" was deepened to include a recognition of "death."[42] And it was none other than Japan's warrior class that had been responsible for this.

Suzuki waxed ecstatic in his description of the warrior class and its close connection to Zen. Not only were warriors the "most Japanese-like" of all classes, it was the superior character of their culture that allowed them to play the leading role in Japan's development. This led Suzuki to the following breathtaking conclusion:

> It is the warrior spirit that can be rightly said to represent the Japanese people. I believe that if the warrior spirit, in its purity, were to be imbibed by all classes in Japan – whether government officials, military men, industrialists, or intellectuals – then most of the problems presently troubling us would be swept away as if at the stroke of a sword.[43]

As for Zen's contribution to the warrior spirit, Suzuki found this in the need for warriors to act intuitively. While Suzuki admitted that this intuitive mode was related to the pre-Buddhist "pure and clear spirit" of the Japanese, he nevertheless maintained that it was only Zen that incorporated it fully:

> Once [the warrior] sets his goal, it is intuition that allows him to rush towards it having transcended advantage and disadvantage, profit and loss. This intuitive nature is a pronounced characteristic of Zen. Zen is

straightforward [lit. a short sword thrust directly into]. If someone asks, "What is the Buddha?" the master answers, "What did you say, fool!" and strikes them with a rod. If someone says, "I'm troubled by the question of life and death," the master answers, "You fool! Where is there something called life and death?" Then he grabs the questioner by the breast and throws him out of the room.[44]

For Suzuki, then, action based on careful, rational and discriminating thought is the very antithesis of Zen's call for action based on intuition alone. Furthermore, it was exactly this feature of Zen that made it attractive to the warrior class. Not only that, Suzuki maintained that Zen had a uniquely Japanese heritage because "no matter where you go in the world, you will never come across anything like it."[45] Yet, what was the connection between Zen's intuitive nature and the ever-present danger that the warrior might be called upon to die at any moment? Suzuki explained this connection as follows:

> Warriors always exist in the interval between life and death. When they step across their doorsills, or even if they don't, they always face the possibility of death. There is no time for hesitation. That is why Zen is the ideal religion for warriors.[46]

Suzuki further insisted that while Zen may have started as the ideal religion for Japan's warriors, it was certainly no longer limited to them alone. On the contrary, Zen thought had long since penetrated "into every nook and cranny of Japanese culture." This led Suzuki to conclude: "A foreign scholar once said that Zen is the character of the Japanese people. That is true, for the Zen view of life and death is now that of the Japanese people as a whole."[47]

Shinto and Confucianism

In comparing Suzuki's views with those of the anonymous authors explaining the military's view of life and death, the similarity between both is readily apparent. As one might expect from a Zen scholar, Suzuki's comments were more detailed than those of the military authors, but Suzuki's detail only elaborates, without contradicting, their position. In fact, it is almost as if the military authors had based their comments on one of Suzuki's many discussions of this topic. Further, for those readers who have been led to believe that Suzuki opposed the Asia-Pacific War, or at least remained aloof from it, his statement that the adoption of the warrior spirit by all classes in Japan would instantly solve the country's problems may come as something of a shock.[48]

In acknowledging a Shinto role in developing the national character of the Japanese people, especially their view of life and death, Suzuki is once again in basic accord with the views of the military authors who wrote:

The view of life and death observable in our country's mythical age contains within it praise of the phenomenal world and belief in the immortality of the soul. Furthermore, it rejects the position that physical death marks the end of everything. Thus we can see the germ of the idea that life and death are one.[49]

No doubt Suzuki would have rejected the view that the "germ" of the Zen view of the oneness of life and death was already present in pre-Buddhist Japan in that it gives too much credit to the indigenous Shinto tradition. Yet, Suzuki did recognize that the national characteristics produced by these two religions were at least "related."

This said, there is one area in which Suzuki and the military authors appear to have disagreed, for nowhere does Suzuki refer in his article to a Confucian contribution to the development of the Japanese view of life and death. The military authors, however, had this to say:

In the Tokugawa period [1600–1867] Bushido was systematized by Confucianism, leading warriors to ignore the question of life and death and rush toward a place where they believed right existed. Thus they sought to acquire life within the context of the larger society even if that meant their death as individuals. That is to say, they took as their ideal a spirit in which they discarded their small [egocentric] self and lived in their large [true] self.[50]

Was Suzuki wrong to have ignored Confucianism's contribution? In his defense it can be said that while in the Tokugawa period Japanese Confucianists successfully divorced themselves from Buddhism, Buddhists, particularly those in the Zen school, never even so much as contemplated divorcing themselves from Confucianism. This is because such Confucian values as loyalty and filial piety had long been part of Zen teachings, especially as directed toward the laity.

Historically speaking, this is not surprising since it was the Zen school that had first introduced and propagated neo-Confucian thought in Japan in the Kamakura period (1185–1333). By the end of the fourteenth century the famous neo-Confucian Ashikaga Academy located at Shimozuke had several thousand students, all of whom, like their teachers, were Zen priests.[51]

That the Zen school, first in China and then in Japan, had so readily embraced neo-Confucianism is explained in part by the fact that the latter, while identifying itself as the true form of a revitalized Confucianism, had nevertheless been deeply influenced by Buddhist metaphysics. For example, although the booklet's military authors introduced the terms "small self" and "large self" as belonging to Confucianism, the Zen school had long employed these same terms, holding the large self (daiga) to be the equivalent of the more traditional Zen term of "non-self" (muga). The goal in either case was to free oneself from attachment to the small, egocentric self.

Further, Suzuki's failure to discuss Confucianism can be seen as a reflection of his earlier assertion that the Zen school had been the most successful of all Buddhist schools in integrating the thought-patterns of the Chinese as well as Indian peoples. Thus, if Suzuki failed to discuss Confucianism it may well have been because he saw no need to separate out of Zen something that had for so long been an integral part of its character.

Something similar can be said for the integration of Shinto and Shinto-inspired national chauvinism into Zen. For example, as early as the Kamakura period it was possible for Rinzai Zen Master Ean (1225–77) to proudly proclaim: "To the end of the end of the last generation will this land of Ours surpass all other lands."[52] Similarly, Rinzai Zen Master Hakuin, introduced above, asserted that "though Our Land is situated out of the Way, everlasting is its Imperial Rule, noble are its people. Thus Our Land surpasses others by far.... This Land of Ours is pure and divine." [53]

General Wada

Returning to the *Field Service Code*, it will come as no surprise to learn that the imperial military continued to promote the Code and its values in its own writings. In August 1942, for example, Reserve Lt. General Wada Kameji (1870–1945), former head of the Military Staff College, published a 302-page book entitled *The Spirit of the Army* (*Rikugun-Damashii*). That General Wada's book represented the military's thinking is shown by the Army Ministry's seal of approval on its cover as well as the calligraphic endorsements of three serving generals, including Tōjō Hideki in his capacity as Minister of the Army.

The overall purpose of Wada's book was to call on the Japanese people, both soldiers and civilians, for ever greater dedication to the war effort based on the "glorious fruits of battle" that Japan had acquired up to that point. While admitting that Japan's material resources were limited, Wada explained that Japan had been victorious in the "magnificent and great holy war" then underway because of its "unlimited spiritual power." [54] In the first instance this power had its origins in the *Field Service Code*'s teaching that "faith is power," but he also made it clear that this power could be seen throughout Japan's long history in those innumerable warriors (and their present-day soldier successors) who had "transcended life and death" through their realization of the "unity of life and death." [55]

But what was at the core of this spiritual power? Just as with the Code's authors, Wada devoted a section of his book to an explanation of what he called the "Pure View of Life and Death." Like Tōjō, Wada found the core of this power in the Bushido code as expressed in the *Hagakure*. The famous phrase "I have discovered that Bushido means to die," according to Wada, "reveals the way in which warriors can live for all eternity." And he continued, "From ancient times, warriors who were truly loyal possessed an unshakable view of life and death." [56]

Yet, what was the ultimate source of this unshakable view of life and death? Rather than answer this question himself, Wada turned to an Army officer who by 1942 had been eulogized many times over as a "god of war," Lt. Colonel Sugimoto Gorō (1900–37). Readers of *Zen at War* will recall that Sugimoto was a long-time lay disciple of Rinzai Zen Master Yamazaki Ekijū (1882–1961), chief abbot of the Buttsūji branch of the Rinzai sect and head of the entire sect by the end of the war (1945–6).

Although Sugimoto had been killed in action in northern China in September 1937, he left behind a collection of writings that was published posthumously the following year as *Great Duty* (*Taigi*). Sugimoto's book sold more than 100,000 copies and was especially popular among young officers. In addition, it was praised and endorsed by not only high-ranking government officials and generals like Wada but by leading Rinzai and Sōtō Zen figures as well. Sugimoto described the importance of his Zen training as follows:

> The reason that Zen is necessary for soldiers is that all Japanese, especially soldiers, must live in the spirit of the unity of sovereign and subjects, eliminating their ego and getting rid of their self. It is exactly the awakening to the nothingness (*mu*) of Zen that is the fundamental spirit of the unity of sovereign and subjects. Through my practice of Zen I am able to get rid of my self. In facilitating the accomplishment of this, Zen becomes, as it is, the true spirit of the imperial military.[57]

Sugimoto then added: "Zen training clarifies life and death, thereby making possible the *elimination of life and death*. Further, Zen training makes it possible for me to become completely pure, thereby fulfilling my wish to be a true military man [Italics mine].[58]

What was of particular interest to Wada was Sugimoto's claim to have "eliminat[ed] life and death." For this reason Wada inserted a long quotation from *Taigi* that he felt expressed the essence of Sugimoto's view of life and death. Appropriately, the quotation began with Sugimoto's reference to the famous Rinzai Zen priest Kanzan Egen (1277–1360), spiritual advisor to Emperor Hanazono (r. 1308–18) and founder of the imperial-sponsored Myōshinji monastic complex in Kyoto. Sugimoto wrote:

> When National Teacher Kanzan was asked about his view of life and death, it was his custom to roar: "From the outset I've never had [anything that can be called] life and death!" For those masters who have abandoned body and mind, it may truly be said there is no life and death.
>
> Life and death are not to be found in everyday affairs, nor are they to be found in other activities. There is only "no life and death." However, the transformed view of life and death held by those great masters who have undergone the unparalleled Great Death, cannot be comprehended by

those of mediocre ability; for the living bodies of these masters, having transcended life and death, are totally free.

Even should ordinary persons succeed in extinguishing their body and mind and enter into the realm of non-attachment, they will not become bodhisattvas, Buddhas or gods. The reason for this is that they must have the strength to save all sentient beings. If there are those who leave behind either acts or writings that cause future generations to rouse themselves on behalf of our imperial nation, it is they who will become gods, bodhisattvas, and Buddhas.[59]

Needless to say, the Zen influence is clear and unmistakable in the above, not least of all by Sugimoto's reference to "Great Death" (*Daishi-ichiban*), a term unique to Zen that appears in the forty-first case of the famous *kōan* collection, *Hekigan-roku* (*Blue Cliff Record*). The term refers to a Zen practitioner who, having emptied the mind of all discriminating thought, has experienced a spiritual rebirth, that is to say, realized enlightenment.

Given Sugimoto's preference for Zen, it is not surprising to learn that he was critical of other religious orientations. In this connection, the reader will recall the anonymous authors of the Department of Military Education's four booklets who provided the official commentary on the Code. They praised the Zen sect for having "overthrown the earlier belief in rebirth in Amitābha Buddha's western Paradise and replaced it with the teaching that one's very mind is the Buddha, coupled with a call to rely on one's own efforts [to achieve salvation]." As the following reveals, Sugimoto shared these authors' critique of the Pure Land tradition:

The true life of religion is to create people who have no attachments, who have no life and death. Today, however, there are religions that fail to encourage the abandonment of body and mind and produce more and more people full of attachments, more and more people for whom there is life and death. These religions distinguish life from death and talk about transmigration and cause people to become attached to [the idea of] rebirth in Paradise. Such religions ruin the nation.[60]

The idea of gaining something through one's practice has, of course, long been anathema to the Zen ideal of complete non-attachment, not least of all to life and death as well as to enlightenment itself. However, Sugimoto's Zen-inspired non-attachment was not an end in itself, for it was meant to serve an even loftier ideal – absolute loyalty to the emperor. Wada concluded his Sugimoto quotation with the following:

In pure loyalty there is no life and death. Where there is life and death there is no pure loyalty. Those who speak of life and death are not yet pure in heart, for they have not yet abandoned body and mind. In pure loyalty there is no life and death. Therefore, simply live in pure loyalty. No, it is too easy to say, "*live* in pure loyalty." Pure loyalty is all there is; nothing lies outside of it. This is truly [the meaning of] pure loyalty.[61]

Having shown how Sugimoto wed a Zen-inspired view of life and death, based on total non-attachment and elimination of discriminating thought, to the requirement for absolute loyalty to the emperor, Wada was now ready to conclude his own discussion of life and death. He did so with the following rousing exhortation:

> Therefore, youth of Japan, take care to constantly cultivate your body and mind, and, exerting yourself to the utmost, strive to accomplish your duty and acquire an unshakable view of life and death while not neglecting to train your spirit. Death itself is truly the way to live for all eternity![62]

Inasmuch as the war would continue for another three long years, millions of Japanese youth, like Sugimoto Gorō before them, would yet be given the opportunity to "live for all eternity."

Civilian influence

While the *Field Service Code* was required reading for all military personnel, it is critically important to realize that its influence was not limited to the military alone. In fact, Hata Ikuhito, one of Japan's leading military scholars, argues that the Code had an even greater impact on civilians than it did on the military:

> Although the *Field Service Code* was originally created with combat personnel in mind, it was much talked about by both civilians and quasi-military personnel, with the result that it spread rapidly throughout the general populace. A related phenomenon was an explosion of interest in the *Hagakure*, well-known for its statement: "I have discovered that Bushido means to die".... Not only that, many commercial publishers brought out books for the general public with such titles as: *Reader on the Field Service Code* (*Senjinkun Tokuhon*); *Detailed Commentary on the Field Service Code* (*Senjinkun Seikai*); and *True Meaning of the Field Service Code* (*Senjinkun Hongi*).[63]

In reviewing these books, one finds that they are primarily anecdotal in nature, filled with war-related stories from various periods in Japanese history designed to demonstrate the seamless connection between Japan's modern military spirit and Bushido. As one might expect, there were not only anecdotes on particularly brave and loyal samurai warriors, but even more stories on modern military figures like General Nogi Maresuke, Zen-inspired hero of the Russo-Japanese War.

Just how much influence these books and related articles had on the civilian population is impossible to gage precisely. What can be said, however, is that the authors of these materials fully intended Japanese civilians to adopt the values underlying the Code. This is demonstrated, for example, by the 1942 book, *The Field Service Code and the Spirit of Japan (Senjinkun to Nihon Seishin)*. The book's author, Okuda Kyūji, included the following in his introduction:

> The *Field Service Code* is a ready wartime reference for the people of this nation and, as such, is the most urgent and important guiding principle for our daily life. It clearly expresses the course we are to take from this point onwards. Those who obey this Code and put it into practice are those who can truly give their all to the state. The embodiment of the *Field Service Code* by all the people of this country will bring victory to our imperial land for all eternity.[64]

Tomomatsu Entai

Books like the above were not, however, composed entirely of anecdotes, and there was still room for explanatory material, not least of all concerning the Code's view of life and death. This was demonstrated by an essay that appeared in the preceding book contributed by Tomomatsu Entai (1895–1973), one of Japan's best-known Buddhist scholar-priests and professor at Jōdo (Pure Land) sect-affiliated Taishō University. Entai's essay was entitled: "The Japanese People's Philosophy of Death" and began with a statement designed to show just how different the Orient is from the West:

> There is a pronounced tendency in western civilization to stubbornly affirm a strong sense of life. A natural result is that strife runs rampant both within their societies and between nations. While there are exceptions, western civilization is, first and foremost, a civilization of strife, while oriental culture has a peaceful feeling running through it. This is because Oriental culture is conscious of death.[65]

In echoes of D. T. Suzuki, Entai describes Japan's earliest inhabitants as having had an optimistic and cheerful nature, yet very warlike because they had "never directly faced the question of death." It was, of course, Buddhism's introduction to Japan that changed this, for it taught that "all living things must die." This in turn produced the Japanese people's philosophy of death, the content of which Entai explained as follows:

> Our philosophy of death is definitely not a denial of life. Instead, it urges rejection of a wrongful attachment to life in order to grasp true life. While there may be differences in degree, we have all received this Buddhist-influenced education since childhood. Thus it can be said that we are well prepared for death, having truly resigned ourselves to its inevitability.

To say that we are well prepared for, or resigned to, death sounds grim, but in reality it simply means that we Japanese have developed a taste for death, or at least that we have been trained for it. Thus, unlike westerners, we have little fear of death. While death is certainly not desirable, we are resigned, or should I say reconciled, to the fact that all living things must die.[66]

One of the most significant aspects of Entai's writing is his emphasis on the Japanese as having been trained since childhood to accept death. Here we have yet another indication that at least some of the values espoused by Japanese militarism were not the instant creations of a modern totalitarian ideology but did in fact resonate with traditional Japanese cultural if not religious values. What army would not welcome soldiers into its ranks who had resigned themselves to death even before heading for the battlefield?

Similarly, although Entai was affiliated with the Jōdo (Pure Land) sect, the similarity of his views with those of D. T. Suzuki suggests that the latter was correct in asserting that the Zen view of life and death had, as a result of its incorporation into the Bushido code, become the commonly accepted view of the Japanese people regardless of class or sectarian affiliation. Entai, perhaps aware of the criticism of men like Sugimoto Gorō, makes no claim that his is a uniquely Pure Land interpretation of death but instead emphasizes that he is reiterating a universally-held Buddhist view. As chapter 9 will reveal, the same thing may be said for the Nichiren sect as well.

Entai is clearly concerned, even obsessed, with demonstrating that the Japanese people's view of life and death is quite different from, and moreover superior to, that held by westerners. Thus he ends his essay with an attempt to show just how "rational" and "practical" the Japanese people's view of death really is. In this respect, at least, we see a certain divergence from Suzuki's views:

It appears that westerners often marvel at the tradition of "*harakiri*" [lit. cutting the stomach open]. This tradition stems from the fact that the Japanese people know "there is something more precious than life itself." Thus they are prepared to lay down their lives for that more precious something. This, too, comes from the influence of Buddhism in that "living" is not held to be all there is to "life." That is to say, in order to live truly one must be aware of a realm where there is no reluctance to lay down one's life. To think in this way has nothing to do with superstition nor is it a denial of life. Rather, it is a result of having properly reflected on life in a rational and practical manner. That is to say, in order to truly live properly it is necessary to accept death as well as life.[67]

In discussing the willingness to die for something more precious than life itself, Entai's thinking may be seen as validating the Code's requirement that a soldier choose death rather than endure the shame of being taken prisoner. While this requirement may not seem to apply to civilian non-combatants, it was soon interpreted as being very relevant: it came to mean "Death with honour!" for all Japanese, civilian and military alike, as it became increasingly clear that the sacred land of Japan would itself endure the shame of invasion.

Zen at work

While the writings of Buddhist scholars like D. T. Suzuki and Tomomatsu Entai undoubtedly had some influence on the Japanese people's readiness to die in the war effort, their scholarly influence pales in comparison with the effect of a much larger group – the 200,000 Buddhist priests of all sects whose temples were located in every rural community and city throughout Japan. Since they collectively enjoyed a virtual monopoly on funerary rites, it was at their temples, not Shinto shrines, where individual funerals were held for the hundreds of thousands of Japanese war dead. More than any other single group, it was they who valorized the deaths of Japan's soldiers on the battlefield, and, at the same time, rallied resistance to an Allied invasion of Japan that appeared increasingly likely from late 1943 onwards.

The *Field Service Code* became the text of choice for many of these priests, for as has been seen, it offered ample opportunity to reaffirm what had long been held to be the Buddhist view of life and death. Not surprisingly, the Rinzai and Sōtō Zen sects took the lead in promoting the Code among their adherents, recognizing as they did that the Code, in its underlying ideology, was a child of their own making.

To give but one example, the administrative headquarters of the Sōtō sect printed the entire code in the 1 February 1941 issue of the *Sōtō Shūhō*, the sect's administrative organ. In introducing the Code's text, sect editors noted, like so many of their contemporaries, that the Code was as applicable to civilians on the home front as it was to soldiers on the battlefield. This was because the country was engaged in total war in which all of the nation's citizens, regardless of position, must be of "one body and one mind" (*ittai-isshin*). The introduction ended with these words: "The main text of the Code follows with the hope that it will be used in evangelization efforts."[68]

That the Sōtō sect was quite serious about this proposal is demonstrated by the fact that by 15 March 1941 the sect's administrative headquarters had printed thousands of copies of the Code including an additional section entitled: "Military Spirit and Zen." Advertisements for this sectarian version of the Code ran month after month in the *Sōtō Shūhō*, including price discounts for those temples that ordered in bulk. But just how could temples use a military field code as evangelism material?

Kumazawa Taizen

The answer is provided by no less a Sōtō Zen representative than Kumazawa Taizen (1873–1968), chief abbot of Eiheiji since the beginning of 1944. As Eiheiji was founded by Zen Master Dōgen in 1246, its chief abbot has traditionally been considered to most fully embody the enlightened mind of Dōgen himself. Thus, there is no higher honour for a Sōtō Zen monastic than to serve as its head.

While Eiheiji was tucked away in relative physical isolation in Fukui Prefecture near the Japan Sea coast, Taizen was anything but a monastic recluse. On the contrary, few Zen masters have travelled more than he did during the war years, visiting hundreds of the 14,244 Sōtō Zen temples (as of 1935) attended by some 20,000 priests. And just what did Taizen have to say about the *Field Service Code* during his travels? We are fortunate to have a record of one of his talks as recorded in the May 1944 issue of the pan-Buddhist magazine *Daihōrin* (Great Dharma Wheel). Appropriately, the article was entitled: "How to Avoid the Coming of Life and Death" (*Shōji Tōrai Ikan ga Kaihi-sen*).

> For some thirty-four years I served as abbot of Eigenji located in Tsuruga [Fukui Prefecture]. There is a regiment stationed there, and I served as regimental chaplain for some fifteen years. As a result, military men often came to my temple to practice Zen meditation, and I gave them lectures on Zen as well.
>
> I often addressed the question of life and death, typically using the following passage written on the very first page of the *Military Regulations for Internal Affairs*: "Military barracks are a soldier's home. It is here he shares both hardships and life and death with his fellow soldiers. It is here that he recognizes that life and death are the same...."
>
> In the military the transcendence of life and death is considered a matter of prime importance in a soldier's education. More recently, the writers of the *Field Service Code* were kind enough to include the following view of life and death in Section Seven, chapter 2 of the Code. This section reads as follows: "That which penetrates life and death is the lofty spirit of self-sacrifice for the public good. Transcending life and death, earnestly rush forward to accomplish your duty. Exhausting the power of your body and mind, calmly find joy in living in eternal duty."
>
> We can see that the Code reveals not only how to promote military spirit but how to transcend life and death as well.[69]

Taizen's comments are quite revealing for a number of reasons, not least because they show that he, like so many of his fellow Zen masters, had been closely connected to the Japanese military for many years. Equally, they reveal that long before the advent of the *Field Service Code*, Zen masters like Kumazawa had identified passages within military regulations that conformed to their own view of life and death, e.g. the phrase "life and death are the same." That Kumazawa discovered this phrase in the *Military Regulations for Internal Affairs* is significant because, as the reader will recall from chapter 2, it was these same regulations that, following revision in 1907 (and promulgation in 1908), incorporated a distinct Zen influence.

In light of this, it can be said that asking how influential the *Field Service Code* was in and of itself is asking the wrong question, for there was really nothing new in the Code's underlying ideology, especially concerning its view of life and death. Readers of *Zen at War* will recall that as early as the Russo-Japanese War of 1904–5, Buddhist chaplains like Shaku Sōen expressed a wish to: "... inspire, if I could, our valiant soldiers with the ennobling thoughts of the Buddha, so as to enable them to die on the battlefield with the confidence that the task in which they are engaged is great and noble."[70]

The important question, then, is not the effectiveness of the *Field Service Code* by itself, but rather, the overall effectiveness of the Japanese military's program of "spiritual education" that had roots reaching back to the Sino-Japanese War of 1894–5 but really came into its own after 1907. Before addressing this question, however, there is yet another question that is of even greater importance. That is to say, just what connection did any of this really have to do with Zen?

Taizen was fully prepared to address this point, and he began, like so many of his Sōtō Zen contemporaries, by noting that Dōgen had placed the highest priority on the need for Buddhists to clarify the meaning of life and death. And further, Dōgen taught that if the Buddha existed within life and death, then there was no life and death. Taizen then repeated a famous teaching by Dōgen included in the *Shūshōgi*: "Simply be aware that life and death are identical with Nirvāṇa, for then there is nothing to loathe in life and death nor desire in Nirvāṇa. You will, for the first time, be able to free yourself from life and death."[71]

Yet, quoting Dōgen still doesn't answer the question of the connection between Zen and the military. Taizen continued:

The Japanese people, possessed of a radiant history, must do their utmost to extinguish self and serve the public good, thereby bringing no shame on their ancestors. Japanese boys must not only serve their country but find a place to die. And where does one find a place to die?

It doesn't necessarily mean going to the battlefield. It may be right where you are.... Expressed in different words, the place where your mission in life is fulfilled is precisely your place of death. And equally, the place where you fulfil your mission in death is precisely your place of life.

This is because life and death are most definitely not separate entities. When water freezes it becomes ice, and when it melts, it becomes water. Then it rises to become clouds and falls as rain. Even though its form changes its essence does not. Life and death are like this, for life and death are one absolute reality (*shōji ichi-shinnyo*). Upon recognizing this, you are able to transcend life and death, exercising great freedom for the first time. Ordinary people, believing that life and death are separate entities, view life from a relative point of view, unable to progress to the realm of true freedom. This is not just true for life and death. It is wrong to tie pleasure and pain, or poverty and wealth to a relative viewpoint. Cut yourself off from relative viewpoints in all things.[72]

Zen as death

In Taizen's exhortation to "find a place to die" it is difficult not to be reminded of the following passage in the *Hagakure* where another Zen priest, Yamamoto Jōchō, described the purpose of Zen meditation as follows:

> Meditation on inevitable death should be performed daily. Every day when one's body and mind are at peace, one should meditate upon being ripped apart by arrows, rifles, spears and swords, being carried away by surging waves, being thrown into the midst of a great fire, being struck by lightning, being shaken to death by a great earthquake, falling from thousand-foot cliffs, dying of disease or committing *seppuku* [ritual disembowelment] at the death of one's master. And every day without fail one should consider himself as dead.
>
> There is a saying of the elders that goes, "Step from under the eaves and you're a dead man. Leave the gate and the enemy is waiting." This is not a matter of being careful. *It is to consider oneself as dead beforehand* [Italics mine].[73]

It is exactly here that the "practical outcome" of the Japanese military's Zen-derived view of life and death is to be found. Thanks to Zen, the Japanese soldier (at least the well-indoctrinated soldier) fully expected to die on the battlefield. The only question for the soldier was where and under what circumstances he would die, i.e. would he die with his honour and that of his family intact. In his 1943 book entitled *Japan's Military Masters – The Army in Japanese Life*, Hillis Lory describes spiritual training as "the religion of the Army."[74] He then went on to explain:

> Many of the soldiers in the present [Asia-Pacific] War are so determined to die on the battlefield that they conduct their own public funerals before leaving for the front. This holds no element of the ridiculous to the Japanese. Rather, it is admired as the spirit of the true samurai who enters the battle with no thought of return.[75]

In a similar vein, Thomas Allen and Norman Polmar noted the following in their book, *Code-Name Downfall*: "The Japanese soldier, fighting fiercely, dying willingly, confounded – and often frightened – US troops. A dark, *unfathomable acceptance of death* drove the Japanese fighting man [Italics mine]."[76]

If Allen and Polmar paint a rather sinister description of the Japanese soldier's acceptance of death, Meirion and Susie Harries note in their book *The Rise and Fall of the Imperial Japanese Army* that the Japanese soldier was an almost ideal prototype:

> The Japanese soldier was required to display qualities that every army covertly hopes for, even expects, but shrinks from demanding directly.

From the commander's point of view, the most useful practical property of the Japanese soldier was his willingness to die, which removed all limits on what his leaders could attempt. A legacy of the authentic samurai ethic, as the war progressed acceptance of death became ever more heavily stressed – just as it was ever more necessary.[77]

The Harries were not the only observers to point out the "freedom" that the Japanese soldier's readiness to die gave his commanders. Noda Masaaki, a noted Japanese psychiatrist, described the same phenomenon in his 1998 book, *War and the Responsibility of the Accused [Sensō to Zaiseki]*:

In the [Asia-Pacific] war the Japanese people had two battlefields. One of them involved rational thinking based on considerations of military power. The other consisted of an irrational belief in spirit as supreme, making anything possible as long as one were prepared to die.[78]

Nevertheless, it appears that on occasion it was possible to get too much of a good thing. In what might almost be considered an amusing episode had the consequences not been so tragic, Major General Itō Takeo, commander of the 38th Infantry Corps, actually lamented that the soldiers under his command were *too willing* to die. In January 1943, General Itō wrote:

Given our situation, there are none calling themselves Japanese soldiers who are attached to life. On the contrary, they all want to die.... Thus, the problem is not death, but how to accomplish our mission. What I am racking my brains about is not teaching my soldiers how to die laughing or die with peace of mind, but rather how to get them to stay alive even one more day fighting to the last.[79]

Military historian Kawano Hitoshi notes that both Japanese and US soldiers shared the same basic fear of death. The difference between them was in the way they dealt with that fear. In general, US soldiers consciously acknowledged their fear and sought to control it as effectively as possible. Japanese soldiers, on the other hand, sought to deny their fear even existed, or at least drive it from their conscious minds. "By accepting death at the outset," Kawano asserted, "[Japanese soldiers] sought to eliminate their fear of death." [80]

As accurate as the preceding authors were in their descriptions, what they failed to realize was that behind such things as "the authentic samurai spirit" or "spirit as supreme" stood the Zen view of life and death. It was this view that effectively removed all limits on what Japan's military leaders could attempt on the battlefield, no matter how irrational. In reality, the Japanese soldier's "unfathomable acceptance of death" was not the least bit unfathomable, at least when understood within the context of the doctrinal interpretations long promoted by Zen masters like Kumazawa Taizen and his ilk. And in this connection it should not be forgotten that in his 1938 book, *Zen and Japanese Culture*, D. T. Suzuki noted:

> The spirit of the samurai deeply breathing Zen into itself propagated its philosophy even among the masses. The latter, even when they are not particularly trained in the way of the warrior, have imbibed his spirit and are ready to sacrifice their lives for any cause they think worthy. This has repeatedly been proved in the wars Japan has so far had to go through.[81]

For Suzuki, the willingness of the Japanese people to sacrifice themselves on behalf of "any cause they think worthy" without the slightest hesitation or regret was the greatest contribution Zen had made to not only the warrior but Japanese society as a whole. In the same book, Suzuki quotes the following medieval Zen-influenced poem to show that this self-sacrificial attitude was also the key to victory:

> Victory is for the one,
> Even before combat,
> Who has no thought of himself,
> Abiding in the no-mind-ness of Great Origin.[82]

Given that Japan was still three years away from its attack on Pearl Harbour when Suzuki wrote the above, his words seem almost prophetic. Or, since these words were written in English for a western audience, did he mean them more in the nature of a warning?

Soldiers speak

Up to this time we have listened primarily to the voices of observers, both Japanese and western, outside of the Japanese military itself. What were Japan's military men thinking? Needless to say, most of the voices remaining from the war period are those of "good soldiers" and their remarks naturally reflect the values of their superiors. This, however, does not lessen the fact that a very large number of Japan's fighting men had, as they were trained to do, "resigned themselves to death."

This resignation can be seen as early as the Russo-Japanese War. In *Human Bullets (Nikudan)*, one of the most famous books to come out of that war, author Captain Sakurai Tadayoshi related the following story concerning the assault on the Russian stronghold at Port Arthur:

> We left Japan fully determined to turn into dust, ... saying, "Here I stand ready to die!" Our hearts were impatient but the opportunity was slow in coming. More than one hundred days had passed since we had left for the front.... At night sleeping on our arms or in the day exposed to the hail-

storm of bullets, we had never forgotten our desire to return the imperial favour and beneficence with death and death only. Thousands of our comrades had died without the joy of seeing the final success.... We were eager to avenge them....

How was it that we were still alive, after fighting one, two, three, already four battles without having fallen ... on the battlefield! I had been fully resolved to die on Mt. Taku, but still I was left behind by a great many friends. Surely this time, in this general assault, I must have the honour and distinction of offering *my little self* to our beloved country. With this idea, this desire, this determination I started for the battle [Italics mine].[83]

As revealed above, there was a very close connection between resignation to death and the idea of self-sacrifice, the "offering of my little self." Shortly before the *Yamato*, Japan's greatest battleship, left port in April 1945 on a one-way suicide mission to Okinawa, Second Sub-Lieutenant Yoshida Mitsuru confided the following to his diary: "With a few days' rest, I will gain the mental strength to turn the tide of war and will cultivate my fighting spirit for sure death in a state of selflessness (*muga*)."[84]

Had he read Yoshida's words, Lt. General Chō Isamu, second in command of the ill-fated Japanese garrison on Okinawa, would surely have nodded in approval. As will be detailed in chapter 9, General Chō was himself a newly-ordained Buddhist priest who wrote the following parting message to his own Buddhist master: "I am filled with joy at having found the best place in all of Japan to die!"[85]

Finally, the preceding comments would all have been warmly welcomed by Imperial Army General Kawabe Masakazu (1886–1965). In 1942 General Kawabe served as Chief of Staff of Japanese forces in China and in 1943 became Commander-in-Chief of the Burma Area Army. More importantly, Kawabe had been Inspector General of Military Training from January 1939 to March 1940 when work on the *Field Service Code* was in its initial stages. In postwar years Kawabe recorded that he had been very satisfied with the Code's final content, noting: "The Code clarified the way in which the entire army and navy, being of one body and mind, could enter into a state of selflessness (*botsuga*), transcending life and death."[86]

Zen selflessness

That "selflessness" is one of the cornerstones of Zen (and Buddhist) teachings hardly bears repeating here. In Japanese it is variously expressed as *muga* (non-self/selflessness), *mushi* (no "I"), *daiga* (great-self), *botsuga* (disappeared-self), *bōga* (forgotten-self), and *messhi* (extinguished-self). Just how Zen leaders employed these terms to promote the supremacy of the state, most especially loyalty to the emperor, is dramatically revealed in the following June 1935 article entitled: "The People's Spirit and Non-Self" (Kokumin Seishin to Muga):

Zen Master Dōgen wrote: "To study the Buddha Dharma is to study the self, to study the self is to forget the self." Entering into the "realm of the forgotten-self (*bōga*)" is a fundamental teaching of Buddhism. Gaining peace of mind and acquiring religious faith comes through having reverently taken refuge in the Buddha, having forgotten the self and realized the non-self (*muga*).

It goes without saying that Zen enlightenment consists in moving away from the small self and emptying the self through entering into the absolute truth of the large self (*daiga*). Therefore, all of the saints and sages of this world have taught that, having forgotten and emptied the self, the supreme good consists of serving other individuals and society. Having entered this realm of the forgotten-self and non-self, it then becomes possible to render filial piety to one's parents and loyalty to one's sovereign.[87]

This article was published in *Sanshō*, a periodical published by Sōtō Zen head monastery Eiheiji a full two years before Japan entered into war with China, i.e. long before the emergence of the patriotic fervour (if not hysteria) that inevitably accompanies modern warfare. In addition, it is readily understandable that the non-existence of the self should lead to an acceptance of death; for if the self as we know it does not exist, then death no more marks the end of life than birth marks its beginning.

As early as the Tang dynasty (618–c.907), a Northern Chan monk by the name of Yuangui (644–716) is recorded as having demonstrated his fearlessness in the face of death. According to this story, when Yuangui sought to convert the tutelary god of Mt. Song to Buddhism, the god threatened to kill him for having failed to show the proper respect. Responding to the god's threat, Yuangui said: "Since I am unborn, how could you kill me? My body is empty and I see myself as no different from you: how could you destroy emptiness, or destroy yourself?"[88] In post-Meiji era Japan, this interpretation of the non-existence of the self became the foundation of not only absolute loyalty to the emperor but an unquestioning willingness to die on his behalf.

Japanese boys

The reader will recall that Zen Master Kumazawa Taizen urged Japanese "boys" to find a place to die. This may seem strange until one realizes that from late 1943 Japanese boys were literally the only group of Japanese males left, apart from the elderly, who might still be called up for military service. Draft deferments for students in universities, technical colleges, and higher schools had ended in September 1943, and there were even quotas established for 15–17-year-old youth "volunteers" to take part in Manchuria–Mongolia Development Youth Patriotic Units.

As the following comments reveal, Taizen was well aware of these developments and more. He clearly understood that an invasion of Japan's home islands was no longer a question of "if" but only "when." What was the civilian population expected to do about this?

> Today we have arrived at a point where all of our people are soldiers. Thus the *Field Service Code* is not just instruction for soldiers alone, but for all one hundred million citizens. Especially today when the factory is the battlefield and the home is the battlefield, all of us must keep this fact in our minds and in our hearts. The execution and practice of this Code will result in the accomplishment of certain victory in the Greater East Asia War now underway.
>
> Section Seven, chapter 1 of the Code expresses this spirit as follows:

> Faith is power; he who has faith and fights resolutely will always be victorious. Confidence in certain victory is the result of thorough and realistic training. Utilizing every moment, spare no effort in cultivating the power to achieve certain victory over the enemy. On victory or defeat hangs the future of the empire. Reflect on the glorious history of the Army, remembering always your obligation to our tradition of a hundred battles and a hundred victories. In doing this you cannot fail but be victorious.

> In reflecting on these words, we see that all one hundred million of us must truly become red-hot balls of fire in anticipation of certain victory. . . . This is truly what it means to find a place to die. All one hundred million of us must be of one mind, sacrificing ourselves for the public good. This is the manifestation of the true appearance of a Japanese. In the present emergency, we must resolutely fight to the end. In this effort Zen faith and practice are of great importance. We must practice this Zen *kōan* in order to protect Japan and fulfil our duty to bring prosperity to all of Greater East Asia.[89]

Here Taizen reveals himself to be in complete agreement with the previously introduced authors who regarded the *Field Service Code* as being as applicable to civilians as to the military. We also see that Zen faith and practice were critical to Japan's "certain victory." Yet, what exactly did Taizen expect his civilian readers to do?

> When the invasion comes, all men and women must become soldiers to ward off the enemy. Our slogan must be "one person kills one person," meaning that if one hundred thousand of the enemy come, then we will kill all one hundred thousand, each person killing one. I hear that military practice with bamboo staves has already begun. This is exactly the spirit and practice we need. . . . This is unquestionably the time that all the people of this country must rouse themselves to action. Now is the time to truly face the problem of death.[90]

In this connection, it should be noted that Taizen was not advocating anything more than other leading Zen figures were advocating as well. For example, Sōtō Zen Master Harada Daiun published the following in July 1944 under the title: "Be Prepared, One Hundred Million [Subjects], for Death with Honour!":

> It is necessary for all one hundred million subjects [of the emperor] to be prepared to die with honour.... If you see the enemy you must kill him; you must destroy the false and establish the true – these are the cardinal points of Zen. It is said that if you kill someone it is fitting that you see their blood. It is further said that if you are riding a powerful horse nothing is beyond your reach. Isn't the purpose of the *zazen* we have done in the past to be of assistance in an emergency like this?[91]

That Taizen and Harada's thinking ran exactly parallel to that of Japan's military leaders is revealed by the following entry, made in July 1944, in the then secret *War Journal of Imperial Headquarters:* "We can no longer direct the war with any hope of success. The only course left is for Japan's one hundred million people to sacrifice their lives by charging the enemy to make them lose the will to fight."[92]

Suicidal strikes were, of course, nothing new to the imperial military. As early as May 1944 Japan had employed the tactic of purposely crashing manned aircraft, and later manned underwater torpedoes, into Allied ships, thereby ushering in the era of the infamous *kamikaze* attacks. One of those who rode a torpedo to his death in an attack on Allied ships on 24 July 1945 was a naval ensign by the name of Seki Toyoiki. Shortly before departing on his suicide mission, Seki wrote: "At last I have reached the point where death is unavoidable. Thus I will seek eternal life.... In the Bushido of Japan, nothing is more important than cutting off attachment to life and preparing for death."[93]

These suicide attacks inspired Dr. Masunaga Reihō (1902–81), a Sōtō Zen scholar-priest, to write a series of articles in the Buddhist newspaper, *Chūgai Nippō*, from 25 May to 1 June 1945 entitled: "The Source of the Spirit of the Special Attack Forces." According to Reihō:

> The source of the spirit of the Special Attack Forces lies in the *denial of the individual self* and the rebirth of the soul which takes upon itself the burden of history. From ancient times Zen has described this conversion of mind as the achievement of complete enlightenment [Italics mine].[94]

In a similar vein, Lt. Colonel Inokuchi Rikihei, a staff officer in a Special Attack Force Unit said the following to a postwar American Board of Inquiry on Wartime Bombing: "Originally, the *Kamikaze* Suicide Units were possessed of a *spiritual character.* As far as technical skill was concerned, a member could achieve the aims if he had the skill of an ordinary pilot."[95]

Just how important developing the "spiritual character" of its suicide units was to the Japanese military is demonstrated by the fact that it was common practice to send unit members for training to nearby Zen temples. In his 1983 book *Everything is Emptiness (Issai wa Kū)*, Hirata Seikō (b. 1924), current head of the Tenryūji branch of the Rinzai Zen sect, provided the following account:

> At the time, Tenryūji, too, had its share of those who had to hurl themselves into enemy ships in a month's time. They practiced meditation with the novice monks and chose a posthumous Buddhist name *(kaimyō)* for themselves. Then, leaving behind a mortuary tablet with their name engraved upon it, they plunged to their deaths. Lots of these mortuary tablets remain at Tenryūji today.

And what were unit members taught while training at Tenryūji? Seikō continued:

> You must not think that the gracious life of the Buddha is a cycle of living and then dying. That is to say, "life-and-death" is not a question of water in a river flowing from higher to lower. It is not a question of something alive turning into something dead. The gracious life of the Buddha knows neither life nor death; it is only a matter of [the unity of] life-and-death.[96]

If suicide unit members received training and instruction of this kind at Zen temples, it is important to remember that from 1943, if not before, all of the Japanese people were exhorted to demonstrate the same suicidal "spiritual character" that the young members of the Special Attack (i.e. *Kamikaze*) Forces possessed and, in fact, that the entire Japanese military had always been expected to possess. In this effort, Zen leaders and the Buddhist clergy as a whole played a leading role, for the time was fast approaching when literally the entire Japanese nation was expected to find a "place to die."

Decisive battle

The anticipated Allied invasion of Japan was referred to in Japanese as *hondo kessen* or the "decisive battle for the mainland." As seen above, preparations, both practical and "spiritual," had already begun in 1943. These preparations involved the mobilization of virtually the entire adult population and led, in early 1945, to the formation of civilian militia units composed of all males from the ages of fifteen to sixty and females from the ages of seventeen to forty-five. The "weapons" supplied to these units often consisted of no more than sharpened bamboo spears or even merely awls. One mobilized high school girl, Kasai Yukiko, was given an awl and told: "Killing even just one American soldier will do. You must prepare to use the awls for self-defense. You must aim at the enemy's abdomen."[97]

In his 1953 book, *The Psychology of the Japanese (Nihonjin no Shinri)*, Minami Hiroshi explained the rationale behind these preparations as follows:

When defeat drew near, the shocking idea of complete annihilation resting upon "spirit as supreme" (*seishin-shugi*) was discussed among the leaders of the arm for the defense of Japan proper, who took a crushing defeat of all the armies and *the sacrifice of a whole people* for granted – "Even if we were to be wiped out on each battlefield, a 'spiritual charge' would be further carried out on a nationwide scale." In this logic of a "spiritual charge," a bamboo spear resistance could never be considered reckless [Italics mine].[98]

Saipan

Just how seriously Japanese civilians took these preparations was first demonstrated at the time of the Allied invasion of the strategically important island of Saipan in the Marianas on 15 June 1944. Saipan was defended by nearly 30,000 Japanese troops of whom 97 per cent had fought to the death by 9 July, leaving only 921 survivors. This was, incidentally, very similar to the earlier 98.8 per cent Japanese casualty rate at Attu in the Aleutians, the 99.7 per cent casualty rate at Tarawa in the Gilbert Islands, and the 98.5 per cent casualty rate at Roi-Namur in the Marshalls.

What made Saipan different from previous battles was the significant population of Japanese civilians living there, numbering at least 20,000. Of this number upwards of 1,000 chose suicide over surrender. In his book *Downfall*, Richard Frank described what happened at Marpi Point on 11 July 1944, two days after the fighting officially ended:

> Hundreds of civilians spurned invitations to surrender from Marines and even pleas from fellow Japanese, who described the good treatment they experienced by surrendering. In a carnival of death that shocked even battle-hardened Marines, whole families waded into the sea to drown together or huddled to blow themselves up with grenades; parents tossed their children off cliffs before leaping to join them in death.[99]

Those civilians who did survive talked of having received lectures on the spirit of the *Field Service Code* as part of the Japanese garrison's preparation for the Allied invasion.

Okinawa

What transpired on Saipan was, at least in terms of scale, only a dress rehearsal for the invasion of Okinawa starting 26 March 1945. There the Allies faced a total Japanese force in excess of 100,000 men of whom 76,000 were trained soldiers and the remainder poorly-trained and armed Okinawan militia units. Utilizing tunnels and caves in the southern part of the island, the Japanese military fought a war of attrition in an attempt to forestall the Allied invasion of the mainland for as long as possible. By late June, however, organized resistance came to an end leaving more than 92,000 dead. Total US casualties, including both dead and wounded, came to 72,358 on Okinawa proper, not to mention additional losses on offshore Allied ships subjected to wave after wave of suicidal *kamikaze* attacks. In addition, somewhere between 62,000 to as many as 150,000 Okinawan civilians perished.[100]

Historian, and postwar Okinawa prefectural governor (1990–98), Ōta Masahide points out that the *Field Service Code* even influenced the strategy selected for the island's defense. This was because, tactically speaking, it would have made sense to place at least some troops in defensive positions in the mountainous region in the north. The military strategist for the defending Japanese 32nd Army, Colonel Yahara Hiromichi, later admitted that he would have had no hesitation in doing so had the Code "not contained the article on death in battle as honourable and life after defeat as shameful."[101]

Ōta went on to note it was the samurai tradition that prevented military leaders from making rational decisions. In his eyes, "the price that Okinawan civilians were forced to pay for the sake of 'samurai honour' was simply too great."[102] Ōta's reference to civilians comes from the fact that many Okinawans were still hoping to be *protected* by the Japanese military. Military leaders, on the other hand, not only demanded the deaths of their military subordinates but Okinawan civilians as well, ordering both groups to commit suicide rather than surrender. "In short, the civilians (the government and the people) were regarded as partners of the military, destined to carry out a final 'honourable suicide' (*gyokusai*) and were never regarded as subjects of military protection."[103]

Allied attitudes

Based on what happened on both Saipan and Okinawa, as well as what the Allies knew of the ongoing formation of civilian militia on Japan's main islands, the US Joint Chiefs of Staff published, on 25 May 1945, the outline of a plan to invade Japan, tentatively scheduled to begin on 1 November 1945. One vital assumption of the plan read as follows: "The enemy will continue the war to the utmost extent of their capabilities, and the invaders will confront not only Japan's armed forces but also a fanatically hostile population."[104] By 21 July 1945, one 5th Air Force intelligence officer, cognizant of Japan's publicly broadcast word to mobilize the entire population, declared: "The entire population of Japan is a proper Military Target.... THERE ARE NO CIVILIANS IN JAPAN."[105]

It was exactly this massive military mobilization that led historian Herbert Bix to declare: "... the whole nation had become enveloped in the imagery of national salvation through mass suicide."[106] Writing more concretely, military historian Richard Frank notes:

By mustering millions of erstwhile civilians into the area swept by bombs, artillery, and small-arms fire, Japan's military masters willfully consigned hundreds of thousands of their countrymen to death. Moreover, by deliberately eliminating any distinction between combatants and non-combatants, they would compel Americans to treat all Japanese as combatants or fail to do so at their peril. It was a recipe for extinction.[107]

If there is the slightest doubt that this suicidal mobilization of the entire Japanese people was exactly what the Japanese military had in mind, it is dispelled by the carefully researched 1995 book, *The Decisive Battle for the Mainland – It Was No Phantom* (*Hondo Kessen – Maboroshi dewa nakatta*). The book's Japanese authors pointed out that the civilian militia units, known in Japanese as *giyūhei* (loyal and courageous soldiers), were organized on a national scale in June 1945. Two months earlier, imperial military headquarters issued orders that all units involved in the defense of the mainland were forbidden to retreat, no matter what the circumstances. Similarly, not only was it forbidden to send injured soldiers to the rear for medical treatment, all medical treatment was to be held in abeyance for as long as the fighting continued.

In light of these factors, not to mention the lack of weapons, training, etc. the authors identified the military's plan as a "structure for the annihilation of the Japanese people" (*kokumin mina-goroshi no taisei*).[108] Yet, they did note that one group would have definitely survived the Allied invasion, no matter how severe. This group was the emperor and his immediate entourage together with the military staff of the Imperial headquarters. Their survival was guaranteed because of a massive series of bombproof tunnels that had been built for them in mountainous Nagano Prefecture using the forced labour of some 6–7,000 Koreans, an unknown number of whom died in the process.

The existence of these tunnels, ready for occupancy from June 1945, led Ohinata Etsuo, one of the book's authors, to comment that from its very inception the plan to relocate Imperial military headquarters to Matsushiro in Nagano Prefecture contained within it the egoism of the political elite albeit under the guise of a "national objective." This small group was "willing to sacrifice the overwhelming majority of the Japanese people to achieve their goals."[109] In the tunnels of Nagano Prefecture, had they been used, there would have been no "selflessness."

On 11 August 1945, only four days before the emperor officially announced Japan's surrender, and after the atomic bombing of both Hiroshima and Nagasaki, Japanese newspapers carried the following statement by Army Minister Anami Korechika (1887–1945): "Even though we may have to eat grass, swallow dirt, and lie in the fields, we shall fight on to the bitter end, ever firm in our faith that *we shall find life in death*. [Italics mine].[110] Literally to the last few days of what had been fourteen years of nearly constant warfare for Japan (1931–45), the Zen identification of life and death found expression at the highest levels of the Japanese military.

It was this unwavering attitude on the part of Japan's military leaders that led Rinzai Zen Master Nakajima Genjō, introduced in chapter 1, to confide the following during a second visit I paid to his temple in January 2000: "The atomic bombs were a good thing. Imperial military headquarters would never have ended the war without them." While this statement is only speculation on the part of a naval petty officer, Genjō was certainly better qualified than most to understand exactly what the Zen-inspired Japanese military spirit was all about, and what it would take to stop it.

Equally important, there is ample testimony from civilians that they, too, were prepared to follow the military into death. One example is provided by Kurosawa Akira, then a young propaganda filmmaker who would become one of Japan's best known directors in the postwar era. Kurosawa wrote that had the emperor so directed:

[Japanese] people probably would have done as they were told, and died. And probably I would have done likewise. The Japanese see self-assertion as immoral and self-sacrifice as the sensible course to take in life. We were accustomed to this teaching and had never thought to question it.[111]

In light of everything we have seen above, it is difficult to deny the truth of Genjō and Kurosawa's assertions.[112]

Plate 8 Female student corps at Meiji University undergoing bayonet training. Courtesy Mainichi Shimbun-sha.

Conclusion

At this point the question must be raised as to the *moral responsibility* of Japanese Zen leaders for what actually occurred and what likely would have occurred if "technology," in the form of two atomic bombs, had not altered the course of history.

To answer this, let us look at what appears on the surface to be a totally different phenomenon – the practice on death row in American prisons for a guard to call out: "Dead man walking!" when condemned prisoners make their last walk down the corridor to the execution chamber. Based on the evidence presented above, it is clear that Japan's wartime Zen leaders did everything in their power to turn not only Japanese soldiers, but nearly the entire civilian population, into a mass collection of "walking dead." They did so by interpreting the Buddhist doctrine of the non-existence of the self, coupled with the oneness of life and death, in such a way as to produce an unquestioning willingness to die on behalf of the emperor and the state.

In infusing the suicidal Japanese military spirit, especially when extended to civilians, with the power of religious belief, Japan's wartime Zen leaders revealed themselves to be *thoroughly and completely morally bankrupt.* That the Allied invasion never took place, and therefore the mass "spiritual charges" never occurred, does not fundamentally alter the question of moral responsibility, for Zen leaders did everything they could to ensure a suicidal response on the part of both the military and most especially the civilian population.

To be sure, Japan's political and military leaders bear an even greater moral responsibility for having initiated and prosecuted the war in the first place. Further, advocates of State Shinto also share responsibility for having promoted national chauvinism and the worship of a divine emperor as a descendant of the Sun Goddess. This said, it must not be forgotten that Japanese Zen had long since embraced both Shinto national chauvinism and Confucian social ethics, especially the latter's insistence on loyalty to one's superiors within a social hierarchy. Furthermore, none of these other groups ever claimed that what they said or did represented the "true Buddha Dharma."

D. T. Suzuki

For those readers who suspect that I may have exaggerated the ideological role played by Zen within Japanese militarism, and/or that my condemnation of Zen's wartime conduct is too severe, I note, somewhat ironically, that my comments are supported by no less a figure than D. T. Suzuki. In 1946 Suzuki wrote a short yet lucid essay entitled "Reform of the Zen World" (*Zenkai Sasshin*) in which he claimed that because "today's Zen priests lack intelligence," he wanted "to increasingly develop their power to think about things independently."[113]

As to why such reform was necessary, Suzuki pointed to the wartime words and deeds of Zen leaders who, he claimed, justified their war support as follows:

It will be sufficient if we [Zen priests] simply follow the dictates of our political leaders, for in doing so we will be aiding Japan. If we are told to say that a horse is a deer, then all we need say is, "Fine, a horse is a deer," for in that way we will be able to continue eating. It's not the responsibility of Zen priests to comment about what's going on in the world."[114]

Suzuki was, of course, highly critical of the above rationalization. He went so far as to assert that those Zen priests who claimed to be enlightened, yet who were unable to think for themselves, "should have their enlightenment taken to the middle of the Pacific ocean and sent straight to the bottom!" But what really upset Suzuki was the call by Zen leaders for what amounted to national suicide:

It was they [i.e. Zen leaders] who went around urging the people to face tanks with bamboo spears. Claiming to speak the truth, they even went so far as to say that once the Americans landed, every woman would be dishonoured and every man castrated. As a result I'm told that a large number of women fled to the countryside.

It is of course possible to defend these Zen leaders using the excuse that they spread their tales as a result of having been ordered to say that a horse is a deer. But should not Zen priests like these be ousted from Zen circles? Should we not be astounded by the level of intelligence displayed by these Zen priests who claimed to be specialists in "enlightenment"?[115]

No doubt many readers, myself included, would share Suzuki's dismay, if not anger, at the profound ignorance displayed by wartime Zen leaders. Yet, as revealed earlier in this chapter, it was Suzuki who wrote in 1942 that Japan's problems could be solved instantly if only all social classes would simply embrace a pure warrior spirit. While Suzuki's wartime writings were notably free of the demagogic emperor-worship of his contemporaries, it was nevertheless the Zen view of life and death he promoted that served as a foundational element of the Japanese military spirit. As a *postwar* advocate of Zen "reform," someone should have reminded Suzuki of the old adage, "Physician heal thyself!"

War atrocities

Finally, the question must at least be raised as to a possible relationship between the Japanese military's Zen-inspired embrace of death and the barbarity and cruelty visited on Japan's prisoners of war. To give but one example, of the 254,473 US and UK prisoners reported captured by Germany and Italy together, only 4 per cent (9,348) died in the hands of their captors. This compares with 27 per cent of Japan's Anglo-American POWs (35,756 of 132,134) who did not survive.[116] Given figures like these, the question must be asked as to whether Japanese soldiers, having resigned themselves to their own deaths, could respect or care about the lives of Allied POWs who wanted to live?

Gavan Daws addressed this question in his 1994 book, *Prisoners of the Japanese.* After interviewing hundreds of former Allied POWs, Daws came to the following conclusion: "In the eyes of the Japanese, white men who allowed themselves to be captured in war were despicable. They deserved to die."[117] Given the well-documented brutality of Japanese troops directed toward other Asian soldiers, especially Chinese, Daws was mistaken in having singled out "white men" only. Japanese contempt and maltreatment of prisoners was not so much a question of skin colour as it was the latters' failure to have died "honourably" on the battlefield, just as they themselves were prepared to do.

In the postwar era, a number of former imperial soldiers, especially in the lower ranks, have come forward to reveal that they never "joyfully" embraced death in the first place. Instead, they were coerced, often brutally so, into accepting death by their military superiors. Private First Class Matsubara Kazuo, for example, was one of the few survivors of the 1942–3 battle for Guadalcanal. In a postwar interview, Matsubara explained that he had never expected to return alive from military service, "all I wanted was to go into battle with a full stomach and die!"[118]

More importantly, in explaining why he and his fellow soldiers raped and pillaged in Nanjing, Azuma Shirō, the Japanese soldier first introduced in chapter 1, noted that the highest honour an imperial soldier could achieve was to come home dead. That is to say, dying for the emperor was a soldier's greatest glory while being taken prisoner alive was his greatest shame. Azuma continued: "*If my life was not important*, an enemy's life became inevitably *much less important*. . . . This philosophy led us to look down on the enemy and eventually to the mass murder and ill treatment of captives [Italics mine].[119]

No doubt there were many other Japanese soldiers like Matsubara and Azuma, especially as training and morale deteriorated in the latter stages of the war. Given this, it is hardly surprising (though none the less tragic) that such soldiers would rape and murder those weaker than themselves, utterly convinced their own turn would come soon. There is a crude yet accurate Anglo-Saxon aphorism that states: "Shit rolls down hill." To this might well be added: ". . . and so does the Zen view of life and death as expounded by Japan's wartime Zen leaders." Is this not the very stuff out of which "fanaticism" is made?

Buddhist collaboration with Japanese militarism was, of course, far broader and deeper than merely the Zen school. As Part II will reveal, while Zen may have been the leading player in this collaboration, especially in having promoted a selfless resignation to death, it had no shortage of company among its fellow Buddhists.

Part II

8

BUDDHIST WAR BEREAVEMENT

From a theoretical or doctrinal point of view, Buddhist bereavement for the families of fallen soldiers is an oxymoron. That is to say, Buddhist ethical values are based on universal love and compassion for *all* living beings. No fewer than three categories of the Noble Eightfold Path, namely Right Speech, Right Action and Right Livelihood, give concrete expression to those values by proscribing the types of action from which all wars are born.

Moreover, when it comes to the specific precepts Buddhists are expected to follow in their daily lives, the very first of them is the prohibition against killing. This precept applies to *all* Buddhists, lay or cleric, and regardless of sectarian affiliation. The Mahāyāna school in particular has long made non-killing a critical element of the conduct expected of its ideal – the self-sacrificing bodhisattva. Buddhist scholar Har Dayal described the traditional Indian view of a bodhisattva as follows:

> A bodhisattva does not use weapons of any kind. He does not hate any being, and cannot kill a living creature even in thought. He understands that all things originate in causes, and cultivates pity and compassion.... He also condemns and shuns the barbarous custom of war among states and kings of the world. War has its origin in hatred, avarice, cruelty and selfishness, and the glory of victorious kings is stained with blood. It is better for a king to abdicate than to wage war.[1]

If the meaning of these words is taken at face value, there can be no doubt that the Zen and other Buddhist leaders introduced in this book were in grievous breach of the bodhisattva ideal. Yet, the case is not as simple as it might seem, for Dayal goes on to point out: "[Mahāyānists] have rather stultified themselves by teaching the strange doctrine that a bodhisattva may violate any or all of the precepts... if he is moved by compassion for others. This view has led to much subtle casuistry."[2]

The Buddhist leaders and scholars introduced below were firmly convinced that their words and actions flowed from their deep compassion for those of their fellow citizens who had lost their loved ones on the battlefield. What is more debatable, however, is just how "subtle" the casuistry they displayed was. This question, however, is best left for the reader to decide.

The historical reality is that, its bodhisattva ideal notwithstanding, the Mahāyāna school has often found itself deeply and directly involved in the wars fought by its secular rulers. While it is beyond the scope of this book to examine this development in detail, suffice it to say that Buddhist bereavement in modern Japan was not some uniquely Japanese aberration or invention, but one that had a long history within the Buddhist tradition of both pre-modern Japan and other Asian countries. What follows is therefore more in the nature of a classic case study of the way in which certain Buddhist doctrines were recast so as to offer consolation to the bereaved families of soldiers who had fallen on Japan's modern battlefields.

Early attempts

In post-Meiji Japan, Buddhist chaplains accompanied troops to the battlefield as early as the Sino-Japanese war of 1894–5. Their job was not only to give "morale-building" talks to the soldiers, but to conduct funerals for those who fell in battle as well as notify the relatives of the deceased in Japan itself. Even in times of peace, the need for chaplains was recognized, with the Nishi (West) Honganji branch of the True Pure Land sect (Jōdo-Shinshū), for example, despatching forty-six priests to more than forty military bases throughout Japan as early as 1902.[3]

In the same year Nishi Honganji produced a booklet entitled *Bushidō* as part of a series called "Lectures on Spirit" (Seishin Kōwa). The connection between the two events is clear in that it was Ōtani Kōen (1850–1903), an aristocrat and the branch's administrative head, who both despatched the military chaplains and contributed a foreword to the booklet. Kōen explained that the booklet's purpose was "to clarify the spirit of military evangelization."[4]

As its title suggests, Nishi Honganji intended this booklet to provide the doctrinal basis for its outreach to the military. That this outreach had a broader focus than the soldiers themselves can be seen from the inclusion of a concluding chapter entitled "To the Parents and Family of Military Men." Although in 1902 Japan was at peace, there was an increasing awareness of the possibility of war with Russia. Thus, sectarian leaders like Kōen realized that soldiers' parents and family members would be concerned that their loved ones might die in battle. However, before pursuing this issue further, let us first see how this branch of the True Pure Land sect defined itself so as to be relevant to the military profession.

War-related doctrines

The booklet's author was Satō Gan'ei (1847–1905), a military chaplain as well as clerical head of a Nishi Honganji-affiliated laymen's association known as the Yuima-kai (Skt. Vimalakîrti). The military character of this association is clear in that three high-ranking Imperial Army officers were members, each contributing a calligraphic endorsement to the booklet. One of the three, Lt. General Ōshima Ken'ichi (1858–1947), later served as Minister of War in two cabinets and Privy Counselor during the Asia-Pacific War.

In his introduction, Gan'ei explained that the purpose of religion in Japan was "to be an instrument of the state and an instrument of the Imperial Household." More specifically, the government had granted Buddhism permission to propagate itself in order "to ensure that citizens fulfill their duties [to the state] while at the same time preserving social order and stability." Gan'ei claimed that it was religionists like himself who had been charged with making sure this important task was accomplished.[5]

Yet, what did all this have to do with the military? In a section entitled "The Way of the Martial Arts and the Way of the Buddha," Gan'ei explained:

> The bodhisattva of the Way of the Buddha is the warrior of the Way of the martial arts; the warrior of the Way of the martial arts is the bodhisattva of the Way of the Buddha. This is due to a mysterious convergence between bodhisattva and warrior. That is to say, the warrior in the Way of the martial arts is made knowledgeable of life and death through duty and loyalty, while the bodhisattva in the Way of the Buddha is able to destroy evil, know the future, and exist freely within the realm of life and death. Therefore, if a warrior believes in the Way of the Buddha, he will be doubly advantaged, with the courage derived from his sense of loyalty and duty further strengthened even as he loses his fear of death.[6]

These words may surprise some readers in that they would seem more appropriate coming from the mouth of a Zen master. After all, wasn't it Zen, not the True Pure Land sect, that had nurtured the warrior spirit over the centuries?

Gan'ei was in fact quite aware of this contradiction and readily admitted that Zen had a special relationship to the warrior class, noting that such Zen luminaries as Eisai, Dōgen and Hakuin had all contributed to this relationship. He further acknowledged that many medieval warriors had ridden into battle holding a banner of the Nichiren sect inscribed with the words "*Namu Myōhō Renge-kyō* (Homage to the *Lotus Sūtra*). The numbers of these Nichiren warriors, however, "were never a match for those affiliated with the Zen sect."[7]

Gan'ei emphasized that despite the popularity of Zen among the warrior class, many medieval warriors, including the great seventeenth-century unifier of Japan, Tokugawa Ieyasu (1542–1616), had been Pure Land adherents. For him it was not a question of 'either-or' but 'both-and.' Gan'ei explained this seeming paradox as follows:

> I think that for military men of today who wish to calm their minds ... only the Zen and True Pure Land sects can meet their needs. In looking at these two sects, when asked if it isn't best to limit oneself to one or the other of

them, I would say that is true. This said, for those persons who are straightforward, full of life and refined, Zen is best. On the other hand, for those who take things one step at a time and harbour a great deal of ambition, then the True Pure Land sect is best.

Although both of these sects have a practical focus, the Zen sect is on the extreme end of relying on one's own power [to realize enlightenment] while the True Pure Land sect is on the extreme end of relying on another's power [i.e. Amitābha Buddha]. These two teachings appear to be exact opposites, but the strange thing is that these two extremes are actually identical with one another.[8]

For Gan'ei, the critical feature of both sects is their "practical" (*jissai-teki*) nature. In addition, he noted that both of them had the ability to "conform to the times." But what exactly was it about the True Pure Land sect that made it so practical? How did faith in Amitābha Buddha translate into martial prowess on the battlefield? Gan'ei explained:

By virtue of believing in the compassion of the Buddha, your person has already become one that will inevitably realize Buddhahood in the future. With both body and mind residing peacefully in the precious mind of the Tathāgata [Buddha], your person as a bodhisattva lacks for nothing in its quest to realize Buddhahood; for everything you do becomes the practice of a bodhisattva.

As a living bodhisattva filled with the Buddha's compassion, you pitch camp; take up a sword overflowing with compassion in your compassionate hand; and together with Amitābha Buddha, thrust your sword home, dispatching both friend and foe to the Pure Land in the West.[9]

Gan'ei concluded the chapter by offering his military readers this parting advice:

Soldiers, first find a spiritual home in the great matter of life and death. Then, when facing battle, realize that yours is the religious practice of a bodhisattva. In so doing you will naturally come to realize the meaning of the unity of the Way of the Buddha and the Way of the martial arts.[10]

With this background in mind, let us next turn to the chief focus of this chapter – the manner in which Buddhist doctrine was made relevant to soldiers' families, especially to the war bereaved.

Family members

Overall, it must be said that Gan'ei's comments directed toward soldiers' families were somewhat superficial in nature, more in the nature of an afterthought as revealed in their shortness (eleven pages) as well as their location at the booklet's very end. This is understandable in that, with Japan at peace, the possibility of death in battle was more theoretical than real though this would soon change with the outbreak of the Russo-Japanese War in 1904. In any event, Gan'ei's comments marked an early attempt to find Buddhist doctrines that would console the living as well as the dead in the coming age of total war.

Unsurprisingly, the primary Buddhist doctrine Gan'ei invoked was that of karma. Karma, of course, is the moral law of causality which states that one's thoughts, words and actions have consequences that affect the doer, for better or worse, in both this life and future lives. Gan'ei explained the military relevance of this doctrine as follows:

> Everything depends on karma. There are those who, victorious in battle, return home strong and fit only to die soon afterwards. On the other hand, there are those who are scheduled to enter the military yet die before they do so. If it is their karmic destiny, bullets will not strike them, and they will not die. Conversely, should it be their karmic destiny, then even if they are not in the military, they may still die from gunfire. Therefore there is definitely no point in worrying about this. Or expressed differently, even if you do worry about it, nothing will change.[11]

As the preceding quotation reveals, there can be no question here of soldiers dying because of mistaken decisions made by their political or military leader(s). As Gan'ei tirelessly pointed out, the Imperial military was under the direct control of its commander-in-chief, His Majesty, the Emperor, whose "bountiful benevolence cannot fail but bring tears of gratitude to the eyes of all parents and family members."[12] Thus, a soldier's death is attributable solely to the past karma of that particular soldier. In short, he had it coming.

If this explanation seems rather harsh to western ears, it should be noted that Buddhist compassion also had its role to play in allaying family fears. The concern here, however, was not so much the possibility of dying on the battlefield as it was the possible mistreatment of soldiers, especially recruits, within the Japanese military itself. Gan'ei maintained that there was no longer anything to worry about, for as he explained:

> The existence of some cruel elements in the military is a thing of the past. The belief then was that if you kicked [a soldier] his slovenliness would be cured; or if you struck him, his willfulness would disappear. Those soldiers who were unable to endure this rough treatment fled or hid themselves, ending up as deserters. For some, the pain was so great that they became dazed and lost control of themselves.
>
> Today, however, in step with pedagogical progress, educational methods have been thoroughly revamped. We have reached a point where the treatment of soldiers may be thought of as being even too compassionate.[13]

In reading of an Imperial military that was "even too compassionate," readers of *Zen at War* may recall the words of Sōtō scholar-priest Kurebayashi Kōdō (1893–1988) who in 1937 claimed: "Wherever the Imperial military advances there is only charity and love.... In other words, brutality itself no longer exists in the officers and men of the Imperial military who have been schooled in the spirit of Buddhism."[14]

Gan'ei, endeavouring to convince the families of soldiers that their loved ones were safe, would surely have welcomed Kōdō's comments. How could a family member possibly object to a loved one serving in a military engulfed by compassion; where a soldier's life or death was, thanks to the doctrine of karma, solely the just dessert of that soldier's past deeds?

Shaku Sōen

During the subsequent Russo-Japanese War of 1904–5 we also find Zen voices seeking to assuage the grief of those left behind. One of these voices belonged to Rinzai Zen Master Shaku Sōen, previously introduced as the abbot of Kamakura's Engakuji monastery and D. T. Suzuki's master. Sōen was better acquainted with the realities of war than most; for he had personally gone to the battlefield as a chaplain attached to the headquarters of the 1st Army Division commanded by His Imperial Highness Prince (and General) Fushiminomiya Sadanaru (1858–1925). In a book published in 1906 entitled *Sermons of a Buddhist Abbot*, Sōen explained his motivation for having become a chaplain as follows:

> I wished to have my faith tested by going through the greatest horrors of life, but I also wished to inspire, if I could, our valiant soldiers with the ennobling thoughts of the Buddha, so as to enable them to die on the battlefield with the confidence that the task in which they are engaged is great and noble. I wished to convince them of the truths that this war is not a mere slaughter of their fellow-beings, but that they are combating an evil, and that, at the same time, corporeal annihilation really means a rebirth of [the] soul, not in heaven, indeed, but here among ourselves.[15]

While these words were clearly meant for soldiers, not their families, we find here yet another invocation of karma to assuage the fear of death. Sōen found a positive element in this doctrine that Gan'ei had overlooked, i.e. the certainty that death would lead to subsequent rebirth in human form, not as punishment for past misconduct, but as a reward for the soldier's sacrifice in combating evil. Sōen explained the significance of this process as follows:

> There is but one great spirit and we individuals are its temporal manifestations. We are eternal when we do the will of the great spirit; we are doomed when we protest against it in our egotism and ignorance. We obey, and we live. We defy, and we are thrown into the fire that quencheth

not. Our bodily existences are like the sheaths of the bamboo sprout. For the growth of the plant it is necessary to cast off one sheath after another. It is not that the body-sheath is negligible, but that the spirit-plant is more essential and its wholesome growth of paramount importance. Let us, therefore, not absolutely cling to the bodily existence, but when necessary, sacrifice it for a better thing. For this is the way in which the spirituality of our being asserts itself.[16]

In promising soldiers the possibility of life "eternal," Sōen sounds almost Christian in his approach. However, Sōen did not place the war dead in a Christian heaven; but asserted, true to the doctrine of karma, that "what we actually see around us is that the departed spirits are abiding right among ourselves."[17] Needless to say, this was an attractive possibility not only to soldiers facing death on the battlefield but to their family members as well. Yet, Sōen was clearly not overly concerned about consoling the war bereaved, for he concludes his discussion by noting:

As for us who are left behind, no superfluous words are in place, only we must not disgrace the honor and spirit of the dead who have solemnly bequeathed to us their work to perfect. Mere lamentation not only bears no fruit, it is a product of egoism, and has to be shunned by every enlightened mind and heart.[18]

In describing lamentation at the time of death of a loved one as "a product of egoism," Sōen is taking an impeccably Buddhist position. Yet, one cannot help but wonder if he would really have dared direct those remarks to the families of soldiers who had just received notification of their loved one's death. After all, as Sōen would be the first to admit, not all Japanese were possessed of an "enlightened mind and heart." Who would address the spiritual needs of the "unenlightened"?

Yamada Reirin

In Sōtō Zen scholar-priest Yamada Reirin (1889–1979), we find a somewhat "softer" Zen voice addressing the question of war bereavement. In postwar years, Reirin served as the abbot of Zenshūji temple in Los Angeles, president of Komazawa University, and the seventy-fifth head of Eiheiji monastery. Reirin's wartime comments are included in a 1942 book entitled *Evening Talks on Zen Studies* (*Zengaku Yawa*). Together with his praise for the imperial military's "wonderful fruits of battle," Reirin, like both Gan'ei and Sōen before him, found the key to Buddhist consolation in the doctrine of karma.

As the following passage reveals, Reirin sought to offer karmic hope not so much to soldiers on the battlefield as to the families they left behind:

The true form of the heroic spirits [of the dead] is the good karmic power that has resulted from their loyalty, bravery, and nobility of character. This will never perish. . . . The body and mind produced by this karmic power cannot be other than what has existed up to the present. . . . The loyal, brave, noble, and heroic spirits of those officers and men who have died shouting, "May the emperor live for ten thousand years!" will be reborn right here in this country. It is only natural that this should occur.[19]

Whereas Sōen had gone to the battlefield to inspire soldiers to willingly sacrifice their lives in a cause that was "great and noble," Reirin, writing for a home audience, hoped to console grieving family members with the thought that every baby born in Japan was potentially their lost loved one. He did deny, however, that the bereaved would ever recognize which particular child was theirs. Nevertheless, there could be no doubt that the "good karmic power" (zengōriki) the heroic spirit had acquired through his death on the battlefield would result in his rebirth in Japan. That much was "absolutely certain" (hitsujō). Given this, what need was there for grief?

Tomomatsu Entai

Perhaps the most ambitious Buddhist attempt to console grieving survivors was provided by Tomomatsu Entai, the Pure Land sect scholar-priest whose views on life and death were previously introduced in chapter 7. Entai's comments are contained in an 82-page booklet published on 25 December 1941, only days after Japan's attack on Pearl Harbour. Entitled A Reader for Bereaved Families (Izoku Tokuhon), the booklet was published by the army's "Military Relief Department" (Juppei-bu).

The Buddhist influence on the booklet is clear even from its subtitle: "Turning Illusion into Enlightenment (Tenmei Kaigo). Section headings reveal a similar influence, e.g. "Turning the Mind," "Nirvāṇa," and, of course, "Karma." This does not mean, however, there was no Shinto influence, for according to Entai: "Following their death in battle, your children or husbands are no longer ordinary human beings but have, at a single bound, become [Shinto] gods and Buddhas . . ."[20] Similarly, there were the inevitable references to Japan's divine emperor.

In employing Buddhist terminology, Entai did not necessarily limit himself to the traditional meaning of these terms. One of the best examples of this was his use of the Zen-related term tenshin (lit. turning the mind). As noted above, this was also the title of one of the booklet's sections. The initial aim of this section was to help the war bereaved overcome their grief by recognizing its futility, i.e. no amount of crying would bring their loved ones back. Once the war bereaved realized this, Entai explained what happened next as follows:

At this point you will come to understand that it was you yourself who chose to make your life gloomy. The term tenshin is definitely not limited to what Zen practitioners so stringently refer to as "enlightenment" (*satori*). Instead it means that you are capable of returning to your natural self; capable of discarding your former ill-natured self and need no longer needlessly worry about the future. Becoming aware of your true self is what *tenshin* really means. That is to say, it is no more than simple "self-discovery"; no more than discovering your true self; no more than becoming normal; no more than becoming ordinary; no more than returning to your original self.[21]

Needless to say, from a traditional Buddhist point of view, returning to one's original self in the absence of an enlightenment experience is to return to the illusory self, not one's "true self." For Entai, however, this distinction was of little or no importance, for his goal was to get the war bereaved back to normality whether enlightened or not. It is interesting to note, however, that Entai did not entirely dismiss the idea of enlightenment as a goal toward which the war bereaved should be striving, at least in the long run. In fact, Entai believed that the war bereaved were, thanks to their bereavement, in a better position than most to realize enlightenment.

In a section entitled "Seeking Solitude," Entai explained that there comes a time in the grieving process where the bereaved simply wish to be left alone, even from close relatives and friends. This, Entai asserted, was "the first step on the road toward enlightenment."[22] As to why this was so, Entai called on no less a personage than Śākyamuni Buddha for an explanation:

> Buddhism's founder, Śākyamuni, repeatedly emphasized the virtue of the "world of solitude." Human beings must of necessity be alone with themselves. One day, Śākyamuni emphasized to his disciples: "No two of you should take the same road." This means that if, little by little, you follow a particular path, you will find that the road will open up before you as you proceed.
>
> The genuine article is never to be found residing in "a mind that depends on others." The bereaved will never be saved as long as they take too strong an interest in the outside world, thinking "I wonder if someone is going to come to visit me." Instead, you must realize that in the final analysis you are on your own.... You must become a light unto yourself.[23]

In admonishing the bereaved to become "a light unto yourself," Entai is once again impeccably Buddhist. The Pali *Maha-parinibbana Sutta* (Skt. sūtra) records Śākyamuni Buddha as having said the following to Ananda, one of his chief disciples, shortly before his death: "Therefore, Ananda, you must all be lamps unto yourselves. You must rely on yourselves and on no one else. You must make the Dharma your light and your support and rely on nothing else."[24]

The significance Entai gave to Śākyamuni's admonition to his disciples to take separate roads, however, cannot be upheld: the reason Śākyamuni directed his disciples to do this was to ensure that the Dharma was spread far and wide during India's dry season. It was not meant as a directive to seek solitude.[25] Entai, however, was ever ready to sacrifice context in his ongoing quest to comfort the bereaved by attributing spiritual significance to death on the battlefield.

Persimmons

In addition to invoking Buddha Śākyamuni, Entai was quite capable of calling on his own experiences to promote his didactic goals. One such experience involved three old persimmon trees on the grounds of Hōzenji temple where Entai spent his youth. Old though they were, these trees were particularly fruitful, and Entai always eagerly awaited the coming of fall when they would ripen and turn sweet.

Nevertheless, Entai was puzzled by one fact. As he cleaned the temple garden every day, he always found a number of small, unripe persimmons laying on the ground. "What a waste!" he thought. Yet, by the end of October he noted that every branch would have two or three bright red pieces of fruit left hanging from it. Given the weight of the fruit he realized that had all the fruit come to maturity the tree's branches would have snapped under the weight and none of the fruit would have ripened. "The persimmons that had fallen from the tree had, through their very act of falling, accomplished their purpose. By negating themselves they had preserved the tree and allowed the remaining persimmons to ripen."[26]

And what was the connection of fallen persimmons to the war bereaved? No doubt the reader can already guess the connection, but this is how Entai explained it:

> It is thanks to those who have fallen in battle that Japan is secure, making it possible for our young men to return safely.... The war bereaved have a heavy burden to bear; they have sacrificed a great deal. That is fine, for in so doing they have brought happiness to many. If through their suffering, they are able to bring happiness to even one more household, what could be more gratifying? This magnanimous spirit is what is meant by the mind of a bodhisattva.
>
> The fallen persimmon already lies on the broad earth. It doesn't seek to have more of its fellow persimmons join it. Rather it merely looks up at the beautiful, ripe fruit still left on the tree branches, delighting in their bright red colour. When you are able to do likewise, then you will have realized a superb enlightenment.[27]

Karma

Like his predecessors, Entai could not avoid a discussion of karma. While he had little to say that was new, he did reinforce conclusions that had a profound effect on the way the Japanese people viewed the war at the time and even today:

There are those who say that it is no more than chance that someone dies on the battlefield, or becomes a widow early in life, or becomes an orphan without having seen their father's face. However, there is not so much as a single bullet flying from the enemy that happens by chance. It is definitely the work of karma, for it is karma that makes it strike home. . . .

Your husband died because of his karma. . . . It was the inevitability of karma that caused your husband's death. In other words, your husband was only meant to live for as long as he did. In those bereaved who have recovered their composure, one sees the realization that their husband's death was due to the consistent working of karma. No one was to blame [for his death] nor was anyone in the wrong. No one bears responsibility for what happened, for it was simply his karma to die.[28]

As early as 1906 D. T. Suzuki, in his English writings, had strongly opposed the idea that Buddhists, especially Zen Buddhists, were infected with any kind of "blind, fatalistic conceptions as is sometimes thought to be a trait peculiar to orientals."[29] Nevertheless, Entai employed his own brand of "oriental fatalism" to cover not only those who had died on the battlefield but those left behind as well. He explained: "The fact that you became a widow at twenty-six is due to your karma."[30] As the following reveals, this was the same rigidly deterministic interpretation of karma held by Suzuki's own master, Shaku Sōen:

We are born in a world of variety; some are poor and unfortunate, others are wealthy and happy. This state of variety will be repeated again and again in our future lives. But to whom shall we complain of our misery? To none but ourselves![31]

Even today the world struggles to understand why the Japanese people as a whole, unlike the Germans, have had such enormous difficulty in coming to grips with their war responsibility. At least part of the explanation is to be found in the doctrine of karma as formulated by the likes of Entai who asserted that "no one was to blame nor was anyone in the wrong." On the one hand, karma appears to place a premium on the moral behaviour of the individual. Yet, when it comes to evaluating the behaviour of a society's leaders who decide on war or peace, it has almost nothing to say. Instead, individuals in society get no more nor no less than what they deserve. How could the war responsibility of Japanese leaders be determined in the face of the "consistent working of karma"?

Nirvāna

Finally, given its pre-eminent position within Buddhism, a word needs to be said about the connection Entai saw between Nirvāṇa and the war bereaved. That is to say, was Entai ready to give the war bereaved special entry to Buddhism's ultimate goal?

The answer is that Entai was, for he entitled the final chapter of his booklet "A Life of Tranquility." The Japanese word Entai used for tranquility, i.e. *seijaku*, is a traditional alternative designation for Nirvāṇa (*Nehan*). According to Entai, those who have entered this realm could be characterized as follows:

> They neither make a pretense of being courageous nor do they refuse to admit defeat. They neither seek sympathy nor look upon the world with prejudiced eyes. Instead they display a calm, natural countenance that defies description just as if nothing special had occurred in their households.[32]

Needless to say, the preceding is not a traditional Buddhist description of enlightened persons. Rather, Entai used it with reference to a special group of war bereaved that he had recently encountered. They were special because not only had they "graduated from complaining" about their misfortune but were now filled with a spirit of gratitude for everything that had happened to them. Most especially, they appeared in Entai's eyes to be overcome with "reverence for the gracious benevolence of the emperor."[33]

This special group of bereaved was composed of those who had lost their loved ones in August 1937 when Japanese troops made a costly landing in Shanghai one month after the outbreak of full-scale war with China. While, like all bereaved, this group had initially been consumed by grief, with the passage of time, i.e. by September 1941, Entai found they had transcended their grief. Now their demeanor exuded a kind of "indescribable brilliance" characterized by "unassailable majesty."[34]

Entai did not seek to deny the difficulties this group of bereaved had encountered along the way to their new state of awareness. It had come, he claimed, only as "the fruit of three years of tears and constant anguish." In particular, parents had come to realize that their sons had not died recently on the battlefield but had "been among the war dead from the very beginning." The bereaved, having trained themselves to the utmost, no longer had "the least sign of attachment."[35]

Entai concluded his final chapter with the following admonition to the ever-increasing numbers of war bereaved:

> I have only been talking about one group of war bereaved here, but I am confident that throughout this country there are those whose loved ones died two or three years ago who have reached the same state of mind. I see in them a superb model for those who have only recently lost their loved ones. Moreover, they provide a silent lesson to all the people of this nation. I pray that all bereaved will reach this final stage just as soon as possible.[36]

Ultimately the family and friends of some three million Japanese war dead would be given the opportunity to achieve, in Entai's words, a "life of tranquility" as well as express their "reverence for the graciousness of the emperor." Given the parallels Entai saw between war bereavement and the realization of enlightenment, Entai should have been pleased.

Conclusion

In reading the preceding attempts to validate if not valourize the deaths of millions on the battlefield, it is difficult not to be overwhelmed by the ability of the human mind to twist words like "Nirvāṇa," "compassion," "karma" etc. until they fit a predetermined outcome – the justification if not glorification of death on the battlefield. Nevertheless, it is important to realize that these wartime Japanese Buddhist leaders were neither the first nor the last to have done so. In China, for example, similar efforts can be traced back at least 1500 years.

One example is Emperor Wen (r. 581–604) of the Sui Dynasty (c.581–618 CE) who enlisted the spiritual aid of Buddhist monks in his military campaigns by constructing temples at sites where he and his father had won important battles. He ordered priests residing in these temples to hold memorial services for the souls of his fallen soldiers in order to assure his still-living followers that were they to fall on some future battlefield, their souls, too, would be looked after.[37]

Emperor Wen was also determined to use Buddhism as a method of unifying all of China. Like his earlier counterpart in India, the famous King Aśoka (270–230 BCE), Wen built numerous stupas enshrining sacred relics of the Buddha throughout his empire in order "to propagate Buddhism as an instrument of state policy."[38] In turn, Wen's efforts served as a model for Prince Shōtoku (574–622 CE), Japan's first great patron of Buddhism, to employ Buddhism in his own campaign to unify Japan. The inevitable price of such patronage, however, was Buddhism's subservience to the state and its rulers.

Convinced of his righteousness, Wen went on to promote himself as a Cakravartin or "Universal Monarch," claiming that "the Buddha had entrusted the true Dharma to the ruler of the realm."[39] Soon after establishing the Sui dynasty in 581 CE, Wen declared:

> With the armed might of a Cakravartin King, We spread the ideals of the ultimately benevolent one [the Buddha]. With a hundred victories and a hundred battles, We promote the practice of the ten Buddhist virtues. Therefore, *We regard weapons of war as having become like incense and flowers* [presented as offerings to the Buddha] and the fields of this visible world as becoming forever identical with the Buddha land [Italics mine].[40]

Significantly, even today Buddhist leaders in various Asian countries continue to use Buddhism to justify warfare. David Little, for example, points out in his book *Sri Lanka – The Invention of Enmity* that Buddhist leaders of the Sinhalese majority condone the use of violence directed against the rebellious non-Buddhist Tamil minority in order "to protect the *Saṃgha* and Buddhist teachings ...

rationaliz[ing] the use of violence against the 'other,' even though it contravenes the basic tenets of Buddhism."[41]

Given this background, questions related to the use of Buddhist doctrine to console both the living and the dead in wartime Japan cannot be dismissed as nothing more than a momentary aberration within the Buddhist tradition. If indeed Buddhist doctrine as described above was "twisted," then that twisting is but one of many such examples in Buddhist history and remains as alive today as it was more than a thousand years ago. To deny this is to deny the unsettling reality that Buddhism, like other of the world's religions, has often justified, if not encouraged, the slaughter of human beings.

Commenting on the universal aspect of this all-too-prevalent religious phenomenon, Martin Marty of the University of Chicago wrote:

> Positive thinkers and public relations officers for the faiths would repudiate this notion or evade the fact. They want religion to be nothing but *godspel*, or good news. Apologists for the faiths usually minimize the distress that can come with religion or that religion can produce. You will not read about the destructive element in religious impulses in the advertisements for the church of your choice. Yet if the pursuit of truth is still to be cherished as a foundational theme in the academy, one must note the feature of religion that keeps it on the front page and on prime time: it kills. Or, if, as the gun lobbies say of weapons – that they do not kill; people do – one must say of religion that if it does not kill, many of its forms and expressions motivate people to kill.[42]

As much as Buddhists, this author among them, would like to deny the applicability of Marty's words to their faith, as this and other chapters reveal, at least in Japan's modern history if not long before, large numbers of Buddhist leaders did everything in their power to prove him right.

9

CONFESSIONS OF A BUDDHIST
CHAPLAIN

Introduction

As revealed in the previous chapter, Buddhist priests, from as early as the Sino-Japanese War of 1894–5, were deeply involved on the home front in comforting the war bereaved through valorizing the deaths of those who fell in battle. Their role, however, was not limited to Japan's home islands alone as demonstrated by priests like Shaku Sōen, abbot of the Rinzai Zen monastery of Engakuji in Kamakura. The reader will recall that during the Russo-Japanese war of 1904–5, Sōen went to the battlefield "to inspire, if I could, our valiant soldiers with the ennobling thoughts of the Buddha, so as to enable them to die on the battlefield with the confidence that the task in which they are engaged is great and noble."[1]

Sōen was, of course, far from the first Japanese Buddhist priest to minister directly on the battlefield. In fact, this custom can be traced back at least as far as the fourteenth century, when loyalists revolted against the military government in Kamakura from 1331–33. It was then that itinerant Buddhist chaplains belonging to the Pure Land tradition were assigned to warriors in the field. Their role was to ensure that their warrior patrons recited the name of Amitābha Buddha ten times at the time of death, thereby ensuring rebirth in the Pure Land.

As historian Sybil Thornton points out, the activities of these chaplains quickly expanded beyond a purely religious function, and they ended up not only burning, burying and praying for the dead, but caring for the sick and wounded as well. When their warrior patrons were not engaged in battle, the chaplains amused them with poetry and assumed a role close to that of a personal servant. Given that chaplains appear to have been beholden to their patrons for food, clothing, and shelter, this latter role is hardly surprising.[2]

Eventually, these chaplains came to play what might best be described as a "paramilitary" role, i.e. actively aiding and protecting their warrior patrons when needed. This, however, provoked a reaction from ecclesiastical superiors who, in one letter written in 1399, admonished their chaplains to "never touch things like bows and arrows and weapons ... because they are used to kill." On the other hand, chaplains were allowed to hold their master's body armour and helmet "because they are things that protect the body."[3] Should the chaplains violate these prohibitions, or their warrior patrons force them to, the ecclesiastical authorities warned they were quite prepared to cancel the rebirth of the offending party in the Pure Land. Whatever one might think of these prohibitions, standards of conduct for all parties did exist.

By the sixteenth century, things had changed. On the one hand, the battlefield neutrality of priests affiliated with the earlier Itinerant branch (Yugyō-ha) of Pure Land Buddhism continued to be recognized by the authorities. On the other hand, historian Sybil Thorton notes that priests in other sects were forced to provide warlords with "camp-priests who acted as couriers, bodyguards, and body servants to warriors in the field."[4] As the following material reveals, this latter development was but a precursor to the role of Japan's modern Buddhist chaplains. No longer were there any standards of conduct based on combatant versus non-combatant status. The demand for service to one's country, sovereign, and his designated military representatives was absolute and recognized no exceptions whatsoever.

It is perhaps for this very reason that few, if any, Buddhist chaplains have come forward to recount their experiences during the Asia-Pacific War. This is compounded by the postwar efforts of Japan's Buddhist leaders to hide, or at least ignore, their own sect's fervent war support while projecting a positive image of themselves as advocates of world peace. No doubt it is also due to feelings of shame connected with what the Buddhist chaplains themselves either saw or did on the battlefield. In the following story, which was not published until 1988, the last of these reasons is probably the most important, though all of them are closely connected.

The following comments are those of Nichiren sect priest, Fukushima Nichi'i (1909–1987), late abbot of Renjōji temple in Mito city, Ibaragi Prefecture. Brief as these comments are, they are all the more valuable because there is so little else like them. I would like to express my gratitude to Nichi'i's successor, Sekitō Keiun, for allowing this story, originally published in *The Japanese People's War* (*Nihonjin no Sensō*), to appear here in slightly altered translation.

The *Lotus Sūtra* on the battlefield

On 26 October 1937 I was directed by the administrative head of the NIchiren sect to become a military chaplain for the North China Expeditionary Army and assigned to the headquarters of the 26th Division stationed in Dadong. I served in this capacity for some seven years until I myself was drafted into the army as a member of the Division's Takahashi unit.

Although I was a chaplain, I was occasionally ordered by a major in the artillery to assist in the operational planning for positioning artillery pieces. Within the headquarters unit itself, I was assigned to the adjutant's office.

Lieutenant Colonel Suzuki served as the senior adjutant with Major Sumibe as his assistant. Colonel Chō Isamu [1895–1945] was chief of staff.

Colonel Chō received permission from the division commander to postpone his lunch for one hour everyday in order to devote himself to the religious practice of reading the *Lotus Sūtra* under my guidance. It was only then that he had lunch. It was this karmic relationship that led to the chief of staff becoming my disciple and entering the priesthood of the Nichiren sect. Chō delighted in this because, having truly understood the significance of reciting the holy title of the *Lotus Sūtra*, he entered the priesthood for the sake of the nation, the emperor, the people of Japan, and the future of our country's military. I therefore gave him the Buddhist name of "Jikōin Nichiyū" (Courageous Sun [residing in] the temple of Abundant Compassion).[5]

Not long thereafter, Chō was promoted to Major General and attached to the headquarters of the Guandong (Kwantung) Army [in Manchuria]. From there he was ordered to the General Staff Office [in Tokyo]. In July 1944, Chō, now a Lt. General, was sent to become chief of staff of the 32nd Army in Okinawa, commanded by Lt. General Ushijima Mitsuru [1887–1945]. Facing defeat, both Generals Ushijima and Chō committed suicide by ritual disembowelment early on the morning of 23 June 1945 at the entrance to [their headquarters in] Mabuni cave. The last message I received from Chief of Staff Chō ended with: "I am filled with joy at having found the best place in all of Japan to die!"

In 1978, on the thirty-third anniversary of my disciple's death, I went to Mabuni to pray for the repose of his soul. At that time I also erected a stone monument directly below the hillside cave in which he died. Using Chō's own handwriting as a model, the monument was inscribed with the words: "Adoration to the Wonderful Dharma *Lotus Sūtra*." In addition, I had a poem written by Chō to his second son inscribed on this monument in large letters. Just as I was conducting the solemn service for the repose of both Chō's soul and those of the other Okinawan war victims, a rain squall hit and my newly purchased robes got drenched. For me it was a once in a lifetime experience that I shall never forget.

Returning to the chaplaincy, whenever a unit attached to our headquarters was despatched on a military operation, the commander of that unit almost always had me sit immediately to his left as we headed for the battlefield. I got the impression that my presence made the commanders feel secure.

Those soldiers who fell on the battlefield may well have been fated to do so. Confucius, for example, survived life-or-death crises on three separate occasions and lived to complete his mission in life, dying at age seventy-three. Nichiren was nearly executed at Tatsunokuchi and then banned to Sado island for three years. After being pardoned, Nichiren founded a temple on Mt. Minobu and lived on for nine more years.

Major Sumibe, the assistant adjutant who cared deeply for me, was saddened to learn that his entire family in Tokyo had died as martyrs [due to Allied bombing raids] in our country's darkest hour. Every time there was a battle there were casualties, and we had to cremate our fallen comrades among the wooded hills of the north. Prior to burning their bodies we set up camp, using four heavy machine guns to protect us.

On one occasion an enemy bullet pierced a soldier's thigh and a second went through his steel helmet before coming to rest in his head. I picked up his blood-soaked corpse and took it to the rear, my own military uniform getting smeared with blood in the process.

At the front we reduced villages to ashes as we searched for spies. There were always prisoners. It made no difference whether they were young or old, we first had them dig their own graves and then forced them to kneel down beside them. Following this, soldiers were selected who were skilled swordsmen.

Initially the soldiers struck the nape of the victim's neck with a pop, using the back of their military sword to dislocate the bone joint. Then they lopped off the head. If they did their work well, the head fell forward and blood forcefully spurted out of the carotid artery like two fountains. When all the blood from the heart was exhausted, the victim expired and fell down into the open grave. We then continued marching without even covering the corpses. On the battlefield it was always a question of kill or be killed – there was no other way.

After heavy rains we frequently encountered scenes in which either the heads or the bodies of our victims had been carried along by the current and half buried further down the river. The war was like a medieval picture scroll depicting [a Buddhist view of] hell. The battlefront consisted of the three evil realms of: 1) hell, 2) hungry ghosts, and 3) beasts. There were times when our soldiers even ended up fighting each other. While it was called a "holy war" fought by an "Imperial Army," terms like these turned out to be totally meaningless.

Author's response

The preceding remembrances of Fukushima Nichi'i mark the last of the "blood and guts" depictions of war in this book. This is not, however, the last time the reader will be forced to confront the question of how it was possible that men professing the Buddhist faith, based as it is on compassion and nonviolence, could have been so monumentally blind to the morality of their actions. How was it possible that General Chō, despite reciting the greatest of the Mahāyāna scriptures, the *Lotus Sūtra*, day after day, did not experience any pangs of conscience as he oversaw the destruction of village after village of Chinese peasants and the beheading of countless "spies"? How was it possible that Nichi'i, his Buddhist master, could have given his disciple the name "abundant compassion" and not recognized any moral conflict with his disciple's (or his own) military duties?

To be sure, there are no easy answers to these questions. One of the mechanisms Nichi'i used to legitimate death on the battlefield was his belief in the Buddhist-derived concept of "fate" (*shukumei*).[6] In other words, those who died on the battlefield were fated to do so. We have previously seen this idea, closely connected with the popular Buddhist understanding of *karma* and karmic retribution, at work in Ōmori Zenkai's justification of social inequality in chapter 7. It was even more strongly present in the previous chapter. What it does so well is erase any thought of individual, let alone group, responsibility for society's myriad shortcomings, not least of all the mass slaughter that inevitably accompanies modern warfare. "*Shikatta ga nai*" (it can't be helped) has long been a "culturally correct" reaction in Japanese society to various forms of injustice that appear beyond the power of the individual to change.

Given this, it is more than a little ironic to read that unit commanders always wanted Nichi'i to ride close to them when they went on field operations. As Nichi'i notes, "I got the impression that my presence made the commanders feel secure." The reader will recall from chapter 1 that Yamamoto Gempō told his disciple not to worry because "even if a bullet comes your way, it will swerve around you." These are only two examples of the popular Japanese belief in Buddhism's magical powers, popularly portrayed as superhuman in nature. In peacetime, these powers are invoked for such purposes as curing illnesses, locating suitable marriage partners, or securing entrance into prestigious schools. In wartime, however, they were thought to protect the believer from harm, no matter how much harm the believer may be doing to others! Needless to say, Buddhism is far from the only world religion to foster such notions.

General Chō Isamu

The reader will recall that Lt. General Chō was first introduced in chapter 7. Chō was known for his quick, inquiring mind and boundless energy. Yet, while widely admired for his brilliance, he also had a reputation as a fiery, hard-driving man who placed heavy demands on his subordinates. Nichi'i captured both sides of his disciple's personality in a description he wrote in 1980:

> General Chō was a career staff officer of acute intellect. He had such excellent powers of observation that the Devil himself would have been scared out of his wits had their paths crossed. Not only that, he also possessed a superior ability to foresee the outcome of events.
>
> Chō had mastered German and loved to read detective stories and science fiction. In reading these books he attempted to anticipate the author's intent and reach the conclusion on his own. It was exactly because he had such a fine mind and outstanding temperament that he would not tolerate anything that was unreasonable.[7]

Interestingly, in light of his brilliant and fiery nature it can be argued that Chō's personality was not unlike that of Nichiren, the thirteenth-century founder of the sect in which he became a priest. Nevertheless, the fiery part of his nature might well be considered a character defect in a high-ranking officer like Chō. Okinawan historian Ōta Masahide notes, however, that as far as the Battle of Okinawa is concerned, this was not the case; for Chō was "the perfect foil for General Ushijima's calm and competent dignity."[8]

General Chō was clearly one of those many, many "true believers" in the Imperial Army who, despite his priestly status, saw not the least contradiction between the Buddhist faith and his statement: "I am filled with joy at having found the best place in all of Japan to die!" In fact, it was his acceptance of what was regarded as the Buddhist view of life and death that enabled the general to so confidently address his master as he did.

It is noteworthy that Chō first revealed his ultranationalist leanings while still a major attached to the Army Ministry in Tokyo. It was there that, as a member of a clandestine group of middle-ranking officers known as the "Cherry Blossom Society" (Sakura-kai), Chō helped plan a major military-led *coup d'etat* later known as the "October Incident" (Jūgatsu Jiken) of 1931. Chō was set to command a unit assigned to attack a Cabinet meeting, killing everyone from the prime minister on down.

However, as was so often the case in the 1930s, the plot was uncovered shortly prior to its execution, not by the police but by senior Army leaders, including General Araki Sadao. Although the *coup* leaders, Chō included, were momentarily arrested by military police, the whole incident was quickly hushed up with the *coup* plotters receiving no more than reprimands. Chō's "punishment" consisted of no more than reassignment to duty on the continent.

Chō was first stationed in Beijing and then in Hangkou, followed by service as an infantry battalion commander on Taiwan. His subsequent military career progressed until, with the outbreak of full-scale war with China, he became an intelligence staff officer with the Shanghai Expeditionary Force. Chō would later claim that it was he who issued the orders to "kill all captives" at the December 1937 Rape of Nanjing.[9] In claiming this we are once again forced to consider a possible link between the acceptance of one's own death on the battlefield and the total indifference displayed by Japanese military leaders like Chō towards the heartless massacre of tens of thousands of their captives.

Moreover, Chō's callousness was by no means limited to his enemies, be they foreign or domestic. Prior to the Allied invasion of Okinawa in the spring of 1945, Chō, as chief of staff, was asked by a newspaper reporter what civilian residents should do when enemy troops landed. Chō replied: "It is too late to say this, but all civilians should accept military instructions like soldiers. In other words, each civilian ought to have a fighting spirit to kill ten enemy soldiers and destroy our enemy." And he added:

When the enemy lands and our food supply gets cut off, the military is not in a position to provide civilians with food even if you plead with us that civilians will starve to death. The military's important mission is to win the war. We are not allowed to lose the war in order to save civilians.[10]

As on the Japanese mainland itself, everyone, soldiers and civilians, men and women, young and old, were expected to die. If this statement sounds too extreme, consider the following orders adopted by the 32nd Army on Okinawa in January 1945. Entitled "Outline of the Plan of Operations for the Imperial Army and Navy," the orders clearly state that Okinawa was to be sacrificed "in order to buy time for the protection of the national polity.... Everything up to and including a single tree or blade of grass is to be turned into military power. Military, public officials and civilians are to be united, living *and dying* together [Italics mine].[11]

It was orders like the above, showing such total disregard for the safety of civilians that later prompted Okinawan poet Shimabukuro Tetsu to write the following poem entitled "The Battle of Okinawa and Consoling the Spirits":

The 32nd Division was the "sacrifice" offered by Imperial headquarters and the Emperor.
It was just as in Saipan and Iōjima.
They were the "sacrifices" placed into the hands of the US military as a means of biding time, in the face of imminent defeat.
Soldiers who killed the defenseless in China now, in Okinawa, were themselves killed by overwhelming forces, embroiling Okinawan civilians into the battle, even more defenseless.
It was just as in the Philippines....
The irresponsibility, recklessness, terrorism, stupidity, debauchery, amorality, and cruelty of the Imperial Army had no confines.
Do not tell lies to those fallen.
If you want to console their spirits, speak to them of the true rationale for their deaths.[12]

Conclusion

It is my heartfelt prayer that this book will contribute to explaining "the true rationale for their deaths." This said, I cannot help but ask once again how it was possible for a Buddhist priest like Nichi'i to witness daily what were so clearly war atrocities committed against Chinese civilians, "young and old," without having confronted the moral implications of his acquiescence to this mindless brutality. Needless to say, there is no question here of the Japanese Army having executed spies convicted by a military court or any other court. To be "suspected" of spying was all the proof needed for execution. In the face of a foreign invasion, who would not become "spies" for their country?

To be sure, in his earlier 1980 memoirs, Nichi'i did attempt to explain his actions, especially after he had been turned into an infantry soldier in 1943, forced to abandon his previous position as a Buddhist chaplain:

> When war finally comes, and you find yourself exposed to enemy fire in the midst of battle, there is not an ounce of human kindness to be found. In the face of fierce fighting, it is a choice of killing or being killed, striking or being struck. There are no other choices. It is a world in which ideas, philosophy, ideals, religion, ethics and morality no longer exist.[13]

On the one hand, it is difficult to argue with Nichi'i's description of the brutal reality of the battlefield. Nevertheless, the question must be asked as to whether religion, ethics, etc. truly no longer exist on the battlefield. Is it not more likely that Nichi'i consciously *chose* to believe, even *prior* to going into battle, that such things no longer existed so as to justify, if only to himself, the carnage of which he was a part? If there is a shred of Buddhist morality present in Nichi'i's writings, it is the fact that he did at least recognize the battlefield as being the very incarnation of the traditional East Asian Buddhist view of hell. But here, too, one suspects that the traditional depictions of multi-layered Buddhist hell(s) provide almost a justification for his *acceptance* of a hellish world rather than any moral imperative to actively work to end the suffering of the sentient beings trapped within it.

Taking this question to the extreme, had Nichi'i been assigned as a chaplain to a German SS unit stationed at Auschwitz, is there any reason to suspect he would have acted differently than he did in China, or his disciple General Chō Isamu, for all his "abundant compassion," acted in both China and on Okinawa?

10

BUDDHISM – THE LAST REFUGE OF WAR CRIMINALS

Many readers will immediately recognize that the title of this chapter is a remake of the old aphorism: "Patriotism is the last refuge of scoundrels." In addition, the title alludes to 'taking refuge' in the Buddha, Dharma, and Saṃgha, something recognized in all schools of Buddhism as the fundamental act required to become a Buddhist. This chapter, however, is not primarily about Japanese war criminals who converted to Buddhism. Rather, it focuses on the uses to which Buddhism was put to in the immediate postwar years including everything from hiding suspected war criminals to providing convicted war criminals with a means of "transcending life and death" even as they faced the hangman's noose.

In one sense it can be argued that for suspected or convicted war criminals to seek refuge in Buddhism was nothing new. The history of Buddhism in China and Japan is full of examples of men and women who entered Buddhist monasteries not because they were seeking enlightenment but rather to escape secular troubles, including imprisonment and execution. There is, for example, the famous Rinzai Zen nunnery of Tōkeiji in Kamakura, popularly known as *kakekomi-dera* (lit. temple for taking refuge), which offered married women in medieval Japan one of the few possibilities of leaving their husbands. The price of freedom from their marital ties, however, was a willingness to live the celibate life of a Buddhist nun.

As for men, the most dramatic example in medieval Japan was the Zen sect-related *komusō*. *Komusō* were, at least in the beginning, itinerant Zen monks who played a Japanese bamboo flute known as a *shakuhachi* as part of their religious practice. However, because they wore a conical wicket basket over their head, it was possible to completely disguise their identity, a fact that gradually attracted an assortment of shady characters who found it advantageous to disguise themselves. This latter practice became so widespread during the Edo period (1600–1867) that the government outlawed *komusō* altogether.

Finally, in both China and Japan, it has long been a practice for poverty-stricken parents to place one or more of their children, both boys and girls, in monasteries and nunneries at a young age due to their own inability to provide for them. This was also the case if, for whatever reason, the children became orphaned. On the other end of the scale, during the middle ages, Japanese emperors found it convenient, under a system known as *Insei*, to ostensibly retire to a Buddhist monastery while actually continuing to conduct affairs of state from behind monastic walls.

The first part of this chapter deals with none of the classical uses (or abuses) of Buddhist monastic life. Instead it focuses on the use to which a number of Buddhist temples were put following Japan's surrender on 15 August 1945. The fighting may have ceased, but the question of the apprehension and prosecution of war criminals had only just begun. As the following story reveals, not all of the alleged war criminals were willing to entrust their fate to what appeared to them as "victor's justice." The relative anonymity provided by the Buddhist *Saṃgha*, i.e. the community of monks and nuns, might yet have its uses.

SECTION ONE: COLONEL TSUJI MASANOBU GOES UNDERGROUND

Colonel Tsuji Masanobu (1902–68?) was one of the Japanese Army's most brilliant strategists, having played a key role in planning the successful attack on British forces in Singapore in February 1942. In his own eyes, he was a champion of Asian unity and a resolute anti-Communist, the latter trait proving key to his postwar survival. Nevertheless, as Meirion and Susie Harries have pointed out, he was also consumed by "megalomaniac ambition, violent prejudices, and a ruthless disregard for human life."[1] Among other things, it was Tsuji who supervised the infamous Bataan Death March of Allied captives in the Philippines in April 1942. Of the 70,000 POWs who began this march only 54,000 arrived safely in Japanese custody at Camp O'Donnell.[2]

August 1945 found Tsuji attached as a staff officer to the Bangkok headquarters of the 18th Army Corps in ostensibly neutral Thailand. After first getting word, on 10 August 1945, that Japan was preparing to surrender, Tsuji, like other staff officers, pondered his options. By the morning of 14 August, Tsuji put together the following rather surprising plan which he presented to his commander, Lt. General Nakamura Aketo (1889–1966):

> Although there has not yet been a formal announcement, we have no choice but to admit that the Japanese government has accepted the Potsdam Declaration [of 26 July 1945]. If Japan surrenders uncondition-ally, there can be no doubt that the imperial military will be forced to lay down its arms. Although this is truly heartbreaking, I don't think it means the end of Japan. Therefore, in preparation for the day when our nation rises again, please allow me to go underground here in Bangkok![3]

Responding to General Nakamura's query for more details, Tsuji explained that he intended to go "underground" by disguising himself as a Buddhist priest. To assist him, he had selected seven young "special attack," i.e. *kamikaze*, pilots who had been unable to carry out their suicide missions because there were no aircraft left for them to fly in the southern command. As a result, these seven were trained for a new mission – infiltrating behind enemy lines to act as spies and saboteurs. Some readers may recall the famous case of Second Lt. Onoda Hiroo who had been given a similar mission. Onoda managed to hold out on Lubang Island in the Philippines until March 1974.

Tsuji did not select his subordinates by chance, for they had one additional crucial attribute – they were all Buddhist priests. Four of them were affiliated with the Zen sect (three Sōtō and one Rinzai), with one each from the Pure Land, True Pure Land, and Nichiren sects. Inasmuch as they were scheduled to "disguise" themselves as monks in the southern Theravāda school, their sectarian differences within the northern Mahāyāna school could be put aside. Ironically, not only would their newfound ecumenism have been difficult to duplicate in Japan itself, it was directed toward a military goal, that of spying and sabotage, not to mention aiding a suspected war criminal to escape prosecution.

Underground in Bangkok

On the evening of 15 August, following the emperor's surrender speech broadcast that afternoon, Tsuji and his companions gathered at the Thailand Hotel for a final banquet. Following their meal, they all changed into the saffron-coloured robes of a Theravādan monk; discarding their shoes in favour of a monk's bare feet and, excepting Tsuji, shaving their eyebrows in accordance with Thai Buddhist custom. Conveniently, there was a power failure in Bangkok that night, and in the darkness they headed, reciting sūtras as they walked, for Wat Ratchaburana temple located on the banks of the Chao Phraya river. Tsuji had selected this temple because a small two storied Japanese-style funerary hall had been built on its grounds to hold the cremated remains of Japanese nationals who died while in Thailand.

Interestingly, though dressed in Theravādan robes, Tsuji and his companions had no intention of hiding their Japanese identity. They would claim to have travelled first to Burma and then, as the war situation worsened, to Bangkok in order to study the Theravādan tradition. Initially at least, both Thai immigration officials and police, not to mention temple officials, accepted their story. Nevertheless, it soon became clear that their collective presence in the small Japanese funerary hall was attracting too much outside attention. Tsuji therefore ordered six of the monks to move to the much larger Wat Mahathat temple while he remained in the funerary hall with only one attendant, Sōtō Zen priest Fukuzawa Ekō.

Much to the surprise of his priestly companions, Tsuji succeeded in memorizing in only three days both the short *Heart Sūtra* (*Hannya Shingyō*) and the much longer "Revelation of the [Eternal] Life of the Tathāgata" (*Nyorai Juryōhon*) chapter of the *Lotus Sūtra*. These were the sūtras that they had agreed to recite in common despite their sectarian differences. These were not, however,

Plate 9 The Japanese funerary hall located in the grounds of the Wat Ratchaburana temple in Bangkok, Thailand. Colonel Tsuji Masanobu and his priestly subordinates went into hiding here at the time of Japan's surrender on 15 August 1945. Photograph courtesy of Michael Drummond.

the only sūtras that Tsuji knew, for he had been raised in a devout True Pure Land sect family and had memorized the main sūtras of that sect at his mother's side. In addition, as a young officer he had studied Buddhism under the guidance of Akegarasu Haya, abbot of the True Pure Land temple of Myōdatsuji in Matsutō city, Ishikawa Prefecture.

In September 1945 British troops finally arrived in Bangkok under the command of Admiral Lord Louis Mountbatten (1900–79), Supreme Allied Commander in the South East. Their primary mission was to disarm Japanese troops remaining in Thailand, but they were also responsible for the apprehension of suspected war criminals, Tsuji being at the top of their list. Although Japanese military commanders told the British that Tsuji had died in battle, the British refused to believe them. For his part, Tsuji feared that Ekō might be arrested if he stayed with him and therefore ordered his remaining attendant to move to Mahathat temple with the others, leaving him alone in the funerary hall. Tsuji was, however, not totally defenceless, for he had hidden his officer's sword, hilt just visible, behind the hall's Buddha altar.

Escape from Bangkok

On the evening of 28 October 1945 Tsuji received the news he had gradually come to expect: "The British and Thai military police will arrive early tomorrow morning to arrest you."[4] Hearing this, Tsuji immediately boarded a train for Laos with the aid of another underground organization operating in Bangkok, the Nationalist Chinese secret police. Once in Laos he took a boat down the Mekong River and then made his way to Hanoi. From there he crossed into China and travelled to Zhongjing (Chungking), China's wartime capital.

Given Tsuji's long involvement in Japan's invasion of China, including his direct responsibility for the massacre of some 5–7,000 overseas Chinese civilians in Singapore in March 1942, one might expect that the Chinese authorities would have immediately imprisoned, if not executed, Tsuji themselves. However, by this time Generalissimo and Nationalist leader Jiang Jieshi (Chiang Kai-shek) was embroiled in a rekindled, bitter civil war with China's Communists led by Mao Zedong (Mao Tse-tung). Thus, not only did Tsuji escape arrest, but, thanks to his staunch anti-Communist credentials, he was quickly recruited by Jiang to serve as one of his military advisers. Thus did Tsuji undergo yet another transformation – from monk to mercenary.

In the meantime, the British had discovered the true identity of Tsuji's seven accomplices in Bangkok. They were arrested and repeatedly questioned as to Tsuji's whereabouts though, true to their original mission, they all feigned ignorance. Finally, unable to prove anything to the contrary, the British repatriated them to Japan in August 1946 where they returned to their priestly duties. Their relationship with Tsuji, however, was by no means at an end.

Back in Japan

Tsuji initially endeared himself to Jiang Jieshi by sharing a decade's worth of Japanese strategic planning against communism in Manchuria and north China. At Tsuji's urging, Jiang released a number of imprisoned Japanese war criminal suspects and invited them, too, to serve as his military advisors, capitalizing on their knowledge of the hated Communist enemy.[5] Nevertheless, by the beginning of 1948 it was clear that the Nationalists would ultimately lose, and Tsuji decided to gamble yet again by returning to Japan. Claiming to have been a Japanese university professor of ancient Chinese cultural history at Beijing (Peking) University, Tsuji joined some 800 former Japanese soldiers and civilians in Shanghai awaiting repatriation to Japan.

Once again his gamble paid off, and Tsuji successfully fooled the American military police who questioned him when he stepped off the boat in Sasebo. But where could he hide in Japan? As he quickly discovered, even his distant relatives were under constant surveillance by Japanese police acting on the orders of the Occupation authorities. Thus, on the evening of 4 June 1948 Tsuji once again looked to Buddhism for refuge – specifically, the Sōtō Zen-affiliated Hōshōji temple in Tokyo, headed by his former attendant, Fukuzawa Eikō.

Without the slightest hesitation, Eikō offered to assist his former commander, convinced this was an excellent way "to oppose the Allied occupiers of his country."[6] Thus began an odyssey lasting more than two years in which Tsuji was moved from one remote country temple to another, assisted by one or another of his seven former subordinates. While in hiding, Tsuji continued his pretence of being a university professor though now he claimed to be teaching at Sōtō Zen sect-affiliated Komazawa University in Tokyo.

Because so many of Komazawa's teachers were also priests, temple parishioners often assumed that Tsuji must be a "scholar-priest" (*gakusō*) himself, especially when he stayed at remote mountain temples that no longer had their own resident priests. Tsuji, for his part, did not attempt to correct the parishioners' false assumption if for no other reason than that it produced increased donations of food to the temple. In poverty-stricken postwar Japan, and without any other source of income, these donations were most welcome additions to Tsuji's own gardening efforts.

The parishioners of Seiryūji in the mountains of Hyōgo Prefecture were especially glad to have Tsuji in residence. Passing by the temple, they heard Tsuji loudly reciting the sūtras he had learned in Bangkok. In gratitude they brought donations of rice, fermented soy bean paste, and sweet potatoes to the temple saying, "It's been a long time since we've heard sūtras being recited in this empty temple." As he placed their donations on the temple's Buddha altar, Tsuji replied, "Your donations represent the broad and unlimited grace of the Buddha."[7]

Post-occupation Japan

Even before the formal end of the Occupation in 1952, Tsuji had been able to show himself in public without fear of arrest; for in 1949 the Allied attempt to apprehend and punish suspected war criminals came to an abrupt end for reasons of Cold War-induced political expediency. Being cautious, Tsuji initially elected to remain in hiding, but by June 1950 he felt safe enough to publish a book entitled *Underground for Three Thousand Leagues* (*Senkō Sanzen-ri*) detailing his many adventures since first disguising himself as a monk in Bangkok. Needless to say, this book had been written while staying in one or another of his temple hideouts.

Not only did Tsuji's book become a best seller, but the fame it brought its author served as a springboard for still another career change – from wanted fugitive to national politician. In 1952, following restoration of Japan's sovereignty, Tsuji successfully ran for a seat in the Lower House of the Diet where he was reelected every two years until 1959 when he switched to the Upper House. If it seems strange that a suspected war criminal like Tsuji could so readily emerge as a political leader in postwar Japan, it should be remembered that Kishi Nobusuke (1896–1987), also suspected of being a war criminal, was not only elected to the Lower House in 1952 but served as prime minister for three years from 1957. Like Tsuji, Kishi had first distinguished himself in colonized Manchuria where his economic policies were rated so highly that Prime Minister Tōjō Hideki selected him to serve as his minister of commerce from 1941 onwards.

While postwar Germany made a clear and conscious break with its Nazi past, as men like Tsuji and Kishi (let alone the emperor) reveal, Japan's wartime and postwar periods remained closely connected. Which is not to say that all of Japan's suspected war criminals escaped prosecution; for, as will be seen below, a handful of Japan's top military and civilian leaders did stand trial for their wartime actions. While Tsuji successfully used Buddhism, at least organizationally, to escape all responsibility for his wartime barbarity, what of these other leaders? Did they, too, seek refuge in Buddhism?

SECTION TWO: FINDING RELIGION ON DEATH ROW

The Tokyo War Crimes Tribunal, officially known as the International Military Tribunal for the Far East (IMTFE), opened on 3 May 1946 and remained in session for some two-and-a-half years, completing its work on 12 November 1948. This trial, however, represented only a small part of the overall Allied effort to bring suspected Japanese war criminals to justice throughout the Asia-Pacific region. In all, some 5,700 Japanese were put on trial in such places as the Philippines, China, Indonesia, and Russia, not to mention Japan, resulting in death sentences for 984 convicted war criminals and imprisonment of varying lengths for another 3,500.

In Tokyo, eighty persons suspected of being Class A war criminals were detained in Sugamo prison beginning in 1945. Of these, twenty-eight were eventually brought to trial, including nine civilians and nineteen professional military men. The indictment accused the defendants of promoting a scheme of conquest that

> contemplated and carried out ... murdering, maiming and ill-treating prisoners of war [and] civilian internees ... forcing them to labour under inhumane conditions ... plundering public and private property, wantonly destroying cities, towns and villages beyond any justification of military necessity; [perpetrating] mass murder, rape, pillage, brigandage, torture and other barbaric cruelties upon the helpless civilian population of the overrun countries."[8]

Of the original twenty-eight defendants, two died of natural causes during the trial while one defendant appeared to suffer a mental breakdown on the trial's very first day. This defendant, civilian ultranationalist leader Ōkawa Shūmei (1886–1957), was subsequently transferred to a psychiatric ward only to be pronounced cured and released in 1948. The remaining twenty-five, however, were all found guilty, many on multiple counts. Of the convicted, seven were sentenced to death by hanging, sixteen to life imprisonment, and two to lesser terms. All seven of those sentenced to death were found guilty of having incited, or otherwise been part of, massive atrocities. Significantly, while three of the sixteen sentenced to life imprisonment died between 1949 and 1950 in prison, the remaining thirteen were paroled between 1954 and 1956, having served less than eight years of their life sentences.

Hanayama Shinshō

With this background in mind, we turn to an examination of the seven condemned men's relationship to Buddhism, especially in the intervening weeks between their convictions in mid-November and the day of their execution by hanging in the first few minutes of 23 December 1948. One reason for this focus is because of the leading role these seven men played in wartime Japan. Secondarily, of all those imprisoned, only these seven left a record, partial though it be, of their spiritual life prior to execution.

The existence of this partial record is due to the efforts of True Pure Land sect-affiliated scholar-priest, Hanayama Shinshō (1898–1995). Hanayama's sectarian affiliation was no accident for this sect had long provided the great majority of prison chaplains since the formal establishment of a chaplaincy system in September 1881. In 1939, for example, 159 out of a total of 163 chaplains came from one or the other of the two branches of the True Pure Land sect. As a result, statues of Amitābha Buddha were enshrined in almost every prison in Japan.[9]

Hanayama's scholarly credentials derive from the fact that he was a European-educated, widely published professor of Buddhist Studies at Tokyo University. He accepted the additional duty of Buddhist chaplain in Sugamo prison in February 1946. As such, he was the only Japanese to have direct contact with all Japanese war criminals condemned to death who were awaiting execution. Much of the following account is based on Hanayama's prison recollections contained in *The Road to Eternity – My Eighty-Two Years of Life* (*Eien e no Michi – Waga Hachijū-nen no Shōgai*), first published in 1982.

Hirota Kōki

Baron Hirota Kōki (1878–1948) began his adult career as a diplomat, eventually rising to the post of ambassador to the Soviet Union from 1928–31 and then Japan's foreign minister from 1933–6. In 1936 he left diplomatic service to become the nation's prime minister. Although his cabinet lasted less than a year, Hirota was in office long enough to treble the military's budget and make secret arrangements for increasing the army's size from seventeen to twenty-four divisions, a 41 per cent increase. He also took the initial steps to place the economy on a wartime footing, employing deficit financing to fund the military's expansion. In short, it was Hirota who made it militarily and financially possible for Japan to launch its full-scale invasion of China in July 1937.

The collapse of his cabinet did not bring an end to Hirota's government service. On the contrary, he went on to become Japan's foreign minister once again, only this time the army was in the midst of committing the Nanjing massacre and other atrocities. More than anything else, it was Hirota's connection to these atrocities that later resulted in his becoming the only wartime civilian leader to be sentenced to death as a war criminal. This said, one of the eleven Allied judges, B. V. A. Roeling of the Netherlands, opposed his conviction on the basis that Hirota could neither have known of the atrocities nor prevented them.

Be that as it may, one further feature unique to Hirota was that, in name at least, he was a Rinzai Zen priest. That is to say, while Hirota's childhood name was "Jōtarō," he received the name 'Kōki' (lit. broad strength) upon entering the Zen priesthood while yet in primary school. Significantly, even after leaving the Rinzai Zen temple of Shōrinji in Gifu Prefecture where he trained, Hirota retained both his priestly name and his Zen affiliation for the rest of his life. Thus, formally at least, Hirota lived and died as a Zen priest.

It would, however, be mistaken to read too much into Hirota's priestly status, for he left Shōrinji during his middle school years and eventually became a protégé of Tōyama Mitsuru, the notorious ultranationalist leader previously introduced in chapter 4. It was Tōyama's connections to Japan's political leaders that first enabled Hirota to enter the diplomatic service and then move on to a political career.

In prison, Hirota's Zen affiliation was well-known to Hanayama Shinshō who made no attempt to dissuade him from his faith. The two men did, however, have the following exchange during their third private meeting held on Friday afternoon, 26 November 1948:

Shinshō: Have you composed any poetry or put your thoughts down on paper?
Hirota: Inasmuch as my record as a public official is there for all to see, I have
    nothing to add at this point.... I simply want to die naturally... returning to
    nothingness (*mu*). Since I have already said what had to be said and done
    what had to be done, I have nothing more to say. Living naturally and dying
    naturally – that is my creed.
Shinshō: I understand that you practiced Zen?
Hirota: Yes, I did as a youth, but from middle school onwards I studied the
    teachings of Wang Yangming.
Shinshō: Well, his teachings are pretty close to Zen, aren't they?
Hirota: Yes, they are.[10]

As tantalizing as the above exchange is, it offers little on which to base an assessment of Zen's influence on Hirota. Nevertheless, Hirota's hope to "die naturally ... returning to nothingness" does suggest that Zen was once again being used to overcome the fear of death. Though no definitive answer is possible, the question must be asked as to whether Hirota's own acceptance of "nothingness" made it easier for him to initiate policies that led to the deaths (i.e. the return to nothingness) of millions.

To be sure, Hirota does mention that following his childhood practice of Zen he studied the neo-Confucian philosophy of Wang Yangming (1472–1529). As Shinshō noted, however, Wang Yangming's teachings share a deep affinity with Zen, not least of all because Wang emphasized the importance of having a personal and intuitive experience of the identity of self with all things. A book on Wang entitled *Life Chronology* (*Nian-pu*) contains the following description of his personal realization: "He [Wang] had already given up and put behind him all thought of personal success or failure, honour or disgrace, and only the question of life and death remained to be overcome. Thus day and night he stayed in silent, solitary meditation...."[11] Shortly thereafter, Wang experienced "great enlightenment," leading him literally to jump for joy and give a shout, awakening his amazed companions in the process. Wang claimed to have realized that "the way to sagehood lies within one's own nature."[12]

It was experiences like these that led contemporary scholar of neo-Confucian thought Wing-tsit Chan to comment that the philosophy of Wang and his predecessors "has often been called Zen in Confucian disguise" though Chan added that Wang also stressed "active involvement in human affairs and a dynamic approach to the mind."[13] For Wang, however, mind meant essentially the will, with sincerity of will being the critical element necessary to all human endeavour. Believing this, Wang demanded of his followers the utmost in determination, firm purpose, self-examination and self-mastery, all grounded in personal experience and expressed in "forthright, direct, and spontaneous action."[14]

In this connection it may be well to recall the words of D. T. Suzuki as he described the connection between Zen and Japan's warrior class:

> Zen discipline is simple, direct, self-reliant, self-denying; its ascetic tendency goes well with the fighting spirit. The fighter is to be always single-minded with one object in view: to fight looking neither forward nor sidewise. To go straight forward in order to crush the enemy is all that is necessary for him.... Zen is a religion of will-power, and will-power is what is urgently needed of warriors, though it ought to be enlightened by intuition.[15]

For his part, Wang Yangming claimed, albeit metaphorically, that he had realized his own doctrines only after undergoing "a hundred deaths and a thousand sufferings."[16]

If, as appears to be the case, Zen and the Zen-influenced Wang Yangming school were the two main spiritual influences on Hirota's formative years, we are faced yet again with the question of what influence, if any, these "Siamese twins" exerted on his subsequent embrace of militarism. Was Hirota, for example, able to apply such things as "will-power," "firm purpose," and "forthright, direct, and spontaneous action" to his militarist goals? Or did he, perhaps, merely utilize intuitive insight, short-circuiting as it does the need for rational thought, let alone concern for the moral consequences of one's acts. In the postwar era, Nakamura Hajime, one of Japan's greatest postwar scholars of Buddhism, described the danger stemming from this latter way of thinking as follows:

> The Japanese inclination to lay too much emphasis upon particular facts or specific phases amounts to an anti-intellectual standpoint of no theory or anti-theory. It ends up with the contempt of rational thinking and the worship of uncontrolled intuitionism and activism. Herein lies the intellectual cause of the failure of Japan in the past, and the danger still lies in this direction today. In order not to repeat the same failure, we ought from now on to learn to seek universal "reason" through specific "facts."[17]

There is, of course, no way of knowing how Hirota would have responded to Nakamura's words had he heard them. Yet, if the old aphorism "where there's smoke, there's fire," contains an element of truth, then there may well be a deeper connection between Hirota Kōki the militarist and Hirota Kōki the Zen priest than merely his priestly name and childhood training. Leaving further exploration of this question to the future, one must, at the very least, question Hirota's claim that dying on the gallows, let alone on the battlefield, can legitimately be described as "dying *naturally.*"

Doihara Kenji

A second of the seven who had a clear Zen connection was General Doihara Kenji, Commander of the Guandong (Kwantung) Army in Manchuria from 1938–40. Doihara (1883–1948) was also a member of the Supreme War Council from 1940–43 and army commander in Singapore between 1944–5. Deeply involved in the army's drug trafficking in Manchuria, Doihara later ran brutal POW and internee camps in Malaya, Sumatra, Java and Borneo.

In a meeting with Hanayama Shinshō held on Monday afternoon, 22 November 1948, Doihara described his interest in Zen as follows:

> I started my practice of Zen in the Rinzai tradition as a youth even though my family was Shinto. I both practiced *zazen* and read Zen-related books.
>
> On the one hand, I can say that I had a theoretical grasp of such teachings as the unity of mind and matter, great compassion, and "all is emptiness." On the other hand, these were not things that I had personally experienced.
>
> Recently, however, I have had the opportunity to read repeatedly such materials as the biography of [True Pure Land sect founder] St. Shinran [1173–1262], the three Pure Land sūtras, and the *Song of True Faith (Shōshin-ge)*. Further, having devoured the biographies of [True Pure Land sect patriarch] Rennyo [1415–99] and [Pure Land sect founder] Hōnen [1133–1212], I have come to deeply realize that for people like me there is no

other method of salvation. As a result I have fervently recited the name of Amitābha Buddha (*nembutsu*) with the result that the more I did so the more grateful I became.

Nevertheless, I think my practice was still incomplete. No doubt this was because I was still attached to "life." But when my [death] sentence was announced, everything cleared up; and I was able to devote myself completely to reciting the name of Amitābha Buddha. The result is that I am now overcome with the joy of the Dharma (*hōetsu*).[18]

Interestingly, Doihara was not content to gain assurance of his own salvation. Rather, he urged his entire family to place their faith in the Pure Land school. In explaining why this was so important to him, he once again made use of his inability to gain salvation through Zen and requested that a letter containing the following passage be given to his family:

I think my children are well-suited for faith in the Pure Land. Given that even I failed at Zen, there can be no doubt that my children would fail as well. Further, reciting the name of Amitābha Buddha creates peace within the family. Thus, if family members will devote themselves to their occupations based on the spirit of reciting the name of Amitābha Buddha, the resulting spirit of gratitude will create in them a desire to serve society. Within the home, this spirit will serve as the foundation for all their acts bringing with it true happiness. For this reason I ask my family to discard their present [Zen] affiliation and embrace faith [in the Pure Land], seeking true happiness for themselves.[19]

In reflecting on the above quote, one cannot help but be impressed by Doihara's deep, if newly found, faith in the Pure Land school. As Doihara himself later admits, "Had I not been sentenced to death, I probably would have never experienced the joy [of the Dharma]. Rather, I would have died without experiencing the true value of life."[20]

Given that Doihara was awaiting execution, few if any would begrudge him the right to climb the gallows' steps with peace of mind however acquired. Yet, one searches in vain for the slightest recognition on Doihara's part that he had been part of a monstrous military machine that had denied the right of millions of human beings, both friend and foe, to face death with any "peace of mind" whatsoever. That is to say, there is nothing in Doihara's comments to indicate that he felt personally responsible for Japan's aggression, or even that he recognized that Japan had been an aggressor. He did, however, indicate his concern for the future when he noted that both Japan and the Far East as a whole were then embroiled in the midst of some "troublesome thoughts."[21]

While Doihara did not elaborate on what these troublesome thoughts might be, he was likely referring to the postwar spread of left-wing thought in Japan and especially China, not to mention Korea. "I sincerely pray," Doihara wrote, "for the appearance of a great man who can save us at this critical juncture." Just who this "great man" might be, Doihara did not say, but he nevertheless finished his letter to his family with the all too familiar words, "May the emperor live for ten thousand years!"[22]

Tōjō Hideki

Doihara was not alone in turning to faith in Pure Land Buddhism while in prison. General Tōjō Hideki (1884–1948), no doubt the best known of the seven, provides a second example of the influence of this Buddhist school. Tōjō had first risen to prominence as commander of Japan's notoriously brutal military police (*kempeitai*) in Manchuria in 1935. He went on to become a councillor in the Manchurian Affairs Bureau in 1936; chief of staff of the Guandong Army from 1937–8; vice minister of war in 1938; army minister from 1940–44 and, concurrently, prime minister from 1941–4. As far as the Allies were concerned, Tōjō was the arch-instigator of the Asia-Pacific War and, as such, his conviction and death sentence were foregone conclusions.

On Thursday afternoon, 2 December 1948, Hanayama Shinshō met Tōjō for the fourth time. In the course of their conversation, Shinshō noted that Hirota was the only one of the seven facing death to maintain his Zen affiliation. Hearing this, Tōjō replied:

> I could never practice Zen, for I'm just an ordinary person. Even such a distinguished [Sōtō Zen] monk as Ryōkan [1758–1831] wrote:
>
>> I am happy knowing the salvation of Amitābha Buddha is available to those as foolish as me.
>
> Given this, it is unthinkable that I might realize enlightenment through my own efforts (*jiriki*). I am deeply attached to Ryōkan's poem and repeat it frequently.[23]

Tōjō went on to explain why it was impossible for someone like him to realize enlightenment on his own. He claimed it was because "People like me are the stupidest of the stupid, the vilest of the vile.... In the eyes of the Buddha I am an 'extremely evil person' (*gokujū-akunin*)."[24] But just what had Tōjō done to make him so "evil"? Tōjō explained:

> For example, we human beings eat such things as meat and rice, not realizing that they, too, have life. We need look no further than food to realize that since we have to eat something in order to live we are all "extremely evil persons." If we fail to realize this then we cannot understand the meaning of "extremely evil persons" [as taught in the Pure Land sūtras]. In reality it is our puny intelligence that is the source of the

problem. It is for this reason that intellectuals find it so difficult to have faith.[25]

As far as Tōjō was concerned, his evil acts were none other than an inevitable part of the human condition, i.e. the need to consume other forms of life to survive. Thus, by virtue of being human, we are all equally guilty. Tōjō did not, however, seek to deny all personal responsibility for the war. On the contrary, at their very first meeting on the afternoon of 18 November, Tōjō told Shinshō:

> I feel relieved now that the trial is over and the question of responsibility [for the war] has been decided. As far as my own punishment is concerned, I feel it is appropriate. However, I do regret that I was unable to shoulder the entire burden myself, thereby making trouble for my colleagues. This is truly regrettable. Yet, I take some comfort in the fact that during the trial I was able to prevent His Majesty from becoming implicated in the proceedings.[26]

Tōjō's sense of war responsibility clearly extended no further than his fellow colleagues in the government and the military, including of course the emperor himself. It had nothing to do with a feeling of remorse for the many millions who had died as a result of his orders. In accordance with the traditional Japanese concept of duty, Tōjō was doing no more than accepting responsibility for Japan's defeat, not for having launched the war in the first place. That he saw no problem with the war itself is evident from his remark that "there will come a time when, thanks to the level-headed comments of informed people, the true meaning of Japan's actions will *finally* come to be appreciated. [Italics mine].[27]

While Tōjō did not acknowledge any pangs of conscience relating to the war itself, he did identify one area of moral failing on his part, i.e. the atrocities committed against prisoners of war. In his view, this conduct was "extremely regrettable." It was, furthermore, entirely his fault, for he had "failed to drive home in the military both the ancient Japanese spirit of benevolence as well as the emperor's graciousness." Tōjō expressed the hope that the people of the world would recognize that these atrocities stemmed from the erroneous actions of only a portion of the military and were not representative of the military as a whole, let alone the entire Japanese people.[28]

No doubt there is much truth in Tōjō's claim that neither the entire Japanese military nor the Japanese people as a whole were brutal rapists, sadistic torturers, and cold-blooded murderers of unarmed civilians and prisoners of war. Equally, Tōjō himself cannot be held solely responsible for the horror that was Japanese militarism, if for no other reason than that, even during the war, he was not the ultimate authority in Japan. This is demonstrated, among other things, by his removal as both chief of the general staff and prime minister in July 1944, more than a year before the war's end. Clearly this could not have occurred unless there were person(s) more powerful than Tōjō acting behind the scenes.

Tōjō hinted at who at least one of these persons might have been when he noted his satisfaction in having prevented questions related to the emperor's war responsibility from surfacing during the course of his trial. Postponing the question of the emperor's actual role for later discussion, Tōjō's acceptance of total responsibility for Japan's wartime actions can readily be seen as a way of shielding the emperor from scrutiny even at the cost of his own life.

Inasmuch as Tōjō's protection of the emperor was no more (or less) than what was expected of a loyal subject, one might think that Tōjō had been determined to do so from the day of Japan's surrender. This, however, was not the case, for Tōjō shot himself in an attempted suicide on 11 September 1945 just as US military police arrived at his home to arrest him. Tōjō explained the rationale behind his act as follows: "Inasmuch as I had, in the *Field Service Code*, directed my subordinates to choose death rather than become a prisoner of war, I simply followed suit."[29]

Ironically, it was only after having been nursed back to health in a US military hospital that Tōjō became seriously interested in Buddhism. Tōjō did, however, admit to having been nominally a Buddhist since childhood, for his mother had been affiliated with the True Pure Land sect even though his father identified with Shinto. For Tōjō, Shinto was not a religion since it consisted in nothing more than "showing respect for one's ancestors."[30] On the other hand, Tōjō had come to realize that "Buddhism was everything."[31] It even held the key to world peace:

> Buddhist faith deals with the fundamental nature of human life. It is only after resolving this fundamental nature that various surface problems in society can be resolved.... Contemporary politicians ought to read the *Longer Amitābha Sūtra* (*Daimuryōjū-kyō*) in attempting to rejuvenate politics, for it is this sūtra that explains the fundamental nature of life. People talk of the "United Nations" and "world peace" but these things will only be possible when human beings eliminate desire. It is this that will create "peace" in society.
>
> Desire is the true nature of human beings. Thus, the establishment of the state is also a product of desire. When such attractive words as the "existence of one's country" or "self-defense" are spoken, these too are an expression of the state's "desire." In the final analysis this is what causes war.[32]

As interesting as Tōjō's analysis is, if societal and world peace can only be achieved following the elimination of human, let alone state, "desire," then the human race faces a very bleak future indeed. This said, Tōjō's words certainly indicate a dramatic change in a man who only a few years previously had presided over the single largest and most brutal (in terms of numbers killed) empire the peoples of Asia have ever known. As for Tōjō's newfound faith in Buddhism, it is hard to escape the conclusion that it was "too little, and *much* too late."

Tōjō's interest in Buddhism was not, however, primarily dictated by his concern for establishing world peace. On the contrary, his interest was essentially no different than that which had driven such imperial soldiers as "god of war" (*gunshin*) Lt. Colonel Sugimoto Gorō to practice Zen, namely as a method of overcoming the fear of death. After noting that at the moment of execution there was no need for sūtras of any kind, Tōjō added:

> The only thing necessary is [the recitation of] "*Namu Amida-Butsu*" (Homage to Amitābha Buddha). When you've reached the end of the road, there is nothing other than "*Namu Amida-Butsu*." *Human beings must transcend life and death* [Italics mine].[33]

When the time for his execution came, Shinshō reports that Tōjō first shouted: "May His Majesty, the Emperor, live for ten thousand years!" He then walked to the execution chamber where he climbed the gallows' steps at one minute past midnight on 23 December 1948. His last audible words were "*Namu Amida-Butsu*."[34]

Matsui Iwane

The last of the seven to have a Zen connection, albeit a tenuous one, was General Matsui Iwane (1878–1948). Matsui had been a personal appointee of the emperor to the Geneva Disarmament Conference of 1932–7 and then commander of the China Expeditionary Force in 1937–8. It was troops under Matsui's overall command who committed the infamous Rape of Nanjing in December 1937 and related atrocities. Although Matsui no longer took an active role in military affairs after his retirement in 1938, he was nevertheless held responsible by the War Crimes Tribunal for his troops' earlier actions.

Matsui's Zen connection stemmed from the fact that he came from a traditional samurai family. Like so many other warriors, Matsui's forebearers had been affiliated with the Zen school during the Middle Ages. At the beginning of the Meiji period, however, Matsui's father consciously rejected his family's Zen affiliation and switched to Shinto exclusively. This switch was not untypical of an era in which institutional Buddhism as a whole was severely repressed by local and national government officials sympathetic to Shinto. Though this repression was short-lived, it had some long-lasting effects.[35]

Matsui himself drew closer to Buddhism in 1939 when he personally ordered the construction of the Kōa Kannon temple on a hillside outside of the city of Atami in Shizuoka Prefecture. The temple's connection to Japan's wartime effort was apparent in its name: "Avalokiteśvara for the Development of Asia." On 24 February 1940 Matsui said the following at the temple's formal dedication:

> The China Incident [of 1937 onwards] has resulted in massive loss of life through the mutual killing of neighbouring friends. This is the greatest

tragedy of the last one thousand years. Nevertheless this is a holy war to save the peoples of East Asia. . . . Invoking the power of Avalokiteśvara, I pray for the bright future of East Asia.[36]

Matsui also had a second and much larger ceramic statue of Avalokiteśvara placed on the temple grounds next to the main worship hall. This latter statue was approximately six feet tall and made out of the blood-soaked earth the general had brought back from his battlefields in China. He regarded it as a memorial to "console the spirits" of both Japanese and Chinese war dead.

Having previously mourned the war dead of both countries, Matsui was perhaps the best prepared of the seven to admit his own war guilt. In the fourth conversation Matsui had with Shinshō on the afternoon of 9 December 1948 he spoke at length about the events at Nanjing:

I am deeply ashamed of the Nanjing Incident. After we entered Nanjing, at the time of the memorial service for those who had fallen in battle, I gave orders for the Chinese victims to be included as well. However, from my chief of staff on down no one understood what I was talking about, claiming that to do so would have a disheartening effect on the morale of the Japanese troops. Thus, the division commanders and their subordinates did what they did.

In the Russo-Japanese war I served as a captain. The division commanders then were incomparably better than those at Nanjing. At that time we took good care of not only our Chinese prisoners but our Russian prisoners as well. This time, however, things didn't happen that way.

Although I don't think the government authorities planned it, from the point of view of Bushido or simply humanity, everything was totally different. Immediately after the memorial service, I gathered my staff together and, as supreme commander, shed tears of anger. Prince Asaka was there as well as theatre commander General Yanagawa. In any event, I told them that the enhancement of imperial prestige we had accomplished had been debased in a single stroke by the riotous conduct of the troops.

Nevertheless, after I finished speaking they all laughed at me. One of the division commanders even went so far as to say, "It's only to be expected!"

In light of this, I can only say that I am very pleased with what is about to happen to me in the hope that it will cause some soul-searching among just as many of those military men present then as possible. In any event, things have ended up as they have, and I can only say that I just want to die and be reborn in the Pure Land.[37]

For those many Japanese political leaders and historians who even today deny that anything like a rape of Nanjing ever occurred, Matsui's admission should make sober reading (assuming, of course, these leaders were interested in the truth). This said, Matsui clearly sought to distance himself from any personal responsibility for what took place even though, as the senior military officer, he could have always resigned his commission in protest. Instead, Matsui returned to Japan in triumph and on 26 February 1938 was summoned to the imperial summer villa in Hayama. There, in the company of Hirohito's granduncle, Prince Asaka Yasuhiko (1887–1981), and General Yanagawa Heisuke [1879–1945], the emperor personally awarded him a pair of silver vases embossed with the imperial chrysanthemum. Matsui would later repay this imperial beneficence when, in a pretrial deposition, he shifted blame for events at Nanjing to lower ranking division commanders, thereby protecting a prince of royal blood.[38]

None of this means, however, that Matsui's faith in Avalokiteśvara was any less sincere. In fact, his parting words to Shinshō on 9 December were: "I recently told my wife that the reason I am able to be reborn in the Pure Land is due entirely to the compassion of Avalokiteśvara, something for which I must be grateful."[39] Matsui also mentioned that he had told his wife to return the family to the Buddhist faith from Shinto, conducting all funerary rites accordingly. Moreover, once his wife had died, his house was to be donated to the temple he had established to provide for its upkeep.

It is interesting to note that Matsui was not the only one of the seven who felt a special affinity to Avalokiteśvara. While perhaps not with the same intensity, Tōjō Hideki also expressed his faith in this bodhisattva though in a most unusual way. After having told Shinshō yet again just how evil he was, Tōjō removed a handkerchief from his pocket given to him by one of his American jailers and said:

Avalokiteśvara came to visit me unexpectedly in the form of this handkerchief that was recently given to me. Avalokiteśvara kindly changed herself into this form though I must admit I find the whole thing very strange. I don't mean to be superstitious, and it may only be an accident, yet from the Buddha's point of view nothing is an accident.

You see, the brand name for this handkerchief is "Cannon," signifying an artillery weapon in English. However, pronounced in Japanese, the same sounds properly stand for "Kannon" [Avalokiteśvara]. It is for this reason that I say that Avalokiteśvara kindly changed herself into this form.[40]

If in these words Tōjō appears to be literally grasping at straws, it must not be forgotten that he was, after all, facing imminent death. Thus, any signs of supernatural intervention, real or otherwise, could not help but have been welcome. In addition, as incongruous as his identification of artillery weapons with Avalokiteśvara, the Mahāyāna personification of boundless compassion, may have been, it should be remembered that during the war years, the Rinzai Zen sect had done likewise. It revived a medieval sectarian practice of bestowing the traditional military title of *Shōgun*, i.e. Generalissimo, on this same bodhisattva.[41] Thus, Tōjō was by no means alone in his identification of the personification of compassion with war.

Finally, for those readers who may find it strange that Matsui looked to Avalokiteśvara rather than Amitābha Buddha for rebirth in the Pure Land, Shinshō described a letter that had been sent to Matsui in prison by Mitsunaga Taiyū, abbot of Zenkōji temple in Nagano Prefecture. After pledging to worship Avalokiteśvara for as long as he lived, Taiyū wrote: "Avalokiteśvara is identical with Amitābha Buddha; Amitābha Buddha is identical with Avalokiteśvara." Upon hearing of Taiyū's words from Shinshō, Matsui replied, "Please tell that priest that it's just as he said."[42]

Itagaki Seishirō

The reader will recall from chapter 7 that as a young officer, Itagaki Seishiro (1885–1948) had been interested in Zen. Nevertheless, in later life General Itagaki changed allegiance to the Nichiren school, the most overtly nationalist of Japan's traditional Buddhist sects. Itagaki had a long military career that included service as chief of staff of the Guandong Army in 1636–7; army minister in 1938–9; chief of the army general staff in 1939; commander in Korea in 1941; membership on the Supreme War Council in 1943; and commander in Singapore in 1945. Itagaki was also responsible for prison camps in Java, Sumatra, Malaya, and Borneo where troops under his command terrorized both military and civilian prisoners.

Itagaki's switch to the Nichiren school was connected to his acceptance of the apocalyptic world view advocated by another famous Nichiren-affiliated military leader, General Ishiwara Kanji (1889–1949). From May 1929 Itagaki assisted Ishiwara in drawing up plans for the 1931–2 seizure of Manchuria and the establishment of Japan's puppet state of *Manzhouguo* (*Manchukuo*). According to General Araki Sadao, then chief of the Operations Division of the General Staff, Itagaki and Ishiwara were an ideal combination: "Itagaki was a straightforward, uncomplicated fellow; Ishiwara was a man of lightning intellect, but both got on well together."[43]

In Ishiwara's mind the establishment of *Manzhouguo* was the first step in preparing for Japan's inevitable confrontation with the USA, inevitable because the USA was the chief source of the democratic ideology threatening to undermine Japan's founding principles centred on the emperor. War with the USA would, he claimed, lead to an unprecedented global world conflict, or "final war," the successful resolution of which would usher in a reign of universal and eternal peace.

Ishiwara had first developed these views after joining the National Pillar Society (Kokuchū-kai) in 1920. Readers will recall from chapter 5 that this Buddhist lay society had been established by former Nichiren sect priest Tanaka Chigaku in 1914. Tanaka propagated a doctrine he called "Nichirenism"

(*Nichiren-shugi*), a virulent mix of Japanese nationalism (including anti-Semitism) and absolute faith in the *Lotus Sūtra*. However, despite the centrality of the *Lotus Sūtra*, Tanaka also preached the supremacy of the emperor and asserted that Japan was the centre of the universe. This latter assertion led Tanaka to proclaim: "Japan is the Truth of the World, Foundation of Human Salvation, and Finality of the World."[44]

With this background in mind, it possible to understand what Itagaki meant when he shared his own "world-view" with Shinshō during their fourth interview held on the afternoon of 9 December 1948:

> Prior to the occurrence of the recent war, there were those who claimed this would be the world's final war, and I was one of those who supported this idea, or better said, I was one of those who believed it. We thought the world's final war would occur within twenty years. Japan had to prepare for that as well as be ready for the final "peace" that would follow.
>
> We did our very best to prepare for this. But, contrary to our hopes, the China Incident occurred [in July 1937]. Recognizing its seriousness, we sought to conclude this incident just as soon as possible. At the time I was serving in the War Ministry and tried my best [to resolve it] but failed. In the end it led to World War II, and Japan lost its fighting power as far as the "final war" is concerned.
>
> If, as the prophets have foretold, a final world war does occur, this will put Japan at a disadvantage now that it has renounced war. On the other hand, if such a war makes it possible for Japan to achieve its ideal of "true peace," I think we may have to endure it for a while.... In this event Japanese Buddhism will have an extremely important role to play.[45]

The "prophets" Itagaki referred to are, of course, Nichiren in the first instance as well as Tanaka Chikaku and Ishiwara Kanji among others. Nichiren believed that as of the year 1050 CE the world had entered a period of turmoil and degeneracy known as the "latter Dharma" (*mappō*). In his *Senjishō* (*Selection of the Time*) Nichiren predicted this would eventually lead to "a great struggle, unheard-of in times past" (*zendai mimon no dai-tōsō*). This was the source of Itagaki's belief in a "final war" though the idea that it would occur "within twenty years" can be traced to Ishiwara.

Nichiren also predicted that this great struggle would be followed by a period of universal and eternal peace where the *Lotus Sūtra* would reign supreme. Since, however, Nichiren believed that only he had properly understood the *Lotus Sūtra* in the age of the latter Dharma, Japan was destined to become the wellspring of true faith for the entire world. Japan would become the wellspring of a new "golden age" in which government and the *Lotus Sūtra*, as interpreted by Nichiren, would unite as one to preside over world regeneration, peace, and harmony.[46] Here is the origin of Itagaki's claim that *Japanese* Buddhism would have a special role to play in the coming era of true peace.

Given the fact that Itagaki was one of those primarily responsible for conducting a war that had caused the deaths of upwards of ten million Chinese, his claim to have sought to end Japan's full-scale invasion of China proper as quickly as he could rings hollow indeed. Yet, it is true that his mentor, Ishiwara Kanji, did actively oppose war with China to the point that, on 1 March 1941, then War Minister Tōjō Hideki forced Ishiwara to retire from active duty despite Itagaki's attempts to protect his old friend and mentor.

It must be stressed, however, that neither Ishiwara nor Itagaki were opposed to war itself, only a protracted war with China which they feared would divert Japan's attention and limited resources away from its true enemies. Japan should, they argued, seek to make China its ally in preparation for a possible war with the Soviet Union over control of Manchuria. Manchurian resources had to be retained in Japanese hands if Japan were to have any chance of defeating it's ultimate enemy, the United States. The war with China simply didn't fit in with Ishiwara and Itagaki's Nichiren-based, apocalyptic ideology of war and peace.

The American historian Mark Peattie sees a close connection between Ishiwara's fate and that of Kita Ikki, the Nichiren-affiliated ultranationalist civilian ideologue who, the reader will recall, was executed for his role in the Young Officers' Uprising of February 1936. Peattie writes: "In their shared apocalyptic vision, their militant sense of righteousness, their willingness to confront authority, their disdain of consensus, and their ultimate banishment for their views, they paid the price for their convictions."[47]

Needless to say, in their intolerance of others these men were doing no more than following the example of Nichiren himself. And herein lies the ultimate irony of Nichiren-based nationalism, for as "nation-centred" as it may be, it has never been wholeheartedly embraced by the state due to its claim to be in exclusive possession of religious truth. Down through the ages, Nichiren adherents have put forth various social and religious views which they demanded the state adopt *en toto*. While the modern Japanese state, at least initially, welcomed Nichiren-inspired nationalism, it was ultimately no more willing than its predecessors to subordinate itself to the dictates of Nichiren leaders of whatever stripe. In short, the very doctrinal support Nichiren adherents offered for assigning Japan a privileged role in spreading the one and only "true faith" led to its repeated rejection by the state.

Unlike Ishiwara, Itagaki did not pursue his faith in "Nichirenism" to the point of being removed from active duty. Although he was given lesser military commands due to his closeness to Ishiwara, he nevertheless faithfully executed the orders of his military superiors to the end of the war (hence he, rather than Ishiwara, was sentenced to die as a war criminal). One thing Itagaki did retain from his previous interest in Zen was the Zen-inspired view of life and death. During his second interview with Shinshō on the afternoon of 22 November 1948, Itagaki explained his view as follows:

First of all, even though I die I will continue to live through my descendants. Second, even though my outer form disappears, I will become one with all of nature. That is to say, when the desires attached to this despicable body disappear, I will become a god and a Buddha, one with eternal truth, one with nature itself. Third, I have no doubt that history will vindicate me, and thus I will not die. Therefore I believe my life and those of the others [who are to die with me] to be eternal.[48]

Itagaki continued by explaining that even after death he was determined to become a "nation-protecting spirit." When Shinshō asked him what he meant by the word "spirit" (*tamashii*), Itagaki replied:

Out of trepidation I chose the word "spirit" instead of "god." When I spoke to my children I told them that when they are at work on behalf of their country I will most certainly be there beside them. By discarding my outer shell I will acquire supernatural powers that can be used at any time. This is not a claim I make myself. Rather, Śākyamuni Buddha said, "Be diligent and acquire true awakening [enlightenment]. Don't be slothful!" His words may be a little different than mine, but that is what he said nonetheless.[49]

When Shinshō next informed Itagaki that the execution date for himself and the others had been postponed, Itagaki replied:

The postponement is annoying, for I would prefer that they kill me as soon as possible. On the other hand, it does give me an opportunity to come to a deeper appreciation of the debt of gratitude I owe the Buddha. When life and death have been transcended, one reaches this state of mind.[50]

And finally Itagaki handed a piece of calligraphy to Shinshō on which he had written in Sino-Japanese: "The secular world is empty and vain. The Buddha alone is Truth."[51]

Mutō Akira

General Mutō Akira (1892–1948) was vice chief of staff of the China Expeditionary Force in 1937; director of the Military Affairs Bureau in 1939–42; army commander in Sumatra in 1942–3; and army chief of staff in the Philippines in 1944–5. Troops directly under his command participated in both the Rape of Nanjing and the final Rape of Manila at the time of the Allied counter-invasion in February and March of 1945.

Both of Mutō's parents had been devoted adherents of the True Pure Land sect of Buddhism, and as a child he had taken part in the local temple's annual spring festival celebrating the birth of Śākyamuni Buddha. As a young officer, Mutō studied a number of religious traditions on his own, starting with Pure Land, but including Zen, Nichiren, and Christianity as well. Of these, Christianity attracted him the least, but he made no formal commitment to any of them.

Following his imprisonment, Mutō came to regret not only his own personal indifference to religion but the indifference of society as a whole. At his fourth meeting with Shinshō on the afternoon of 2 December 1948 he said: "Although the state concerns itself with such things as politics and the economy, were it to take 'religion' more seriously, I think it would undergo a complete transformation. Up to this point I have to admit that people like me have lived thoughtlessly without paying much attention to men of religion, heedlessly dismissing what they had to say."[52]

Nevertheless, Mutō did admit to having resumed his childhood practice of reciting the name of Amitābha Buddha. He did not claim, however, to have "transcended life and death" like so many of the others. On the contrary, he employed Zen imagery to show just how attached he remained to life, saying:

> For we human beings I think [attachment to life] is instinctive. For those who are enlightened, it may well be [as sixteenth-century Rinzai Zen master Kaisen Jōki said] that if you extinguish the discriminating mind even fire is cool. Those of us who are not enlightened, however, retain an instinctive attachment to life no matter what. While we may overcome this [attachment] intellectually, it is important to admit we have these feelings even though we be called unmanly or cowardly.[53]

Despite his ongoing attachment to life, Mutō was ultimately able to find a larger purpose to his death while, at the same time, reconciling himself to its inevitability. He expressed his feelings in the following poem:

> To become a pillar of peace is an extreme honor
>   for someone as insignificant as me.
> Inasmuch as I should have died on the islands to the South,
>   how can I be reluctant to lose my life?[54]

True to his somewhat ambivalent attitude toward religion, Mutō shared the following at his last individual meeting with Shinshō on the morning of 22 December 1948, less than twenty-four hours before he and his six companions were scheduled to be hung. Mutō said: "I don't know whether the Buddha exists or not, but without really meaning to do so I have been repeating "*Namu Amida-Butsu.*" You know, without really meaning to do so."[55]

Kimura Heitarō

General Kimura Heitarō (1888–1948) was chief of staff of the Guandong Army in 1940–1; vice minister of war in 1941–3; a member of the Supreme War Council in 1943; and army commander in Burma in 1944–5. Kimura helped plan the China and Pacific wars, including the numerous surprise attacks which played such a prominent role in it. Involved in the brutalization of Allied POWs, Kimura was the field commander in Burma when civilian and POW slave labour died in the construction of the Siam–Burma Railway including, of course, the infamous "Bridge on the River Kwai."

Of the seven, Kimura was the closest to being a Christian. This was, due more to the influence of his family members, however, than his own inclinations. His mother, younger sister, and daughter either had been or were Roman Catholics, and his wife was also sympathetic to this faith. One manifestation of this was that his family members asked a German priest to visit Kimura in prison in hopes that he would agree to be baptized prior to his execution. Kimura, however, refused to do so, and he later explained why to Shinshō at their first meeting on 19 November 1948. "I do have faith," Kimura said, "but I haven't chosen any particular religion, be it 'Buddhism' or 'Christianity.'"[56]

Because Kimura, at the age of sixty-one, was hearing-impaired, Shinshō found it difficult to communicate with him. Hence, nearly all of their relatively short conversations were concerned either with his family or events related to his impending execution. Perhaps the person who was most concerned with Kimura's religious faith was his 20-year-old Christian daughter, Yuriko. On 10 December 1948, Yuriko was waiting for Shinshō's arrival at the entrance to Sugamo Prison. She told him: "I'm concerned that because I believe in Christianity and my father is following Buddhism, he may feel constrained about leaving any words behind for his family. Please tell him not to fail to leave behind his teachings for us."[57]

Shinshō agreed to do so, and Kimura left behind a number of letters for his family including this parting poem:

> I pray that this mortal frame
>   may be reborn seven times,
> as a pillar of peace to repay
>   the debt of gratitude I owe my country.[58]

Emperor Hirohito

Needless to say, Emperor Hirohito was never indicted, much less convicted, as a war criminal at the Tokyo War Crimes Tribunal. In fact, his wartime role was never examined by the Allies in any public forum. Nevertheless, as American historian Herbert Bix has convincingly demonstrated in his recent book *Hirohito and the Making of Modern Japan*: "From the very start of the Asia-Pacific war, the emperor was a major protagonist of the events going on around him."[59]

In reaching this conclusion, Bix dispels the postwar myth that the emperor was a helpless puppet in the hands of the military and suggests that the real reason Hirohito's wartime role escaped scrutiny was, once again, due to Cold War-induced political expediency on the part of the USA and its western allies.[60]

This parallels Tōjō's previous testimony that he took satisfaction in "having not implicated the emperor during the course of the trial."

While, thanks to Bix's book, the question of Hirohito's war responsibility has been established at last, there was a related, almost unbelievable, plan that is far less known, a plan that would have seen Hirohito become a Buddhist priest in postwar years. It is unbelievable because wartime Shinto-based mythology portrayed Hirohito as a "living god" (*arahito-gami*), the latest in Japan's allegedly "unbroken line" of divine emperors extending back for some 2,600 years. Given this, it seems preposterous to think that either Emperor Hirohito or his advisers would ever have entertained the idea that a living god might transmute into a mortal Buddhist priest. Yet, preposterous or not, the historical reality is that it was given serious consideration.

The reasoning behind this consideration was that, like his loyal subjects introduced above, Hirohito might be tried as a war criminal. The worst case scenario envisioned the possibility that the victorious Allies would do away with the imperial institution altogether. In the minds of Hirohito and his advisers, the imperial institution had to be saved at all costs. But could Buddhism help preserve the throne?

A number of Hirohito's confidants, centred on Prince (and twice prime minister) Konoe Fumimarō (1891–1945), thought it could. On 20 January 1945 Konoe made an unexpected visit to the Shingon sect-affiliated temple of Ninnaji in Kyoto, ostensibly to pray for "the completion of the holy war." Ninnaji was the ancestral temple of Konoe's noble family, descendants of the Fujiwara clan who had served and intermarried with the imperial family since the seventh century. More importantly, Ninnaji had an impressive imperial pedigree in that it had been founded in 888 CE by Emperor Uda (r. 887–97) who later moved his palace inside the temple precincts and assumed the title of "*Hō-ō*" (Skt. *Dharma Rāja* or Dharma King), a traditional title for kings in India, China, and Japan who took upon themselves the role of protector of Buddhism. In Japan, the title *Hō-ō* was bestowed on an emperor once he entered the priesthood upon retirement.

Konoe, following his prayers for victory, convened a secret meeting at his nearby villa. Apart from himself, the other three participants were Navy Minister and Admiral Yonai Mitsumasa (1880–1948), former prime minister Okada Keisuke (1868–1952) and Ninnaji's abbot, Okamoto Jikō (1867–1957). Jikō was both the thirty-ninth in the line of Ninnaji abbots and the administrative head of the Omuro branch of the Shingon sect comprising some 800 temples in all. Konoe opened the meeting by saying: "In light of the precedent established by Dharma King Uda, I would like to propose that His Majesty be invited to Ninnaji to enter the priesthood. I can't imagine that the Allies would bother an emperor who had become a priest."[61]

All present supported Konoe's proposal including Jikō who agreed to step aside for the sake of the emperor, bestowing on him the priestly name of "Yū-nin Hō-ō." Yū-nin, meaning "abundant benevolence," was an alternative Chinese-derived pronunciation of the same Chinese characters used for Hirohito's secular name. Following this meeting, Konoe sought the support of Prince Takamatsu (1905–87), the emperor's second brother and a professional naval officer. Takamatsu's support was critical; for according to Konoe's plan, Hirohito would abdicate in favour of his small son, Akihito, while Takamatsu took over as regent until Akihito reached majority.

Once installed as Ninnaji's new abbot, Hirohito would devote the rest of his life to praying for the repose of the souls of all those who had given their lives in his service. Hirohito biographer Edward Behr records that Konoe spent nine hours trying to convince Takamatsu of the wisdom of his plan but to no avail. How, Takamatsu asked, could the Americans and British, who were Christians, be expected to understand the religious motivation behind an emperor giving up his throne in order to become a Buddhist priest? Weren't the Allies more likely to regard Hirohito's move as an attempt to escape war responsibility, thereby actually confirming his guilt in their eyes? The plan, he felt, was simply too risky to be implemented.[62]

Failing to gain either Takamatsu's support or that of other leading members of the emperor's inner circle, Konoe was ultimately forced to abandon his plan. It must be stressed, however, that this abandonment had nothing to do with the appropriateness of using the Buddhist priesthood as a means of protecting a possible war criminal. The fact that millions had been ordered to their deaths in the emperor's name was, morally speaking, of no more concern to Konoe than it was to Ninnaji's abbot, Okamoto Jikō, even though Buddhist precepts require the expulsion from the *Samgha* of any member who is guilty of taking human life. In agreeing to step aside, Jikō was doing no more than following a tradition of Buddhist subservience to the state that in his own temple's case already had a history of more than a thousand years.

Ironically, it was Konoe, not the emperor, whom the Allies chose to investigate as a possible war criminal. Faced with the prospect of being questioned about his wartime role, Konoe chose suicide by swallowing a cyanide capsule in the early morning hours of 15 December 1945. The question of the emperor's war responsibility, on the other hand, was never once raised by Allied prosecutors during the two-and-a-half years of the Tokyo War Crimes Tribunal. At no time did the Allies propose that Hirohito step down or accept the least responsibility for his wartime actions. Thus, at least this time, Buddhism did not become the last refuge for a man whom many, this author among them, regard as having been Japan's greatest war criminal.[63]

Conclusion

Tsuji Masanobu

Let me first note that, as strange as it may seem, Tsuji Masanobu's imitation of a Buddhist priest did not end in postwar Bangkok. In 1961 Tsuji, still a member of the Upper House of the Japanese Diet, once again donned the saffron robes of a Theravādan monk in the Laotian capital of Vientiane. This time, however, Tsuji's disguise was even less convincing than before. For one thing he had been unable to find any robes in Vientiane long enough to fit his relatively large frame. Second, he was wearing a style of eyeglasses not seen in Laos, where almost no priests wore glasses in the first place. And finally, Tsuji once again refused to shave his eyebrows as was also the custom for Laotian monks. In short, Tsuji was inviting trouble if he seriously hoped to convince anyone in Laos that he was a monk. But just why was he trying to disguise himself in the first place?

The answer once again involved war though this time it was not a war of Japan's making. Instead, Tsuji's concern was the civil war raging in neighbouring Vietnam. Specifically, he had come to Laos in order to gather intelligence on Vietnam in advance of a meeting between Japanese Prime Minister Ikeda Hayato (1899–1965) and President John F. Kennedy scheduled for May 1961. Based on past experience, Tsuji realized there was no better way of moving freely through roadblocks, checkpoints, and even across borders, than dressed in a monk's robes. Tsuji expressed a desire to visit Hanoi in order to meet Ho Chi Minh. "When I meet President Ho Chi Minh," he said, "I will try to convince him to stop this stupid war between the north and the south since both parties to it are Vietnamese."[64]

The last time Tsuji was seen alive was early on the morning of 21 April 1961. Two Japanese residents of Vientiene drove him to the city's outskirts where he met a Laotian priest who had agreed to serve as his guide. The two of them quickly disappeared into the mists of the Laotian highlands as they walked along the road leading to Luang Prabang.

Various theories have been put forward as to what happened to Tsuji next. One theory claims that he was captured and eventually executed as a spy by Communist Pathet Lao soldiers. A second theory asserts that he was killed by the CIA. A third theory has him reaching Hanoi and then leading North Vietnamese troops into battle. Nevertheless, in the absence of anything to indicate that he was still alive, Japanese courts declared him officially dead seven years later, on 20 July 1968. He would have been 65 years old.

Tsuji, it appears, was quite aware of the possibility he would not return. In March 1961, just one month before his departure for Laos, Tsuji visited the Sōtō Zen temple of Jiganji in Osaka to make a somewhat unusual request. He informed the abbot, Ōtake Ippō, that he wanted to change his sectarian affiliation from the True Pure Land to the Sōtō Zen sect. The reason Tsuji gave was that he was dissatisfied with the shortness of the posthumous Buddhist names bestowed on the deceased in the True Pure Land sect. Instead, he wanted a longer name as was customary in the Sōtō sect. Ippō, impressed with his earnestness, accepted Tsuji into the Sōtō sect and informed him that upon death he would receive the posthumous name of "Layman Radiant Nation Masanobu [residing in] the Temple of Great Serenity." Ippō added, "I felt something Zen-like about Tsuji's features and the way he moved his body."[65]

If there was indeed something "Zen-like" about Tsuji, it may have been best captured by D. T. Suzuki in his description of Zen-influenced warriors:

Zen did not necessarily argue with [warriors] about the immortality of the soul or righteousness or the divine way *or ethical conduct,* but it simply *urged going ahead with whatever conclusion rational or irrational a man has arrived at.* Philosophy may safely be left with intellectual minds; Zen wants to act, and the most effective act, once the mind is made up, is *to go on without looking backward.* In this respect, Zen is indeed the religion of the samurai warrior [Italics mine].[66]

If Suzuki's description may be taken as a model for the life of a Zen-inspired warrior, it would be difficult to deny that Tsuji Masanobu had, throughout his life, embodied it to the full. To those who would argue that despite his belated switch to Sōtō Zen, Tsuji never formally underwent Zen training, Suzuki had this to say:

The spirit of the samurai deeply breathing Zen into itself propagated its philosophy even among the masses. The latter, even when they were not particularly trained in the way of the warrior, have imbibed his spirit and are ready to sacrifice their lives for any cause they think worthy.[67]

As quixotic as his final imitation of a Buddhist priest appears to have been, Tsuji was fully prepared to sacrifice his life for a cause he, at least, found worthy.

Class A war criminals

In reflecting on the similarities between the Class A war criminals described above, we find that in their final days, at least six of the seven found spiritual solace in the Buddhist faith. Yet, with the possible exception of Itagaki Seishirō, it cannot be claimed that Buddhism *per se* served as the inspiration for any of them to participate in aggressive warfare. As for Itagaki, it is certainly debatable as to whether his adherence to Ishiwara Kanji's apocalyptic vision of a "final war" is an authentic expression of the Nichiren tradition. No less debatable is the question of whether Nichiren-inspired nationalism is an authentic expression of the Buddha Dharma. As interesting as these questions are, they lay beyond the scope of this book.

Few people would deny the right of condemned men to seek in religious faith a means of reconciling themselves to their impending death. Even their Allied executioners made certain that the spiritual needs of the condemned were ministered to. It is nevertheless striking to see how many of the condemned consciously looked to Buddhism, regardless of sectarian affiliation, as a means of *transcending life and death.* As previously revealed in chapter 7, this is exactly what led the Japanese military to incorporate the Zen teaching on life and death into such military documents as the *Field Service Code.*

It is also striking that, their faith in Buddhism notwithstanding, few if any of the condemned assumed moral responsibility for their acts. Matsui Iwane appears to have been the exception in that he genuinely regretted the brutality of the Japanese military following the fall of Nanking in 1937. Yet, he goes on to absolve himself of any personal responsibility, claiming that he was helpless in the face of his subordinates' unwillingness to restrain their troops. For his part, Tōjō Hideki appears to have come to regard himself as an "extremely evil person," at least within the Pure Land understanding of that term. Yet, he was equally convinced that despite the millions who died following his orders, "the true meaning of Japan's actions will *finally* come to be appreciated."

Whatever their differences, Matsui and Tōjō did share one thing in common, i.e. the strong Shinto influence exerted on them through their fathers. Given the ultranationalist and emperor-centric features found in prewar State Shinto, it is not surprising that they, as senior officers in what was known as the "emperor's military" (*kōgun*), should have been attracted to this faith. Yet, Shinto is a religion that offers surprisingly little spiritual solace to men facing the hangman's noose. Buddhism, on the other hand, especially in its True Pure Land formulation, offers the promise of personal salvation to all who seek it no matter how "evil" they might have been in the past.

Some readers may find it strange, or at least incongruous, to see how many of the condemned ultimately turned to the True Pure Land school for spiritual sustenance, especially when a number of them had earlier practiced Zen. Does the Pure Land school, like Zen, have a militarist dimension as well?

The reader will recall a previous discussion of this question at the beginning of chapter 8. It was there Satō Gan'ei was quoted as having said, "I think that for military men of today who wish to calm their minds ... only the Zen and True Pure Land sects can meet their needs." Further, as noted in the introduction to chapter 9, some of Japan's earliest military chaplains were itinerant Pure Land priests. Not only that, but the historical reality is that over the centuries some of Japan's fiercest battles have been fought by adherents of the True Pure Land sect.[68]

Readers of *Zen at War* will recall the deep impression Pure Land faith made on the Japanese officer corps during the Russo-Japanese War of 1904–5 as they observed the way in which adherents of this school were able, even though seriously wounded, to die on the battlefield without crying out for help. Instead, they simply recited *Namu Amida-Butsu*. "I was deeply moved," said General Hayashi Senjūrō (1876–1943), "by the power of the Buddhist faith as revealed in these soldiers' actions."[69]

Yet, what exactly was it that made the Pure Land faith so attractive to Japan's modern soldiers? The noted True Pure Land scholar-priest Ōsuga Shūdō (1876–1962) explained the underlying rationale as follows:

Reciting the name of Amitābha Buddha makes it possible to march onto the battlefield firm in the belief that death will bring rebirth in paradise.

Being prepared for death, one can fight strenuously, knowing that it is a just fight, a fight employing the compassionate mind of the Buddha, the fight of a loyal subject. Truly, what could be more fortunate than knowing that, should you die, a welcome awaits in the Pure Land of Amitābha Buddha?[70]

If there is a difference between Zen and the Pure Land tradition, it is simply this: Zen-influenced warriors were promised that by undergoing spartan, demanding, and highly regimented Zen practice, most especially the meditative practice of *zazen*, they would acquire a form of spiritual power that would directly enhance their martial prowess on the battlefield. Pure Land leaders, on the other hand, did not promise to make them better fighters, but they did offer "peace of mind" based on guaranteed entrance into paradise upon death. The common factor in both schools was their provision of a method for "transcending life and death."

Interestingly, generals like Doihara Kenji and Tōjō Hideki were not the only military men to have turned to the True Pure Land school in defeat, having decided that Zen salvation acquired through their own efforts was not possible for them. General Imamura Hitoshi, first introduced in chapter 7, was also attracted to Pure Land in the postwar era. Imamura's biographer, Tsunoda Fusako, noted that "[Imamura] was deeply moved by the idea of universal salvation as taught by Shinran." Yet, she also quoted Imamura as saying: "Having failed to bring victory to the nation, I must bear the great sin of causing many of my troops to die meaninglessly. After death I will be unable to go to either the Pure Land or Heaven."[71] Tsunoda explained the contradiction by claiming that Imamura had too strong a sense of responsibility to unconditionally accept the Pure Land tradition's offer of universal salvation.

Finally, it is noteworthy that the Pure Land faith was not only attractive to right-wing military men. Even a left-wing Rinzai Zen priest, Mineo Setsudō (1885–1919), found himself turning to it when facing a similarly hopeless situation. Setsudō had been sentenced to life imprisonment for his role in the "High Treason Incident," (*Taigyaku Jiken*) of 1910, an alleged anarcho-Communist plot to assassinate Emperor Meiji. While in prison, Setsudō wrote *"A Passage on My Repentance"* (*Waga Zange no Issetsu*) in which, after reflecting on his own weakness, he declared his faith in the vows made by Amitābha Buddha.[72] If, as D. T. Suzuki claims, Zen is a religion for those who seek an "iron will," then the Pure Land tradition is for those who discover that iron wills are of little value to the vanquished.

Hirohito and D. T. Suzuki

While, ultimately, Hirohito did not enter the Buddhist priesthood, this did not signify a lack of interest in Buddhism on his part. In fact, only eight months after Japan's surrender, Hirohito summoned no less an authority on Buddhism than D. T. Suzuki to instruct both him and Empress Nagako in the fundamentals of this faith. Suzuki delivered his lectures before their Royal Highnesses on 23–4 April 1946.

Fortunately, Suzuki published the content of his lectures, with some additions, the following year in a 136-page booklet entitled *An Outline of Buddhism* (*Bukkyō no Tai-i*). As its name suggests, it was a general introduction to Buddhist thought, not unlike what one might received today in an introductory course on Eastern religions. It did, however contain some surprises.

In the first instance, Suzuki took pains to defend Buddhism in particular, and religion in general, from those who asserted that religious belief was no more than superstition or

> even worse, religion is an opiate used by capitalists and bureaucrats to intoxicate the masses so as to make them act blindly, doing just as they are told. Those who reject religion think that god(s) are no more than objects toward whom one prays for selfish reasons.[73]

Needless to say, Suzuki is describing the militantly atheistic stance of Japan's newly reorganized Communist Party, the only sizable, prewar political organization to have spoken out, albeit ineffectually, in opposition to Japan's military aggression. Given the fervent and unconditional support for Japanese militarism that characterized all of Japan's religious traditions, from Buddhism and Shinto up to and including Christianity, it is hardly surprising that the Communist credo was attracting an increasing number of followers in 1946, especially given the desperate poverty in which the majority of the Japanese people found themselves.

To counter arguments like these, Suzuki emphasized the importance of a proper understanding of the "spiritual world" (*reiseiteki sekai*). According to Suzuki, this understanding could be acquired through "intuition that transcended discriminating thought," by realizing that the spiritual world and the ordinary world of our daily experience are "only one world." Misfortune (*fukō*) comes to human beings from the fact that "they think that the spiritual world and the discriminating world of the senses mutually clash with one another when what is needed is to penetrate through to the harmonious world of a single reality."[74]

Suzuki admitted that the term "spiritual world" was a designation he had given to such Buddhist terms as: "Nirvāṇa," "realizing Buddhahood," "rebirth in the Pure Land," etc. He warned, however, against the common (mis)understanding of these terms: these words should not be thought of as representing a world entered into only after death. The spiritual world Suzuki described could be entered *in this life* if "as the Zennists say, one kills the intellect."[75]

Suzuki explained the importance of killing the intellect as follows:

> The world of analysis and discrimination is ruled over by the firm conviction of the existence of the self. Thus, as long as one does not slay the

self, it is impossible to enter the world of non-discrimination and equality. The killing of the intellect is none other than the slaying of the self.[76]

Lest his words sound too warlike, Suzuki hastened to explain that the killing of the intellect really meant the *transcendence* of the intellect, something accomplished by the realization of a state of "no mind" (*mushin*) or "no thought" (*munen*). Should all of this remain too abstract, Suzuki quoted an unnamed Zen master who said: "Give the discriminating mind that is always spouting off about something or other a sound trouncing. Then feed what's left to the dogs!"[77]

Readers familiar with Suzuki's other writings will recognize the preceding comments as merely representative of his overall thinking, including the fact that he seldom if ever suggested that meditation, i.e. *zazen*, was either necessary or even desirable for someone seeking to enter the spiritual world. Also missing, of course, were his wartime comments identifying the warrior class as "the most Japanese-like" of all classes and asserting that most of Japan's problems could be solved instantly "if the warrior spirit, in its purity, were to be imbibed by all classes in Japan."

Nevertheless, at the end of his second lecture, Suzuki once again attempted to apply Buddhist doctrine to the political realm. This time, however, he came to a dramatically different conclusion. "We must," Suzuki claimed, "expand our vision beyond the confines of the nation-state as a vehicle for group living to include a 'world government' or a 'world state.'" The relationship of Buddhist doctrine to such a state Suzuki explained as follows:

> The ego of the nation-state is a form of self-attachment. Wherever the self exists there is always fighting. The reason for this is that those who cut themselves off from the world and don't know what is going on cannot help but be filled with fear and suspicion. At the same time they engage in the conceit of exaggerating their own importance. It is only natural that those who block the road leading to the outside world should end up like this. The final result is that they bring about the ravages of war.[78]

One can only speculate on the reaction of their Royal Highnesses to Suzuki's proposal for the creation of a "world state." After all, it is difficult to envision a place for either an "emperor," much less an "empress," in such a state. Perhaps that was exactly the message Suzuki intended to deliver. One would like to believe that he had learned something from the many millions who had "transcended life and death" to die selflessly for the emperor and state. Yet, if Suzuki had ultimately come to the realization that the state's ego was a form of self-attachment, the human cost of such a realization was very high indeed.

On the other hand, a more cynical observer might argue that not only Suzuki but the emperor himself were but adapting themselves to the new realities of a postwar Japan in which a commitment to peace was not only expected but required by the Allied Occupation authorities. Among other things, this meant that Hirohito had to distance himself from his former close association with the Shinto faith.

On 1 January 1946 Hirohito was forced, in his New Year's greetings, to renounce his Shinto-derived status as a living god. Then, only six days after the second of Suzuki's lectures, the Occupation authorities ordered Hirohito to cease honouring Japan's war dead through visitations to the Shinto-affiliated Yasukuni shrine in Tokyo where these "heroic spirits" (*eirei*) were enshrined.

Seen in this light, calling on Suzuki, whose prewar writings were already known and respected in the West, to deliver lectures on Buddhism at the imperial palace may well have been part of the larger effort then underway to "salvage the imperial mystique."[79] Were this the case, Suzuki was but doing his part in assisting yet another "war criminal" to take refuge in Buddhism.

11

BUDDHISM – A TOP SECRET
RELIGION IN WARTIME JAPAN

On a winter's day in early 1999 I was conducting research deep in the bowels of the library at Hitotsubashi University in Tokyo. In the midst of searching for a dictionary on leading ultranationalists in prewar Japan, I came across a book, the title of which immediately caught my eye: *Buddhism and Social Movements (Bukkyō to Shakai Undō)*. What, I wondered, was a book on Buddhism doing in a section of the library devoted to right-wing political organizations and personages?

Out of curiosity, I opened the book to find that it had been published in February 1939 by the Criminal Affairs Bureau of the Ministry of Justice. Its author was listed as Ogata Hiroshi, a public prosecutor in the Kanazawa district court system. What really surprised me was the stamp on the book's inner cover: "Top Secret" (*Gokuhi*). What, I asked myself, could possibly have made Buddhism in wartime Japan such a sensitive topic that a top secret designation was required to read about it?

Inasmuch as the book consisted of 497 pages in all, no more than a fraction of its content can be introduced here. Thus, I have chosen to focus on only two aspects of the book's contents. The first aspect concerns what the Japanese government feared in Buddhism, i.e. what the government feared from both left-wing and right-wing Buddhists whom it viewed as threats to public security.

The second aspect focuses on the book's conclusions, for here was an official government document that spelled out in some detail the role Buddhism was expected to play in Japan. If there were any question that the Japanese government opposed Buddhism during the war years, this section of the book should lay that issue to rest. There were, however, clear government expectations of the social, political and even religious values which a truly *Japanese* Buddhism should embrace. The crucial question is – did the government get what it wanted?

The Ministry of Justice's fears

Fear of the Left

Significantly, Ogata added the following subtitle to his book: "Primarily Concerned with the Incident Involving the 'Youth League for Revitalizing

Buddhism' (*Shinkō Bukkyō Seinen Dōmei*)." As this subtitle and the more than 200 pages devoted to this topic reveal, the original impetus for Ogata's book came from the government's October 1937 crackdown on this pan-Buddhist reform group. Inasmuch as I had previously introduced the League and its activities in *Zen at War*, I was curious to see what the League looked like from the government's viewpoint.[1] Just what was it that made the League such a threat?

Since some readers may not have seen this original introduction, let me begin with an excerpt from the League's founding declaration as made public on 5 April 1931 by the League's chairman, Nichiren lay activist Seno'o Girō (1889–1961):

> A revitalized Buddhism must deny currently existing Buddhism which has already lost its capacity for confrontation while, at the same time, calling on all Buddhists to return to the Buddha. A revitalized Buddhism must recognize that the suffering in present-day society comes chiefly from the capitalist economic system and must be willing to cooperate in a fundamental reform of this system, working to preserve the well-being of the masses. We must revolutionize bourgeois Buddhism and change it to a Buddhism for the masses.[2]

Between 1931 and 1934, the League published a total of six pamphlets detailing its positions on various issues. Of these six, two were written by Seno'o himself and the others by leading League members. Not surprisingly, Seno'o wrote the first pamphlet published which was entitled simply: "A Lecture on the Revitalization of Buddhism" (*Shinkō Bukkyō no Teishō*). In this pamphlet he presented a more detailed rationale for the founding of the League together with the doctrinal basis of its program.

A second pamphlet by Seno'o, published in 1933, was entitled: "On the Road to Social Reform and the Revitalization of Buddhism" (*Shakai Henkaku Tojō no Shinkō Bukkyō*). As its name implies, Seno'o focused on the need for social reform based on a Buddhist understanding. For example, he put forth the proposition that international cooperation, rather than narrow nationalism, was the Buddhist approach to world peace. When nations seek only to promote themselves, he wrote, they inevitably resort, sooner or later, to military force to achieve their self-centred goals. Such efforts, Seno'o stated, were clearly at odds with the Buddhist doctrine of "selflessness" (*muga*).

Seno'o maintained that the ideal Buddhist society, i.e. the *Saṃgha*, was a communal organization. As such it was in direct contradiction to the personal acquisitiveness fostered by a capitalist economic system. In particular, Seno'o saw Buddhist temples as the natural agents for the promotion of such a communal society in Japan.

Together with the capitalist system, it was Japanese Buddhism's leaders who came in for the harshest criticism. Among other things, Seno'o accused sectarian leaders of having turned the central object of worship in each of their sects (e.g.

Amitābha Buddha in the True Pure Land sect) into absolute deities who had the power to "save" the faithful. According to Seno'o, early Buddhism was clearly atheistic in orientation, with no place for salvation figures to act as religious opiates.

In addition, Seno'o accused temple priests of being "sermon thieves" (*sekkyō dorobō*). They deserved this title, in his opinion, because they took the position that social ills and inequities could all be solved, if only people would become more spiritually inclined. Behind the scenes, however, these same priests took care to insure that they themselves were well provided for through their solicitation of large donations. In so doing they effectively became pawns of the ruling classes who used their services to help support the status quo.

For Seno'o there was little if no hope that currently existing Buddhism would be able to reform itself from within. He made this clear in the final sentences of his pamphlet:

As the saying goes, one should not serve new wine from old wineskins. Members of the Youth League for Revitalizing Buddhism should advance resolutely. You should carry the Buddha on your backs and go out into the streets! Go out into the farm and fishing villages![3]

Needless to say, sentiments like these were no more welcomed by the Japanese government than they were by institutional Buddhist leaders. The government moved to censor the League's organ, *Revitalized Buddhism (Shinkō Bukkyō)*, as early as the November 1931 issue. Over the next five years the police, on more than ten occasions, either forbade the sale of the offending League publication altogether or required certain articles to be deleted prior to distribution. As Ogata noted, the League's publications, as well as its activities, were clearly aimed at "revolutionizing the national polity and denying the system of private ownership."[4]

As a consequence, government repression did not stop with censorship alone. League-sponsored public lectures were frequently terminated by police in the audience starting as early as May 1933. Seno'o himself was first arrested in September 1934 when he attempted to speak at a rally in support of Tokyo's striking streetcar conductors. Although he was only held overnight, he was beaten by a guard the next morning before his release.

In February 1936 Seno'o was arrested once again, this time together with another League member, Matsuura Fumio. The police were convinced that the League was either connected to the Communist Party or a Communist organization using Buddhism as a cover. Unable to force admissions of Communist affiliation from either man, the police finally released the two League leaders after having held them without charges for nearly one month.

Ogata makes clear that what was so disturbing about the League from a police perspective was the way in which its members took their organization's motto to heart. That is to say, members did indeed carry the Buddha out into the street. For example, as early as August 1932 League members began collecting signatures on the street for a petition drawn up by the Japan Farmers Union (*Nihon Nōmin Kumiai*). The League was collectively able to gather more than 2,000 signatures on this petition which demanded, among other things, that the government act to increase the incomes of tenant farmers and other workers so as to alleviate the growing disparity between the upper and lower classes.

In addition to its efforts on behalf of farmers, the League also took a strong stance against various government and judicial measures which helped perpetuate discrimination against Japan's traditional outcaste community, members of which were commonly referred to as *burakumin*. Still further, League members supported the activities of the "Anti-Nazi Fascism Annihilation League" (*Han-Nachisu Fassho Funsai Dōmei*) and took part in many anti-war labour strikes. Seno'o himself also became an editor of the left-wing *Labour Magazine* (*Rōdō Zasshi*).

Seno'o's activism came to an abrupt end on 7 December 1936 when he was arrested once again. This time he was charged with the crime of treason, punishable by death, for having allegedly plotted the destruction of both the emperor system and capitalism. At first Seno'o denied the police accusations, insisting that the League's goals were to *reform* capitalism, work for world peace, and oppose fascism and militarism. After enduring more than five months of relentless police questioning, however, he finally broke down and confessed that all of the charges against him and the League were true. Not only that, he promised that henceforth he would unconditionally support both the emperor and the nation.

Seno'o's confession was used by the police as the pretext for the wholesale arrest of more than 200 League members scattered throughout Japan starting in October 1937. Of those arrested, twenty-nine were eventually prosecuted including Seno'o, who despite his pledge of loyalty was sentenced to five years in prison on 29 August 1939. Given this background, it is little wonder that Ogata characterized the League as "possessed of a radical and lawless objective that, in the final analysis, puts an extremely distorted emphasis on Buddhist 'harmony' and 'love'."[5]

Fear of the Right

If the number of pages devoted to the topic is any indication, Ogata was far less concerned about Buddhist-inspired right-wing activities than he was about those on the left. He devoted only 27 pages to this topic, describing the activities of just one man, Inoue Nisshō (1886–1967), yet another Zen-trained ultranationalist who led a band of assassins popularly known as the "Blood Oath Corps" (*Ketsumeidan*).

Inoue began his Zen training in Manchuria in October 1912 while working for the Japanese-owned South Manchuria Railroad Company. Inoue's first master was a Japanese Sōtō Zen priest and "missionary" by the name of Higashi

Soshin. Inoue relates that under Soshin's guidance, he meditated on a daily basis for more than a year "almost forgetting to eat or sleep."[6] Inoue claimed to have passed a number of *kōan* during this period and, in recognition of his accomplishment, Soshin granted him the lay name of "Yuishin" (Mind-only).[7]

Although Inoue eventually left Soshin to become a spy and translator for the Japanese Army in northern China, he later noted that Soshin's parting words had a profound impact on his religious life:

> When I went to bid farewell to Zen Master Higashi Soshin, he said to me: "Had we had more time, I would have liked to instruct you on the *Lotus Sūtra*." At the time I didn't think much about it, but in later years this master's words were to have a major impact on my spiritual life."[8]

Inoue returned to Japan permanently in February 1921 and in the early summer of 1922 resumed his religious training in an abandoned Buddhist nun's hermitage known as Santoku-an located near his home village of Kawaba in Gumma Prefecture. Here, Inoue once again engaged in the intensive practice of *zazen*, though this time he trained completely on his own. Sometime later, however, Inoue felt that his practice of *zazen* was, if anything, actually increasing the level of distress he felt not lessening it. He wrote:

> After having practiced *[zazen]* for some time, I noted that during the time I was seated my mind became clear. However, when I had to stand up to do things like relieving myself, there was no change in my state of mind, and I continued to be afflicted by the same doubts as before. Since I didn't know of any other method [of training], I continued to practice *[zazen]* day and night but my mental anguish only increased.[9]

As a result, Inoue eventually switched to something he called *daimoku-zammai*, i.e. the state of *samādhi* (mental concentration) achieved through the repetitive invocation of the phrase, i.e. *Namu-myōhō-renge-kyō* (Adoration to the Marvellous Dharma of the *Lotus Sūtra*). It should be noted, however, that the inspiration for this latter practice came not from any contact with the Nichiren sect but was, rather, the result of Soshin's earlier influence coupled with a subsequent vivid dream Inoue had while still in China. In this dream, he had seen the phrase invoking the *Lotus Sūtra* engraved on a stone pagoda in the midst of what seemed to be a life-threatening situation.

Enlightenment

After further months of *daimoku-zammai* practice accompanied by still more visions, Inoue finally had an initial enlightenment experience in the spring of 1924. Significantly, Inoue employed classic Zen terminology to describe his breakthrough:

I experienced a oneness in which the whole of nature and the universe was my Self. I was overwhelmed with the feeling that "heaven and earth [and I] are of the same root," and "the ten-thousand things [and I] are of one substance." This was something I had never felt before, a truly strange and mysterious state of mind. I thought to myself "This is really weird!" And then I thought, let me examine my past doubts in light of the enlightened realm I had just entered. As I quietly reflected on these doubts, I was astounded to realize that my doubts of thirty years standing had melted away without a trace."[10]

The two phrases Inoue quoted above are contained in the fortieth case of the *Blue Cliff Record* (J. *Hekiganroku*/Ch. *Biyan Lu*), the famous twelfth-century collection of one hundred *kōan* that has been described as containing "the essence of Zen."[11] In the case in question, the conversation partner of the famous Zen master Huairang (677–744) cites a passage from an earlier essay written by Sengzhao (384–414) describing the oneness of heaven, earth, and humanity.[12] Significantly, Sengzhao is known for the deep influence Daoist thought and terminology exerted on his understanding of Mahāyāna philosophy, especially the Mādhyamika school's teaching of "emptiness" (Skt. *śūnyatā*, J. *kū*).

Good and evil

One of the doubts that had long plagued Inoue was how to determine standards for good and evil, right and wrong. Here, too, the Zen "solution" to this question is evident, for Inoue stated:

It is truly a case in which, from the very beginning, "good and evil do not differ [from one another]." Rather, when our thoughts and actions are in accord with the truth of a monistic universe, this is good. When they are not, this is evil.... This said, concrete manifestations of good and evil do differ from one another according to the time, place, and those involved. Thus, there is no need to be attached to a particular concept [of good and evil] or think about what is right or wrong.[13]

As will be seen shortly, Inoue did at least live up to his own perception of right and wrong. Or perhaps more accurately, when he subsequently embarked on his career as the leader of a band of ultranationalist assassins, he would find no need to "think about what is right or wrong."

Further Zen training

Although Inoue did not resume formal Zen training until sometime after his solitary experience of "enlightenment," he did, again in the best Zen tradition, realize the need for "post-enlightenment"(*gogo*) training. As he explained:

The reason that strange phenomena don't occur very often during the practice of *zazen* is because one's spirit is unified through the use of *kōans*, facilitating the rapid acquisition of wisdom. In my case, the strange phenomena that I experienced were an initial stepping-stone toward the realization of wisdom.

Undergoing religious practice by oneself is dangerous, for having entered the realm where strange phenomena occur, one may either go mad or become conceited. In Zen practice, on the other hand, if one displays any signs of strangeness, the waking stick (*keisaku/kyōsaku*) is employed as a warning to prevent these abberations.[14]

The temple Inoue chose for his post-enlightenment training was the famous Rinzai temple of Ryūtakuji, that the reader will recall was founded by medieval Rinzai Zen reformer, Hakuin. It is true, however, that Inoue chose to continue his Zen training only after having first visited the Nichiren sect's headquarters on Mt. Minobu where he found the training "unsatisfactory."[15] In addition, he also attended a week-long seminar conducted by ultranationalist Tanaka Chikaku, creator of previously introduced "Nichirenism" (*Nichiren-shugi*). As to why he ultimately chose to stay with Zen rather than adopt Nichirenism, Inoue wrote:

The reason I chose Zen is that, while Nichirenism is all right, it is full of discussion and debate. Furthermore, this discussion is of a scholarly type in which putting theory into practice only comes later, if at all. . . . What the nation and our people need now, however, is not theory but actual reform. That is to say, implementation must come first, and theory later. As far as I'm concerned, theory can be left up to those specialists who call themselves scholars. Given this and my own personality, which eschews both doctrines and creeds, I realized that Zen was best for me.[16]

Nevertheless, Inoue did write of his deep admiration for Nichiren as a historical personage, a man whose life of perseverance in the face of great adversity seemed to parallel his own. Yet even this statement must be qualified by noting that Inoue had first studied Nichiren's life only after having had his initial enlightenment experience.[17]

Inoue first went to Ryūtakuji in the fall of 1926 where he came under the guidance of a Rinzai Zen master now quite familiar to readers: Yamamoto Gempō. While at Ryūtakuji, Inoue was particularly attracted to the practice of *yaza*, the solitary late-night practice of meditation. Inoue recounted: "After bedtime at 8 p.m. I would enter the Hakuin Memorial Hall where I practiced *zazen* until around eleven. At times I continued my practice until 1 a.m."[18] In addition, Inoue participated in week long intensive meditation periods, i.e. *sesshin*, that were held at this temple on a monthly basis. Eventually Inoue was put in charge of the temple kitchen, one of the most responsible and difficult positions at a Zen temple.

Thanks to his previous right-wing connections, Inoue received an invitation in April 1928 to participate in the founding of a small temple in the village of Oarai not far from the city of Mito, north of Tokyo. This temple was to be built in conjunction with the construction of a nearby hall memorializing Emperor Meiji (*Meiji Kinenkan*). Whereas the centrepiece of the *Meiji Kinenkan* was to be a bronze statue of Emperor Meiji, the centrepiece of the temple was to be a bronze statue of Nichiren, selected for his well-known dedication to the defense of Japan. The Nichiren (and nationalist) orientation of this new temple is also reflected in the name selected for it, i.e. *Risshō Gokokudo* or Temple to Protect the Nation [by] Establishing the True [Dharma].

It should be pointed out, however, that Inoue was, at least initially, an interested bystander in the construction of this temple. The planning and fund-raising for its construction was in the hands of former imperial household minister Count Tanaka Mitsuaki (1843–1939) and the president of Ibaragi Transport Company, Takeuchi Yūnosuke. As temple records indicate, contributions toward the temple's construction came from scores of Japan's top political and military leaders, for from its outset this temple was designed to become the "foundation for the reform of the state" through training Japanese youth.[19] Nevertheless, Inoue initially declined the invitation to head the temple, for the simple reason that the temple, lacking traditional parishioners, had no reliable source of income.

Once persuaded to direct the temple's activities, Inoue did put on the robes of a Buddhist priest, though this was an act entirely of his own making, unsanctioned by any Buddhist organization or sect. It was this "imitation" of a Buddhist priest, coupled with the presence of Nichiren's statue in the temple, that would later result in both Japanese and non-Japanese scholars alike mistakenly identifying Inoue as a "Nichiren priest." Inoue never made this claim for himself, his robes notwithstanding.

Having agreed to head the temple, Inoue threw himself into the work of training a group of youths who would eventually number some twenty in all. Inoue's goal was to create a band of volunteers with a "do-or-die" spirit. Toward this end he employed a variety of training methods that included *zazen* practice in the morning and evening; assigning *kōan* and conducting private interviews with his disciples, i.e. *dokusan*; *daimoku* recitation; and fasting. In fact, youths seeking admittance to his group were first required to undergo a seven-day fast. Inoue explained the rationale for this requirement as follows:

Without doing this [i.e. fasting] the youths would talk big and spout nothing but theory, unable to undergo true [Buddhist] training. The reason that numerous training centres ended in failure was because they forgot this essential element in the hardening-up process.[20]

Although Inoue initially conceived of his band as engaging in legal political activities, by 1930, under the prodding of young military officer sympathizers,

Inoue realized he must take more resolute measures. He justified this new direction as follows: "In an emergency situation, emergency measures are necessary. What is essential is to restore life to the nation. Discussions over the methods for doing this can come later, much later."[21]

And toward what goal were Inoue and his band's "emergency measures" directed? Inoue explained: "We had taken it upon ourselves to engage in destruction, fully aware that we would perish in the process. Therefore we had no interest in developing constructive proposals of any kind."[22] Yet, how was Inoue able to justify such "destruction" on the basis of his Buddhist faith?

In actual fact, Inoue found no difficulty in doing so, for his Zen training provided him with the rationale, i.e. the taking of life was none other than an expression of Buddhist compassion. During lectures at his temple on the thirteenth-century Zen collection of *kōan* known as the *Mumonkan*, Inoue maintained that it was Buddhist compassion that had motivated Nansen (Ch. Nanquan, 748–834) to kill the monastery cat in case number fourteen. Building on this, Inoue claimed:

> Revolution employs compassion on behalf of the society of the nation. Therefore those who wish to participate in revolution must have a mind of great compassion toward the society of the nation. In light of this there must be no thought of reward for participating in revolution. A revolution that does not encompass a mind of great compassion is not Buddhist. That is to say, revolution is itself the mind of great compassion.[23]

Time for action

As the next step in achieving their goals, Inoue and key members of his band shifted their base of operations to Tokyo in October 1930. Finding a home with other ultranationalist groups in the nation's capital, Inoue continued his recruitment of youths, including some from Japan's most prestigious universities, who were prepared in his words to become "sacrificial stones" (*sute-ishi*).[24] Employing Zen terminology, one of Inoue's band members later explained: "We sought to extinguish Self itself."[25]

That Zen terminology should have continued to play a prominent part in the discourse of even those band members recruited in Tokyo is not surprising in light of the fact that the band members' "religious training" had by no means come to an end. In a 1998 personal interview, 90-year-old Yotsumoto Yoshitaka (b. 1908), a Tokyo University student at the time Inoue recruited him, informed the author that the band members frequently practiced *zazen* at the Rinzai temple of Ryū-un-in located in Tokyo's Bunkyō ward.[26] It was here that Yamamoto Gempō conducted *zazen-kai* (one or two-day Zen training sessions) on his regular visits to the Tokyo area. There is, however, no record indicating that Gempō was directly involved in Inoue and his band's plans for "revolution."

Yet, why had Inoue and his band chosen assassination as their method of revolution? Were there no other more humane ways of bringing about the fundamental reform of Japanese society which Inoue sought? Inoue stated:

> In explaining why "assassination" was the most appropriate method to have employed, I would point out that … this method required, whether successful or not, the least number of victims.… The critical issue is that there was no better method than implementing what I felt sure was best for the country, untainted by the least self-interest.[27]

It was exactly this point that Inoue believed distinguished his revolution from those that had taken place in western countries. In the French and Russian revolutions, Inoue claimed, the revolutionaries had worked to insure their own survival in order that they might secure a leadership role for themselves in the post-revolutionary era. As a consequence they were quite willing to kill any and all persons who stood in their way. The result was a massive loss of life.

Inoue and his band members, however, were prepared from the outset to perish themselves in the process of the revolution. The "selflessness" of their Buddhist faith enabled them to willingly sacrifice themselves, firm in the belief that others, particularly their comrades in the military, would follow after and construct the ideal society they sought. By being prepared to sacrifice themselves, they could insure that as few persons as possible would fall victim to revolutionary violence. A youthful band member by the name of Onuma Shō (1911–78) clarified Inoue's thinking in this regard as follows:

> Our goal was not to harm others but to destroy ourselves. We had no thought of simply killing others while surviving ourselves. We intended to smash ourselves, thereby allowing others to cross over [to a new society] on top of our own bodies. I think this is what our master Inoue meant when he told us that our goal was not to sacrifice personal affections on the altar of justice but to destroy ourselves. In the process of destroying ourselves it couldn't be helped if there were [other] victims. This was the fundamental principle of our revolution. A mind of great compassion was the fundamental spirit of our revolution.[28]

Inoue himself summed up his attitude in the following short poem: "Dew taken up in the palm of the hand fades away in the summer morning."[29]

Assassination

Of the more than twenty intended victims, only two were actually killed by members of Inoue's youthful band. The first of these was Inoue Junnosuke (1869–1932), a former finance minister, who was shot on the evening of 9 February 1932 as he entered Komamoto Elementary School in Tokyo to deliver an election speech. His assassin was twenty-two year old Onuma Shō, introduced above, a one-time baker's assistant and carpenter's apprentice. In subsequent court testimony, Onuma explained that he had debated with himself over whether to strike before Junnosuke spoke or afterwards. In the end he decided to strike before due to his concern that innocent well-wishers might be injured if he waited until Junnosuke's departure.

This, however, was not Onuma's only concern, for he was beset by anxiety over the act of assassination itself. Especially on the morning of the assassination day, he had been so upset he wondered whether he would be able to carry out his assignment. It was at this point that he sought strength from his Buddhist training as he began to quietly recite four sections of the *Lotus Sūtra* to calm himself. Thereafter he recited the *daimoku* four or five times and finally began to practice *zazen* in the full lotus posture. About this, Onuma said:

> After starting my practice of *zazen* I entered a state of *samādhi* the likes of which I had never experienced before. I felt my spirit become unified, really unified, and when I opened my eyes from their half-closed meditative position I noticed the smoke from the incense curling up and touching the ceiling. At this point it suddenly came to me – I would be able to carry out [the assassination] that night.[30]

Nearly four weeks later, on the morning of 5 March, Baron Dan Takuma (1858–1932), managing director of the Mitsui holding company, was shot just as his car pulled up to the side entrance of the Mitsui Bank Building. This time the assassin was a twenty-one year old band member by the name of Hisanuma Gorō (b. 1911). By this time Inoue himself had taken refuge in the "House of Heavenly Action," a student hostel run by the Black Dragon Society and located next door to the home of the previously introduced ultranationalist leader, Tōyama Mitsuru. Six days after Dan's death, and realizing his arrest was imminent, Inoue chose to turn himself in to the police.

Although Inoue's direct involvement with assassinations ended with his arrest, his indirect involvement did not. Only two months later, on 15 May, a small group of young naval officers, army cadets, and civilians, who had earlier plotted together with Inoue, launched a second wave of violence. This time the victim was no less than Inukai Tsuyoshi (1855–1932), prime minister and head of the Seiyūkai political party. Inukai's death, coupled with the earlier assassinations, marked the end of party-based government in Japan which in turn contributed substantially to the eventual military takeover. Thus did Inoue and his band's self-proclaimed dedication to "destruction" become a reality.

Court trial

Inoue's trial began on 28 June 1933. According to one description, the courtroom atmosphere was "as melodramatic as a revival meeting" thanks not only to the religiously impassioned court testimony of Inoue and his "right-minded" young followers, but the similarly emotional pleadings of the defendants' lawyers as well.[31] The trial so captured the nationalistic imagination of the nation that when, six weeks later, the presiding judges attempted to limit testimony to events directly related to the assassinations, the defendants, in an almost unheard of move, successfully demanded the presiding judges step down from the case due to their alleged "inattention."[32]

When the trial finally resumed on 27 March 1934, the new chief judge gave the fourteen defendants, Inoue among them, the right to wear formal *kimono* (not prison uniforms) in the courtroom as well as expound at length on the "patriotic" motivation for their acts. Inoue's testimony made it abundantly clear that his Buddhist faith lay at the heart of his actions:

> I was primarily guided by Buddhist thought in what I did. That is to say, I believe the teachings of Mahāyāna Buddhism as they presently exist in Japan are wonderful.... No matter how many sects Mahāyāna Buddhism may be divided into [in Japan], they all aim for the essence, the true form of the universe.[33]

If Inoue took a rather ecumenical stance in his testimony, it is also true that he went on to express his indebtedness to both the Pure Land and Nichiren sects for having contributed to his "salvation." With regard to Zen, however, he said: "I reached where I am today thanks to Zen. Zen dislikes talking theory so I can't put it into words, but it is true nonetheless."[34]

Inoue made another reference to an especially "Zen-like" manner of thinking when he was asked about the particular political ideology that had informed his actions. He replied: "It is more correct to say that I have no systematized ideas. I transcend reason and act completely upon intuition."[35]

Inoue went on to describe the contribution Buddhism had made to his band's acts. He first noted that Buddhism was a religion that taught the existence of "Buddha nature" (*Busshō*). Although Buddha nature is universally present, he asserted, it is concealed by passions, producing ignorance, attachment, and degradation. Japan is likewise a country that possesses a truly magnificent national polity, a polity that is in fact identical with the "absolute nature of the universe itself." Yet here too, human desires for such things as money, power, etc. had worked to conceal this incomparable national polity and resulted in dualistic ways of thinking, leading to the failure to comprehend the fundamental truth that matter and mind are one. Thus, even though Japan's national essence is excellent, degradation can occur.

At this point the judge interrupted to ask: "In the final analysis, what you are saying then is that the national polity of Japan, as an expression of universal truth (*shin'yo*, Skt. *tathatā*), has been clouded over?" Inoue replied: "That's right. It is due to various passions that our national polity has been clouded over. It is we who have taken it on ourselves to disperse these clouds."[36]

Yamamoto Gempō's defense

The 15 September 1934 morning edition of the *Asahi Shimbun* carried the following headline: "Zen Master Yamamoto Gempō, spiritual father of Inoue Nisshō, arrives in Tokyo to testify in court. Yamamoto claims, 'I'm the only one who understands his [Inoue's] state of mind.'"[37] Commencing his testimony at 11.10 a.m., Gempō said:

The first thing I would like to say is that Inoue has engaged in spiritual cultivation for many years. This led him to a direct realization of the most important element in religion – the true nature of the mind, something Buddhism calls perfect wisdom. Perfect wisdom is like a mirror that reflects humans, heaven, earth, and the universe. Inoue further realized that the true form of humans, heaven, earth, and the universe is no different than the true form of the self. The manifestation of this truth of the universe is the Spirit of Japan, that is to say, the polity of Japan. It is in these things that Inoue's spirit is to be found.

In light of the events that have befallen our nation of late, there is, apart from those who are selfish and evil, no fair and upright person who would criticize the accused for their actions in connection with the Blood Oath Corps and 15 May Incidents. Since agreeing to appear in court on behalf of the defendants, I have received several tens of letters. All of these letters, with but one exception, have expressed support for the defendants, identifying their actions as being at one with the national spirit. Notwithstanding this, however, it is utterly impossible to express by the spoken or written word the true meaning and intent of either Inoue or those allied with him in these two incidents.

No doubt there are those who would ask why, in light of his devotion to religion, a believer in Buddhism like Inoue would act as he did? This is especially true given that Buddhism attaches primary importance to social harmony as well as repaying the four debts of gratitude owed others and practicing the ten virtues.[38]

It is true that if, motivated by an evil mind, someone should kill so much as a single ant, as many as one hundred and thirty-six hells await that person. This holds true not only in Japan, but for all the countries of the world. Yet, the Buddha, being absolute, has stated that when there are those who destroy social harmony and injure the polity of the state, then even if they are called good men killing them is not a crime.

Although all Buddhist statuary manifests the spirit of Buddha, there are no Buddhist statues, other than those of Śākyamuni Buddha and Amitābha Buddha, who do not grasp the sword. Even the guardian Kṣitigarbha Bodhisattva holds, in his manifestation as a victor in war, a spear in his hand. Thus Buddhism, which has as its foundation the true perfection of humanity, has no choice but to cut down even good people in the event they seek to destroy social harmony.

Although Inoue came to visit me in the midst of his spiritual training, I most definitely did not give him my sanction [i.e. confirming him as being fully enlightened] nor say that his practice was complete.

Thus on 14 December of last year [1933], I received a letter from Inoue stating that now more than ever he wished to become a Buddha, that is to say, to realize the fundamental unity of the universe and self and become one with all things. Since then I have visited him [in prison] and verified his intention. The [Buddha] Dharma is like a great ocean, the further one enters into it the deeper it becomes. I believe that Inoue's true work is set to begin from this point onwards. However, in the event he were sentenced to death, his wish would remain unfulfilled. This much I can vouch for.

Inoue's hope is not only for the victory of Imperial Japan, but he also recognizes that the well-being of all the coloured races (i.e. their life, death, or possible enslavement) is dependent on the Spirit of Japan. There is, I am confident, no one who does not recognize this truth.

Although there is much more I would like to say, I have no doubt that both the lawyers for the defense who have thoroughly researched this case, as well as each one of the judges present who, possessed of a truly pure mind, graciously adjudicate it, are well aware of what I have to say.

At this point the defendants are not thinking of themselves, but state they have entrusted themselves to the judgement of the law. For my part I am absolutely certain they have truly become one with the spirit of the gods and Buddhas.[39]

Verdict and aftermath

Inoue and the members of his band were all found guilty and sentenced on 22 November 1934. As Gempō had hoped, none of the defendants were sentenced to death. Inoue and the two actual assassins were given life sentences while the others received sentences ranging from fifteen down to as few as three years. In rendering his verdict, the presiding judge described the motivation of Inoue and his band as follows:

[The defendants maintain that] to overthrow the old system of organization is a destructive or negative act. To establish the new system of organization is a constructive or positive act. Without destruction, however, there can be no construction. Since ultimate denial is the same as genuine affirmation, destruction is itself construction, and the two are one and inseparable.[40]

While the sentences were, especially by Japanese standards, clearly on the lenient side, what is more surprising is that eleven of the accused were amnestied and

217

released from prison in early 1935. Inoue himself had his sentence made progressively shorter until in 1940 he, too, was freed only to be invited a short time later to become a personal adviser to the then Prime Minister Konoe Fumimarō.

When Ogata published his report in early 1939 he was, of course, unaware that Inoue would be released the following year let alone become the prime minister's adviser. Nevertheless, there is ample reason to believe that Ogata would have welcomed these developments, for following an interview with Inoue in Tokyo's Kosuga prison, Ogata came away "unable to overlook the mysterious power that allowed Inoue to have a peace of mind so vast that nothing could disturb it."[41] Whether public prosecutor or prime minister, who would not seek for "peace of mind" like this or admire those who possessed it?

The Reformation of Japanese Buddhism

As demonstrated above, Ogata clearly saw left-wing forms of Buddhism as deviating from Buddhism's proper role in Japanese society. Right-wing figures, on the other hand, were far more tolerable, even admirable. This did not mean, however, that Ogata was satisfied with mainstream institutional Buddhism, for in his opinion the time for significant reform had arrived.

In the fourth and concluding section of his book, Ogata devoted two chapters to describing the nature of that reform. While the second chapter focused on specific proposals for improvement in the work of prison chaplains, the first chapter, entitled "The Necessity for Reform of Japanese Buddhism," contained an outline of Buddhism's ideal form, something Ogata (and his contemporaries) called "Imperial Way Buddhism" (*Kōdō Bukkyō*).[42] As an officially sanctioned "top secret" government document, Ogata's outline represents more than simply the religious prejudices of its author. Rather, it comes closer than anything else now available in describing not only the government's understanding of Buddhism but its expectations as well. For this reason, and despite its somewhat repetitive nature, the first chapter is included below in its entirety.

Chapter One

Religion represents a person's attitude toward life as well as their view of the world. Religion is most definitely not a simple question of ideology. Rather, it is composed of the entire experience of the real life of humankind. Buddhism, too, is like this, for it is based on the cognitive life of Śākyamuni who was delivered from life's suffering. Thereafter Buddhism could not help but develop and progress through the ages in accordance with the objective changes taking place in an ever changing society. Changes to its form and contents signify no more than the way in which it brings relief from suffering in accordance with the age in which it finds itself.

The true nature of the universe is that time changes incessantly and culture changes gradually. Nothing is permanent, and Buddhism is no exception. Buddhism's future is ensured exactly when it develops in concert with the age in which it finds itself, for therein lies the power for its development. On the one hand, the Buddhist goal of delivering various types of individuals [from suffering] cannot be regarded as of secondary importance. Yet the basis for contemporary practice must include both individual deliverance and the altruistic deliverance of society as a whole. Furthermore, Buddhism must seek the development of both the individual and society.

It is for this reason that Buddhism in Japan must focus on the Japanese people and state. That is to say, a Japanese Buddhism that has lost sight of Japanese tradition, history, and the Spirit of Japan is unthinkable. In this respect, the object of Buddhism's teachings must be the Japanese nation. The distinctive quality of Japanese Buddhism lies in its exaltation of the Spirit of Japan.

When we quietly reflect on the history of Japanese Buddhism, we find that it has had its share of ups and downs. Nevertheless, its true character was developed by the national polity of our country, producing an Imperial Way Buddhism characterized by its [historical] willingness to "pacify and protect the state" (*chingo kokka*) and "promote Zen for the protection of the state" (*kōzen gokoku*).

However, what is the actual situation Buddhism finds itself in today? The anti-religion movement [advocated by the Communists] rejects religion as an opiate that stupefies the masses. The Youth League for the Revitalization of Buddhism does likewise in that it denounces contemporary Buddhism for its failure to move beyond the realm of ideas while vainly compelling resignation and subservience, absent any guiding principles or vitality. The League argues that a religion that is not only unable to save the country but lacks guiding principles is nothing more than an empty shell.

In thinking about this issue, I find that contemporary Buddhism (and Christianity for that matter) truly have a number of aspects in need of reform. Needless to say, those anti-Japanese doctrines and teachings of the various sect founders must be reformed, for they were developed during [Japan's] Dark Ages when the national polity was obscured. Chief among these is the belief that Shinto deities are mere manifestations of Buddhist bodhisattvas. In addition, there is a need to convert temples into juridical persons, clean up priestly institutions, and undertake countless other reforms. This said, there can be no reform more important than the establishment of guiding principles for the salvation of our nation.

In this connection I would like to candidly and boldly propose the reorganization of the chief objects of worship. The essence of Buddhism is to be found in the Buddha, Dharma, and *Samgha*. Furthermore, Buddhism teaches that a Buddha possesses three forms: 1) his Dharma body, 2) his physical body, and 3) his reward body.[43] Inasmuch as in our country it is the Sun Goddess who, both in history and in fact, embodies all three of these forms, there can be no question that the chief object of worship for Japanese Buddhism must be the Sun Goddess, for she is the Truth of the universe. When this Truth is deified, it appears in physical form as the Sun Goddess. Therefore, it follows that today's sectarian-based Buddhism should unite together as one in reverence to the Sun Goddess.

Buddhism's ideal is to be a unified whole without sects. Furthermore, the guiding principle of Buddhism in Japan is the salvation of our homeland. The future development of Imperial Way Buddhism cannot exist apart from the exaltation of the Spirit of Japan. Thus, Buddhist sects should cease wrangling with one another and make the Sun Goddess, who is the Truth of the Japanese Spirit and the common ancestress of our people, their main object of worship. This is the practical observance of Buddhism in the present age.

Furthermore, as previously indicated, the Imperial Way of Japan and the true nature of Buddhist "wisdom" most definitely do not contradict one another. Therefore, making the Sun Goddess the chief object of worship while retaining Buddhist doctrine is the right thing to do. However, maintaining that Shinto deities are mere manifestations of Buddhist bodhisattvas is to revere India and China's past and must be rectified.

Japanese Buddhism has a hallowed history, having long been separated from its origins [in India]. Thus in form it has grown into something that is uniquely Japanese. Nevertheless, in terms of content it has developed some bad features, having degenerated into a religion that reveres statuary as its essence. The reform of present-day Buddhist doctrine requires a return to the past.

While it is true that Buddhism must be reformed, it should not be rejected. No, it absolutely must not be rejected! The reason for this is analogous to the situation in which my mother, having come to my father as his bride from another family, gave birth to me. My father would have no reason to reject me as his child simply because I was born from my mother.

Japanese Buddhism originated in India and was introduced into Japan by way of China and as such does contain alien ideas. Nevertheless, contemporary Japanese Buddhism is a religion and culture with an enduring history and tradition stretching back some 1,400 years since its introduction. To some extent at least, it has ended up being Japanized. That is to say, while it is true that Buddhism encountered opposition when it was first introduced as well as in recent years, it is also true that the Imperial Court deigned to fervently embrace Buddhism and establish it as a state religion with influence on political affairs. Furthermore, in the Middle Ages Buddhism spread widely among the general populace.

In any event, although it has had its ups and downs, Buddhism has in times past occupied the greater part of the intellectual and cultural life of our ancestors. Even more, our ancestors worked extremely hard to Japanize it. For example, granted that it was no more than a disguise, their efforts gave birth to the idea that Shinto deities were manifestations of Buddhist bodhisattvas leading to the amalgamation of Buddhism and Shinto.

The Buddhism of the Nara and Heian periods [646–794/794–1185] both had the important duty of pacifying and preserving the Imperial Court. This duty was subsequently given expression by [Rinzai Zen sect founder] Eisai in his treatise entitled "The Promotion of Zen and the Defense of the Country" and Nichiren in his "The Establishment of Righteousness and the Security of the Country." Added to these was the teaching of [True Pure Land sect] priest Rennyo who wrote: "Revere the law of the Sovereign and preserve the Buddha Dharma deep in your heart." Given that we know of these things even today, no one can deny that the deeds and thoughts of our ancestors have been transmitted to us as an ineradicable part of our blood.

Buddhism has, over the course of its fourteen-hundred-year history [in Japan], given birth to Japanese Buddhism. That is to say, while Buddhism is a heretical teaching, thanks to having bonded with the Japanese race, it has produced a distinctively Japanese Buddhism. Thus Buddhism cannot now be rejected for the same reason that my father cannot reject me.

The construction of a Buddhism for the new age must be based on its fourteen-hundred-year history while taking into account both the present and the future. To think of such construction, while trampling under foot Japanese Buddhism's distinctive character and history, is more in the nature of pure ignorance than mere recklessness. This is clearly demonstrated by the failure in recent times of the anti-Buddhist movement [of the Meiji period]. The rioting that occurred in various parts of the country at that time was not an expression of resistance to the new [Meiji] government on the part of an ignorant populace still attached to the old shogunal government. Rather, it was a backlash against the barbarism of those government officials who disregarded Japanese Buddhism's history. Although it can be described as similar to a religious uprising, its substance was completely different from the Buddhist-related peasant uprisings [of the premodern period].

Given this, it is clear that within the anti-Buddhist movement of today can be discerned the remnants of the anti-Buddhist thought existing at the time of the Meiji Restoration. While I can't be sure, this may be the reason Buddhist adherents have, of late, suddenly and confusedly spoken of the need to devise countermeasures. Yet one cannot but feel annoyed to discover that not a single one of their countermeasures addresses the root of the problem.

The core of the needed reforms is the abandonment of "blind attachment." Why is it that Buddhists teach others to rid themselves of blind attachment yet fail to do so themselves? Why is it that they teach others to do good and lead upright lives yet fail to practice these things themselves?

If contemporary Buddhists wish to discard their blind attachment to statuary and see the true Buddha in Japan, there is no more perfectly enlightened personage than the Sun Goddess. As I previously mentioned in my discussion on the essence of the Imperial Way, the gracious source of the creation and evolution of the universe is to be found in the Sun Goddess. If the Spirit of Japan is the distinctive quality of Japanese Buddhism, then the object of absolute devotion of Japanese Buddhists must be the Sun Goddess.

The reason I put forth this argument is not an expression of some narrow nationalism. Rather, I have clarified the special characteristics of both the Imperial Way and Japanese Buddhism in order to arrive at this conclusion. Were I to give a more detailed explanation of my reasoning, I would first point to the fact that in the True Pure Land sect, Amitābha Buddha is the chief object of worship. The reason that the phrase "*Namu Amida-Butsu*" [Homage to Amitābha Buddha] is recited in this sect, however, is not to gain worldly favors. Shinran clearly taught this when he said: "Reciting the phrase *'Namu Amida-Butsu'* is done as an expression of joy emanating from one's faith" (as quoted in Akegarasu Haya's book, *Amida no Hongan*).

Thus, one should not recite the name of Amitābha Buddha out of a desire to gain entrance into the Pure Land. Rather, such recitation is an expression of one's gratitude, one's desire to repay the debt of gratitude owed Amitābha Buddha. Even were one to express one's thanks over and over again, it would be impossible to completely satisfy one's feelings of religious devotion. Therefore the recitation of "*Namu Amida-Butsu*" is no more than the result of the need to give vent to such feelings. In short, it is no more than an expression of gratitude for those who have truly awakened to the road of life. If this were not so, and the name of Amitābha Buddha were recited with the goal of gaining worldly favors, then such a faith would be no different from the faith of those aborigines who worship phallic symbols. The same reasoning applies to the chief objects of worship of all Buddhist sects.

The repayment of the debt of gratitude we owe others is what Buddhists refer to as the four debts of gratitude.[44] In a country with a national polity such as ours, however, the truth is that three out of the four, no, four out of the four, ought to be respectfully reduced to the immense debt of gratitude owed the emperor. Further, as explained in the previous paragraph, the divine virtue of the Sun Goddess is unsurpassable. The gracious essence, virtue, and power of the emperor is most definitely nothing but an expression of his non-differentiated great compassion for others. As far as Buddhists are concerned, he truly ought to be worshipped as the essence of the various Buddhas and bodhisattvas.

If this is so, the emperor as a living god should also be considered the gracious appearance of the Sun Goddess in the present world. Thus, there should never be a case in which tenets arise [in Buddhism] asserting that it is wrong to pledge absolute faith in the emperor, that is to say, that it is wrong to worship the Sun Goddess.

It is also possible to discuss this issue from another point of view – that of ancestor veneration. I am confident that the highest form of ancestor veneration is to be found in the veneration of our common ancestors. At the same time, Buddhists already perform memorial services for our individual ancestors thereby acquiring considerable financial reward, designating it as the eternal recitation of sūtras on behalf of the deceased. These services bring in the bulk of the temples' income thereby insuring their financial stability. Given this, it would be illogical for there to be a theory claiming that it was wrong to hold worship services on behalf of our common ancestors.

It would be good for Buddhists to consider this – the ancestors who are beneficiaries of eternal sūtra recitations were, as citizens of this land, once joined as one to the gods. It is exactly this unity of gods and humans that has been the most precious and powerful legacy bequeathed to the Japanese people in every age. With their deaths these same ancestors entered into the realm of the Buddhas where their life as priests is assured. Given this, it is truly incomprehensible that Buddhists would fail to venerate their common ancestors who lie at the very core of their existence and with whom they share the same roots. Note that what I am saying here is neither the idea that Shinto deities are manifestations of Buddhist bodhisattvas nor some newfangled theory I have just invented.

At the end of the Tokugawa era [1615–1867], and prior to the promulgation of the edicts separating Shinto from Buddhism, every feudal domain was filled with a fairly intense anti-Buddhist movement. Moreover, as noted in my previous discussion of this movement, there were a considerable number of domains that took concrete steps to promote this movement. At that time, Buddhists, fearing the destruction of Buddhism, enshrined the Sun Goddess in their temple sanctuaries as a method of preserving the Dharma. The [Pure Land sect] temple of Zōjōji in the Shiba district [of Tokyo] is but one example of many that did so.

Yet another example involves the famous traditional temples located on Mt. Kōya dating back to the time of [Shingon sect founder] Great Teacher Kōbō [aka Kūkai]. Shocked by the severity of the anti-Buddhist movement, the sect's administrative body decided that in order to preserve the Dharma they would rename the entire mountain as "Hironori Shrine" [using the Japanese pronunciation of the Chinese characters for Kōbō].

Shaku Unshō [1827–1909], among other Shingon priests, opposed this decision and, in the end, this Shinto shrine never saw the light of day.

What should one think of this proposal? If asked, I would reply that it does not represent the mixture of gods and Buddhas. The reason is that gods and Buddhas ought not be enshrined together, for Buddhists should enshrine only Shinto gods. The argument that there is something wrong with Buddhists enshrining gods, or worshipping them, or placing one's faith in them, ought never arise anywhere. If such an argument were to arise, I dare say such talk would soon degenerate to the point that it would be claimed it is wrong for Buddhists to pay reverence to the emperor.

The basis for the future development of Japanese culture depends on the thoroughgoing yet critical adoption of a culture of [Buddhist] wisdom placed on top of a "culture of blood" and a "culture of race." Should this be forgotten, it will lead to a repetition of the same stupidity as advocated by the Freemasons.[45] Thus, it makes no difference who you are, for as long as you are a Japanese you must have faith in the Sun Goddess as our common ancestor and the center of our race. In other words, the Japanese people must absolutely embrace this faith, for the philosophical principles associated with the Sun Goddess represent the acme of our racial culture.

Today we are in the August Reign of Emperor Shōwa [Hirohito]. Domestically this is a time of enhancing the life of farmers while in foreign affairs, Imperial Japan's mission is to promote concord with all nations, knowing that we are now on the brink of accepting the heavy responsibility of guiding the entire world. Truly, this is the fall for Buddhists to be reborn.

It is unbearable to think about the situation which now prevails with Buddhists vainly esteeming ancient India while chasing after statuary and paying no attention to present-day Japan. If they truly wish to appreciate the national polity and clearly manifest Buddhism's true value, then they must rid themselves of former customs and, uniting together under the umbrella of the Imperial Will, take their first step forward as a reborn Imperial Way Buddhism conforming to the national polity.

Buddhism takes as its first principle the removal of attachment to all relative viewpoints and, further, criticizes polemics. Isn't it true that Buddhism rejects those who take pleasure in polemics as "foolish disputants"? Buddhism regards everything as being completely empty, without form or self. It recognizes and teaches that the Buddha, Dharma and *Samgha*, as well as the precepts and faith, should constantly evolve. Buddhism must not have sectarian egos or divisions. These divisions are even more abnormal than in the secular world and are the most despicable things imaginable.

Buddhism should make a principal of its original ideal of a unified teaching without sectarian differences. Japan has a national polity consisting of unconditional support for the Imperial Way. Though there are various sectarian doctrines, great compassion is one all-encompassing unity. When great compassion is merged with devotion to the Sun Goddess, then the true nature of Imperial Way Buddhism can be manifested. If Buddhism fails to wake up from its feudal dream, then momentum will build, and its success or failure will be left to chance. Just wait and see what happens then!

Author's conclusion

No doubt I am not alone in finding this chapter of Ogata's book, at least in its conclusions, to be one of the most fanatical pieces of religious writing imaginable. Further, Ogata's proposals for Buddhism's "reform" make abundantly clear the nature of the conflict between a race-based, nationalistic faith in a Shinto Sun Goddess (with a divine emperor as her living incarnation) and such universal tenets in Buddhism as "wisdom" and "compassion."

Since Ogata's writings were then "top-secret," he was clearly writing to influence the views of those relatively few government officials who would have had access to his report. Thus, he sought to defend Buddhism from those who even then regarded Buddhism as an "un-Japanese" religion. To do this, Ogata not only aligned Buddhism with the Imperial Court but demonstrated just how supportive Buddhist sectarian founders had been of the state during their lifetimes. In that sense, Ogata sought to convince his readers that the "Imperial Way Buddhism" he advocated was really nothing new.

Yet Ogata was clearly not satisfied with the Buddhism of his day, for he claimed it remained lost in its "feudal dream." While Buddhism was to be allowed to retain its "doctrine(s)," it ought to discard its sectarian statuary in favor of the Sun Goddess alone as the sole Truth of the universe. If there appear to be echoes of monotheism in this proposition, it must be remembered that the Sun Goddess was identified *en toto* with the "Japanese race." In essence, then, Buddhism was being called upon (if not coerced) to abandon its supranational objects of worship in favor of a national (if not tribal) deity.

Perhaps the most frightening aspect of Ogata's writing is that, as fanatical as he may now appear, he was ignorant of neither Buddhist doctrine nor practice. In fact, early chapters of his book contained quite lucid and detailed descriptions of not only Mahāyāna Buddhism prior to its introduction to Japan, but the earliest teachings of Buddhism in India as well. Thus, no matter what other faults Ogata may have had, simple ignorance of Buddhist doctrines and history was not one of them. Nevertheless, his knowledge of Buddhism did not prevent him from fervently embracing and promoting the race-based and nationalistic religious fanaticism of his age.

Ogata's writing is also interesting because of an implied admission he made with regard to the Sun Goddess: beyond a belief in the ultimacy of the Sun Goddess (and her imperial descendants ruling over a divine land), Ogata had almost nothing to say of any doctrinal content related to the broader Shinto faith. This suggests (though it does not prove) that while Shinto was indispensable as a "race-based" religion, by itself it was insufficient for anyone looking for a more sophisticated understanding of the human condition, most especially anything connected to personal salvation. Such matters were Buddhism's preserve, and Ogata was not prepared to cast it aside for a Shinto-only policy. Buddhism was, after all, nothing less than his (and the Japanese people's) "mother."

On the one hand, it can be argued that the Sun Goddess-centric form of Buddhism advocated by Ogata never came into existence. His urging notwithstanding, Japan's Buddhist sects never went so far as to replace their various objects of worship with representations of the Sun Goddess exclusively. Yet, it would be a mistake to interpret this as in any way demonstrating resistance to either Japanese aggression abroad or emperor-worshipping, totalitarianism at home. As this book and *Zen at War* have revealed, institutional Buddhist leaders were united as one in their fervent promotion of the war effort.

As far as the Zen school is concerned, it was "god of war" Lt. Col. Sugimoto Gorō who noted:

The Buddhist statues that are enshrined in temples should, properly speaking, have the emperor reverently enshrined in the center and such figures as Amitābha Buddha or Mahāvairocana at his sides. It is only the various branches of the Zen sect in Japan who have His Majesty enshrined in the center.... All of Japanese Buddhism should have His Majesty, the Emperor as their central object of worship.[46]

Sugimoto's stance is not the least surprising given Rinzai Zen Master Yamazaki Ekijū's own unambiguous endorsement of the emperor. Ekijū, Sugimoto's master, wrote: "The faith of the Japanese people is a faith that should be centered on His Imperial Majesty, the Emperor." A study of the literature of the period reveals that Ekijū's endorsement was shared not only by his fellow Zen masters but the leaders of all of institutional Buddhism.

Thus, if Japanese Buddhism succeeded in maintaining something of its traditional Buddhist character as far as its objects of worship were concerned, this must be considered as something of a hollow victory. In terms of the government's demand for absolute loyalty and obedience, institutional Buddhism did not hesitate to promote government policy as its own. Nor in fact did it hesitate to adopt the phrase "Imperial Way Buddhism." By March 1943, for example, both branches of the True Pure Land sect were using this phrase to describe themselves. The Nishi Honganji branch went so far as to claim: "In the True Pure Land sect there can be no teaching that does not advocate submission to the imperial national polity."[47]

That things could have been different is demonstrated by the existence of the Buddhist Youth League for the Revitalization of Buddhism. Its leaders clearly saw and opposed the growth of Japanese militarism and were prepared to risk imprisonment and maltreatment, even protesting against Nazi anti-Semitism as early as May 1933. On the other hand, the League can be faulted for having adopted an ideological stance that made it difficult to know where Buddhism left off and socialism and communism began. In any event, the combination of government repression and the opposition of institutional Buddhist leaders condemned this movement to failure from the outset.

In the final analysis, at least politically speaking, what the government wanted from Buddhism is exactly what the government got. The reader will recall that in 1943 Yasutani Haku'un wrote:

> In the event one wishes to exalt the Spirit of Japan, it is imperative to utilize Japanese Buddhism. The reason for this is that as far as a nutrient for cultivation of the Spirit of Japan is concerned, I believe there is absolutely nothing superior to Japanese Buddhism.

In identifying the "Spirit of Japan" with Japanese Buddhism, Yasutani was in complete accord with Ogata. And all too tragically, up until 15 August 1945 there was indeed "absolutely nothing superior to Japanese Buddhism" in cultivating not only that spirit but the brutality, inhumanity, and fanaticism it produced.

EPILOGUE

Where do we go from here?

The preface to my earlier *Zen at War* ended with the following Chinese maxim: "A journey of ten thousand leagues begins with the first step." Hopefully readers will recognize this current volume as constituting a second step along the path toward understanding. This said, a second step remains far, far, from the end of a journey of any significance. Were the phenomenon of holy war safely behind Buddhists, one might even question the whole purpose of "dragging up the past." Sadly, however, questions related to Buddhist-sanctioned warfare remain alive even today as demonstrated by the involvement of Singhalese Buddhists in Sri Lanka's bitter civil war.

When we look beyond Buddhism, we see millions of believers of all the world's major faiths, from the Balkan states, to the Mideast, to Indonesia, justifying the killing of their fellow human beings in the name of (or at least with the support of) religion. There is, of course, nothing new in this, for the historical reality is that all religions have engaged, at one time or another, in what are variously called "holy wars," "*jihad*," "just wars," etc. It is, for example, only in retrospect that the Christian Crusades from the eleventh–thirteenth centuries are recognized as having fallen short, far short, of the teachings of Jesus of Nazareth.

Closer to our own times, it must not be forgotten that the leaders of both the Protestant and Roman Catholic churches on the European continent remained silent, on the whole, in the face of Hitler's Holocaust against Jews and other "inferior races." Even more recently, in the war between Iran and Iraq of the 1980s, both of these self-proclaimed Islamic countries claimed to be engaged in a religious *jihad* against the other. "For God and Country/In the name of Allah, the *Merciful*" etc., are battle cries that continue to reverberate throughout the world, seemingly without end.

If I have one hope as author, it is that this book, like its predecessor, will serve as a catalyst for thoughtful adherents of all the world's faiths to look critically at the historical relationship of their own faith to state-initiated warfare. Couched in Christian terms, is there any world religion whose adherents in large numbers can claim to have always, or even consistently, or *even once* "loved one's enemy and done good to those who abuse you"? How is one to explain the tremendous gap that exists in all religions between their highest ideals of peace and universal well-being and the historical reality of their consistent endorsement of governmental war policies?

Rinzai Zen scholar-priest Ichikawa Hakugen went so far as to write that, in the face of death, war *requires* the unity of killing and the "peace of mind" derived from religion.[1] Expanding on this theme, sociologist Peter Berger wrote:

> Whenever a society must motivate its members to kill or to risk their lives, thus consenting to being placed in extreme marginal situations, religious legitimations become important.... Killing under the auspices of the legitimate authorities has, for this reason, been accompanied from ancient times to today by religious paraphernalia and ritualism. Men go to war and men are put to death amid prayers, blessings, and incantations.[2]

As early as 1932, the noted German-American Protestant theologian, Reinhold Niebuhr, described just how easy it is for the adherents, especially the leaders, of *ALL* religions to be found among "the worst liars of wartime." Niebuhr wrote:

> The nation is always endowed with an aura of the sacred, which is one reason why religions, which claim universality, are so easily captured and tamed by national sentiment, religion and patriotism merging in the process. The spirit of the nationally established churches and the cult of "Christentum and Deutschtum" of pre-war [i.e. World War I] Germany are interesting examples. The best means of harmonizing the claim to universality with the unique and relative life of the nation, as revealed in moments of crisis, is to claim general and universally valid objectives for the nation. It is alleged to be fighting for civilization and for culture; and the whole enterprise of humanity is supposedly involved in its struggle.
>
> In the life of the simple citizen this hypocrisy exists as a naive and unstudied self-deception. The politician practices it consciously (though he may become the victim of his own arts), in order to secure the highest devotion from the citizen for his enterprises. The men of culture give themselves to it with less conscious design than the statesmen because their own inner necessities demand the deceptions, even more than do those of the simple citizens. The religious or the rational culture to which they are devoted helps them to realize that moral values must be universal, if they are to be real; and they cannot therefore give themselves to national aspirations, unless they clothe them in the attributes of universality. A few of them recognize the impossibility of such a procedure. Among most, the force of reason operates only to give the hysterias of war and the imbecilities of national politics more plausible excuses than an average man is capable of inventing. So they become the worst liars of wartime.[3]

Sadly, Niebuhr's words remain as relevant today as they were in 1932. In a 1995 visit to Yokota Air Force Base outside of Tokyo, the author came across the following interview with Major Gary Perry, a local Protestant chaplain, in the base newspaper *Fuji Flyer*. When asked about the relationship between the Christian teaching prohibiting killing and the US military, Maj. Perry replied:

> I interpret killing as a willful taking of life for personal gain, or because of hate or convenience. I view the military as an institution that when going to war, *takes life to save people.... I believe it's sometimes necessary to kill in order to preserve life.* Of course, I would always encourage actions short of that [Italics mine].[4]

Major Perry's position is, of course, one that has a long history within the Christian tradition, reaching back to what eventually came to be known as a "just war," first advocated by St. Augustine at the end of the fourth century and further elaborated on by St. Thomas Aquinas in the thirteenth century. Whereas the subsequent Protestant Reformation changed the interpretation of many doctrines of the early church, the doctrine of a "just war" remained widely accepted. For example, Martin Luther made the following comments in 1523 in a treatise entitled *Secular Authority: To What Extent It Should Be Obeyed*:

> If your opponent is your equal, your inferior, or of a foreign government, you should first offer him justice and peace, as Moses taught the children of Israel. If he is unwilling, then use your best strategy and defend yourself by force against force .... And in such a war *it is a Christian act and an act of love confidently to kill, rob, and pillage the enemy*; and to do everything that can injure him until one has conquered him according to the methods of war .... *Such happenings must be considered as sent of God*, that He may now and then cleanse the land and drive out the knaves [Italics mine].[5]

In these quotations, I suggest, we hear a clear echo of wartime Sōtō Zen scholars Hayashiya Tomojirō and Shimakage Chikai who wrote: "Japanese Buddhists believe that war conducted for a [good] reason is in accord with the great benevolence and compassion of Buddhism.... We now have no choice but to exercise the benevolent forcefulness of 'killing one in order that many may live'."[6]

When their countries go to war, Buddhist and Christian believers alike are encouraged to ignore the ethical prohibitions against killing so fundamental to their respective faiths. Equally important, there is no suggestion of any personal responsibility for their murderous acts. Instead, it is an expression of Buddhist compassion to kill; it is God's will to kill. Separated by differences of hundreds of years, let alone culture and religious affiliation, how is one to account for this similarity?

Clearly much work remains to be done if we are to understand, let alone prevent, future "holy wars." This work cannot be done by scholars of religion alone, but must be conducted with the assistance of experts in a broad range of disciplines, most especially historians, sociologists, anthropologists, psychologists, political scientists, and even economists. In the absence of such multidisciplinary studies, the prospects for future holy wars are all too clear. As peace activist and Jesuit, Daniel Berrigen notes:

> Everybody has always killed the bad guys. Nobody kills the good guys. The Church is tainted in this way as well. The Church plays the same cards; it likes the taste of imperial power too. This is the most profound kind of betrayal I can think of. Terrible! Jews and Christians and Buddhists and all kinds of people who come from a good place, who come from revolutionary beginnings and are descended from heroes and saints. This can all be lost, you know. We can give it all up. And we do. Religion becomes another resource for the same old death-game.[7]

Clearly, the overwhelming majority of the world's religious adherents do not wish to see their faith become "another resource for the same old death-game," let alone used to "motivate people to kill." For this to be prevented, however, the world's major religions must call their adherents to a higher universal or global ethic – an ethic that transcends ethnic, national, or even religious identities, an ethic in which one is called to "love one's neighbour as oneself," wherever and whoever that "neighbour" may be.

In building support for such a universal ethic, religious leaders should remember that their role is one of leading by personal example and exhortation, inspiring others to adopt, of their own free will, the highest ethical standards of their respective faiths. Coercive methods of any kind must be clearly recognized as being the very antithesis of the authentically religious life. For this reason, religious leaders must resist the siren call of the state to use its coercive powers to enforce the particularistic moral dictates of their personal faith.

Despite the difficulties involved, failure to adhere to a universal global ethic is to invite continued repetitions of the recent tragedies in the former Yugoslavia, Uganda, not to mention New York, 11 September 2001, on an ever-grander scale. In the long term it could also make spaceship earth uninhabitable for the human species. Even more importantly, for those, like myself, who believe in the liberating function of the religious experience, it is to betray the heritage of religious sages like Śākyamuni Buddha who taught "never is hatred by hatred overcome, rather, it is overcome by love. This is an ancient law."

Shalom

POSTSCRIPT

In Chapter 1, I noted that none of the many branches of the Rinzai Zen Sect has ever admitted, let alone apologized for, their fervent support of Japanese militarism. Happily this is no longer the case, for on 27 September 2001 the 100th session of the Myōshinji Branch General Assembly held in Kyoto issued a proclamation containing the following passage:

> As we reflect on the recent events [of 11 September 2001] in the USA, we recognize that in the past our country engaged in hostilities, calling it a "holy war," and inflicting great pain and damage to various countries. Even though it was national policy at the time, it is truly regrettable that our sect, in the midst of wartime passions, was unable to maintain a resolute anti-war stance and ended up cooperating with the war effort. In light of this, we wish to confess our past transgressions and critically reflect on our conduct.

A follow-up statement by branch administrators on 19 October 2001 said:

> It was the publication of the book *Zen to Sensō* [i.e. the Japanese edition of *Zen at War*] that provided the opportunity for us to address the issue of our war responsibility. It is truly a matter of regret that our sect has for so long been unable to seriously grapple with this issue. Still, due to the General Assembly's adoption of its recent "Proclamation," we have been able to take the first step in addressing this issue. This is a very significant development.

Myōshinji, it should be noted, is the largest branch of the Rinzai Zen sect with more than 3,400 affiliated temples and 1.6 million adherents. In addition, the smaller Tenryūji branch issued a similar statement earlier in the 2001, once again citing my book as the catalyst. Kubota Jiun, current head of the Sanbō-kyōdan, also apologized in the spring of 2001 for the "errant words and actions" of Yasutani Haku'un during the wartime era.

232

As welcome as these long overdue admissions are, they represent no more than the first step on the road to restoring Zen to its rightful place within the Buddhist tradition. The challenge now is for all those whose lives, like my own, have been enriched by this tradition to create the second, third and subsequent steps.

NOTES

PREFACE

1 Quoted in Brian Victoria, *Zen at War* (New York: Weatherhill, 1997), p. 101.
2 Christian Brothers, *A Treatise on Modern Geography* (Dublin: W. Powell, 1870), p. 301. Modern spellings for some words have been employed.
3 Heinrich Dumoulin, S. J., *A History of Zen Buddhism* (Boston: Beacon Press, 1963), p. 290.
4 Quoted in Peter Harvey, *An Introduction to Buddhist Ethics* (Cambridge: Cambridge University Press, 2000), p. 34.
5 Ibid., p. 254.
6 See, for example, D. T. Suzuki's discussion of "Zen and Swordmanship II" in *Zen and Japanese Culture* (Princeton: Princeton University Press, 1959), pp. 139–214. On p. 144 of this section Suzuki informs us: "Without the sense of an ego, there is no moral responsibility, but the divine transcends morality." On p. 147 Suzuki describes this ego-less state as what Zen calls either "no-mind" (*mushin*) or "no-thought" (*munen*).
7 John Daido Loori, *The Heart of Being* (Boston: Charles E. Tuttle Co., 1996), p. 24.
8 Quoted in Peter Harvey, *An Introduction to Buddhist Ethics*, p. 254.

1 THE ZEN MASTER WEPT

1 Nakajima Genjō's war memoirs are primarily contained on pp. 41–68 of his book: *Yasoji o Koete* (Numazu, Shizuoka Prefecture: Shōinji, 1998).
2 Yoshida Yutaka, "Nankin Daigyaku-satsu o dō toraeru ka" (How to Grasp the Great Nanking Massacre?) in *Nankin Daigyaku-satsu to Genbaku* (Osaka: Tōhō Shuppan, 1995), p. 128.
3 Quoted in Iris Chang, *The Rape of Nanking* (London: Penguin Books, 1998), p. 48.
4 Ibid., p. 176.
5 Ibid., p. 49. Note that the romanized Chinese here, as in other places, has been converted to *pin-yin* format from Wade-Giles. The original read "Pikankan." While it is impossible to say for certain without seeing the original Chinese characters, the word "pi" (bi) can refer to a woman's vagina. Given the context, this (rather than "hip") is the more likely meaning of the term used by Azuma and his fellow soldiers.
6 Ibid., p. 218.
7 Quoted in Onuma Hiroaki, *Ketsumeidan Jiken Kōhan Sokki-roku*, vol. 3 (Tokyo: Ketsumeidan Jiken Kōhan Sokki-roku Kankō-kai, 1963), p. 737.
8 See Victoria, *Zen At War*, pp. 86–94, for further discussion of this point.

9 Quoted in Kenneth Ch'en, *Buddhism in China* (Princeton: Princeton University Press, 1964), p. 357. Liang Su was an important figure in Chinese intellectual and literary circles during the last quarter of the eighth century. He was among the first to recognize the possibility of a synthesis of Buddhism and Confucianism that eventually led to the creation of Neo-Confucianism. Liang studied Tiantai Buddhism under the guidance of Chanjan (711–82) who revived this school in the late eighth century.

10 Genjō provided the name of his torpedoed ship and estimated casualties in a second personal interview that took place at Shōinji on 25 January 2000. Of special interest is the fact that the Japanese ship that first rescued Genjō was itself torpedoed shortly thereafter, and Genjō found himself in the water yet again. It was his good fortune, however, to have been rescued a second time.

2 MONKS AND SOLDIERS MOVE ON THEIR STOMACHS

1 Quoted in Victoria, *Zen At War*, pp. 183–4.

2 Tanaka Gi'ichi was also a firm believer in the unified military state, yet another insight he picked up from his study in Russia where, as noted in the text, he had seen how domestic unrest could hamper if not badly damage a nation's ability to wage war abroad. In 1907, the same year this episode took place, Tanaka played a leading role in drafting a new Imperial National Defense Policy which called for a rapid military buildup to protect Japan's new interests in Korea and Manchuria. Promoted to the rank of major general in 1910, lieutenant general in 1915, and full general in 1921, Tanaka was a strong proponent of the Army policy that "a good soldier equals a good citizen." Accordingly, Tanaka left active military service in 1925 to become president of the Seiyūkai political party and then prime minister in 1927. As prime minister Tanaka ruthlessly suppressed domestic left-wing dissent while pursuing an expansionist policy in China. Tanaka died shortly after leaving office in 1929.

3 Ōe Shinobu, *Kogarashi no Toki* (Tokyo: Chikuma Shobō, 1985), p. 43.

4 Ibid., p. 46.

5 Ibid., p. 47.

6 For further information on the role of spiritual education in the Japanese military, see Victoria, *Zen at War*, pp. 114–16.

7 Originally Zen priests, together with the peasantry, ate unmilled brown rice (*genmai*). As milled white rice became more affordable due to the introduction of milling machines, however, pressure to switch to the more easily eaten and tastier white rice grew. Nutritionally, white rice has far fewer vitamins than unmilled brown rice. Eventually a compromise was reached in most contemporary Zen monasteries where barley, rich in vitamins, is mixed in with rice that has been milled for only 70 per cent as long as required to create standard white rice. As for the monastic evening meal, it should be remembered that mendicant Buddhist monks were originally forbidden from eating after noon in the hot climates of India and Southeast Asia. In the cold climates of China and East Asia, however, this prohibition was broken under the guise that the food eaten in the evening was taken for medicinal purposes.

8 Mizukami Tsutomu, *Ikkyū* (Tokyo: Chūō Kōron-sha, 1997), p. 42.

9 D. T. Suzuki, *Zen and Japanese Culture*, p. 62.

10 Quoted in ibid., p. 114.

3 THE ZEN OF ASSASSINATION

1 In addition to the incident described in this chapter, the most important of these assassinations were first, the shooting of Prime Minister Hamaguchi Ōsachi (1870–1931) on 14 November 1930 (died 26 August 1931); second, the shooting of

Prime Minister Inukai Tsuyoshi (1855–1932) on 15 May 1932; and third, the murders of three leading political figures (together with the wounding of one more and the escape of three) during the abortive Young Officers' Uprising of 26 February 1936.

2 This phrase is later quoted by Fukusada Mugai in defense of his disciple, Lt. Col. Aizawa Saburō's actions. It was employed repeatedly by countless Zen masters and other Buddhist leaders during the Asia-Pacific War (and before) to justify their endorsement of Japan's military actions abroad. Its origin can be traced to the famous Chinese Buddhist treatise entitled *Sanlun Xuanyi* written by the Sui Dynasty priest, Jicang (643–712). It forms one of the fundamental tenets of the Sanlun (Three Treatises, J. Sanron) school based on the Mādhyamika philosophy of Nāgārjuna. However, the "destruction" called for in this school originally had nothing to do with taking the lives of other sentient beings. Instead, it refers to "destroying" the mind of attachment, such "destruction" being in and of itself the establishment of the True.

3 For a detailed exposition of the February 26th Incident, see, for example, Richard Storry, *The Double Patriots*, pp. 177–91; Hugh Borton, *Japan's Modern Century*, pp. 386–9; or David Bergamini, *Japan's Imperial Conspiracy*, pp. 809–58.

4 The incident is described in Meirion and Susie Harries, *Soldiers of the Sun* (New York: Random House, 1992), pp. 181–2.

5 Quoted in David Bergamini, *Japan's Imperial Conspiracy* (New York: William Morrow, 1971), p. 802. It is also noteworthy that Yamazaki Ekijū (1882–1961), one of those Rinzai Zen masters whom I identify in *Zen at War* (see pp. 121–9) as a staunch supporter of Japanese militarism, conducted a memorial service for Major General Nagata following his assassination. It can therefore be said that at least in this instance prominent Rinzai and Sōtō Zen masters found themselves on opposite sides of the fence, though both remained, nevertheless, closely connected to the Japanese military. For further discussion of Ekijū's role see Ichikawa Hakugen, *Nihon Fashizumu ka no Shūkyō*, pp. 42–4, 81.

6 Quoted in Sugawara Yutaka, *Aizawa Chūsa Jiken no Shinsō* (Tokyo: Keizai Ōrai-sha, 1971), pp. 180–1. Prince Higashikuni was well-known for his interest in Buddhism. For details of some of the uses to which he put his Buddhist faith, see David Bergamini, *Japan's Imperial Conspiracy*, pp. 813–5, 1374–5. Readers unfamiliar with Bergamini's work, however, are cautioned against accepting at face value the author's always flamboyant and sometimes inaccurate description of events.

7 Ibid., p. 181.

8 Ibid., p. 181.

9 Quoted in Yamada Kyōdō, *Mugai-san no Fūkei* (Sendai: Hōbundō, 1991), p. 191.

10 Quoted in Sugawara, *Aizawa Chūsa Jiken no Shinsō*, p. 81.

11 Ibid., p. 203.

12 Quoted in Katano Tatsurō, *Kongō-hōzan Rinnōji Gohyaku-gojū-nen-shi* (Sendai: Kongō-hōzan Rinnōji, 1994), p. 191.

13 Ibid., p. 193.

14 Quoted in Hugh Byas, *Government by Assassination* (London: Bradford & Dicken, 1943), p. 111.

15 Ibid., pp. 111–2.

16 Ibid., p. 113.

17 Quoted in James W. Heisig and John C. Maraldo, eds., *Rude Awakenings* (Honolulu: University of Hawaii Press, 1994), p. 22.

18 R. H. Blyth, *Zen and Zen Classics: Mumonkan*, vol. 4 (Tokyo: Hokuseido Press, 1966), p. 123.

19 Quote in Katano Tatsurō, *Kongō-hōzan Rinnōji Gohyaku-gojū-nen-shi*, p. 189.

20 Ibid., p. 190.

21 Ibid., p. 190.

22 Ibid., p. 190.

23 Ibid., p. 193.
24 Quoted in Victoria, *Zen at War*, p. 37.
25 D.T. Suzuki, *Zen and Japanese Culture*, p. 63.
26 Ibid., p. 84.
27 In Japanese, the two assassinations referred to are collectively known as the "*Ketsumeidan Jiken*," i.e. the Blood Oath Corps Incident. The Blood Oath Corps was a band of assassins headed by Inoue Nisshō, lay disciple of Rinzai Zen Master Yamamoto Gempō introduced in chapter 1. As noted in the text, the Zen connection to this incident will be introduced in chapter 11. See also Victoria, "The Zen of Assassination: The Cases of Fukusada Mugai and Yamamoto Gempō," published in *ARC, The Journal of the Faculty of Religious Studies*, McGill University, 27, 1999, pp. 5–36. Note, too, that the assassination of Prime Minister Inukai Tsuyoshi on 15 May 1932 was an extension, or second phase, of the Blood Oath Corps Incident.

4 ŌMORI SŌGEN

 1 Dōgen Hosokawa, *Omori Sogen – The Art of a Zen Master* (London: Kegan Paul International, 1999), pp. *xi–xiii*.
 2 See Victoria, *Zen at War*, pp. 112–13, 160–2.
 3 Ibid., pp. 188–90.
 4 Quoted in Dōgen Hosokawa, *Omori Sogen – The Art of a Zen Master*, pp. 71–2.
 5 Quoted in Ōmori Sōgen, *Sanzen Nyūmon* (Tokyo: Kōdan-sha, 1986), pp. 248–9.
 6 Quoted in Victoria, *Zen at War*, p. 188.
 7 Quoted in Hosokawa, *Omori Sogen – The Art of a Zen Master*, p. 28.
 8 Ibid., p. 58.
 9 Ōmori Sōgen, *Yamaoka Tesshū* (Tokyo: Shunjū-sha, 1983), p. 212.
10 Quoted in Dōgen Hosokawa, *Omori Sogen – The Art of a Zen Master*, p. 73.
11 Ibid., p. 81.
12 Ibid., p. 95.
13 Contained in Arahara Bokusui, *Dai-Uha Shi* (Tokyo: Dai-Nippon Issei-kai Shuppan), pp. 21–2.
14 Quoted in Hori Yukio, *Uha Jiten* (Tokyo: Sanryō Shobō, 1991), p. 123.
15 Ibid., p. 125.
16 Ibid., p. 312.
17 Quoted in Dōgen Hosokawa, *Omori Sogen – The Art of a Zen Master*, p. 41.
18 Ibid., p. 40.
19 Hori Yukio, *Uha Jiten*, p. 311.
20 See Ben-Ami Shillony, *Revolt in Japan* (Princeton: Princeton University Press, 1973), p. 42.
21 Arahara Bokusui, *Dai-Uha Shi*, p. 432.
22 Contained in ibid., p. 431.
23 Quoted in Hori Yukio, *Uha Jiten*, p. 416.
24 Quoted in Dōgen Hosokawa, *Omori Sogen – The Art of a Zen Master*, p. 43.
25 Quoted in Naimushō Keiho-kyoku, *Shuppan Keisatsu-hō*, No. 73 (September 1934), p. 166.
26 Arahara Bokusui, *Dai-Uha Shi*, p. 432.
27 Ben-Ami Shillony, *Revolt in Japan*, p. 112.
28 Quoted in Toyoda Jō, *Kakumeika Kita Ikki* (Tokyo: Kōdan-sha, 1991), p. 409.
29 Quoted in Hori Yukio, *Uha Jiten*, p. 294.
30 Quoted in ibid., p. 294.
31 See Ben-Ami Shillony, *Revolt in Japan*, p. 128.
32 Ibid., p. 132.
33 Quoted in Dōgen Hosokawa, *Omori Sogen – The Art of a Zen Master*, p. 45.

34 Quoted in Ben-Ami Shillony, *Revolt in Japan*, p. 164.
35 Quoted in ibid., p. 173.
36 Herbert Bix, *Hirohito and the Making of Modern Japan* (New York: HarperCollins, 2000), p. 305.
37 Quoted in Dōgen Hosokawa, *Omori Sogen – The Art of a Zen Master*, p. 45.
38 Quoted in Civil Intelligence Section; General Headquarters, US Far East Command, *The Brocade Banner – The Story of Japanese Nationalism* (unpublished, typed report issued on 23 September 1946), p. 92.
39 Ibid., p. 91.
40 Quoted in Hosokawa, *Omori Sogen – The Art of a Zen Master*, p. 47.
41 For more on Seki Seisetsu's political views, especially his strong support for Japan's military actions, see Victoria, *Zen at War*, pp. 112–13.
42 Ibid., p. 47.
43 Ibid., p. 47.
44 Ibid., p. 51.
45 Civil Intelligence Section, *The Brocade Banner – The Story of Japanese Nationalism*, p. 129.
46 Quoted in Dōgen Hosokawa, *Omori Sogen – The Art of a Zen Master*, p. 51.
47 Ibid., p. 49.
48 For further details in Victoria, *Zen at War*, p. 190.
49 Dōgen Hosokawa, *Omori Sogen – The Art of a Zen Master*, p. 51.
50 Quoted in ibid., p. 51.
51 See Victoria, *Zen at War*, p. 189.
52 Quoted in Dōgen Hosokawa, *Omori Sogen – The Art of a Zen Master*, p. 51.
53 Ibid., p. 51.
54 Ibid., p. 52.
55 Quoted in Hori Yukio, *Uha Jiten*, p. 308.
56 Ibid., p. 308.
57 Ibid., p. 308.
58 Ibid., p. 309.
59 Ibid., p. 234.
60 Dōgen Hosokawa, *Omori Sogen – The Art of a Zen Master*, pp. 76–7.
61 Quoted in ibid, pp. 90–91.
62 Quoted in James W. Heisig and John C. Maraldo, eds., *Rude Awakenings*, p. 20.
63 Collected by Echū in 1660.
64 Quoted in Dōgen Hosokawa, *Omori Sogen – The Art of a Zen Master*, p. 92.
65 Ibid., p. 98.
66 Described in Ben-Ami Shillony, *Revolt in Japan*, pp. 216–17. For a more complete discussion, see Masao Maruyama, *Thought and Behaviour in Modern Japanese Politics* (London: Oxford University Press, 1963), pp. 26–33, 65.
67 Quoted in David Titus, *Palace and Politics in Prewar Japan* (New York: Studies of the East Asian Institute, Columbia University, 1974), p. 275.
68 Herbert Bix, *Hirohito and the Making of Modern Japan*, p. 305.
69 Quoted in David Titus, *Palace and Politics in Prewar Japan*, p. 287.
70 Herbert Bix, *Hirohito and the Making of Modern Japan*, pp. 302–6.
71 David Titus, *Palace and Politics in Prewar Japan*, pp. 286–7.
72 Quoted in ibid., p. 285.
73 Ōmori Sōgen, *Ken to Zen* (Tokyo: Shunjū-sha, 1966), p. 69.

5 ZEN MASTER DŌGEN GOES TO WAR

1 Victoria, *Zen at War*, p. 167.
2 For an introduction to Ichikawa Hakugen, see Victoria, *Zen at War*, pp. 166–74.

3   Ibid., pp. 137–8.

4   Ibid., p. 137.

5   Ibid., p. 168.

6   For further discussion of this topic, including further references to both Nakaseko and Kodera's research, see Heinrich Dumoulin, *Zen Buddhism: A History, Japan*, n. 3–4, p. 106.

7   Quoted in Philip Kapleau, *The Three Pillars of Zen* (Tokyo: John Weatherhill, 1965), p. 29.

8   No. 7, December 2, 1980.

9   No. 11, December 11, 1980, p. 4.

10 David G. Goodman and Masanori Miyazawa, *Jews in the Japanese Mind* (New York: The Free Press, 1995), pp. 106–7.

11 This quotation is taken from an article by J. H. Hunting entitled "The Protocols of the Elders of Zion," that first appeared in the March 1978 issue of *Vineyard*. The complete article is available on the Internet at: http://www.cdn-friends-icej.ca/antiholo/protocol.html.

12 Tanaka Chigaku, *Shishi-ō Zenshū Daisan-shū*, vol. 6 (Tokyo: Shishi-ō Bunko, 1937), p. 353.

13 Ibid., pp. 353–4.

14 Additional background information contained in Leonard Mosley, *Hirohito, Emperor of Japan*, p. 186.

15 Quoted in John Dower, *War Without Mercy* (New York: Pantheon Books, 1986), p. 224.

16 Ibid., p. 225.

17 Quoted in Victoria, *Zen At War*, p. 50.

18 Ibid., p. 42.

19 Quoted in Ananda K. Coomaraswamy, *Buddha and the Gospel of Buddhism* (London: George G. Harrap, 1916), p. 137.

20 Quoted in Victoria, *Zen At War*, p. 43.

21 Quoted in Okano "Women's Image and Place in Japanese Buddhism" in *Japanese Women*, Kumiko Fujimura-Fanselow and Atsuko Kameda, eds. (New York: The Feminist Press, 1995), p. 16.

22 Quoted in Brian Victoria, "Zen Master Dōgen's Social Consciousness" in *Journal of Asian Culture*, vol. 1, no. 1 (Spring 1977), pub. Graduate Students Association, UCLA, p. 13.

23 Quoted in Nakamura Sōichi, *Zenyaku Shōbōgenzō*, vol. 4 (Tokyo: Seishin-shobō, 1972), p. 9.

24 Quoted in Richard J. Smethurst, "The Military Reserve Association and the Minobe Crisis" in *Crisis Politics in Prewar Japan* (Tokyo: Sophia University, 1970), p. 9.

25 Quoted in Herbert Bix, *Hirohito and the Making of Modern Japan*, p. 315.

26 Edward J. Drea, *In Service of the Emperor* (Lincoln: University of Nebraska Press, 1998), p. 32.

27 Quoted in Victoria, *Zen At War*, p. 168.

28 Ibid., p.168.

29 Harada Sōgaku, "Nihon Seishin to Daijō Zen" (The Japanese Spirit and Mahāyāna Zen) in *Chuō Bukkyō* (March 1934), p. 298.

30 Yasutani Haku'un, "The Crisis in Human Affairs and the LIberation Found in Buddhism" in *ZCLA Journal* 3/3–4 (1973), p. 46.

31 David G. Goodwin and Masanori Miyazawa, *Jews in the Japanese Mind*, p. 103.

32 D. T. Suzuki, *Zen and Japanese Culture*, p. 84.

33 Philip Kapleau, *The Three Pillars of Zen*, p. 29.

34 John Dower, *War Without Mercy*, p. 228.

35 Shimano Eido, "White Cloud," in *ZCLA Journal*, 3/3–4 (1973), p. 50.

36 Hashimoto Fumio, "Yoroppa ni okeru Zen" (Zen in Europe) in *Doitsugo to Jinsei: Hashimoto Fumio Ronbun-shū* (Tokyo: Sanshū-sha, 1980), p. 223. In 1949 Hashimoto went on to become a professor of German at Tokyo's Chuō University. Further, from 1952 onwards he participated in Yasutani's lay-oriented Sanbō-kōryū-kai (Society for the Prosperity of the Three Treasures).

37 Ibid., p. 223.

38 Ibid., p. 223.

39 This quote was part of a personal conversation I had with Robert Aitken in mid-1975 in which we discussed Yasutani's attitude toward the Vietnam War. Aitken further confirmed this quotation to me in an e-mail dated 23 March 1999 though he also added: "I don't think he [Yasutani] was necessarily referring specifically to the war in Vietnam.".

40 See Victoria, *Zen at War*, pp. 160–2, 188–90.

41 Josh Baran's comments were included in a review he wrote on *Zen At War* entitled: "Zen Holy War?" The entire review is available on the Internet at: http://www.teleport.com/~zennist/zenholy.htm.

6 CARRYING ZEN TO CHINA

1 For further background information see Victoria, *Zen At War*, pp. 63–5.

2 Ibid., see discussion in chapter 7, pp. 79–94.

3 Takagi Sōgō, *Gempō Rōshi* (Tokyo: Daizō Shuppan-sha, 1963), p. 87.

4 See, for example, "God of War" Lt. Colonel Sugimoto Gorō's comments in Victoria, *Zen at War*, p. 124.

5 Takagi Sōgō, *Gempō Rōshi*, p. 88.

6 Ibid., p. 89.

7 Ibid., p. 88.

8 This incident is described in Tamaki Benkichi, *Kaisō – Yamamoto Gempō* (Tokyo: Shunjū-sha, 1970), p. 32.

9 Quoted in Tamaki Benkichi, *Kaisō – Yamamoto Gempō*, p. 149.

10 For further details of Asahina Sōgen's right-wing activities, see Victoria, *Zen at War*, pp. 162–6; for those of Harada Sōgaku, see pp. 135–8 of the same book; and for those of Yasutani Haku'un see chapter 5 of this book. Note that Yamada Kōun, as Yasutani's chief Dharma heir, became the administrative and spiritual head (*kanchō*) of the Sanbōkyōdan in 1970. The Sanbōkyōdan (Three Treasures Association) was the name given to what was, in essence, a newly established Zen sect, first registered with the Japanese government in January 1954.

11 Quoted in Takagi Sōgō, *Gempō Rōshi*, pp. 84–5.

12 I am grateful to retired Zen Master Robert Aitken for having shared with me a photocopy of the colophon of this sūtra booklet.

13 Quoted in Tamaki Benkichi, *Kaisō – Yamamoto Gempō*, p. 201.

14 Ibid., p. 202.

15 Ibid., p. 202.

16 Quoted in Leonard Mosley, *Hirohito, Emperor of Japan* (London: Prentice-Hall International, 1966), p. 356.

17 The mutual friend was Tanaka Seigen (b. 1906). Tanaka was former secretary-general of the Japan Communist Party who, while imprisoned in 1933, recanted his Marxist beliefs and pledged absolute loyalty to the emperor as a result of Gempō's visits with him in prison.

18 Quoted in Tamaki Benkichi, *Kaisō – Yamamoto Gempō*, p. 154.

19 Ibid., see pp. 155–7 for a fuller discussion.

20 Ibid., p. 156.

21 Ibid., pp. 157–8.
22 Quoted in Hugh Burton, *Japan's Modern Century* (New York: Ronald Press, 1970), p. 570.
23 Quoted in Tamaki Benkichi, *Kaisō – Yamamoto Gempō*, p. 161.
24 Quoted in Richard B. Frank, *Downfall –The End of the Imperial Japanese Empire* (New York: Random House, 1999), p. 347.
25 Ibid., p. 92.
26 Quoted in Chaen Yoshio, *Misshitsu no Shūsen Shōchoku* (Tokyo: Matsudo Shuppan, 1987), p. 41.
27 Ibid., p. 42.
28 Masanori Nakamura, *Japanese Monarchy* (New York: M.E. Sharpe, 1992), p. 87.
29 Ibid., p. 71.
30 Ibid., p. 91.
31 Quoted in ibid., p. 91.
32 Quoted in Tamaki Benkichi, *Kaisō – Yamamoto Gempō*, p. 155.
33 Hugh Borton, *Japan's Modern Century*, p. 463.
34 Matsumoto's comments are quoted in Masanori Nakamura, *Japanese Monarchy*, p. 103, while the relevant text of the American draft is found on p. 100 of the same book. The final version of Article 1 reads as follows: "The Emperor shall be the symbol of the State and of the unity of the people, deriving His position from the will of the people with whom resides sovereign power.".
35 For further details, see Herbert Bix, "Symbol Monarchy" in *The Journal of Japanese Studies*, vol. 21, no. 2 (Summer 1995), p. 336.
36 See Tamaki Benkichi, *Kaisō – Yamamoto Gempō*, p. 158.
37 Masanori Nakamura, *Japanese Monarchy*, p. 100.
38 These comments were provided to the author by Herbert Bix in an email dated 1 April 2000. For further details on Narahashi, including a concocted meeting with the emperor, see Herbert Bix, "Symbol Monarchy" in *The Journal of Japanese Studies*, vol. 21, no. 2 (Summer 1995), pp. 339–40.
39 See, for example, comments in Takagi Sōgō, *Gempō Rōshi*, p. 84.
40 For further details see David Bergamini, *Japan's Imperial Conspiracy*, pp. 682–3.

7 ZEN "SELFLESSNESS" IN JAPANESE MILITARISM

1 These figures were contained in the *Report of International Committee of the Red Cross, 1939–1947*, vol. 2 (1948), p. 316. The corresponding figures on the allied side were 5,893,000 French, 1,811,000 English, and 477,000 US POWs.
2 Hata Ikuhiko, *Nihonjin Hōryō*, vol. 1 (Tokyo: Hara Shobō, 1998), p. 87.
3 Quoted in the 8 January 1941 issue of the *Asahi Shimbun*, p. 7.
4 D. T. Suzuki, *Zen and Japanese Culture*, p. 70.
5 Quoted in Tsunoda Fusako, *Sekinin Rabauru no Shōgun Imamura Hitoshi* (Tokyo: Shinchō-sha,1984), p. 357.
6 Ibid., p. 338.
7 Ibid., p. 190.
8 Ibid., p. 129.
9 Ibid., pp. 129–30.
10 For further details on both Generals Nogi and Kodama, see Victoria, *Zen at War*, pp. 36–7.
11 Quoted in Victoria, *Zen At War*, p. 58.
12 Quoted in Imamura Hitoshi, *Imamura Taishō Kaisō-roku*, vol. 1 (Tokyo: Jiyū Ajia-sha, 1960), pp. 259–60.
13 Ibid., p. 261.
14 Ibid., pp. 264–5.

15 Ibid., p. 265.
16 Ibid., p. 267.
17 Ibid., p. 272.
18 For further information on Shaku Sōen, especially his understanding of the relationship of Buddhism to war, see *Zen at War*, pp. 25–9.
19 Imamura Hitoshi, *Imamura Taishō Kaisō-roku*, vol. 1, p. 281.
20 Quoted in ibid., pp. 279.
21 Ibid., p. 280.
22 Ibid., p. 280.
23 Ibid., p. 273.
24 Ibid., p. 285.
25 Ibid., p. 280–1.
26 Ibid., p. 294–5.
27 Ibid., pp. 292–3.
28 Ibid., p. 294.
29 Quoted in Tsunoda Fusako, *Sekinin Rabauru no Shōgun Imamura Hitoshi* (Tokyo: Shinchō-sha, 1984), p. 139.
30 Ibid., p. 392.
31 Quoted in Tanaka Tadao, *Sawaki Kōdō – Kono Koshin no Hito*, vol. 2 (Tokyo: Daihōrin-kaku, 1995), p. 462.
32 Ōmori Zenkai, "Taisei Yokusan to Daijō Bukkyō" (Assisting Imperial Rule and Mahāyāna Buddhism) in *Sōtō Shūhō*, no. 39 (15 January 1941), pp. 1–3.
33 Ibid., p. 2.
34 See, for example, Victoria, *Zen at War*, pp. 43, 50, and 171–2.
35 Quoted in Charles S. Prebish, *Buddhism: A Modern Perspective* (University Park: Pennsylvania State University Press, 1975), p. 95.
36 Quoted in Victoria, *Zen at War*, p. 111.
37 Kyōiku-sōkanbu, eds., *Seishin Kyōiku Shiryō*, vol. 2 (Tokyo: Kaikō-sha, January 1941), pp. 675–6.
38 Ibid., p. 673.
39 Ibid., pp. 677–9.
40 Quoted in Victoria, *Zen at War*, p. 105.
41 D. T. Suzuki, "Nihonjin no Shōji-kan" (Japanese View of Life and Death) in *Suzuki Daisetsu Zenshū*, vol. 29 (Tokyo: Iwanami Shoten, 1970), p. 31.
42 Ibid., pp. 32–7.
43 Ibid., p. 33.
44 Ibid., p. 33.
45 Ibid., p. 33.
46 Ibid., p. 33.
47 Ibid., p. 37.
48 For further discussion, see Victoria, *Zen at War*, pp. 105–112.
49 Kyōiku-sōkanbu, eds., *Seishin Kyōiku Shiryō*, vol. 2, p. 676.
50 Ibid., p. 678.
51 Joseph Kitagawa, *Religion in Japanese History* (New York: Columbia University, 1966), p. 126.
52 Hajime Nakamura, Philip p. Wiener, ed., *Ways Of Thinking Of Eastern Peoples: India-China-Tibet-Japan* (Honolulu: East-West Center, 1964), p. 434.
53 Ibid., p. 435.
54 Wada Kameji, *Rikugun-Damashii* (Tokyo: Tōsui-sha, 1942), pp. 9, 14.
55 Ibid., see, for example, pp. 71–3, 292–4, *et al.*
56 Ibid., p. 291.
57 Sugimoto Gorō, *Taigi* (Tokyo: Heibon-sha, 1938), p. 178. For further information on Sugimoto Gorō, see Victoria, *Zen at War*, pp. 116–129.

58 Ibid., p. 179.
59 Ibid., p. 292.
60 Ibid., p. 293.
61 Ibid., p. 293.
62 Ibid., p. 294.
63 Hata Ikuhito, *Nihonjin Hōryō*, vol. 1, p. 143.
64 Okuda Kyūji, *Senjinkun to Nihon Seishin* (Tokyo: Gunji Kyōiku Kenkyū-kai, 1942), p. 2.
65 Ibid., p. 312.
66 Ibid., p. 313–4.
67 Ibid., p. 314. As is so typical of East Asian Buddhism, Entai's comments are a mixture of indigenous Chinese thought and Buddhism. The phrase, "there is something more precious than life itself" is a quotation from the Confucian scholar Mencius (372–289 BCE) spoken in connection with his emphasis on the importance of *yi* (J. *gi*), often translated as "righteousness" but better translated as "doing the right (or appropriate) thing." Mencius's teaching was later interpreted to mean "fulfilling one's duty" to one's superiors, most especially to one's sovereign. Quoted in D. C. Lau, *Mencius*, 6A.10 (Harmondsworth: Penguin, 1970), p. 166.
68 *Sōtō Shūhō*, no. 40 (1 February 1941), pp. 4–5.
69 Kumazawa Taizen, "Shōji Tōrai Ikan ga Kaihi-sen" (How to Avoid the Coming of Life and Death) in *Daihōrin* (May 1944), p. 19.
70 Quoted in Victoria, *Zen at War*, p. 26.
71 Quoted in Kumazawa Taizen, "Shōji Tōrai Ikan ga Kaihi-sen" (How to Avoid the Coming of Life and Death) in *Daihōrin* (May 1944), p. 19.
72 Ibid., p. 21.
73 Yamamoto Tsunetomo [Jōchō], *Hagakure*, trans. William Scott Wilson (Tokyo: Kodansha International, 1979), p. 164.
74 Hillis Lory, *Japan's Military Masters –The Army in Japanese Life*, p. 32.
75 Ibid., p. 43.
76 Thomas B. Allen & Norman Polmar, *Code-Name Downfall*, p. 165.
77 Meirion and Susie Harries, *Soldiers of the Sun – The Rise and Fall of the Imperial Japanese Army*, p. 323.
78 Noda Masa'aki, *Sensō to Zaiseki*, p. 289.
79 Quoted in Nagamine Hideo, *Nihongunjin no Shiseikan*, pp. 162–3.
80 Kawano Hitoshi, "Gyokusai no Shisō to Hakuhei Totsugeki" [The Ideology of Death before Dishonour and the Bayonet Charge] in *Sensō to Guntai*, p. 169.
81 D. T. Suzuki, *Zen and Japanese Culture*, p. 85.
82 Ibid., p. 123.
83 Quoted in Hillis Lory, *Japan's Military Masters –The Army in Japanese Life* (Westport, CT: Greenwood Press, 1973, first printed, 1943), pp. 42–3.
84 Minami Hiroshi, *Nihonjin no Shinri* (Tokyo: Iwanami Shoten, 1953), p. 158.
85 Quoted in Fukushima Nichi'i, "Jūgun-sō toshite Chūgoku ni Hachinen" (Eight Years in China as a Military Chaplain) in Asahi Shimbun Têma Danwa-shitsu, eds., *Nihonjin no Sensō* (Tokyo: Heibon-sha, 1988), p. 78.
86 Kawabe Masakazu, *Nihon Rikugun Seishin-kyōiku Shi-kō* (Tokyo: Harashobō, 1980), p. 117.
87 Okamoto Sekiō, "Kokumin Seishin to Muga" (The People's Spirit and the Non-self) in *Sanshō* (June 1935), p. 206.
88 Quoted in Bernard Faure, *Chan Insights and Oversights* (Princeton: Princeton University Press, 1993), pp. 162–3.
89 Kumazawa Taizen, "Shōji Tōrai Ikan ga Kaihi-sen" (How to Avoid the Coming of Life and Death) in *Daihōrin* (May 1944), pp. 19–20.
90 Ibid., pp. 19–21.

91 Quoted in Victoria, *Zen at War*, p. 138. Although frequent reference is made throughout the war period to there being a total of "one hundred million" Japanese, the actual count in the 1944 census was about seventy-two million.

92 Quoted in Richard B. Frank, *Downfall*, p. 89.

93 Quoted in Nagamine Hideo, *Nihongunjin no Shiseikan* (Tokyo: Hara Shobō, 1982), p. 157.

94 Quoted in Victoria, *Zen at War*, p. 139.

95 Quoted in Minami Hiroshi, *Nihonjin no Shinri*, p. 158.

96 Hirata Seikō, *Issai wa Kū*, p. 94.

97 Quoted in Richard B. Frank, *Downfall*, p. 189.

98 Minami Hiroshi, *Nihonjin no Shinri*, p. 162.

99 Richard B. Frank, *Downfall*, p. 29.

100 For further discussion on the number of civilian deaths on Okinawa see Richard B. Frank, *Downfall*, pp. 71–2.

101 Chalmers Johnson, ed., *Okinawa: Cold War Island* (Cardiff, CA: Japan Policy Research Institute, 1999), p. 25.

102 Ibid., p. 25.

103 Ibid., p. 29.

104 Richard B. Frank, *Downfall*, pp. 117–18.

105 Ibid., p. 189.

106 Herbert Bix, *Hirohito and the Making of Modern Japan*, p. 496.

107 Richard B. Frank, *Downfall*, p. 190.

108 Rekishi Kyōiku-sha Kyōgi-kai, eds., *Maboroshi dewa nakatta Hondo Kessen* (Tokyo: Kōbunkyū, 1995), p. 308.

109 Ibid., p. 80.

110 Richard B. Frank, *Downfall*, p. 299.

111 Quoted in Stanley Weintraub, *The Last Great Victory – The End of World War II, July/ August 1945* (New York: Truman Talley Books/Dutton, 1995), p. 572.

112 Whether or not there were realistic alternatives to the use of the atomic bombs remains a subject of much scholarly debate. In *Hirohito – The Making of Modern Japan*, Herbert Bix takes the position that even without the atomic bomb(s), the Soviet Union's entrance into the war against Japan on 9 August 1945 may well have prompted Japan's surrender. On the other hand, Richard Frank in *Downfall* notes that in each month of 1945 somewhere between 100,000 to 250,000 Asian noncombatants are estimated to have died under the brutal conditions of Japanese occupation. Frank asks what gave Japanese civilians a greater right to continue living than these other Asian victims?

113 D. T. Suzuki, "Zenkai Sasshin" [Reform of the Zen World] in *Suzuki Daisetsu Zenshū*, vol. 30, p. 57.

114 Ibid., p. 56. Suzuki's metaphorical use of the words "horse" and "deer" is not accidental, for in Japanese the word for "fool" (*baka*) is written with the Sino-Japanese characters for these two animals. That is to say, in ancient China a hunter (and by extension anyone) who could not tell the difference between a horse and a deer was considered to be a fool.

115 Ibid., pp. 56–7.

116 John Dower, *War Without Mercy*, p. 48.

117 Gavan Daws, *Prisoners of the Japanese* (New York: William Morrow and Co., 1994), p. 18.

118 Quoted in Kawano Hitoshi, "Gyokusai no Shisō to Hakuhei Totsugeki" [The Ideology of Death before Dishonour and the Bayonet Charge] in *Sensō to Guntai* (Tokyo: Iwanami Shoten, 1999), p. 166.

119 Quoted in Iris Chang, *The Rape of Nanking*, p. 58.

8 BUDDHIST WAR BEREAVEMENT

1 Har Dayal, *The Bodhisattva in Buddhist Sanskrit Literature* (London: Routledge & Kegan Paul, 1932), p. 199.
2 Ibid., p. 207.
3 Tsunemitsu Kōnen, *Meiji no Bukkyō-sha*, vol. 1 (Tokyo: Shunjū-sha, 1968), pp. 61–2.
4 Satō Gan'ei, *Bushidō* (Tokyo: Senryūdō, 1902), p. xxii.
5 Ibid., p. 2.
6 Ibid., p. 31.
7 Ibid., p. 45.
8 Ibid., pp. 45–6.
9 Ibid., p. 51.
10 Ibid., p. 52.
11 Ibid., p. 97.
12 Ibid., p. 105.
13 Ibid., pp. 99–100.
14 Quoted in Victoria, *Zen at War*, p. 133.
15 Ibid., p. 26.
16 Ibid., pp. 27–8.
17 Ibid., p. 28.
18 Shaku Soyen, *Sermons of a Buddhist Abbot*, trans. D. T. Suzuki (La Salle, IL: Open Court, 1906), p. 214.
19 Quoted in Victoria, *Zen at War*, p. 132.
20 Tomomatsu Entei, *Izoku Tokuhon* (Kyoto: Rikugun Juppei-bu, 1941), p. 2.
21 Ibid., p. 42.
22 Ibid., p. 9.
23 Ibid., p. 12.
24 Quoted in Mizuno Kōgen, *The Beginnings of Buddhism* (Tokyo: Kōsei Publishing Co., 1980), p. 180.
25 For the historical background to Śākyamuni Buddha's admonition to his disciples, see George N. Marshall, *Buddha – The Quest for Serenity* (Boston: Beacon Press, 1978), p. 88.
26 Tomomatsu, *Izoku Tokuhon*, p. 74.
27 Ibid., pp. 74–8.
28 Ibid., p. 70.
29 Quoted in Victoria, *Zen at War*, p. 105.
30 Tomomatsu Entei, *Izoku Tokuhon*, p. 71.
31 Quoted in Victoria, *Zen at War*, p. 43.
32 Tomomatsu Entei, *Izoku Tokuhon*, p. 80.
33 Ibid., pp. 81–2.
34 Ibid., p. 81.
35 Ibid., p. 81.
36 Ibid., p. 82.
37 Kenneth Ch'en, *Buddhism in China* (Princeton: Princeton University Press, 1964), p. 197.
38 Ibid., p. 201.
39 Ibid., p. 199.
40 Holmes Welch, *Buddhism under Mao* (Cambridge: Harvard University Press, 1972), p. 297.
41 David Little, *Sri Lanka – The Invention of Enmity* (Washington, DC: United States Institute of Peace Press, 1994), p. 94.
42 Martin E. Marty, "An Exuberant Adventure: The Academic Study and Teaching of Religion," in *Academe* 82/6 (1996), p. 14.

9 CONFESSIONS OF A BUDDHIST CHAPLAIN

1 Quoted in Victoria, *Zen at War*, p. 26.
2 Thornton, "Buddhist Chaplains in the Field of Battle" in Donald S. Lopez, Jr., ed., *Buddhism in Practice* (Princeton: Princeton University Press, 1995), pp. 586–7.
3 Quoted in ibid., p. 590.
4 Ibid., p. 589.
5 Note that the statement concerning General Chō's delight in having entered the priesthood is appended here from Nichi'i's description of this event as contained in an earlier book. See Fukushima Nichi'i, *Shōwa Risshō Ankoku-ron*, vol. 1 (Mito: Daisendō, 1980), p. 433.
6 As a technical Buddhist term, the word *shukumei* refers only to one's existence in a previous life. The popular connection of this term to "fate" or "destiny" comes from the fact that the karmic consequences of one's actions in a previous life (or lives) are regarded as determining what will occur in one's present life. Nevertheless, Buddhism does recognize the possibility of changing one's present and future based on the moral quality of one's acts at each point in time. As a technical term, *shukumei* is more properly pronounced in Sino-Japanese as *shukumyō*.
7 Fukushima Nichi'i, *Shōwa Risshō Ankoku-ron*, vol. 1, p. 432.
8 Ota Masahide, *This Was the Battle of Okinawa* (Naha, Okinawa: Naha Shuppan-sha, 1981), p. 30.
9 For further details see David Bergamini, *Japan's Imperial Conspiracy*, vol. 1, p. 30. Bergamini suggests that Chō may have claimed to have issued the orders to kill all captives in order to protect his commander, Prince Asaka Yasuhiko (1887–1981), Emperor Hirohito's uncle, from having to take responsibility for the massacres.
10 Quoted in Chalmers Johnson, ed. *Okinawa: Cold War Island*, p. 29.
11 Quoted in *Himeyuri Heiwa Kinen-shiryōkan Kōshiki Gaido-bukku* (Naha, Okinawa: Himeyuri Peace Museum, 1999), p. 22.
12 Quoted in Julia Yonetani, "On the Battlefield of Mabuni: Struggles Over Peace and the Past in Contemporary Okinawa," in *East Asian History*, no. 20 (December 2000), p. 162.
13 Fukushima Nichi'i, *Shōwa Risshō Ankoku-ron*, vol. 1, p. 428.

10 BUDDHISM – THE LAST REFUGE OF WAR CRIMINALS

1 Meirion and Susie Harries, *Soldiers of the Sun*, p. 342.
2 For a more complete description of this incident, see David Bergamini, *Japan's Imperial Conspiracy*, pp. 1165–70. Bergamini claims that between 2,000 to 3,000 of the 12,000 American POWs were slaughtered, while about 8,000 of the 58,000 Filipinos perished. Another 6,000 Filipinos managed to escape along the way as did a handful of American airmen and officers.
3 Hashimoto Tetsuo, *Tsuji Masanobu to Shichi-nin no Sō*, p. 43.
4 Ibid., p. 48.
5 For further details, see David Bergamini, *Japan's Imperial Conspiracy*, pp. 1342–3.
6 Hashimoto Fumio, *Tsuji Masanobu to Shichi-nin no Sō* (Tokyo: Sanshū-sha,1980), p. 24.
7 Ibid., p. 41.
8 Quoted in "Basic Facts on the Nanking Massacre and the Tokyo War Crimes Trial" available on the Web at: http://www.cnd.org/njmassacre/nj.html.
9 For further details on Japan's prison chaplaincy system see Ogata Hiroshi, *Bukkyō to Shakai Undō*, pp. 491–7.
10 Hanayama Shinshō, *Eien e no Michi – Waga Hachijū-nen no Shōgai* (Tokyo: Nihon Kōgyō Shimbun-sha, 1982), p. 176.

11 Quoted in Wm Theodore de Bary and the Conference on Ming Thought, *Self and Society in Ming Thought* (New York: Columbia University Press, 1970), p. 13.

12 Ibid., p. 13.

13 Wing-Tsit Chan, *A Source Book in Chinese Philosophy* (Princeton: Princeton University Press, 1963), pp. 429–30, 658.

14 Ibid., p. 658.

15 D. T. Suzuki, *Zen and Japanese Culture*, pp. 62–3.

16 Wing-Tsit Chan, *A Source Book in Chinese Philosophy*, p. 656.

17 Nakamura Hajime, Philip p. Wiener, ed., *Ways of Thinking of Eastern Peoples* (Honolulu: East-West Center, 1964), p. 400.

18 Hanayama Shinshō, *Eien e no Michi – Waga Hachijū-nen no Shōgai*, pp. 164–5. The three Pure Land sūtras include: 1) *Amitābha Sūtra*; 2) *Longer Amitābha Sūtra*; and 3) *Meditation Sūtra*, also known as the *Meditation on the Buddha of Infinite Life* (*Amitāyur Dhyāna Sūtra*).

19 Ibid., p. 165.

20 Ibid., p. 167.

21 Ibid., p. 165.

22 Ibid., p. 166.

23 Ibid., p. 254.

24 Ibid., p. 255.

25 Ibid., p. 255.

26 Ibid., p. 236.

27 Ibid., p. 236.

28 Ibid., p. 236.

29 Ibid., p. 245.

30 Ibid., p. 251.

31 Ibid., p. 253.

32 Ibid., pp. 251–2.

33 Ibid., p. 256.

34 Ibid., p. 310.

35 For further details of Buddhism's repression in the early Meiji period, see Victoria, *Zen at War*, pp. 3–11.

36 Quoted in Victoria, *Zen at War*, p. 142.

37 Quoted in Hanayama Shinshō, *Eien e no Michi – Waga Hachijū-nen no Shōgai*, p. 220.

38 See Herbert Bix, *Hirohito and the Making of Modern Japan*, p. 728, n. 56.

39 Quoted in Hanayama Shinshō, *Eien e no Michi – Waga Hachijū-nen no Shōgai*, p. 221.

40 Ibid., pp. 260–1. Tōjō was by no means alone in believing that Avalokiteśvara was capable of assuming a variety of forms in order to compassionately save suffering human beings. The well-known *Kannon-gyō* (*Avalokiteśvara Sūtra*) describes a number of these forms though certainly a handkerchief is unique. See also n. 41.

41 For further historial background information, see Victoria, *Zen at War*, p. 142. Note that this title did not originate with the Rinzai sect. On the contrary, it is to be found in both the *Lotus* and *Śūrańgama Sūtras* where it designates one of Avalokiteśvara's thirty-three incarnations. See, for example, Bunnō Katō *et al.*, trans., *The Threefold Lotus Sūtra* where, on p. 322, Avalokiteshvara manifests himself as a "great divine general" to preach the Dharma and save sentient beings.

42 Quoted in Hanayama Shinshō, *Eien e no Michi – Waga Hachijū-nen no Shōgai*, p. 218.

43 Quoted in Mark R. Peattie, *Ishiwara Kanji and Japan's Confrontation with the West*, p. 95.

44 Ibid., p. 42.

45 Quoted in Hanayama Shinshō, *Eien e no Michi – Waga Hachijū-nen no Shōgai*, pp. 192–3.

46 Mark R. Peattie, *Ishiwara Kanji and Japan's Confrontation with the West* (Princeton: Princeton University Press, 1975), p. 40.

47 Ibid., p. 374.

48 Quoted in Hanayama Shinshō, *Eien e no Michi – Waga Hachijū-nen no Shōgai*, pp. 185.
49 Ibid., p. 186.
50 Ibid., p. 195.
51 Ibid., p. 182.
52 Ibid., p. 231.
53 Ibid., p. 231. Rinzai Zen master Kaisen Jōki (d. 1582) had been invited by the famous warrior and feudal lord Takeda Shingen (1521–73) to become abbot of Erinji in present-day Yamanashi Prefecture. When Takeda's forces were defeated by the equally famous feudal lord Oda Nobunaga (1534–82), some of them took refuge in Erinji. Nobunaga's forces demanded that these refugee warriors be expelled from the temple, but Jōki refused to do so. In retaliation, Nobunaga's forces are said to have burned the temple down with Jōki and all of the monastics gathered together in the second floor of the main entrance gate (*sanmon*). It was then he is alleged to have repeated the words in the text, though they actually form part of Case Forty-Three in the famous Chinese Chan *kōan* collection known as the *Pi-yen lu* (*Hekigan-roku; Blue Cliff Record*).
54 Ibid., p. 230.
55 Ibid., p. 274.
56 Ibid., p. 198.
57 Ibid., p. 211.
58 Ibid., p. 283. Kimura's poem was clearly inspired by a statement made by that famous paragon of loyalty, Shingon sect-influenced warrior Kusunoki Masashige (1294–1336). Facing death in battle, Kusunoki pledged to "be reborn seven times in order to annihilate the enemies of the emperor.".
59 Herbert Bix, *Hirohito and the Making of Modern Japan*, p. 520.
60 Ibid., see especially pp. 567–8, 615–6.
61 Quoted in Mori Taien, "Ninnaji no Rekishi to Shinkō" [Ninnaji's History and Faith] in *Koji-junrei – Kyoto 11 – Ninnaji* (Kyoto: Tankō-sha, 1977), p. 93.
62 Takamatsu's opposition discussed in Edward Behr, *Hirohito – Behind the Myth* (New York: Vintage Books, 1989), p. 284.
63 For a thorough and convincing discussion of Hirohito's war responsibility, see Herbert Bix, *Hirohito and the Making of Modern Japan*, pp. 439–530. Though not as well researched, Edward Behr's book *Hirohito – Behind the Myth*, comes to similar conclusions.
64 Quoted in Hashimoto Tetsuo, *Tsuji Masanobu to Shichinin no Sō*, p. 366.
65 Ibid., p. 380.
66 D. T. Suzuki, *Zen and Japanese Culture*, p. 84.
67 Ibid., p. 85.
68 See, for example, George B. Sansom's description of Oda Nobunaga's struggle in the late sixteenth century to subdue Ishiyama Hoganji in *A History of Japan – 1334–1615* (Kent, England: Wm. Dawson & Sons, 1978), pp. 282–90. Adherents of the True Pure Land school, however, were certainly not the only Buddhists of that era to engage in armed combat.
69 Quoted in Victoria, *Zen at War*, p. 31.
70 Ibid, pp. 31–5.
71 Quoted in Tsunoda Fusako, *Sekinin Rabaul no Shōgun Imamura Hitoshi*, pp. 348–9.
72 For a more complete description of the "High Treason Incident," see Victoria, *Zen at War*, pp. 38–48.
73 D. T. Suzuki, *Bukkyō no Tai-i* (Kyoto: Hōzōkan, 1947), p. 4.
74 Ibid., pp. 8–9.
75 Ibid., p. 12.
76 Ibid., p. 12.

77 Ibid., p. 13.
78 Ibid., p. 133.
79 See Herbert Bix, *Hirohito and the Making of Modern Japan*, p. 619.

11 BUDDHISM – A TOP SECRET RELIGION IN WARTIME JAPAN

1 For additional background material on the League, see Victoria, *Zen at War*, pp. 66–73.
2 Quoted in Victoria, *Zen at War*, p. 67.
3 Ibid., p. 71.
4 Ogata Hiroshi, ed., *Bukkyō to Shakai Undō* (Tokyo: Criminal Affairs Bureau; Ministry of Justice, February 1939), p. 394.
5 Ibid., p. 481.
6 Inoue Nisshō, *Ichinin Issatsu* (Tokyo: Nihon Shūhō-sha, 1953), p. 98. Additional material has been added to this section in order to provide the reader with a clearer understanding of Inoue's connection to Zen.
7 Ibid., p. 99.
8 Ibid., p. 99.
9 Ibid., p. 183.
10 Ibid., p. 197.
11 Heinrich Dumoulin, *Zen Buddhism: A History; Volume 1: India and China* (New York: Macmillan, 1988), p. 249. Note that D. T. Suzuki employed these same phrases to illustrate "Zen aestheticism" in *Zen and Japanese Culture*, pp. 352–4.
12 Sengzhao's essay, entitled "The Namelessness of Nirvāna," was the fourth of four essays contained in the *Zhao Lun* (Treatises of Zhao). For further details on Sengzhao's life and the influence he exerted on the development of Zen (Chan) in China, see Heinrich Dumoulin, *Zen Buddhism: A History; Volume 1: India and China*, pp. 70–4.
13 Inoue Nisshō, *Ichinin Issatsu*, p. 198.
14 Ibid., p. 208.
15 Ibid., p. 221.
16 Quoted in Onuma Hiroaki, *Ketsumeidan Jiken-jōshinsho-gokuchū Nikki* (Tokyo: Ketsumeidan Jiken Kōhan Sokki-roku Kankō-kai, 1971), p. 62.
17 Inoue Nisshō, *Ichinin Issatsu*, p. 220.
18 Ibid., p. 236.
19 Ibid., p. 247.
20 Ibid., pp. 248–9.
21 Ibid., p. 254.
22 Ibid., p. 272.
23 Quoted in Onuma Hiroaki, *Ketsumeidan Jiken Kōhan Sokki-roku*, vol. 3 (Tokyo: Ketsumeidan Jiken Kōhan Sokki-roku Kankō-kai, 1963), p. 184.
24 The reference here is to the sacrifice of one's own game pieces, i.e. 'stones,' in the Japanese board game of *go*, The idea of making a tactical sacrifice in the interests of ultimate victory is similar to that of sacrificing a pawn in the game of chess.
25 Quoted in Onuma Hiroaki, *Ketsumeidan Jiken Kōhan Sokki-roku*, vol. 3, p. 187.
26 The interview took place on 20 January 1998 at the Tokyo offices of the Sankō Industrial Construction Co. which was then headed by the still active Yotsumoto. Ryū-un-in is also known as *Hakuzan dōjō* (training centre) due to its location in the Hakuzan area of Tokyo's Bunkyō ward.
27 Quoted in Onuma Hiroaki, *Ketsumeidan Jiken-jōshinsho-gokuchū Nikki*, p. 30.
28 Quoted in Onuma Hiroaki, *Ketsumeidan Jiken Kōhan Sokki-roku*, vol. 3, p. 188.
29 Quoted in Hugh Byas, *Government by Assassination* (London: Bradford & Dicken, 1943), p. 61.

30 Quoted in Onuma Hiroaki, *Ketsumeidan Jiken Kōhan Sokki-roku*, vol. 3, p. 403.
31 Civil Intelligence Section, *The Brocade Banner – The Story of Japanese Nationalism*, p. 43.
32 Okamura Ao, *Ketsumeidan Jiken* (Tokyo: San-ichi Shobō, 1989), p. 326.
33 Quoted in Onuma Hiroaki, *Ketsumeidan Jiken Kōhan Sokki-roku*, vol. 1, p. 368.
34 Ibid., p. 369.
35 Quoted in Masao Maruyama, *Thought and Behaviour in Modern Japanese Politics*, p. 53.
36 Quoted in Onuma Hiroaki, *Ketsumeidan Jiken Kōhan Sokki-roku*, vol. 1, pp. 87–88.
37 Quoted in Tamaki Benkichi, *Kaisō Yamamoto Gempō*, p. 40.
38 Although there is some variation in the content of the categories, the four individuals/ groups to whom gratitude is owed are typically identified as: 1) one's parents, 2) all sentient beings, 3) one's sovereign, and 4) the Three Treasures of Buddhism (i.e. Buddha, Dharma, and *Samgha*). The Ten Good Practices are typically identified as: 1) not killing, 2) not stealing, 3) not engaging in improper sexual conduct, 4) not lying, 5) not speaking deceitfully, 6) not speaking ill of others, 7) not using flowery language, 8) not coveting, 9) not getting angry, and 10) not holding false views.
39 Quoted in Onuma Hiroaki, *Ketsumeidan Jiken Kōhan Sokki-roku*, vol. 3, p. 737.
40 Quoted in Masao Maruyama, *Thought and Behaviour in Modern Japanese Politics*, p. 53.
41 Ogata Hiroshi, *Bukkyō to Shakai Undō*, p. 261.
42 Ibid., pp. 485–91. For further discussion on the characteristics of Imperial Way Buddhism, see Victoria, *Zen at War*, pp. 79–94.
43 Although definitions and even categories vary somewhat within the Buddhist tradition, the three forms are typically defined as follows: 1) Dharma body (Skt. *Dharma-kāya*) being the highest aspect of the threefold body of the Buddha. It is composed of the absolute nature of the Buddha-mind and is held to be ineffable, unmanifested, and non-substantial; 2) the physical form (Skt. *Nirmāṇa-kāya*) represents the Buddha as he actually manifests himself for the benefit of unenlightened sentient beings, Śākyamuni Buddha being a prime example; and 3) the reward body (Skt. *Saṃbhoga-kāya*) is the body of bliss acquired by bodhisattvas as a result of their religious practice and vows. In effect, it represents the union of the first two bodies.
44 Although there is some variation in the content of the categories, the four individuals/ groups to whom gratitude is owed are typically identified as: 1) one's parents, 2) all sentient beings, 3) one's sovereign, and 4) the Three Treasures of Buddhism (i.e. Buddha, Dharma, and *Samgha*).
45 In the minds of many Japanese leaders, the Free Masons were linked to Jews as a group who, by advocating individualism and liberalism, were part of a sinister plot to destroy Japanese social unity in order to further their goal of world domination.
46 Quoted in Victoria, *Zen at War*, p. 122.
47 Ibid., p. 85.

EPILOGUE

1 Ichikawa Hakugen, *Fudō-chi Shinmyō-roku/Taia-ki* (Tokyo: Kōdan-sha, 1982), p. 44.
2 Peter L. Berger, *The Social Reality of Religion* (Middlesex, England: Penguin University Books, 1973), p. 53.
3 Reinhold Niebuhr, *Moral Man and Immoral Society* (New York: Charles Scribner's Sons, 1932), pp. 96–7.
4 This interview appeared in the *Fuji Flyer* (18 August, 1995), p. 4.
5 John Dillenberger, *Martin Luther: Selections from His Writings* (Garden City, New York: Doubleday, 1961), pp. 398–9.
6 Quoted in Victoria, *Zen at War*, p. 87.
7 Daniel Berrigan and Thich Nhat Hanh, *The Raft Is Not the Shore* (Boston: Beacon Press, 1975), p. 34.

BIBLIOGRAPHY

I. IN WESTERN LANGUAGES

Aitken, Robert. (Fall 1999) "Robert Aitken Responds" in *Tricycle*, 9(1): 67–8.

Allen, Thomas B. and Norman Polmar, N. (1995) *Code-Name Downfall – The Secret Plan to Invade Japan – And Why Truman Dropped the Bomb*, New York: Simon & Schuster.

Anacker, Stefan. "Kaniska" in Charles S. Prebish, (ed.) *Buddhism: A Modern Perspective*, pp. 46–8.

Behr, Edward. (1989) *Hirohito – Behind the Myth*, New York: Vintage Books.

Bergamini, David. (1971) *Japan's Imperial Conspiracy*, New York: William Morrow.

Berger, Peter L. (1973) *The Social Reality of Religion*, Middlesex, England: Penguin University Books.

Berrigan, Daniel and Hanh, T. N. (1975) *The Raft Is Not the Shore*, Boston: Beacon Press.

Bix, Herbert P. (2000) *Hirohito and the Making of Modern Japan*, New York: HarperCollins.

—— (Summer 1995) "Symbol Monarchy" in *The Journal of Japanese Studies*, 21(2): 319–63.

Blyth, R. H. (1966) *Zen and Zen Classics – Mumonkan*, vol. 4, Tokyo: Hokuseido Press.

Borton, Hugh. (1970) *Japan's Modern Century*, New York: Ronald Press.

Brazier, D. (2001) *The New Buddhism – A Rough Guide to a New Way of Life*, London: Robinson.

Bunnō Katō *et al.*, (trans). *The New Buddhism – A Rough Guide to a New Way of Life*, London: Robinson. *The Threefold Lotus Sūtra*, New York: Weatherhill, (1975).

Byas, Hugh. (1943) *Government By Assassination*, London: Bradford & Dicken.

Chan, Wing-Tsit. (1963) *A Source Book in Chinese Philosophy*, Princeton: Princeton University Press.

Chang, Iris. (1998) *The Rape of Nanking*. London: Penguin Books.

Chappell, David W. (ed.) (1999) *Buddhist Peacework – Creating Cultures of Peace*. Boston: Wisdom Publications.

Ch'en, Kenneth. (1964) *Buddhism in China*, Princeton: Princeton University Press.

—— (1973) *The Chinese Transformation of Buddhism*, Princeton: Princeton University Press.

Christian Brothers. (1870) *A Treatise on Modern Geography*, Dublin: W. Powell.

Civil Intelligence Section (General Headquarters, U.S. Far East Command), *The Brocade Banner – The Story of Japanese Nationalism*, unpublished, typed report issued on 23 September 1946, pp. 1–168.

Cook Haruko Taya and Theodore F. Cook. (1992) *Japan At War – An Oral History*, New York: The New Press.

Coomaraswamy, Ananda K. (1916) *Buddha and the Gospel of Buddhism*, London: George G. Harrap.

Daws, Gavan. (1994) *Prisoners of the Japanese – POWs of World War II in the Pacific*, New York: William Morrow and Co.

Dayal, Har. (1932) *The Bodhisattva Doctrine in Buddhist Sanskrit Literature*, London: Routledge & Kegan Paul.

deBary, Wm. (1970) Theodore and the Conference on Ming Thought, *Self and Society in Ming Thought*. New York: Columbia University Press.

Demiéville, Paul. (1973) "Le bouddhisme et la guerre" in *Choix D'études Bouddhiques*, Leiden: Brill.

Dillenberger, John. (1961) *Martin Luther: Selections from His Writings*, Garden City, New York: Doubleday.

Dower, John W. (1996) *War Without Mercy*, New York: Pantheon Books.

Drea, Edward J. (1998) *In Service of the Emperor: Essays on the Imperial Japanese Army*, Lincoln: University of Nebraska Press.

Dumoulin, Heinrich. (1963) *A History of Zen Buddhism*. Boston: Beacon Press.

—— (1988) *Zen Buddhism: A History; Volume 1: India and China*, New York: Macmillan.

—— (1990) *Zen Buddhism: A History; Volume 2: Japan*. New York: Macmillan.

Ehman, Mark A. "The Saddharmapundarika-Sūtra" in Charles S. Prebish, ed., *Buddhism: A Modern Perspective*, pp. 102–7.

Eliot, Charles. (1935) *Japanese Buddhism*, London: Edward Arnold.

Epsteiner, Fred. (ed.) (1985/1988) *The Path of Compassion: Writings on Socially Engaged Buddhism*, Berkeley CA: Parallar Press.

Faure, Bernard. (1991) *The Rhetoric of Immediacy*, Princeton: Princeton University Press.

—— (1993) *Chan Insights and Oversights*. Princeton: Princeton University Press.

Fo Kuang Shan Foundation for Buddhist Culture & Education, (ed.) (1992) *1990 Anthology of Fo Kuang Shan International Buddhist Conference*, Kao-hsiung, Taiwan: Fo Kuang Shan Press.

Frank, Richard B. (1999) *Downfall – The End of the Imperial Japanese Empire*, New York: Random House.

Fuji Flyer. (1995) (Unofficial Publication, Yokota U.S. Air Force Base, Tokyo, Japan), 18 August.

Fujimura-Fanselow, Kumiko and Atsuko Kameda, A. (1995) *Japanese Women*, New York: The Feminist Press.

Gernet, Jacques. (1996) *A History of Chinese Civilization*, 2nd edn., trans. J. R. Foster & Charles Hartman. Cambridge: Cambridge University Press.

Goodman, David G. and Masanori Miyazawa. (1995) *Jews in the Japanese Mind: The History and Uses of a Cultural Stereotype*, New York: The Free Press.

Harries, Meirion and Susie. (1992) *Soldiers of the Sun – The Rise and Fall of the Imperial Japanese Army*, New York: Random House.

Harvey, Peter. (2000) *An Introduction to Buddhist Ethics*. Cambridge: Cambridge University Press.

Heisig, James W. and Maraldo, John C. (eds) *Rude Awakenings*, Honolulu: University of Hawaii Press.

Hosokawa, Dogen. (1999) *Omori Sogen – The Art of a Zen Master*, London: Kegan Paul International.

Ives, Christopher. (1992) *Zen Awakening and Society*, Honolulu: University of Hawaii Press.

Johnson, Chalmers, (ed.) (1999) *Okinawa: Cold War Island*, Cardiff, CA: Japan Policy Research Institute.

Kapleau, Philip. (1965) *The Three Pillars of Zen*, Tokyo: John Weatherhill.

—— (1980) *Zen Dawn in the West*, New York: Anchor Press/Doubleday.

Keel, S. (1978) "Buddhism and Political Power in Korean History" in *The Journal of the International Association of Buddhist Studies* 1(1) 9–24.

Kisala, Robert. (1999) *Prophets of Peace – Pacifism and Cultural Identity in Japan's New Religions*, Honolulu: University of Hawai'i Press.

Kitagawa, Joseph. (1966) *Religion in Japanese History*. New York: Columbia University.

Kotler, Arnold (ed.) (1996) *Engaged Buddhist Reader – Ten Years of Engaged Buddhist Publishing*, Berkeley, CA: Parallax Press.

Kubota, Jiun. (2000) "Apology for What the Founder of the Sanbokyodan, Haku'un Yasutani Roshi, Said and Did during World War II," in *Kyōshō* [Awakening Gong], 281 (March–April): 67–9.

Little, David. (1994) *Sri Lanka – The Invention of Enmity*, Washington, D.C.: United States Institute of Peace Press.

Loori, John Daido. (1996) *The Heart of Being*. Boston: Tuttle.

Lopez, Donald S. Jr (ed.) (1995) *Buddhism in Practice*. Princeton: Princeton University Press.

Lory, Hillis. (1973, first printed, 1943) *Japan's Military Masters – The Army in Japanese Life*, Westport, CT: Greenwood Press.

Marshall, George N. (1978) *Buddha – The Quest for Serenity*, Boston: Beacon Press.

Marty, Martin E. (1996) "An Exuberant Adventure: The Academic Study and Teaching of Religion," in *Academe* 82(6): 14–17.

Maruyama Masao. (1963) *Thought and Behaviour in Modern Japanese Politics*, London: Oxford University Press, 1963.

Mizuno, Kōgen. *The Beginnings of Buddhism*.

Moore, Charles A. (ed.) (1967) *The Japanese Mind*. Honolulu: University Press of Hawaii.

Morris, I. I. (1960) *Nationalism and the Right Wing in Japan*, London: Oxford University Press.

Mosley, Leonard. (1966) *Hirohito, Emperor of Japan*, London: Prentice-Hall International.

Nakamura, Hajime. (1964) *Ways Of Thinking Of Eastern Peoples: India-China-Tibet-Japan*, Philip P. Wiener (ed.), Honolulu: East-West Center.

Nakamura, Masanori. (1992) *Japanese Monarchy*, New York: M.E. Sharpe.

Nhat Hanh, Thich. (1976) *The Miracle of Mindfulness!* Boston: Beacon Press.

Niebuhr, Reinhold. (1932) *Moral Man and Immoral Society*, New York: Charles Scribner's Sons.

Nukariya, Kaiten. (1913) *Religion of the Samurai: A Study of Zen Philosophy and Discipline in China and Japan*, Luzac's Oriental Religions Series, vol. 4. London: Luzac.

Ota, Masahide. (1981) *This Was the Battle of Okinawa*, Naha, Okinawa: Naha Shuppan-sha.

Peattie, Mark R. (1975) *Ishiwara Kanji and Japan's Confrontation with the West*, Princeton: Princeton University Press.

Prebish, Charles S. (ed.) (1975) *Buddhism: A Modern Perspective*, University Park: Pennsylvania State University Press.

—— (1993) "Text and Tradition in the Study of Buddhist Ethics" in *The Pacific World*, pp. 49–68.

Queen, Christopher S., and Sallie B. King (eds) (1996) *Engaged Buddhism: Liberation Movements in Asia*, Albany: State University of New York Press.

Queen, Christopher S. (ed.) (2000) *Engaged Buddhism in the West*, Boston: Wisdom Publications.

Saddhatissa, Hammalawa. (1987) *Buddhist Ethics*. London: Wisdom Publications.

Sansom, George. (1978) *A History of Japan – 1334–1615*, Kent, England: Wm. Dawson & Sons.

Shaku, Soyen. (1906) *Sermons of a Buddhist Abbot*, trans. D. T. Suzuki, La Salle, IL: Open Court.

Sharf, Robert. (1993) "The Zen of Japanese Nationalism," in *History of Religions* 33(1): 1–43.

—— (1995) "Zen and the Way of the New Religions," in *Japanese Journal of Religious Studies* 22(3–4): 417–58.

Shillony, Ben-Ami. (1973) *Revolt in Japan – The Young Officers and the February 26, 1936 Incident*, Princeton: Princeton University Press.

Shimano, Eido (a.k.a. Mui Shitsu) (1973) "White Cloud," in *ZCLA Journal*, 3(3–4): 50–3.

Smethurst, Richard J. (1970) "The Military Reserve Association and the Minobe Crisis of 1935" in *Crisis Politics in Prewar Japan*, Tokyo: Sophia University, pp. 1–23.

Smith, Patrick. (1998) *Japan: A Reinterpretation*. New York: Vintage Books.

Storry, Richard. (1957) *The Double Patriots*, London: Chatto and Windus.

Suzuki Daisetz T. (1959) *Zen and Japanese Culture*. Princeton: Princeton University Press. Originally published in 1938 as *Zen and Its Influence on Japanese Culture*. Kyoto: Eastern Buddhist Society, Otani Buddhist University.

Takeyama, Michio. (1966) *Harp of Burma*, trans. Howard Hibbett, Rutland, VT: Charles E. Tuttle Co.

Titus, David. (1974) *Palace and Politics in Prewar Japan*, New York: Studies of the East Asian Institute, Columbia University.

United States Army, Far East Command, Intelligence, Civil Intelligence Section (1946) "*The Brocade Banner: The Story of Japanese Nationalism,*" Special Report, Mimeographed, pp. 1–166.

Utley, Freda. (1936) *Japan's Feet of Clay*, London: Faber & Faber.

Victoria, Brian. (1997) *Zen At War*, New York: Weatherhill.

—— (1977) "Zen Master Dōgen's Social Consciousness." in *Journal of Asian Culture*. I(1): 1–23. (Spring), pub. Graduate Students Association, UCLA.

Walshe, Maurice, (trans.) (1987) *Thus Have I Heard, The Long Discourses of the Buddha*. London: Wisdom Publications.

Weintraub, Stanley. (1995) *The Last Great Victory – The End of World War II, July/August 1945*, New York: Truman Talley Books/Dutton.

Welch, Holmes. (1972) *Buddhism under Mao*, Cambridge: Harvard University Press.

Welter, Albert. "Official Recognition of Chan Buddhism through the Early Song Dynasty," unpublished paper presented before the 1999 annual meeting of the American Association of Religion, pp. 1–53.

Wright, Dale S. (1998) *Philosophical Meditations on Zen Buddhism* (Cambridge Studies in Religious Traditions, No. 13). Cambridge: Cambridge University Press.

Yamamoto Tsunetomo [Jōchō] (1979) *Hagakure*. trans. William Scott Wilson. Tokyo: Kodansha International.

Yasutani, Haku'un. (1973) "The Crisis in Human Affairs and The Liberation Found in Buddhism," in *ZCLA Journal* 3(3–4): 36–47.

Yonetani, Julia. (2000) "On the Battlefield of Mabuni: Struggles Over Peace and the Past in Contemporary Okinawa," in *East Asian History*, 20: 145–67 (December).

II. IN JAPANESE

Akashi Hirotaka and Matsuura Sōzō, Mo (eds.) (1975) *Shōwa Tokkō Dan'atsu-shi 4 – Shūkyō-jin ni taisuru Dan'atsu (ge)* (History of Suppression by the Special Higher Police Division – Suppression of Religious Persons (Part Two)). Tokyo: Taihei Shuppan-sha.

Arahara Bokusui. (1974) *Dai-Uha Shi, zōho* (A Major History of the Right Wing, enlarged ed.) Tokyo: Dai-Nippon Issei-kai Shuppan.

Asahi Shimbun Têma Danwa-shitsu, (eds.) (1988) *Nihonjin no Sensō* (The Japanese People's War), Tokyo: Heibon-sha.

Chaen Yoshio. (1987) *Misshitsu no Shūsen Chokugo* (Secrets behind the Imperial Edict Ending the War), Tokyo: Matsudo Shuppan.

Fukushima, Nichi'i (1980). *Shōwa Risshō Ankoku-ron* (Treatise on Establishing the True and Pacifying the Country in the Shōwa Era), vol. 1, Mito: Daisendō.

Hanayama Shinshō. (1982) *Eien e no Michi – Waga Hachijūnen no Shōgai* (The Way to Eternity – My Eighty Years of Life). Tokyo: Nihon Kōgyō Shimbun-sha.

Harada Sogaku. (1934) "Nihon Seishin to Daijō Zen" (The Japanese Spirit and Mahāyāna Zen) in *Chuō Bukkyō*, (March), pp. 285–300.

Hashimoto Fumio. (1980) "Yoroppa ni okeru Zen" (Zen in Europe) in *Doitsugo to Jinsei: Hashimoto Fumio Ronbun-shū*, Tokyo: Sanshū-sha, pp. 221–32.

Hashimoto Tetsuo. (1994) *Tsuji Masanobu to Shichinin no Sō* (Tsuji Masanobu and the Seven Buddhist Priests). Tokyo: Kōjin-sha.

Hata Ikuhiko. (1998) *Nihonjin Horyo* (Japanese Prisoners), vol. 1, Tokyo: Hara Shobō.

Himeyuri Heiwa Kinen-shiryōkan Kōshiki Gaido-bukku [Official Guidebook for the Himeyuri Peace Museum] (1999) Naha, Okinawa: Himeyuri Peace Museum.

Hirata Seikō. (1983) *Issai wa Kū* (Everything is Emptiness). Tokyo: Shūei-sha.

Hori Yukio. (1991) *Uha Jiten* (Dictionary of the Right Wing), Tokyo: Sanryō Shobō.

Ichikawa Hakugen. (1975) *Nihon Fashizumu ka no shūkyō* (Religion under Japanese Fascism), Tokyo: NS Shuppan-kai.

—— (1982) *Fudō-chi Shinmyō-roku / Taia-ki*, Tokyo: Kōdan-sha.

Imamura Hitoshi. (1960) *Imamura Hitoshi Taishō Kaisō-roku* (Memoirs of General Imamura Hitoshi) 4 vols, Tokyo: Jiyū Ajia-sha.

Inoue Nisshō. (1953) *Ichinin issatsu* (One Person Kills One Person). Tokyo: Nihon Shūhō-sha.

Katano Tatsurō. (1994) *Kongō-hōzan Rinnōji gohyaku-gojū-nen-shi* (A History of the Five Hundred and Fifty Years of Kongō-hōzan Rinnōji Temple). Sendai: Kongō-hōzan Rinnōji.

Kawabe Masakazu. (1980) *Nihon Rikugun Seishin-kyōiku Shi-kō* (Thoughts on the History of Spiritual Education in Japanese Army). Tokyo: Harashobō.

Kawano Hitoshi. ("Gyokusai no Shisō to Hakuhei Totsugeki" (The Ideology of Death before Dishonour and the Bayonet Charge) in *Sensō to Guntai*, Tokyo: Iwanami Shoten, pp. 154–79.

Kyōiku-sōkanbu. (eds.) (1941) *Seishin Kyōiku Shiryō* (Materials on Spiritual Education), vol. 2, (January) Tokyo: Kaikō-sha.

Kumazawa Taizen. (1944) "Shōji Tōrai Ikan ga Kaihi-sen" (How to Avoid the Coming of Life and Death) in *Daihōrin* (May) pp. 18–21.

Minami Hiroshi. (1953) *Nihonjin no Shinri* (Psychology of the Japanese People). Tokyo: Iwanami Shoten.

Mizukami Tsutomu. (1997) *Ikkyū* (Zen Priest Ikkyū), Tokyo: Chūō Kōron-sha.

Mori Taien. (1977) "Ninnaji no Rekishi to Shinkō" (The History and Faith of Ninnaji) in *Koji-junrei – Kyoto 11 – Ninnaji*, Kyoto: Tankō-sha, pp. 79–95.

Mutō Tōko. (1942) "Dai Tōa Kensetsu to Shōbōgenzō" (The Construction of Greater East Asia and the *Shōbōgenzō*) in *Daihōrin*, (January) pp. 16–25.

Nagamine Hideo. (1982) *Nihongunjin no Shiseikan* (The View of Life and Death of Japanese Soldiers), Tokyo: Hara Shobō.

Naimushō Keiho-kyoku. (1934) *Shuppan Keisatsu-hō* (Report of the Publications Police), No. 73 (September).

Nakajima Genjō. (1998) *Yasoji o Koete* (Beyond Eighty Years), Numazu (Shizuoka Prefecture): Shōinji.

Nakamura Sōichi. (1972) *Zenyaku Shōbōgenzō* (Complete Translation of the *Shōbōgenzō*), vol. 4, Tokyo: Seishin-shobō.

Nishida Norimasa. (ed.) (1941) *Izoku Tokuhon* (Reader for Bereaved Families), Kyoto: Rikugun Juppei-bu.

Noda Masa'aki. (1998) *Sensō to Zaiseki* (War and the Responsibility of the Accused), Tokyo: Iwanami Shoten.

Ogata Hiroshi. (1939) *Bukkyō to Shakai Undō* (Buddhism and Social Movements), Tokyo: Criminal Affairs Bureau; Ministry of Justice (February).

Okamoto Sekiō. (1935) "Kokumin Seishin to Muga" (The People's Spirit and the Non-self) in *Sanshō* (June) published by Daihonzan Eiheji, pp. 206–12.

Okamura A. (1989) *Ketsumeidan jiken* (The Blood Oath Corps Incident), Tokyo: San-ichi Shobō.

Okuda Kyūji. (1942) *Senjinkun to Nihon Seishin* (The Field Service Code and the Spirit of Japan), Tokyo: Gunji Kyōiku Kenkyū-kai.

Onuma Hiroaki. (1963) *Ketsumeidan Jiken Kōhan Sokki-roku* (The Stenographic Record of the Public Trial of the Blood Oath Corps Incident), 3 vols., Tokyo: Ketsumeidan Jiken Kōhan Sokki-roku Kankō-kai.

—— (1971) *Ketsumeidan Jiken-jōshinsho-gokuchū Nikki* (The Blood Oath Corps Incident-Written Statements-Prison Diaries). Tokyo: Ketsumeidan Jiken Kōhan Sokki-roku Kankō-kai.

Ōe Shinobu. (1985) *Kogarashi no Toki* (Time of the Wintry Wind), Tokyo: Chikuma Shobō.

Ōmori Sōgen. (1986) *Sanzen Nyūmon* (Introduction to Zen Practice), Tokyo: Kōdan-sha.

—— (1983) *Yamaoka Tesshū*, Tokyo: Shunjū-sha.

—— (1966) *Zen to Ken* (Zen and the Sword). Tokyo: Shunjū-sha.

Ōmori Zenkai. (1941) "Taisei Yokusan to Daijō Bukkyō" (Assisting Imperial Rule and Mahāyāna Buddhism) in *Sōtō Shūhō*, 39 (15 January), pp. 1–3.

Rekishi Kyōiku-sha Kyōgi-kai, (eds.) (1995) *Maboroshi dewa nakatta Hondo Kessen* (The Decisive Battle for the Mainland was no Illusion). Tokyo: Kōbunkyū.

Satō Gan'ei. (1902) *Bushidō*. Tokyo: Senryūdō.

Sugawara Yutaka. (1971) *Aizawa Chūsa Jiken no Shinsō* (The True Facts of the Lt. Colonel Aizawa Incident). Tokyo: Keizai Ōrai-sha.

Sugimoto Gorō. (1938) *Taigi* (Great Duty/Justice), Tokyo: Heibon-sha.

Suzuki Daisetsu (also Daisetz, D. T.). (1947) *Bukkyō no Tai-i* (An Outline of Buddhism), Kyoto: Hōzōkan.

—— (1970) "Daijō Bukkyō no Sekaiteki Shimei – Wakaki Hitobito ni yosu" (World Mission of Mahāyāna Buddhism – written for Young People) in vol. 29, *Suzuki Daisetsu Zenshū*, Tokyo: Iwanami Shoten, pp. 338–53.

—— (1941) *Isshinjitsu no Sekai*. Tokyo: Kondō Shoten.

—— (1970) "Jijoden" in vol. 30, *Suzuki Daisetsu Zenshū*, Tokyo: Iwanami Shoten, pp. 563–622.

—— (1970) "Nihonjin no Shōji-kan" (Japanese View of Life and Death) in vol. 29, *Suzuki Daisetsu Zenshū*, Tokyo: Iwanami Shoten, pp. 29–37.

—— (1968) *Nihonteki Reisei* (Japanese Spirituality) in vol. 8, *Suzuki Daisetsu Zenshū*, Tokyo: Iwanami Shoten, pp. 3–223.

—— (1947) *Nihon no Reiseika*, Kyoto: Hōzōkan.

—— (1968) *Reiseiteki Nihon no Kensetsu* (Construction of a Spiritual Japan) in vol. 9, *Suzuki Daisetsu Zenshū*, Tokyo: Iwanami Shoten, pp. 1–258.

—— (1969) *Shin Shukyō-ron* (Treatise on New Religion) in vol. 23, *Suzuki Daisetsu Zenshū*, Tokyo: Iwanami Shoten, pp. 1–147.

—— (1970) "Tokkō-tai" (Special Attack Forces) in vol. 30, *Suzuki Daisetsu Zenshū*, Tokyo: Iwanami Shoten, pp. 38–43.

—— (1968) *Tōyōteki Ichi* (Oriental Oneness) in vol. 7, *Suzuki Daisetsu Zenshū*, Tokyo: Iwanami Shoten, pp. 305–442.

—— (1943) *Zen Hyaku-dai*, Tokyo: Daitō Shuppansha.

—— (1970) "Zenkai Sasshin" (Reform of the Zen World) in vol. 30, *Suzuki Daisetsu Zenshū*. Tokyo: Iwanami Shoten, 1970, pp. 410–7.

—— (1941) "Zen to Bushidō" (Zen and Bushido) in *Bushidō no Shinzui*, Handa Shin (ed.) Tokyo: Teikoku Shoseki Kyōkai, pp. 64–78.

Takagi. (1963) *Gempō Rōshi*. Tokyo: Daizō Shuppan-sha.

Takisawa Makoto. (1996) *Gondō Seikyō* (Gondō Seikyō), Tokyo: Pelikan-sha.

Tamaki Benkichi. (1970) *Kaisō – Yamamoto Gempō* (Reminiscences of Yamamoto Gempō). Tokyo: Shunjū-sha.

Tanaka Chigaku. (1937) *Shishi-ō Zenshū Daisan-shū* (Complete Works of the Lion King – Part Three), vol. 6, Tokyo: Shishi-ō Bunko.

Tanaka Tadao. (1995) *Sawaki Kōdō – Kono Koshin no Hito* (Sawaki Kōdo – Heart of an Ancient Man). 2 vols., Tokyo: Daihōrin-kaku.

Tomomatsu Entai. (1941) *Izoku Tokuhon* (A Reader for Bereaved Families). Kyoto: Rikugun Juppei-bu.

Toyoda Jō. (1991) *Kakumeika Kita Ikki* (Revolutionary Kita Ikki). Tokyo: Kōdan-sha.

Tsunemitsu Kōnen. (1968) *Meiji no Bukkyō-sha* (Meiji Era Buddhists), vol. 1, Tokyo: Shunjū-sha.

Tsunoda Fusako. (1984) *Sekinin Rabauru no Shōgun Imamura Hitoshi* (Imamura Hitoshi, the General Responsible for Rabaul), Tokyo: Shinchō-sha.

Wada Kameji. (1942) *Rikugun-Damashii* (The Spirit of the Army), Tokyo: Tōsui sha.

Yamada Kyōdō. (1991) *Mugai-san no Fūkei* (A View of Mugai), Sendai: Hōbundō.

Yamada Reirin. (1942) *Zengaku Yawa* (Evening Talks on Zen Studies), Tokyo: Daiichi Shobō.

Yanagida Seizan. (1980–1) "Tabū e no chōsen – Saikutsu – Nihonshūkyōshi – Sono nazo ni semaru – Dōgen" (Challenging Taboos – Probing Japan's Religious History – Unraveling its Mysteries – Dōgen), 20 part series (18 November–15 January), Chūgai Nippō.

Yasutani Ryōkō (a.k.a. Haku'un). (1943) *Dōgen Zenji to Shūshōgi* (Zen Master Dōgen and the *Shūshōgi*), Tokyo: Fuji Shobō.

Yoshida Yutaka. (1995) "Nankin Daigyaku-satsu o dō toraeru ka" (How to Grasp the Great Nanking Massacre?) in *Nankin Daigyaku-satsu to Genbaku*, Osaka: Tōhō Shuppan, pp. 120–34.

INDEX